What Film Is Good For

What Film Is Good For

On the Values of Spectatorship

Edited by Julian Hanich and
Martin P. Rossouw

Foreword by Mike Figgis
Afterword by Radu Jude

UNIVERSITY OF CALIFORNIA PRESS

The editors gratefully acknowledge the generous support of the Nicolaas Mulerius Foundation.

University of California Press
Oakland, California

© 2023 by The Regents of the University of California

Cataloging-in-Publication Data is on file at the Library of Congress.

ISBN 978-0-520-38680-8 (cloth)
ISBN 978-0-520-38681-5 (pbk.)
ISBN 978-0-520-38682-2 (ebook)

32 31 30 29 28 27 26 25 24 23
10 9 8 7 6 5 4 3 2 1

Contents

Acknowledgments　　ix
Foreword by Mike Figgis　　xi

Introduction: Film Ethics as Delivering the Goods　　1
Martin P. Rossouw and Julian Hanich

PART ONE. ADAPTIVE GOODS

1. ... A Portal to Another World: On Cinema, Climate Change, and a Good Apocalypse　　13
   Jennifer Fay

2. ... Scaling Down: On the Unsustainable Pleasure of Large-File Streaming　　24
   Laura U. Marks

3. ... It's Invaluable: On Film Spectatorship in the Era of Covid-19　　36
   Sarah Cooper

4. ... Stabilities and Mobilities: On the Generic Values of Emplacements, Displacements, and Outplacements　　46
   Timothy Corrigan

PART TWO. EMPATHIC GOODS

5. ... Lies, Loops, or Liberation: On the Dis/Obedience of Feeling More   57
   Michele Aaron

6. ... Public Engagement: On Postcolonial African Cinema's Critical Value   69
   Litheko Modisane

7. ... Shedding Light on Abject Lives: On Global Cinema as Ethical Art   80
   Seung-hoon Jeong

8. ... Empathy: On Its Limitations and Liabilities   91
   Malcolm Turvey

9. ... Political Impact: On the Societal Vibrancy of Film   102
   Jens Eder

PART THREE. SENSITIVE GOODS

10. ... Moral Reflection: On the Reflective Afterlife of Screen Stories   117
    Carl Plantinga and Garrett Strpko

11. ... Challenge and Discomfort: On Situated Elitist Pleasures in Art and Indie Film   128
    Geoff King

12. ... Heterocosmic Connections: On the Many Worlds and World Values of Cinema   138
    Daniel Yacavone

13. ... Depth of Experience: On Early Phenomenology and the Value of Boredom in the Cinema   150
    Christian Ferencz-Flatz

14. ... Striking Beauty: On Recuperating the Beautiful in Cinema   162
    Julian Hanich

PART FOUR. REVIVING GOODS

15. ... Wondering Offscreen: On Cinema's Transformations of Our Relation to the Unseen — 177
Jaimie Baron

16. ... Coming to Wonder: On Cinema's Renewal of Vision — 188
Catherine Wheatley

17. ... Moral Improvement: On How Watching Films Might Make Us Better People — 198
Thomas E. Wartenberg

18. ... Cinematic Ethics: On Film as Transformative Experience — 209
Robert Sinnerbrink

19. ... Spiritual Exercises Before a Screen: On "Film as Philosophy" and Its Transformational Ethics — 221
Martin P. Rossouw

PART FIVE. COMMUNAL GOODS

20. ... Remembrance and Reflection: On Social Justice Cinema in the #BlackLivesMatter Era — 237
Maryann Erigha Lawer

21. ... Making Movie Generations: On the Cultural Work of Hollywood Remaking — 249
Kathleen Loock

22. ... Reaching Unlettered Audiences: On Global Blockbuster Cinema and Its Oral Affinities — 261
Sheila J. Nayar

23. ... Love of Community and Reality: On André Bazin and the Good of Cinema — 274
Dudley Andrew

PART SIX. MEDIAL GOODS

24. ... Projection and Protection: On Cinemagoing as Playing Hide-and-Seek with Reality   289
 Francesco Casetti

25. ... An Animated and Animating Medium: On Hegel, Adorno, and the Good of Film   300
 Nicholas Baer

26. ... The Bigger Picture: On Watching Films on a Cinema Screen   314
 Martine Beugnet

27. ... Quality Time: On Resisting What's Next, or Staying with the Credits   326
 Tiago de Luca

PART SEVEN. UNSETTLED GOODS

28. ... Wanton Destruction: On Cinema's Antisocial Thrills   339
 Adrian Martin

29. ... Alienating Interventions: On What the "Bad" in David Lynch's Films Is "Good" For   349
 Annie van den Oever and Dominique Chateau

30. ... Dangerous Situations: On Whether Cinema Is Poisonous   361
 Michel Chion

31. ... Good for Nothing? On How Films Help Us through the Night   368
 Tom Gunning

32. ... Medium-Sized Matters: On Whether Cinema Has Made Any Difference   378
 Mark Cousins

Afterword by Radu Jude   388
List of Contributors   393
Index   401

Acknowledgments

Since it takes a proverbial village to raise an edited volume, there are several individuals and institutions whom we would like to thank for helping us carry an idea that kept mushrooming on us at every turn.

For financial support, our thanks to the Nicolaas Mulerius Foundation, first, as well as the Groningen Research Institute for the Study of Culture (ICOG) and the Future Generation Professoriate Programme at the University of the Free State.

At the University of California Press, our gratitude goes to Raina Polivka, Sam Warren, Julie Van Pelt, Susan Larsen, and the rest of the team for their enthusiastic and professional support, from start to finish.

We would also like to acknowledge the participants and co-organizers of the research colloquium "Viewing Values: Varieties of Ethical Experience in Cinematic Spectatorship" at the University of Groningen in March 2019—among others, Thomas Wartenberg, Robert Sinnerbrink, Annie van den Oever, Liesbeth Korthals Altes, Margriet van der Waal, Thijs Lijster, and Suzanne Human—since this was the inception of thoughts and collaborations that eventually became this book.

Our thanks also to Jakob Boer, Sjoerd Griffioen, and our anonymous peer reviewers for their engaging and constructive feedback; Iris Zhonga, Sanna McGregor, and Sanet le Roux for their keen editorial assistance in the finalization of the manuscript; and Naomi Morgan for her excellent translation work.

And, last but in fact foremost, to our wonderful collection of contributors to the volume: thank you for joining the conversation and for thinking along with us. Collaborating with you was, for us, clearly *yet another* thing that film is good for.

Foreword

MIKE FIGGIS

At the turn of the twentieth century, human beings created an art form that became, on paper at least, everything that Richard Wagner had aspired to achieve through his operas: a coming together of drama, music, literature, and the visual arts. Cinema changed the world immediately, and once that specific genie was out of the bottle, there was to be no turning back.

As soon as I leave the relative sanctity of my apartment, a place where I still believe I have some control over my cinematic environment, I enter a world where people no longer look up from their screens, no longer listen to the space around them and accept narcissism as a fact of life. Film is more or less responsible for this new "utopia." So the question of what film is good for is somewhat loaded. The artist and philosopher Ad Reinhardt once wrote, "Art is art. Everything else is everything else." Another twentieth-century thinker-artist, John Cage, stated: "I have nothing to say—and I am saying it." I think my own answer regarding film lies delicately balanced between these two statements.

The invention of the printing press clearly led to some wonderful literature being created and distributed to a wide audience. It also enabled a proliferation of pulp and garbage. That's pretty much how I feel about film today. Of course, I am in love with cinema. But I vividly remember being in a conversation with Steven Soderbergh at the Directors Guild of America in Los Angeles (this would have been around 1999) where the

FIGURE 1. The nameless prisoner of war (Roger Jacquet) in *An Occurrence at Owl Creek Bridge* (1962, Robert Enrico).

hot topic was "the future of film in a digital age." I have always been an advocate for greater accessibility to the tools of filmmaking, actively encouraging students to break the rules, shoot on digital cameras, and bypass the studio system. And so, in our conversation, I suggested that in ten years' time there would be ten times more good films available to audiences. Steven sardonically noted that by definition there would also be ten times as many bad films and, as we know, the ratio of bad to good in any art form is weighted on the bad side.

Much of what I see, now more than ever, is "product" and "content." The danger of cinema was always financial. The problem is simply that there is too much stuff out there, and big business has no interest in anything but, well, *bigger* business. A few years ago, I interviewed John Berger, who mused that as a student his one ambition was to be a filmmaker. But then it quickly dawned on him that he would have to get into business with rich folk, and this was one bridge too far for him. I'm still an idealist, though. I've made films in the Hollywood system and I've shot films on zero budget. I use my iPhone and gadgets that I find on the internet (yes, they have their uses). The liberation that came with Apple's Final Cut software was incredible for me. The ease with which I can study film and revisit the countless gems that now form the archive of cinema gives me the kind of freedom as an artist that was not available when I began my journey in the 1970s.

Formats have changed, something long overdue; there was never a sound aesthetic reason why a film had to be 95-minutes long (other than it was good for "business"). For me, one of the most inspiring film experiences in my twenties was watching Robert Enrico's short film *An Occurrence at Owl Creek Bridge/La Rivière du hibou* (1962), in which concepts of time and space and mortality were exquisitely described in purely cinematic terms. I think it's high time that our idea of Cinema, and what exactly a film is, changed. We've become more interested in the news, in documentary, in nature, in ourselves, and, of course, in all things "binge-worthy" that are nowadays churned out on streaming platforms.

But film, like all great art, lives on and still attempts to examine the human condition: life, death, loss, love, and even art itself. These questions will always remain of interest to humanity as it evolves. And film still remains the most relevant medium to explore these core themes of our existence. Within its vastly expanding archive, there is still much treasure to be discovered, treasure that can help form each of us in unique ways. We have in film a technology capable of capturing the essence of ourselves. The combination of a camera and an audio-recording device gives us the ability to control time, freeze time, and then enhance each moment. This recording device also fascinates us because we are fascinated by other human beings. Ingmar Bergman suggested that cinema is essentially the ongoing exploration of the human face. We study other people because it gives us a sense of who we are, and the camera/sound combination, as a kind of social microscope, is the perfect tool for that task.

At its highest level, film can combine the work of poets, painters, and composers in the unique hybrid that we call cinema. We do need to recognize and embrace the fact that barriers have been eradicated through technical innovation and that filmmaking is no longer the domain of an elite group—and it does not need the support of a studio. I'm confident that the power of film is so strong that it will always adapt to the social and economic environment in which it finds itself. As I always encourage young filmmakers: think about the audience you are trying to reach and then simply use any device that you can lay your hands on to connect with that audience.

Yes, film *is* still alive. And those things that it is good at, and *good for*, will live forever more.

Introduction

Film Ethics as Delivering the Goods

MARTIN P. ROSSOUW AND JULIAN HANICH

INTO THE GOODS

It seemed a simple enough idea. We wanted to do a volume on film ethics. So we decided to invite an array of film scholars to respond to what we took to be a decisive yet easy-to-answer question: "What is film viewing *good for*?" By which we meant: "What *values* may we attach to our experiences of the moving image?" Now it just so happens that the issue of "the goods" is also a beloved trope of crime and gangster movies, finding expression in stock antihero statements like "Where're the goods?" or "No—*first* you show us the goods, *then* you get the money!" And, being the film lovers that we are, it's a trope that to our minds nicely covers what this book is about: in gangster parlance, you could say that we asked this group of film studies kingpins to *deliver the goods*—to just give us an indication of *some* goods, *any* goods whatsoever—that film, in their experience, could possibly live up to.

But, as good ideas often go, we weren't quite prepared for some of the reactions our idea of film ethics went on to elicit. (Botched drop-offs of "the goods" is, of course, *also* a gangster trope.) More than a few respected peers turned out to be rather wary of delivering judgments on what film is "good for": *I don't do ethics . . . I never moralize . . . Surely this smacks of instrumentalist thinking . . . ? Why reduce film to the good and the bad . . . ?* And, not to forget: *The "bad" things about movies make for the best part!* Yet little did they know, and did *we* know at

1

the time, that these are *precisely* the sort of conventional responses that our now-completed compilation of essays wants to put into question.

With this volume, we invite those skeptics who might say "I don't do film ethics" to give it a second thought. This requires a basic shift in our approach to the very idea: that doing "film ethics" first and foremost is a matter of addressing *the value* of film as such, and in this case with specific reference to the *value*-able experiences of spectators. Therefore, rather than circumscribing paradigmatic "ethical contents" in film experiences (e.g., moral identification or the fostering of empathy), we want to underline that *any* spectatorial experience may have an ethical dimension inasmuch as cinematic experiences are inevitably valued, or at least have the capacity to be valued, for a multitude of reasons. While we're not unaware of the dangers of endlessly inflating the notion of film ethics, we do find ourselves intrigued by some implications of this shift: namely, that by way of tacit valuations, anyone—the everyday filmgoer, the fan, the filmmaker, the critic—can be thought of as engaging in film ethics at some level, even if only as an unarticulated "lived ethics." But, at the very least, this shift in focus toward value should make it evident that film ethics is far more prevalent in, and fundamental to, film scholarship than people might think initially. Doing film ethics, we propose, is, in a sense, *inevitable*. And considering how often it occurs in the background, our aim here is to make it the main attraction.

IN GOOD COMPANY

To be sure, this volume is about much more than simply wanting to win over those who are agnostic about "what film is good for." With regard to film ethics as a now-burgeoning field, its ambition is to bring to the fore the good of film as the *arch question* of film ethics. In this sense, we admit that our volume is really staging a *retrieval* and *recovery*. For it's a question that has undoubtedly been asked before—even if not as often or as outright as you'd think.

One place where it has recently come up is in the later work of Thomas Elsaesser. In his *Film History as Media Archaeology* (2016), Elsaesser consolidates his career-long interest in the position of cinema within the cultural-technological cycles and formations that have characterized modernity. Yet, in the introductory passages, he is quick to concede that beneath the core questions of his archaeological approach—"*Where* is cinema?" and "*When* is cinema?," expanding upon the classical film-theoretical question of "*What* is/was cinema"—the question of "*Why* is cinema?" or "What is/was cinema *good for?*" also lingers.¹ That is to say, "What role has cinema played—and is still playing—in the larger development of [hu]mankind, or more specifically, in our Western modernity and postmodernity?"² In fact, the same question lurks also in more specific quarters of Elsaesser's work. One finds it, for instance, in his influential statement on complex cinema, "The Mind-Game Film" (2009), where he takes stock of the conditions behind the twists, delusions, and confusions that defined turn-of-the-millennium movies such as *Lost Highway* (1997, dir. David Lynch), *Fight Club* (1999, dir. David Fincher), and *Donnie Darko* (2001, dir. Richard Kelly).³ Here, too, Elsaesser wastes no time in bringing up the question, now only of a particular species of cinematic storytelling: what are *mind-game films* (perceived to be) good for?⁴ Consequently, he considers how mind-game films allow viewers to train their skills of interpretation and interactive engagement as part of the more general affective labor that the modern "control society" demands of us.⁵ That's a compromised good for sure—but a good nevertheless.

Then there is Stanley Cavell, who directly broached the question with the title of his published lecture, "The Good of Film" (2000).⁶ Whereas Elsaesser brings up the good of film in connection with shifting historical forces and fortunes, Cavell raises the question as an extension of one of his most abiding interests: "Emersonian" perfectionism, after Ralph Waldo Emerson—a perfectionism set not on some metaphysical ideal of perfection but on an open-ended process of becoming who you are. As it turns out, Cavell's lecture is mostly about what he understands by a "good film."⁷ But, in the end, Cavell still comes good on the promise of the title: yes, it is an affinity for such perfectionism that makes the likes of Hollywood remarriage comedies *good films,* but it is to work out *our* perfectionist ideas and ideals that these good films are ultimately *good for.*

A number of decades before Elsaesser and Cavell, however, it was Siegfried Kracauer who, in the concluding chapter of his *Theory of Film* (1960), first posed the question in its most famously outright, and dramatic, form.⁸ And it is from this formulation that we take our main cue: "Only now that the inner workings of film have been dealt with is it possible and indeed necessary to come to grips with this issue, which is *most central of all:* what is *the good* of film experience?"⁹ Kracauer didn't pose the question for mere rhetorical effect. His own answer is, in fact, broadcast by the very subtitle of his book: *the redemption of physical reality.* As Kracauer goes on to explain later in his conclusion, "We literally redeem this world from its dormant state, its state of virtual nonexistence, by endeavoring to experience it through the camera."[10] Physical reality has become elusive, sedimented under the abstractive reasoning that drives modernity.[11] But in cinema we have a medium that essentially "incorporates aspects of physical reality with a view to making us experience them," thus mobilizing and turning the unmoored, abstracted fragments of our modern condition against itself.[12] And it is in this restaging of reality that Kracauer locates the good that film experience is for: the potential to retrieve the textures of life from beneath the abstractions of modern science; and the promise to radically reconstitute the modern subject's *lifeworld* as a reconnection *to the* world.

Yet, it is not so much the answer that Kracauer had for his question that is the primary concern of this volume. Our concern, rather, is with the conceptual space *presupposed* and *opened up* by the question itself, and how it can provide a basis for doing film ethics. What we want to propose is that as soon as you consider the value or the good of film, you put yourself on a turf that is unmistakably *ethical*.[13] And this seems true to us regardless of what your answer to the question is, and regardless of the kind or nature of "film" you're talking about, as the mixed bag of Kracauer, Cavell, and Elsaesser above makes clear. For what is ethics if it is not to, in one way or another, busy yourself with that illimitable primitive concept of "the good'? Yet, furthermore, we want to drive home that this is an ethical space that cannot be circumvented. The keen sensitivity we see in Kracauer for how the ontological "what" question of film is imbricated with its ethical "good" question is a model that to some degree holds for *all* thinking about film. The question of the good of film is indeed "most central of all," as Kracauer puts it, because it inevitably *borders on, subtends,* and often so much as *motivates* all the other theoretical questions worth asking. Valuation, even if only by implication, is unavoidable. Therefore, conceptions of what film is good for, even if only nascent or implied, will factor into any film theory worthy of the name.

Of course, our insistence upon this inevitable ethical dimension in reflecting on film is not to ignore the existing and rapidly growing body of work currently done under the banner of "film ethics," especially within contemporary film-philosophy. Next to the work of some of the authors in our volume—such as Michele Aaron, Sarah Cooper, Seunghoon Jeong, Carl Plantinga, Robert Sinnerbrink, Thomas Wartenberg, and Catherine Wheatley—we are thinking, for instance, of Brian Bergen-Aurand, Nadine Boljkovac, Noël Carroll, Jinhee Choi and Mattias Frey, Amy Coplan, Lisa Downing and Libby Saxton, Ward Jones and

Samantha Vice, Joseph Kupfer, Lúcia Nagib, Orna Raviv, D. N. Rodowick, Dan Shaw, Murray Smith, Jane Stadler, and Lisa Trahair. But what bearing does our retrieval of the arch-ethical question of "the good of film" have on film ethics as it is currently pursued by these and many other names? What exactly is this volume's contribution to the existing field? We like to think of our intervention in terms of a double movement: to urge a particular *concentration* within film ethics that goes hand in hand with a simultaneous *expansion* thereof.

On the one hand, our definition of film ethics as addressing questions of value brings to the surface a basic stratum upon which diverse approaches to film ethics converge. For example, as different as phenomenological (e.g., Stadler, Sinnerbrink), new materialist and realist (e.g., Boljkovac, Nagib), or analytical-cognitivist (e.g., Plantinga, Carroll) approaches to film ethics may be, they are *all* premised on particular orders of values and valuation. Undoubtedly, their estimations of the good of film vary as drastically as the difference between the values of intense emotional experience, affirming the transcendence of nature, or the refinement of cognitive insight. But the fact of *value-attributions* at work in these and other approaches still remains—and it allows film ethics as a whole to be more concentrated around a basic point of departure, the question of the good of film, which its diversity of approaches all share.

On the other hand, this concentration that we encourage within film ethics simultaneously also yields, not without a hint of irony, a far more open and ecumenical understanding of what may be admitted under the banner of "film ethics." Our point here is simply this: if we understand film ethics to be primarily about addressing value, and if it can be reasonably posed that assumptions about value and the good of film also thrive in other (seemingly unrelated) fields of film—think of genre theory, historical inquiries, or reception studies—then film-ethical insights can rightly be expected to show up in places far beyond the boundaries of the institutionalized subdiscipline called "film ethics." Hence our claim that film ethics is far better considered as a basic *aspect* of film studies than a mere subfield within it. As we hope our collection of essays from various fields shows, questions about the value of film—and thus film ethics—are within the purview of almost any film scholar.

THE GOOD, THE BAD, AND THE PLENTY

We can imagine that a stickler for definitions reading this might have some pretty hefty philosophical questions brewing by now. *What is* "good," even? How do you define "good" versus "bad"? Could someone value film for something "bad"? Who ultimately decides what is "good"? Given the work that's gone into moral philosophy worldwide over thousands of years, we won't pretend that we can solve these issues in the space of a couple of paragraphs. But how about we at least go back to a few lines from an early landmark, just to get some bigger potential misunderstandings out of the way:

> Every art and every inquiry, and similarly every action and choice, is thought to aim at some good; and for this reason the good has rightly been declared to be that at which all things aim. But a certain difference is found among ends; some are activities, others are products apart from the activities that produce them. Where there are ends apart from the actions, it is the nature of the products to be better than the activities. Now, as there are many actions, arts, and sciences, their ends also are many.[14]

In invoking the opening passage of Aristotle's *Nicomachean Ethics*, and the centrality that it accords to "the good," there are, of course, a number of things we're *not* endorsing here. We're obviously not trying to sell the idea of a neatly hierarchical, teleologically governed universe, with a single "highest good" at the peak of the pyramid. Or the idea that all things (be it a person, a pot, or a Tyler Perry movie) have an immanent form dictating their good. And certainly not the idea that the good of something is universal and unchanging. Today, we know that context is king; there's no denying that values do shape-shift and differ, often drastically, across historical and cultural borders.[15]

Nevertheless, there are things we readily *do* associate with. First is the patent *ubiquity*, the pervasiveness, that Aristotle ascribes to the good. We suggest that a similar ubiquity holds also for the more specific sense of the term we're interested in: "the good" and "goods" as not just any old goal or end, but understood in terms of *values*.[16] Surely no artifact (think: film) or activity (think: spectatorship *and* scholarship!) can function apart from spheres of value; they are unavoidably entangled in webs of human interests, and in this sense they all do "aim," although likely not at "*the* good," certainly at *some* good.

Another aspect we associate with in the passage is Aristotle's intuition for *varieties* of the good: that the good comes in distinct kinds and scales. But, again, we approach this at the level of value, *kinds of* value. This volume thus explores a great diversity of potential values of film: personal, social, educational, political, and—yes—moral-ethical. Some might consider it a tautology to prescribe a moral or ethical value to the good of film. From our standpoint, however, the question of the good of film proceeds from a more fundamental space where *the ethical as such* is about the discovery, clarification, and prioritizing of values. This entails that explicitly "moral" or "ethical" values—the likes of moral understanding, empathy, or transformative experience—at the outset do not per se deserve more attention than other kinds of value that may likewise be enlisted to characterize the good of film. Indeed, several of the essays that follow show how supposedly "nonethical" kinds of value—cognitive values such as education, or aesthetic values such as beauty or wonder—may just as much be part of the wider *axiological* ethics where we negotiate "the good" of cinema spectatorship.

Then there is an especially salient bit of inspiration that we take from Aristotle: reading the *Nicomachean Ethics* today, we can't help being struck by, on top of the ubiquity and variety, the sheer *plenitude* of goods that he sees in the world—irrespective of whether you buy into the ancient philosopher's metaphysical baggage. In fact, we derive this sense of plentitude precisely from the *contextuality* of the good. Now, obviously, the largely conditional and particular nature of the good has its downsides, and we don't deny that a switch of context can make many a supposed good turn decidedly bad. (No doubt: the road to hell is often paved with "good" valuations.)[17] But let us not forget that this selfsame contextuality can also birth new out-of-the-blue specimens of the good. It's a compelling thought: that the things we may regard as good are forever in a process of disclosure and multiplication. New, unforeseen goods of film may and *will* be spawned by new and unforeseen situations: some as big as a technological boom or a planetary crisis, others as small as a secret idiosyncrasy at home. For Aristotle, this might have been too good to be true. Although there is already such an abundance of possible goods in the world, there are *plenty more* still to come.

UNWRAPPING THE GOODS

In the spirit of such plentiful potentials, but also potential pitfalls, we present with this volume no less than thirty-four essays—not only from scholars, but also filmmakers and critics—as a wholeheartedly pluralized perspective on the good of film spectatorship. The best way to come to grips with this abundance of values, we found, is a volume that remains methodologically agnostic and features a number of shorter essays, often voiced in a very personal tone, that approach the good of film from various directions, distances, and determinations. Intended to be thought-provoking, these invited short-form essays put assumptions about the nexus of valuation, the good, and ethics to the test. Also, rather than boxing the essays into a reasonably conventional series of categories, we have opted for seven sections in which hidden affinities can be found and uncovered. We thus aimed for a conversation, even a dialogue, between essays that might encourage readers to draw further connections and conclusions of their own. Taken together, our seven sections, prism-like, refract the light shed on the good of film and thereby break up the assumption that we are presenting a grand theory of film ethics. And who knows: the methodological openness and frequent sense of personal voice that attends each section may even offer new perspectives and ways of doing for more conventional debates in film-philosophy. Following this "ethics" of openness and plenitude we also embrace a fairly flexible understanding of the term "film": even though a fair number of essays focuses on fictional feature films (and some even take the cinema as their natural habitat), others don't hesitate to deal with short films, small-file movies, documentaries, or television series. Examples range from experimental slow cinema to mainstream blockbusters, from Netflix to *Nomadland* (2020, dir. Chloé Zhao), from African cinema to the afterlives of films.

The volume's opening conversation on *Adaptive Goods* revolves around ways that film registers and supports dramatic shifts we are undergoing, and *need* to undergo, in times of global upheaval—whether relating to ecological disaster, migration, or Covid-19. One essay even advocates for an environment with free access to a good that may well prove *invaluable:* watching films. The essays gathered in the section *Empathic Goods* focus on film as an agent of empathy, connection, and dialogue, yet ultimately also the limits and possible dangers of its empathetic potential. *Sensitive Goods,* in turn, deals with film's cultivation of values that converge around overlapping meanings of "sensitivity"—be it sensitivity related to deep or beautiful sensory experiences, moral sensitivity towards others, or a sensitivity to discomforting cinematic experiences. In a phrase, films can be both eye-opening and eye-popping. But films can also harbor edifying, renewing, and transformational capacities, extending from experiences of wonder, through moral improvement, to undergoing profound transformation. That's what our contributors to *Reviving Goods* put on the table.

By all means, films also have the power to convene and consolidate communities of all kinds, as the authors in the *Communal Goods* section argue. Such communities may concern widespread social causes and societal positions, or very specific instances of fanhood and cinephilia.

The essays on *Medial Goods,* by contrast, zero in on values of film that thrive on and emphasize particularities of the medium and the viewing situations in which we encounter films. Here we may think of the cinema as a space of larger-than-life experiences and protection against the vagaries of everyday life, but we can also picture the couch-potato situation of someone who by streaming on Netflix & Co. is deprived of the values nested in an entirely mundane activity: to watch without any rush the credit sequence of a film. But what if the value is not *that* straightforward? What if there is even pleasure to be gleaned from the unpleasant? Ask the authors who feature in our final section on *Unsettled Goods*—"unsettled" both in the sense of values that seem unstable and disquieting and the sense of values that are not yet entirely settled. Is film maybe good for nothing, as one contributor wonders? Not so fast! Even our most doubtful authors are ultimately convinced that film is good for *something.*

In a time of global crisis, strife, and suspicion, this collection of essays aims to sound a more upbeat tone: that watching movies can be profoundly valuable in a rich variety of ways. Of course, this does not deny the simple fact that films are also the product of market forces, often ideologically compromised, and so forth. At the end of the day, and in the greater economic scheme of things, films are still "goods." What the following pages set out to do, though, is to deliver these goods from the still widespread prejudice that money-making entertainment is the *only* thing they're good for.

NOTES

1. Thomas Elsaesser, *Film History as Media Archaeology: Tracking Digital Cinema* (Amsterdam: Amsterdam University Press, 2016), 21 (emphasis ours). Our thanks to Seung-hoon Jeong for drawing our attention to this particular passage.
2. Elsaesser, *Film History as Media Archaeology,* 21.
3. Thomas Elsaesser, "The Mind-Game Film," in *Puzzle Films: Complex Storytelling in Contemporary Cinema,* ed. Warren Buckland (Malden: Wiley-Blackwell, 2009), 13–41.
4. Elsaesser, "Mind-Game Film," 33, 36.
5. Elsaesser, "Mind-Game Film," 34.
6. Stanley Cavell, "The Good of Film," in *Cavell on Film,* ed. William Rothman (Albany: SUNY Press, 2005 [2000]), 333–348.
7. Cavell, "Good of Film," 334–336.
8. Siegfried Kracauer, *Theory of Film: The Redemption of Physical Reality* (Oxford: Oxford University Press, 1960). For two instances where Kracauer

likewise serves as a starting point for thinking about film ethics, although not quite in the way that we propose here, see D.N. Rodowick, "Ethics in Film Philosophy (Cavell, Deleuze, Levinas)," unpublished text (Harvard University, n.d.), https://www.academia.edu/36412056/Ethics_in_film_philosophy_Cavell_Deleuze_Levinas_. Accessed November 6, 2021; and Brian Bergen-Aurand, "Ethics," in *The Routledge Encyclopedia of Film Theory*, ed. Edward Branigan and Warren Buckland (London: Routledge, 2013), 162–166.

9. Kracauer, *Theory of Film*, 285 (emphasis ours).

10. Kracauer, *Theory of Film*, 300.

11. Kracauer, *Theory of Film*, 299–300.

12. Kracauer, *Theory of Film*, 40. See also Miriam Bratu Hansen, *Cinema and Experience: Siegfried Kracauer, Walter Benjamin, and Theodor W. Adorno* (Berkeley: University of California Press, 2012), 37; and Ian Aitken, *European Film Theory and Cinema: A Critical Introduction* (Edinburgh: Edinburgh University Press, 2001), 170.

13. For this and related lines of reasoning here we are indebted to our friend and colleague Liesbeth Korthals Altes.

14. Aristotle, *The Nicomachean Ethics*, trans. David Ross, ed. Lesley Brown (Oxford: Oxford University Press, 2009 [1980]), 1094a1–8.

15. Not that we'd go so far as to reduce all values and valuation to a relativistic free-for-all, though. While values obviously change from one local context to another, there are more fundamentally shared human contexts—"inescapable horizons," to borrow Charles Taylor's coinage, like nature, society, power, and subjective experience, each shining through in this volume—that still provide *some* stability as backgrounds of intelligibility and significance to the values that we forge. See Charles Taylor, *The Ethics of Authenticity* (Cambridge, MA: Harvard University Press, 1991), 31–41.

16. In Aristotle's terms, values represent said higher order, intrinsic ends "apart from the actions" pursued for their own sake, constituting the axiological sphere that determines our notions of what's desirable, ideal, important, and worth striving for.

17. It's for this reason that a figure like Jürgen Habermas—who relies upon a rigorous distinction between *ethics* (concerned with relative and particular goods "for me" or "for us") versus *morality* (concerned with universalizable norms that must unconditionally ensure "the right" for all)—is so skeptical about whether any generalizable claims regarding the good can be made. And it's a position that we have sympathy with. See, e.g., Jürgen Habermas, *Justification and Application*, trans. Ciaran P. Cronin (Cambridge, MA: MIT Press, 1993), 1–18.

PART ONE

Adaptive Goods

I

... A Portal to Another World

On Cinema, Climate Change, and a Good Apocalypse

JENNIFER FAY

WHAT IS A PANDEMIC GOOD FOR?

In April 2020, Arundhati Roy marveled at how the Covid-19 pandemic had afflicted the world's richest countries, "bringing the engine of capitalism to a juddering halt," perhaps not permanently, but long enough for us to consider alternatives to the unjust and toxic status quo. Deadly and targeting the most vulnerable, the virus defied national borders and turned even the most innocuous of handshakes into potential forms of lethal contact. Yet, she asks: "Who could not be thrilled by the swell of birdsong in cities, peacocks dancing at traffic crossings and the silence in the skies?"[1] The fauna took to the abandoned streets, while the forced lockdowns "illuminated hidden things," like gross class inequalities and new features of state violence. While politicians promised a return to normal, Roy bids her readers to take stock of the pandemic's revelatory nature and put these epiphanies to revolutionary ends. With global commerce momentarily halted, the structures of the state newly exposed, and tentative signs of ecological resilience evident everywhere one looks, now is the time to "rethink the doomsday machine we have built for ourselves." The machine is, of course, not only the dysfunctional state but the status of the planet itself. As others have remarked, the pandemic may be yet another consequence of global warming, and the symptoms of the virus are exacerbated by the polluting cultures that gave rise to the Anthropocene.[2] A return to normal is the worst possible outcome. Writes Roy: "Historically pandemics have forced humans to

FIGURE 2. A portal between two apartments in Tsai Ming-liang's *The Hole* (1998).

break with the past and imagine their world anew. This one is no different. It is a portal, a gateway, between one world and the next." We can either drag our ruined world ("the carcasses of our prejudice and hatred, our avarice, our data banks and dead ideas, our dead rivers and smoky skies") with us, or "walk through lightly," ready to create a different mode of existence.³ A pandemic of this planetary dimension is a pause and interruption, a rupture and also a revelation that opens a time and space through which some different version of "we" may pass.

In her provocation, Roy essentially answers the question: "What is a pandemic good for?" Thinking with Roy about pandemics and climate change, I want to ask: "What is film good for?" My answer is that it may achieve, on a smaller scale, what Roy attributes to the global epidemiological emergency: a portal between worlds, a medium that exposes conditions as they are and provides an immersive image of the world as it could be. I am guided in this meditation by Tsai Ming-liang, who imagined a similar pandemic in 1998 and projected it into a future year 2000.

Tsai's portal is literalized as a hole—*The Hole* (1998)—between apartments through which antagonisms fester, body fluids flow, and even body parts pass until our heroine (Yang Kuei-mei) is lifted from near death into the light, and perhaps love, in the apartment above. The pandemic is the cause of her social isolation, but what makes the woman's apartment unlivable is neither the virus (though she contracts it) nor the hole (through which her upstairs neighbor—Lee Kang-sheng—urinates and vomits). It is, rather, that she is caught between the dark, unending, torrential rain outside and the flood caused by the bad plumbing in her apartment inside. The government has shut off the water in her apartment complex to force residents into quarantine quarters. Yet, everywhere water flows out of order.

This would be a story of utter, postapocalyptic despair, but here, as in all of Tsai's films, there is still a minimal hospitality to come, not through a break in the clouds but a hole in the ceiling large enough for a body to pass through. Our heroine leaves behind the overwhelming accumulation of paper products that litter her apartment and accepts a helping hand, literally extended down through the ceiling from the apartment above. From near death from the virus and ruin from the constant rain, our heroine is transported into another space and, it appears, another blissful version of the world. In the final scene, these once unfriendly neighbors are fashionably adorned and sweetly slow dancing. So, what is viral, or catching, in this film is not the flu but hospitality, which compels a character to widen the hole in his apartment floor, transforming the site of ruin into an instrument of neighborly, even world, repair.

If this is a vision of the future from the past, Tsai's *I Don't Want to Sleep Alone* (2006) lingers in the contemporary. A migrant worker (Norman Atun), a waitress (Chen Shiang-chyi), and a homeless man (Lee Kang-sheng) subsist in the damp and deserted spaces of Kuala Lumpur. Smoke from forest fires and planned burning overtakes the city, making breathing nearly impossible, and the three characters resolve their sexual jealousy, chronic loneliness, and fits of coughing by falling asleep on a coveted abandoned mattress. In the quiet ecstasy of the closing credit sequence, the mattress serves as a kind of lifeboat in this smoggy, burning world. It floats its sleeping cargo atop the black, brackish waters that have accumulated in the basement of an unfinished, abandoned construction site, finding some magic in Kuala Lumpur's otherwise halted urban development.

Taken together, Roy and Tsai conceptualize epidemiological and climate emergency as what we might call a secular apocalypse. *Secular* because the virus and environmental conditions function like suprapolitical forces against the combined failures of government and the entrenched systems of global capital, without any promise of divine justice or the redemption of the good and faithful. Roy writes that the virus, "in and of itself holds no moral brief," and it fulfills no particular theodicy.[4] Even in Tsai's film, the little miracles—a couple dancing in a ruined apartment, three people sleeping on an improbably buoyant mattress—are pointedly mundane fantasies borne of this world. These scenarios are *apocalyptic* in the Greek sense of revelation or uncovering something that was there all along (such as the failing infrastructures and ineffectual or brutal governmentality, and gross class and racial inequalities). It exposes the permeability of barriers as well as borders of the state and boundaries of the self. People are vulnerable to the flu, smoke, and general shelterlessness in the world, but these are the same qualities that open them to new forms of intimacy, a revelation that geopolitics and notions of sovereign subjectivity may be preventing us from perceiving and thus imagining as an alternate future.

As Samuel Weber writes, apocalypse is "not simply an uncovering of what has been but a manifestation of what will be: of what is to come. . . . The apocalypse involves a revelation both of the end of one world and the beginning of another." It is a "redemptive *transition* from one world to another, from one life . . . to another and possibly better one."[5] Cinema is the profane instrument of apocalyptic vision through which a new world, including its changing climate, is revealed as latent or hidden in the old. With on-location filming, in particular, backgrounds and foregrounds, scripted action and climatological conditions are in play, often in ways even the filmmaker may not plan for or take any particular notice of. Walter Benjamin coined the phrase "optical unconscious" to characterize the way film and photography not only archive a past that exceeds human perception but also may capture "the spark of contingency" in which "the future nests still today—and so eloquently that, we looking back, may rediscover it."[6] We can find in the archives of film a secret or hidden history of the future unfolding.

What we once presumed to be the stable norms of weather and climate are today becoming the increasing unstable eruption of storms, droughts, and fires. Indeed, in many of Tsai's films, the weather may be more eventful than what we take to be the explicit plot. The background given of climate, typically also in the background of cinema, is now foregrounded or revealed as not only the present tense of a diminished habitat but also a forecast for a less welcoming, less predictable Earth. His characters make slow, minimal adjustments and find different modalities and pleasures for what could be, if not a good life, then a life that is, for the time being, in this ruined world, good enough.

IMAGINING THE END

Tsai, in particular, is the filmmaker who helps us to see in the past and present new rituals of hospitality and latent features of the human in a world beset by constant rain (*The Hole*), drought (*Wayward Cloud*, 2005), smoke, or simply a state of affairs in which the elements are seemingly out of place (*The Hole*; *Rebels of a Neon God*, 1992). In his films, crumbling structures, bad plumbing, water-logged apartments, and profligate plastic bags conspire to evict characters from their homes and worlds. And in many cases, these characters are already vulnerable, displaced, and homeless. At once apocalyptic and utterly banal, the world of his movies projects the effects of rising tides and inclement weather events. As thematized in *Goodbye, Dragon Inn* (2003), staged in a condemned, haunted, leaking Taiwanese movie theater, not even cinema is likely to survive. But, as I remarked earlier, these are not films of despair. The makeshift shelters and invitations to share an apartment, a mattress, or a cigarette belong to a postcatastrophic world full of possibility. His characters are "watching, waiting, lingering, longing, and missing," as Jean Ma writes; they exist "in various states of drift and potentiality."[7]

I wish to emphasize that this form of apocalyptic thinking is quite distinct from mainstream climate fiction and eco-disaster movies and their attendant affects, such as *The Day after Tomorrow* (2004, dir. Roland Emmerich), *The Road* (2009, dir. John Hillcoat), and the *Mad Max* franchise. These are movies that frighten or distress us with the future loss of a familiar world and homey habitat: a projected future without nature. Rather than push us to reorder the status quo, they threaten with scenarios of its withdrawal. Rather than opening a portal to a new and, hopefully, more just world, such dystopic projections want us to want things as they are, to prevent the current world from changing or disappearing. Emblematic in this regard is that oft-mocked scene from *The Road* in which the man and his son share a Coke (product placement for the end times). While the man is transported back to the human world that was—grocery stores full of canned goods, people capable of social interaction, a world he mourns on his son's behalf—the boy is full of carbonated wonder. We know, along with the man, that the can of Coke belongs to a diegetic past we are cued to already miss desperately. In Tsai's films, by contrast, Coke bottles are just another feature of buoyant trash in his many flooded apartments.

Mainstream eco-disaster movies may even trigger what E. Ann Kaplan convincingly diagnoses as pretraumatic stress syndrome, symptoms we suffer not from the violent past, but, proleptically, from the future as it is envisioned on film. In immersive and alarming detail, these eco-disaster movies confront us with a version of a future human subject, some version of ourselves in shattered surroundings, haunted by the loss of the world.⁸ While dread of the future is not new, this particular conceptualization of pretraumatic stress enables us to diagnose how it feels to be living with a pronounced sense of "the end" without the promise of a hereafter. Pretraumatic stress may be one psychological response to an anticipated secular apocalypse.

Writing of an earlier period and a different scenario of end times, Paul K. Saint-Amour has also explored pretraumatic stress as the signature malady for everyone living in nuclear-targeted cities. In the time of mutually assured destruction, nuclear power nations (principally the United States and the Soviet Union) had amassed both sufficient weapons and the will to use them such that they could annihilate each other's citizens and allies in a matter of hours. The uniqueness of nuclear global war was the likelihood of total, planetary destruction—an eradication so geographically and temporally extensive that there would be no "after" in which to experience trauma. For this reason, total nuclear war can be only anticipated and described but not experienced or remembered. The psychological toll is a "collective psychosis of anticipation," a "foreshuddering" in light of a future no one would survive.⁹ To live under the constant looming threat as the price we pay for peace, Cold War citizens were afflicted by what Saint-Amour calls "anticipatory mourning."¹⁰

In the case of post-traumatic stress disorder (usual PTSD), the sufferer reexperiences the violent past in the present (nightmares, hallucinations, and staggering depression). The cure, in part, is to make a temporal adjustment by helping the sufferer to put the shocking experience back in the past, where it may be relegated to memory. Once the trauma is reintegrated into personal history, the sufferer can once again live in the present. The only cure for *pre*-traumatic stress, explains Saint-Amour, is to liberate the future from our catastrophic ideas about it—to relieve ourselves of the crippling stress of "living towards a future that seem[s] . . . to be written in advance" that we prepare for and thus in some way accept.¹¹ In many respects, nuclear criticism is the foundation for much of the early philosophically inflected writing on the Anthropocene and what helps us to pinpoint the challenge of managing, psychically and politically, our planetary crisis. To take just one metric: in 2016, greenhouse-gas emissions surpassed the threshold of 350 parts per million. This is a degree and rate of change that will continue to warm the planet for thousands of years to come, even if we were to halt all emissions immediately.¹² No sooner is the Anthropocene discovered and explained than we learn we are already too late. Srinivas Aravamudan, reflecting on this connection between nuclear projections and climate anxiety, explains the mode of temporal thinking as "catachronism":

> Similar to anachronism that reimagines the past in terms of the present, catachronism re-characterizes the past and the present in terms of a future proclaimed as determinate but that is of course not yet fully realized. To that extent, catachronism cannot function without the operational assumptions of a theological grasp of time, whereby anticipation, belief, and application on the present are integrated as inexorably leading to a known and inevitable outcome.[13]

The dreaded future of the Anthropocene is not the sudden end of the world we get with the nuclear scenario or even a pandemic. It is a slow erosion of familiar conditions, the gradual withdrawal of an environment that envelops all Holocene life: "slow violence," as Rob Nixon calls it.[14] We are left with either crippling anticipation or the melodramatic feeling of belated revelation. Climate-change anxiety forecloses the future and the possibility of action in the present, which we are inclined to keep as it is.

Some eco-disaster movies may even prevent us from seeing that the current state of the world—our giant coastal cities, monocrop agriculture, fossil-fueled mobility—is *itself* the environmental catastrophe. Roland Emmerich's *2012* (2009) and the utterly ludicrous *Geostorm* (2017, dir. Dean Devlin) want us to fear threats to the status quo, and they reassure us that we may arrive on the other side of total environmental collapse with the clichés of America's social order fully intact; automobiles will save and protect us, and little American girls will bond with their heroic fathers looking forward to a bright future continuous with the past.

Between the stress-inducing effects of mainstream climate disaster movies and their general enthrallment with a catastrophic status quo, how may cinema help to rescue the future from our ideas about it? How can it help us to see the current climate catastrophe without also catalyzing pre-traumatic stress that prepares us for a certain future without the will to change it?

TSAI MING-LIANG'S CLI-FI

Answering these questions returns me to Tsai Ming-liang as a master auteur for the Anthropocene, and not only because he features inclement weather, failing infrastructure, and epidemiological emergencies in his films. Rather, his queer narrative arcs and long-take slow cinema reveal characters living in a postapocalyptic world of the present. The catastrophe has arrived and its effects are already being felt, especially by those living on the economic and social margins of Taipei and Kuala Lumpur. In *I Don't Want to Sleep Alone,* smoke drifts into the last quarter of the film. Tsai does not linger with the environmental devastation at its source. Instead, he follows characters who are forced out of, but also freed from, the ideas of normative living and its regulating climate and predictable futures. Kuala Lumpur in this film is still feeling the aftershocks of the Asian financial crisis, with its derelict building projects and abandoned migrant workers. Repurposed for cinema, this world opens out into free-floating desire and intimacy in the slums, tea shops, and half-finished high-rises. Where the rich might have dwelt, the migrant worker sets up a temporary and lovingly decorated shelter.

The story centers on the actor Lee Kang-sheng, Tsai's melancholic muse, who appears in two speechless roles. In the first, he plays a homeless day laborer who is beaten early in the film and tenderly nursed back to life by the Bangladeshi migrant worker. As he regains strength, Lee's homeless character reconnects with the waitress, who is full of unspoken sexual longing. She works in a tea shop and is also the owner's servant, helping her to care for her comatose adult son. In his second role, Lee plays this son of the tea-shop owner. Clothed in a diaper and covered by a sheet, the open-eyed man is nursed (and masturbated) by both his mother (Pearlly Chua) and the waitress. The film is initially structured around these triangles of care and desire. But when the mother has a sexual encounter with the homeless man (played by the same actor who also plays her son), the triangle gives way to a parallelogram of people, none of whom is wholly at home in this world (even the tea-shop owner may be facing eviction) and whose desires stretch far beyond any heteronorms. These attachments and fleeting sexual drives are conveyed through glances and gestures in scenes of care and coercion, through long takes in which bathing, cleaning, arousal, and orgasm unfold in real time. The ambiguity of the narrative is rich: are some of these scenes the dream of the comatose son? Or might the day laborer nurture a fantasy of constant and total care? Is one part of this film "real" and the other a dream? Is there a difference? These are extralinguistic complexities, beyond or simply after language as they rise in the body in relation to other bodies. As Justin Chang observes of Tsai's long-take, dialogue-free cinema: his films teach us "how much you can learn about a person from what they do and how they move often far more than by what they say."¹⁵ As the inheritor of silent cinema's expressive bodies, Tsai's cinema explores the legibility of a person in the world, a phenomenology of feeling borne of genres, posture, and the smallest switches of the face (with Lee, in particular, Tsai ventures into the legibility of even chronic pain over the course of his career). Courting an obsessional mode of spectatorship, Tsai gives us characters who convey themselves. But the environment (natural or otherwise) defies obvious understanding.

The film breaks its silence when smoke from a distant source breaks the frame and permeates all the diegetic spaces. Initially, it overtakes our sleeping subjects like a quiet mist, moving more quickly than people in these otherwise still shots. When we join the scene of Lee in his comatose state surrounded by his mother and the waitress, he is enshrouded in plastic and surrounded by electric fans in a futile effort to diffuse the smoke. A radio broadcast provides the "official" explanation for this atmospheric change: the Malaysian government blames the dangerous smoke on two sources, "illegal workers" incinerating trash in the open and annual forest fires in Indonesia (burning in order to clear fields for palm oil, paper, and pulp plantations). The government will forgive the Indonesian forest fires but certainly prosecute the illegal workers. Listeners are assured that the smoke is *not* coming from the nearby plantation-clearing of Putrajaya (an area close to the city where rubber plantations are being burned to make space for a new government center). With gas masks and ventilators in short supply, people are encouraged to stay indoors and devise their own protection. So much narrative explication in an otherwise speechless film! But the radio announcement is necessary to account for the world-building activities near to and far from new city centers and the monocrop agricultural management that render the world unlivable. This is how the apocalypse arrives, and from here Tsai lingers on how exposed people survive.

Sex is now off the table—the smoke is too much. Kissing gives way to coughing, and eventually coughing gives way to sleeping and sleeping perhaps to dreaming. The final long take, digitally produced and quietly fantastic, finds our three characters asleep and adrift with little more than each other. The soundtrack produces a kind of vertical montage, or a dialectic for a new order. As the heavy mattress floats atop the black water in the dark basement of the unfinished high-rise, we hear an a cappella song in Chinese, an ode to love in the language of spring:

> I want to stay in your arms
> Because you are the only one for me

> Winter has gone and spring is here
> Bridges are filled with flowers again.
> . . . can you hear the canaries sing of love?

These descriptions of budding life are so at odds with the dark and slumbering image. But one hears echoes of Roy's swell of songbirds in the city.

The melody is a theme from Charlie Chaplin's *Limelight*, his 1952 film set in London on the eve of World War I.[16] Chaplin plays a washed-up, alcoholic entertainer who saves a young dancer (Claire Bloom) from suicide. He shelters her in his apartment, offers his own mattress as a space for convalescence, and nurses her back to health, using his own meager savings to pay for the medicine and food she needs (a scenario of care that structures the relationship between Lee's homeless laborer and migrant worker). In one of many pep talks to his despairing patient, Chaplin declares with grand gestures and big feeling: "There is something just as inevitable as death, and that's life, life, life!" Under his stewardship, the dancer resurrects her career and becomes a star of the London stage. Tsai's characters, exhausted and overwrought, are called at the end of the film to the inevitability of sleep, sleep, sleep.[17] Tsai's film is not a wake-up call to the joys of life or to the promises of an adoring public. But neither is it a warning of a coming war or environmental destruction. It does not ask us to preserve this world for the next generation. There is no offer of Coke and a smile. Instead, the film bids us to sleep, to pause, and to consider leaving behind all that was already unwelcoming to these people, a world we should not want to preserve or carry with us beyond the catastrophes of our current moment, or even into our dreams. As an image of *an* end, Tsai offers us a minimal and totally open vision for a future. The mattress with its sleeping lovers drifts to the bottom of the frame, edging its way through the darkness toward an as-yet-unseen portal and promises of another spring.

NOTES

1. Arundhati Roy, "The Pandemic Is a Portal," *Financial Times*, April 3, 2020, https://www.ft.com/content/10d8f5e8-74eb-11ea-95fe-fcd274e920ca. Accessed July 8, 2021.

2. See, e.g., "Coronavirus, Climate Change, and the Environment: A Conversation on COVID-19 with Dr. Aaron Bernstein, Director of Harvard Chan C-CHANGE," Harvard School of Public Health, https://www.hsph.harvard.edu/c-change/subtopics/coronavirus-and-climate-change/#:~:text=expensive%20to%20fix%3F-,Does%20climate%20change%20affect%20the%

20transmission%20of%20coronavirus%3F,and%20our%20risk%20for%20 infections. Accessed July 8, 2021.

3. Roy, "Pandemic Is a Portal."

4. Roy, "Pandemic Is a Portal."

5. Samuel Weber, "Foreword: One Sun Too Many," in Peter Szendy, *Apocalypse-Cinema: 2012 and Other Ends of the World,* trans. Will Bishop (New York: Fordham University Press, 2015), ix–xx, at xi (original emphasis).

6. Walter Benjamin, "Little History of Photography," in *The Work of Art in the Age of Its Technological Reproducibility, and Other Writings on Media,* ed. Michael W. Jennings, Brigid Doherty, and Thomas Y. Levin, trans. Edmund Jephcott and Kingsley Shorter (Cambridge, MA: Harvard University Press, 2008), 274–298, at 276–277.

7. Jean Ma, *Melancholy Drift: Marking Time in Chinese Cinema* (Hong Kong: Hong Kong University Press, 2010), 107.

8. E. Ann Kaplan, *Climate Trauma: Foreseeing the Future in Dystopian Film and Fiction* (New Brunswick, NJ: Rutgers University Press, 2016), see esp. Chapter 1: "Trauma Studies Moving Froward."

9. Paul K. Saint-Amour, *Tense Future: Modernism, Total War, Encyclopedic Form* (Oxford: Oxford University Press, 2015), 23.

10. Saint-Amour, *Tense Future,* 25.

11. Saint-Amour, *Tense Future,* 21.

12. See, e.g., Nicola Jones, "How the World Passed a Carbon Threshold and Why it Matters," *Yale Environment 360,* January 26, 2017, https://e360.yale.edu/features/how-the-world-passed-a-carbon-threshold-400ppm-and-why-it-matters. Accessed July 8, 2021.

13. Srinivas Aravamudan, "The Catachronism of Climate Change," *diacritics* 41, no. 3 (2013): 6–30, at 8. This essay considers how climate-change criticism may build on the methods of nuclear criticism inaugurated in *diacritics* in 1984.

14. Rob Nixon, *Slow Violence and the Environmentalism of the Poor* (Princeton: Princeton University Press, 2011).

15. Justin Chang, "Review: Tsai Ming-liang's 'Days' Is a Quietly Aching Stunner from One of Our Great Filmmakers," *Los Angeles Times,* August 13, 2021, https://www.latimes.com/entertainment-arts/movies/story/2021-08-13/days-review-tsai-ming-liang. Accessed June 10, 2022.

16. Tsai reprises the *Limelight* theme in his most recent film, *Days* (2020), as it magically emanates from a tiny music box exchanged between the film's two characters after a quietly ecstatic scene of intimacy.

17. The Chinese title of the film, *Ring Under Your Eyes,* captures the effects of sleep deprivation as akin to having a black eye.

2

... Scaling Down

On the Unsustainable Pleasure of Large-File Streaming

LAURA U. MARKS

Because of the physical impacts of our movie viewing on other humans and our environment, the ethics of spectatorship involve the materiality of the cinematic medium. In the course of just about a decade, consumers worldwide, but especially those in regions with good infrastructure, have come to expect moving images to be available on demand, on every kind of surface, and often as a replacement for text and audio. These new expectations are the *rebound effects* of cheap and plentiful high-speed internet access: the phenomenon that greater efficiency leads to greater consumption of a resource. Streaming media is calculated to contribute a startling 1% and rising quickly of global greenhouse gases, because most regions of the world obtain electricity from fossil fuels to power their data centers, networks, and devices.[1] That figure contributes significantly to the carbon footprint of information and communication technologies (ICT) as a whole: ICT's electricity use is rising by 6.6% to 7.3% per year.[2] Streaming large files in large quantities, then, ethically implicates spectators in the warming of the planet. Like Laura Mulvey in 1975, I write here about the unacknowledged cost of a certain cinematic pleasure, and I intend to destroy that pleasure.

How does the value of postponing satisfaction by enjoying non-streaming media, accompanied by the ethical awareness that one is not damaging the planet, compare with the luxury of movies on demand? And how does the value of watching brief, low-resolution, often low-tech cinema, accompanied by a similar ethical awareness, compare with

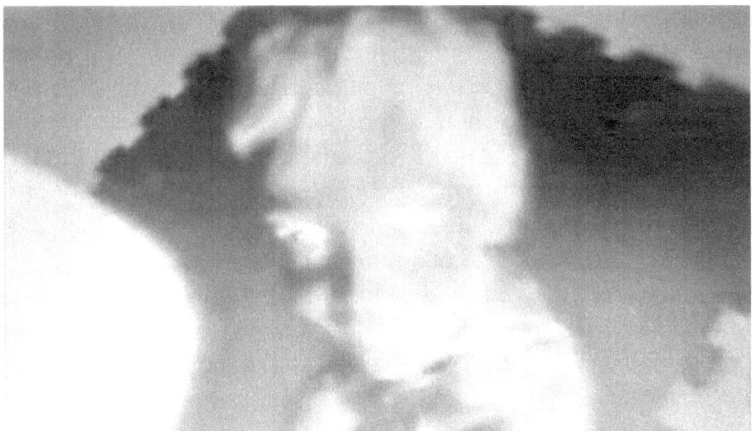

FIGURE 3. Nadia Shams's small-file film *Point Zero* (2020).

the enjoyment of energy-intensive, high-definition streaming? In 2020 I founded the Small File Media Festival to draw attention to this issue and demonstrate that streaming movies can be attractive even when they use minimal bandwidth.

EMBRACING STREAMING INFRASTRUCTURE

Mediation does not separate beings from each other but puts us in contact. Films bring audiences into contact with their pro-filmic worlds. From an aging videotape of a long-ago family gathering, the faces of family members swim up from the magnetic sea. When I Skype a loved one I feel the vibrations of his voice on the keyboard. Video-on-demand platforms like MUBI make rare movies accessible to grateful fans.

Watching movies through these and other media also puts us viewers into contact with the means of mediation. The new field of infrastructure studies makes it more difficult than ever to disavow movies' material, energetic, human, and environmental support. Now when we evaluate what film is good for, we should also evaluate its support, as the means of mediation can be salubrious or insalubrious. Bracketing for now the means of the movie's filming and postproduction, we can evaluate the salubrity of storage medium and playback medium.

Let's first consider a film projected in a movie theater. The film's storage medium entails the use of fossil fuels (for the acetate base) and, if it was shot on film, usually toxic chemicals. The projector is built to last for many years. Audiences gather in the theater to watch the movie, usually multiple times, allowing the environmental costs of production and projection to be divided by the total number of audience members. Yes, we need to account for the carbon footprint of how those audiences reached the theater—driving a gas-fueled car, taking public transit, walking, et cetera. But we also need to measure the less calculable salubrity of the public social occasion of collective viewing—the pleasure of joint action that, as Julian Hanich points out, is missing in solo home viewing.[3]

Turning to private viewing practices, those with a physical storage medium, like videotape, DVDs, Blu-rays, and digital files, all have their different manners of corralling electrons and different degrees of environmental impact. DVDs and Blu-rays have a carbon footprint due to their energy-intensive production and shipping activity, and their plastic packaging. I am certain that, were there the will, it would be easy to engineer a lower-impact physical storage medium. The original private viewing practice without a physical storage medium is, of course, television. Television broadcast transmissions, analog or digital, travel lightly along proprietary segments of the radio spectrum, taking advantage of the free circulation of electrons. Their energy expense lies mainly in the production and use of TVs.

Streaming media are also a private viewing practice without a physical storage medium. Unlike television, however, streaming is narrowcasting: not one-to-many but one-to-one. Each viewer's device requires its own unique transmission. Video files are large; for example, a 1-hour, 720 × 1080p high-definition video with a frame rate of 30 frames per second and bit rate of 5 megabytes per second has a file size of 2.11 gigabytes.[4] They occupy the majority of storage space in servers. They require massive amounts of bandwidth. The streaming audience receives them on mobile phones, computers, and smart TVs that require a great deal of electricity to produce as well as use. Streaming video files travel through underground networks, crossing Indigenous lands and satellite transmitters that crowd the skies in transmissions that "hop" among, by a low estimate, eleven networks before they reach their audience, consuming electricity at each point.[5]

A 2014 study by the engineers Arman Shehabi, Ben Walker, and Eric Masanet has long been used to justify the argument that streaming has a lower carbon impact than DVDs.[6] The authors' comparison was based on the assumption that consumers drive to the video store and watch only five movies per month. They pointed out that the balance would shift if people watched streaming video for more hours a day and/or in higher definition. In fact, the balance shifted that very same year. In 2014, "cord cutters"—consumers who only watch video online—consumed about 100 hours of video per month.[7] Shehabi, Walker, and Masanet's study was limited to content found on DVDs, omitting YouTube-style video clips and videos embedded in social media and websites. Once we take into account total online video viewing, not just movies, the environmental impact of streaming quickly becomes evident.

Given impressive improvements in energy efficiency, the electricity consumption per gigabyte of ICT has decreased dramatically. But only the foolhardy say we are in the clear, as rebound effects mean that efficiency is outstripped by fast-rising demand for data-intensive uses like streaming media, not to mention blockchain, artificial intelligence, and the Internet of Things.[8]

All these devices rely on astonishingly dense electronic circuits, triumphs of Moore's law, whereby the number of transistors on circuit doubles by a factor of 1.4 with each generation. The technological wonder of the electronic circuit relies on ever more efficient channeling of electrons. This increase in efficiency is a function of complementary metal-oxide-semiconductors' ability to work with ever lower supply voltages, known as CMOS scaling. However, with lower voltage, metal-oxide transistors begin to leak exponentially, and what they are leaking is electrons.[9] Engineers are struggling desperately to come up with new ways to ensure energy efficiency. But as engineer Hubert Kaeslin writes:

> While it is utterly clear that there can be no further progress without corresponding improvements in energy efficiency, the thirst for ever higher data bandwidths, the quest for better video resolutions, the current move towards storing everything in the cloud rather than locally, the desire to communicate even with humble objects over the Internet, and similar trends will in all likelihood continue to drive up the energy demand of ICT as a whole. Unfortunately, CMOS scaling alone can no longer be counted upon to yield the same gains in terms of performance, efficiency, and cost reduction as in the past.[10]

Circuits have become so small that the behavior of individual particles really matters. Electrons indentured to move along regimented paths seek liberty. They find it at the expense of circuit efficiency, with the result that Moore's law is coming to an end, and with it the energy efficiency that has powered computer miniaturization for forty years. As we do for farm animals, if we think of an electron's life as worth living, we should consider their freedom, too. I personally find it a splendid joke on us molar-scale beings that electronic freedom threatens to bring decades of computational progress to a crashing halt.

Now let's think about those complementary metals. Semiconductor miniaturization has required the use of increasingly rare metals, including indium, gallium, germanium, tantalum, and the rare earth elements dysprosium, neodymium, praseodymium, vibranium, and yttrium (one of these is fictional).[11] As we know, mining for tantalum in the Democratic Republic of the Congo precipitated humanitarian atrocities and environmental devastation—all because tantalum, twice as dense as steel, durable, highly ductile, and especially easy to weld, is valued for its ability to smooth the flow of electrons in miniaturized circuits.[12] I would like to take a moment to consider how ludicrous it is that the planet's share of these rare and precious metals is fast depleting for purposes that are not good for us: the fetishism of immediacy, platforms designed to addict users, superfluous overbuilding of infrastructure, and the burning of fossil fuels to support them all. The resulting planetary devastation, I argue, trumps any good brought to us by streaming media.

INFRASTRUCTURAL SOUL-ASSEMBLAGES

Infrastructure creates an assemblage, unique in each case, between the source of the movie and its destination. I like to think of these as soul-assemblages. I assume that every entity, however tiny, however dispersed, however immaterial, as long as it is capable of affecting or being affected (Spinoza) has a soul. Hence, my obsession in the above with the labor of electrons and metals, as well as that of humans, technology, and the environment. My soul-assemblage concept draws on Leibniz's concept of the dominated monad, Spinoza's understanding that bodies combine in healthy and unhealthy ways, Whitehead's concept of actual entity, and the assemblage theory of Deleuze and Guattari. The cosmos is a single being, infinitely folded. Entities involved in a common event compose their own set of folds that behaves like a single soul.

So, for example, watching a movie in a theater, my soul folds together with those of other viewers, the screen, the theater furniture, the popcorn, the projector, the electricity powering the projector, the air through which light passes, the movie itself—its story, its characters, its colors and sounds—and with all the souls that made the movie possible. The soul-assemblage of *Black Panther* (2018, dir. Ryan Coogler), for example, encompasses the performers, the crew, set design, equipment, script, editors, et cetera. It also includes the electricity consumption involved at every stage of production and reception, and the resulting greenhouse gases emitted. Around the movie develops an audience soul-assemblage that will be different every time and every place the movie is performed. Assembling with it too are the reviews, the awards, the gossip, the mash-ups on YouTube, the Afrofuturist inspirations, the grieving for the much-missed actor Chadwick Bozeman. The *Black Panther* soul-assemblage is a living, unified, ever-changing entity. We can assess the health of this great soul according to what becomes of the many souls that compose it in the course of their assembling.

We can do the same with the soul-assemblage of a streaming movie. As an example, I consider the much-loved "Beautiful Relaxing Music for Stress Relief ~ Calming Music ~ Meditation, Relaxation, Sleep, Spa" by Meditation Relax Music, which has had almost 37 million views since it was posted to YouTube in 2018. It features three hours of calming looped synthesizer music playing over cycling shots of forests, waterfalls, blue skies, and flowers. The video's soul-assemblage includes the musicians and filmmakers; the production company; the YouTube platform; the millions of human souls that have played it; the uncountable stresses, anxieties, and sleepless nights the viewers suffered; the pleasant feelings of relaxation that washed over them as they listened; the dopamine secreted in the listeners' brains. It includes the devices—phones, laptops, TVs—on which the audience streamed "Beautiful Relaxing Music for Stress Relief," the wired and wireless internet connections, the servers that store YouTube videos, the networks that connect them. It includes engineers, rare metals, and electrons.

YouTube, owned by Google, claims to be carbon neutral at source and receives an A rating from Greenpeace.[13] In fact, this neutrality is achieved in part by cap-and-trade measures, which means an exchange of carbon credits, not an absolute decrease in carbon emissions. Moreover, YouTube accounts for neither the energy source of the other servers and networks through which "Beautiful Relaxing Music for Stress Relief" passes, nor the carbon emissions resulting from production of the devices or their disposal.

You see the irony that a movie made for relaxation from stress and picturing forests actually makes a substantial contribution to the despoliation of the planet. Probably many of its listeners are anxious about global warming yet do not know they are contributing to it. Moreover, streaming a meditation video alone may not be as good for the soul as gathering with friends or going for a walk. By my reckoning, "Beautiful Relaxing Music for Stress Relief" is an overall unhealthy soul-assemblage, whose benefits for stressed individuals are canceled out by the stress their delivery system imposes on the planet.

The point of this lugubrious exercise is not to single out an individual program but to emphasize that the recent habit of streaming large quantities of media on demand is unsustainable, as long as the electricity that powers most of the production and use of data centers, networks, and devices derives from fossil fuels. If you live in a region where energy sources are renewable, bravo! But you still need to factor in the electricity consumption of data centers and networks at streaming sources outside your region, and the energy required to produce your devices. Even were global energy 100% renewable, it still would probably not be enough to support current high and growing levels of streaming. The shift to renewable energy is too slow and uneven to remediate this unsustainable situation before 2030, the year that carbon emissions must be lowered to 2016 levels in order to avoid catastrophic global warming.

If film is to be good for our planetary soul-assemblage, then, change is urgently necessary. Governments should treat high-speed streaming as a luxury. This could be carried out by imposing a carbon tax on streaming platforms, telecoms, and data center and network managers. Of course, those companies would pass these costs on to consumers, deepening the class divide between technological haves and have-nots. Nevertheless, I suggest we not hasten to embrace the carbon-intensive and Western-centric ideal of net neutrality: the idea that all citizens should have equal access to high-speed internet.[14] The Shift Project, citing statistics of the Organization for Economic Co-operation and Development, points out that the digital carbon footprint of an American is sixteen times larger than that of an inhabitant of a developing country, and five times larger than the world average. It argues that regulation is compatible with net neutrality if we consider the criterion that the internet be for the common good.[15] Similarly, as Ramón Lobato writes, net neutrality is "grounded in a first-world idea of the internet, premised on an assumption of unbounded capacity. It does not ring true with how the internet is experienced in many countries."[16]

The United States, China, and the European Union could probably carry out such a regulation internally, but in other countries the internet cannot be regulated at the federal level alone. Therefore, in the shorter term, the onus for change rests on individual practices. Movie lovers of all sorts need to be educated about the carbon footprint of streaming media. Consumers need to understand that the screens on which we watch our streaming movies—especially voracious 4K TVs and phones that last only one or two years—contribute a surprisingly high proportion of global greenhouse-gas emissions. Streaming platforms should be required to default to standard or low resolution, passing to the viewer the responsibility to increase resolution. Viewers in poorly connected regions—those in less-developed countries and outside of urban centers—should become a model for those of us who are "data-rich,"[17] now that the taintedness of our wealth is exposed. Yes, I am saying that people's movie habits in low-bandwidth regions, like Rwanda, Kashmir, and northern Canada, should be aspirational for the rest of us, and not the other way around.[18]

To this bad news and these uncomfortable measures, the cinephilic soul-assemblage curdles in revulsion: to recognize that our seemingly benign streams are flowing with poison; to accept the bitter medicine of relinquishing our convenient and addictive habits. Again, however, I must emphasize that our streaming habits have only taken this unsustainable shape in the last decade or so, thus it is not impossible to massage them into a more Earth-friendly contour. Why not resist the desire for immediate gratification? Why not rent or borrow movies or go to the theater when we want to watch movies in high resolution?

CINEPHILIA AND RESOLUTION

"Hot" media, in Marshall McLuhan's conception, or media that extend a single sense in "high definition," are well filled in with data, leave little to be completed by the audience, and allow less participation. With too much heat and stimulation, passivity and numbness set in.[19] For people in well-infrastructured regions, the numerous streaming-video surfaces that surround us every day emit this video heat, to anodyne effect.

I don't think I'm the only person who finds the marketed appeal of high-resolution, "immersive" media faintly insulting. It assumes we are so forgetful that we can't recall what things look like, so unimaginative that our minds can't fill in details, that our brains and senses have shrunk down to wizened nubs (which, according to McLuhan, they may have). As I demonstrated above, media build a contact between object and viewer, which an engaged viewer can imaginatively realize, even if the video file is low resolution. All media are like executable files—designed to travel small and be unpacked when they reach their destination. Certainly the majority of videos that stream around the world do not need to be high resolution to affect their audience in the intended way. Most instructional and documentary movies, such as news, cat and child videos and other amusements, cooking and meditation videos, sports, and pornography, have the purpose of transmitting information and affect more than providing a rich perceptual experience. Even if they transmit with a very low bit rate and decreased frame rate, the receiver can still learn the information and enjoy the affective response. The same has been long true for online games, though games are becoming sensuously and unsustainably cinematic. I would argue, too, that for the majority of streaming series and narratives, even at very low resolution, narrative and affective content come across easily. (In the first months of the Covid-19 pandemic, Netflix, YouTube, and PlayStation reduced their streams to standard definition, a still quite high 720p, to meet the spike in demand.[20]) Similarly, the faces in video calls and video conferences can be satisfactorily unpacked at the user's end from a small cluster of pixels and a decreased frame rate. And since sound files are much smaller than video files, evocative soundtracks can fill in a great deal of the missing information.

Nevertheless, there are some movies that we want to overwhelm us sensorially. The high resolution, speed, and immersiveness promised in the marketing of every device and telecom package really do matter for films whose meaning rests in the perceptual experience itself. Streaming, with its crafty deployment of compression to replace atmosphere with pixelline approximations, torments the cinephile. But as I have demonstrated, the immersive ideal, very robust bandwidth streaming to a 4K or 8K television, is unsustainable. For the environmentalist cinephile, given the correlation between image quality and global warming, streaming is torture.

SALUBRIOUS SMALL FILES

Finally, some sweetness to follow the bitter pill. Let the song of the small file soothe our souls!

Films that stream at as little as one megabyte per minute can beguile, delight, and satisfy their audiences. To test this hypothesis, I founded the Small File Media Festival, now in its fourth year (smallfile.ca). We invite makers to submit movies of no more than one megabyte per minute, which can be streamed at little cost to the environment. In its first rendition in 2020, the festival screened more than 100 works by artists in sixteen countries, in ten lovingly curated programs, to 165 attendees. The movies included data-spare movies creatively crafted with a wide range of compression algorithms; exquisite, high-resolution works of only 15 seconds; works made with technologies thought to be obsolete; animations; works that rely on still images and rich soundtracks; and many other inventive solutions to our small-file challenge. With small-file movies, the ethical issue is less the content but the file size. Small-file porn, by the criteria I have introduced here, is as ethical as small-file activist documentaries. In fact, however, the movies that fell into our porn category, which in the First Annual Small File Media Festival we renamed "Steamy Bits," challenged the boundaries between erotic, aesthetic, and intellectual enjoyment.[21]

Small-file movies are salubrious in many ways. They embrace the loss of information that occurs with compression. Yet many small-file movies are surprisingly high in quality. It's not necessary to sacrifice resolution to make a file small. Camera and mise-en-scène techniques, such as using a shallow focal length and keeping both camera movement and in-frame movement slow, allow the image to remain crisp when it is compressed. That's because compression algorithms compare sequential frames: when their differences are slight, the disparity in compression is smaller.

Similarly, small-file movies are intensive, not extensive. Most still and video images shot with recent digital cameras expand to fill the needlessly large file size to which the camera defaults. Is a 5 megabyte snapshot created in 2021 more valuable than a 350 kilobyte snapshot created in 2000? In most cases, no. An intensive image pours value into every pixel: every pixel matters. (Azadeh Emadi argues that pixels are the soul of the digital screen, because each one of them undergoes radical transformation to support changes in the picture surface.)[22] In McLuhan's term, small-file movies are "cool" media: they activate the viewer and draw them in. Small-file movies are often haptic, and as a result, erotic; drawn in, we feel the movies with all our senses as much as we perceive them visually; sound plays a large role in this engagement. Small-file movies stimulate the imagination.

Unlike other streaming videos, small-file movies celebrate infrastructure rather than disavow it. They laugh at Moore's law and Koomey's law. They remind us that we form a soul-assemblage with all the human and technical means that facilitate streaming—miners in Africa, assembly-line workers in China, data centers, networks, devices (which can be thoroughly out of date and small-file movies don't mind), electrons, power plants, carbon atoms—and this consciousness of our connection, for once, does not cause pain. By building more salutary connections between viewers, movies, infrastructure, the layers of air that embrace our planet, and the sun, small-file movies connect us to the cosmos in healthy and life-affirming ways.

NOTES

1. The Shift Project, "Climate Crisis: The Unsustainable Use of Online Video" (2019), https://theshiftproject.org/en/article/unsustainable-use-online-video/. Accessed July 27, 2021. After a yearlong survey of the engineering literature, my research group Tackling the Carbon Footprint of Streaming Media, funded by the Social Sciences and Humanities Research Council of Canada, was able to confirm The Shift Project's estimate. You can find our report at https://sfu.ca/sca/streaming-carbon-footprint.html.

2. Bart Lannoo et al., "Overview of ICT Energy Consumption," *Network of Excellence in Internet Science* (2013): 1–59; Ward Van Heddeghem et al., "Trends in Worldwide ICT Electricity Consumption from 2007 to 2012," *Computer Communications* 50 (2014): 64–76; Lotfi Belkhir and Ahmed Elmeligi, "Assessing ICT Global Emissions Footprint: Trends to 2040 and Recommendations," *Journal of Cleaner Production* 177 (2018): 448–463.

3. Julian Hanich, "Watching a Film with Others: Towards a Theory of Collective Spectatorship," *Screen* 55, no. 3 (2014): 338–359.

4. Calculated at https://www.videoproc.com/edit-4k-video/video-size-calculator.htm.

5. Oche Ejembi and Saleem N. Bhatti, "Client-Side Energy Costs of Video Streaming," *Proceedings of the 2015 IEEE International Conference on Data Science and Data Intensive Systems* (December 2015): 252–259, at 255.

6. Arman Shehabi, Ben Walker, and Eric Masanet, "The Energy and Greenhouse-Gas Implications of Video Streaming in the United States," *Environmental Research Letters* 9 (2014): 1–11.

7. Sandvine, "The Global Internet Phenomena Report," Technical Report (2014), https://www.sandvine.com/hubfs/downloads/archive/2014-1h-global-internet-phenomena-report.pdf. Accessed July 27, 2021.

8. Steffen Lange, Johanna Pohl, and Tilman Santarius, "Digitalization and Energy Consumption: Does ICT Reduce Energy Demand?," *Ecological Economics* 176 (October 2020): 1–14.

9. Hubert Kaeslin, "Semiconductor Technology and the Energy Efficiency ICT," in *ICT Innovations for Sustainability,* ed. Lorenz M. Hilty and Bernard Aebischer (New York: Springer, 2015), 105–112.

10. Kaeslin, "Semiconductor Technology," 111.

11. Fairphone, "Scoping Study: Smartphone Material Profiles" (May 2017), https://www.fairphone.com/en/research-resources/. Accessed July 27, 2021.

12. Karen Hayes and Richard Burge, *Coltan Mining in the Democratic Republic of Congo: How Tantalum-Using Industries Can Commit to the Reconstruction of the DRC* (Cambridge: Fauna and Flora International, 2003).

13. Greenpeace, "Clicking Clean: Who Is Winning the Race to Build a Green Internet?" (2017), http://www.clickclean.org. Accessed July 27, 2021.

14. Janine Morley, Kelly Widdicks, and Mike Hazas, "Digitalization, Energy and Data Demand: The Impact of Internet Traffic on Overall and Peak Electricity Consumption," *Energy Research and Social Science* 38 (April 2018): 128–137.

15. The Shift Project, "Lean ICT: Towards Digital Sobriety," Technical Report (2019), https://theshiftproject.org/en/article/lean-ict-our-new-report/. Accessed July 27, 2021.

16. Ramón Lobato, *Netflix Nations: The Geography of Digital Distribution* (New York: New York University Press, 2019), 93.

17. Mathias Leidig and Richard M. Teeuw, "Quantifying and Mapping Global Data Poverty," *PLOS One* 10, no. 11 (2015): 1–15.

18. For more on this question, see Laura U. Marks and Radek Przedpełski, "Bandwidth Imperialism and Small-File Media," in "New Filmic Geographies," ed. Suzanne Enzerink, special issue, *Post45* (2021), https://post45.org/2021/04/bandwidth-imperialism-and-small-file-media/. Accessed July 27, 2021.

19. Marshall McLuhan, "Media Hot and Cold," in *Understanding Media: The Extensions of Man* (London: Routledge, 2001 [1964]), 24–29.

20. Sandvine, "The Global Internet Phenomena Report," Technical Report (2020), https://www.sandvine.com/phenomena. Accessed July 27, 2021.

21. Laura U. Marks, "Small File Movies: Saving the Planet, One Pixel at a Time," *Millennium Film Journal* 71–72 (Spring–Fall 2020): 94–101.

22. Azadeh Emadi, "Reconsidering the Substance of Digital Video from a Sadrian Perspective," *Leonardo* 53, no. 1 (2020): 75–80.

3

... It's Invaluable

On Film Spectatorship in the Era of Covid-19

SARAH COOPER

"Is it good?" I ask my friend, "Is it worth seeing on the big screen?" I listen to her responses and then ponder them as I try to decide whether to book the pricey £16.90 ticket for my closest London cinema—a high-end boutique venue—in September 2020. My pre-2020 academic self would balk at my request for such reductive judgments as well as my own self-interest, which shifts the lofty issue of the value of film into the terrain of (my) time, (my) money, and what I'll get out of this—would it be worth the time, worth the money, worth the trip? Yet behind my articulated questions are unspoken worries about risk and safety, not only for myself but others, too, which arise for reasons that by now will be horribly well known.

In the wake of its initial devastation, Covid-19 had gone into a period of remission at that time in our small corner of the world. Venues that could afford to do so safely were opening up again, and the luxury of being able to go to the cinema was possible once more, albeit momentarily, before a further two national lockdowns. A slew of press articles and other lengthier publications emerged from spring 2020 onward addressing the impact of the virus on the film industry and on cinemas, in particular, some predicting an eventual bounce back, others collapse. Streaming services, meanwhile, fared far better in times when there was no choice but to watch films at home, as well as when people did not want or were not able to make a trip to the cinema in the times of respite. Aside from the different successes of Netflix, Amazon Prime, and

FIGURE 4. Cinema in lockdown, 2020. © Curzon Cinemas.

MUBI, one of the reasons that UK Curzon cinemas were able to keep going during successive lockdowns, when others such as Cineworld and Picturehouse were not, is attributed to the uptake of their home-cinema service. The same is true for some other independent cinemas that managed to adapt to online platforms during a period of ceaseless and unprecedented disruption.

Tomas Eskilsson, head of strategy at the Swedish production company and film fund Film i Väst, suggests that the pandemic has, in fact, just sped up a change that was already under way in the film industry: "The production, distribution and screening of feature films and drama series were already merging and changing character even before the crisis. A paradigm shift is under way. . . . Sars Cov 2/Covid-19 accelerates the development of a new ecosystem, a new movie landscape."[1] This transformation is ongoing: at the time of writing, it is still too difficult to see clearly what the lasting effects of the virus will be, or what this new landscape will look like. With the mutating disease set to be around for an unforeseeable time ahead, although mitigated by vaccines, and with the repayment of debts incurred throughout the pandemic in the United Kingdom alone expected to take decades, the virus continues to take its toll and the aftertimes seem some way away. It is out of this context of crisis and uncertainty that my own reflections on the good and value of film emerge, in tandem with ethical debate on the virus in the broader philosophical sphere.

In a *New York Times* live online discussion held during the first wave of the pandemic, titled "This Isn't *The Good Place*. How Can We Make

It Better?," the philosophers Todd May and Simon Critchley exchanged thoughts on how Covid-19 has brought ethical questions that lie at the heart of moral philosophy to the fore. May, who served as philosophical adviser for the US sitcom *The Good Place*, speaks of the "ethical web" created by the Covid-19 crisis and how the virus has made people think about their obligations to others, those they do not know as well as those they know. Moreover, for Critchley it presents a philosophical moment at which to reflect deeply on the nature of life.[2] Critchley outlines how various areas of moral philosophy have been operative in different ways, sometimes deficiently, during the pandemic: the question of duty to others (deontology); of what people owe to others (contractualism); difficult decisions pertaining to the greatest happiness of the many (utilitarianism); as well as the foregrounding and praise of figures of virtue (virtue ethics) (in the United Kingdom these were the "key workers," especially the carers). Of all these positions in moral philosophy, the question of duty and obligation to others, along with May's web of connectedness, were the most relevant to my own choices on a daily basis, including my possible trip to the cinema in September 2020. But my questions to my friend also brought to mind a connection to some of my earliest scholarly work on film and the distinctive ethical philosophy at its core. My understanding of the good of film in this earlier scholarship is still one to which I adhere. Nevertheless, these changing times call for a more everyday reassessment of what film is good for as the contours of the movie landscape—its ecosystem, as Eskilsson terms it—become open to redefinition.

LOOKING BACK: ETHICS AND FILM

To ask under any circumstances "What's in it for me?" is a deeply unethical question if we think of ethics in the way that philosopher Emmanuel Levinas does. Even the most altruistic person can never entirely avoid such questions, however, and Levinas's ethics of alterity recognizes this by never losing sight of the self, although the sovereignty of this self is in dispute from the outset. His is not a practical ethics of obligation, duty, or connectedness to others; it is, rather, an ethics based on a primordial and perpetual calling into question of the self by the Other. For Levinas, the good transcends essence and belongs to neither Being nor totality: his major works, *Totality and Infinity: An Essay on Exteriority* (*Totalité et infini: Essai sur l'extériorité*, 1961) and *Otherwise than Being or Beyond Essence* (*Autrement qu'être ou au-delà de l'essence,* 1974), seek to maintain a separation between ethics and ontology, thereby challenging a Western philosophical tradition in which he argues the ethical is dependent upon the ontological.[3] The Levinasian ethical dimension is not one of sweetness and light: it is associated with discomfort, exorbitance, and even impossibility—we can never do enough and it asks too much, and yet ethics is born of this. I have always felt in tune with the difficulty of the Levinasian ethical demand, and my reason for turning to his work in the context of my earlier research was that it spoke to particular questions in film scholarship too.

The capacity of film to stimulate ethical reflection has been a longstanding interest of mine. My first book on film, *Selfless Cinema? Ethics and French Documentary* (2006), and a subsequent special issue of *Film-Philosophy,* "The Occluded Relation: Levinas and Cinema" (2007), brought together Levinas's ethics and different forms of filmmaking.[4] In my research on documentary, I had found in existing scholarship that documentary ethics were defined frequently in terms of legal rights. While protecting the rights of documentary participants and filmmakers is essential, little had been done at that time to expand ethical debate beyond the juridical context into the realm of ethics proper. This is where Levinas came in: prior to the juridical is the Levinasian ethical dimension, founded on an originary asymmetrical relation to an Other that exceeds the ability of the self fully to know that Other. My approach to documentary was intended to amplify ethical discussion of film by taking up the Levinasian ethical challenge to ontology and epistemology in relation to questions of representation and spectatorship. *Selfless Cinema?* introduced to film theory and the burgeoning field of film-philosophy a thinker whose writings had rarely been taken up in film studies at that point—his own iconoclastic relation to the image being one of the reasons for this, along with the dearth of references to cinema in his work. My other main writing on Levinas and film focused on the work of filmmakers who consciously engage with his philosophy: the Belgian duo Jean-Pierre and Luc Dardenne. Luc speaks poignantly in his filmmaking diaries of how he and his brother filmed in a manner informed by Levinas's ethics, thinking about sequences and entire films in its light, with his philosophy continuing to interest them in their more recent work.[5]

From research into ethics in the context of French documentary through to the films of the Dardennes, Levinas's work was an inspirational cornerstone of my own. In the field of ethics and film scholarship that flourished thereafter and that is still thriving today, he has an abiding place, in some cases through the work of scholars developing discussion of his ethical philosophy and film,[6] in others with scholars disagreeing with the foundations of his work by turning to the work of other philosophers who do the same and using their critique as a starting point for new debates on ethics and film. For me, though, the good of the film that I wrote about in dialogue with Levinas's thought was never in doubt: it insisted implicitly and explicitly on an irreducible alterity that escaped the possession of the self and in so doing performed and engaged viewers in a profound, compelling ethics.

However, there is something sobering about revisiting this earlier work on Levinas and film in light of Covid-19, as I move now from this specific ethical approach to the good of film to thinking more broadly about what such film scholarship, and film in general, are good for today. It is not that the pandemic has invalidated such film-philosophical work on ethics, or even that it makes a retrospective difference to the arguments. Indeed, in more practical deontological terms, a UK film scholar who was doing their ethical duty by staying at home during successive lockdowns could continue working with ethical philosophy and film if they had access to their films on DVD/Blu-ray or streaming platforms and their texts online. This was obviously only possible if they were unaffected by illness or distractions and more pressing responsibilities—caring or homeschooling—or if they were not dependent on film archives or libraries that had closed. Yet, when it was not practically impossible to forge ahead with such work, even those who had the means and the quiet space confessed to experiencing stultifying periods when it was not feasible to contemplate writing. And for those film scholars who were able to pursue research and writing, it could be argued that their work was no good for anyone other than the person doing it in a time of crisis: it may have provided a form of therapy that distracted from the depressing situation outside, but it had no immediate import for others. It is evident, particularly when the first wave of the virus hit with full force, that many writers and artists, as well as academics in the arts and humanities, felt quite useless in the fight against it, although as lecturers, our quick conversion to online teaching and working was important for, and appreciated by, our students. This prompt reaction notwithstanding, a major part of our role beyond that which we—academics, artists, and writers—played in the everyday ethical web of prevention and protection inheres in responding to the pandemic in more delayed, reflective fashion.

Film scholars, along with other arts and humanities academics, may not have been the pandemic's primary figures of virtue, but we could respond to Covid-19 in the way that we knew how and best. As film researchers, the broader good of our work for others comes in the aftermath of crisis, whether or not it is born of it, and the question of ethical value here begins with the viewing of film. Discussion of ethics and film spectatorship in this different context, whether informed by Levinas or another philosopher's work, must, however, return to the monetary sense of value that opened this essay, as addressing what film is good for in practical terms has hidden costs that the pandemic has served only to accentuate.

ETHICS, VALUE, AND THE ECONOMY OF FILM

Quite apart from its importance for film scholars, the more immediate and palpable good of film during pandemic times for many people would seem to have come by way of spectatorship, giving them something to get lost in, especially if locked down at home with nowhere to go and nothing else to do. The salve for people's mental health came from watching anything absorbing. The virus highlighted and exacerbated existing social inequities in this regard, though, which the transition of screenings from cinema venues to home entertainment did nothing to change. While many a London cinema ticket may be expensive, even if you avoid peak times and high-end venues, it is no consolation that streaming platforms picked up where all cinemas had to leave off, because home-entertainment subscriptions—and, as the difficulties of homeschooling during lockdowns in the poorest families in the United Kingdom attested, devices—were also unaffordable for many. To associate the good of film with permitting the film scholar to carry on working, albeit under constrained circumstances, or with providing a means of escapism for people more generally, will make sense, if at all, only to those who can afford it. Ethical value is trumped by economics here, as spectatorship comes, like so much else, to rest uncomfortably on economic grounds.

This returns me differently to the financial sense of value with which I began: not my own dilemma from a position of relative economic privilege about whether or not to spend money on a ticket and venture to my closest cinema during the early era of Covid-19, but the fact that many are shut out of such a film experience as well as home-entertainment options on economic grounds. The questions that I asked my friend about the film I contemplated going to see in September 2020 point additionally, though, to another issue that I hinted at briefly when referring to my pre-2020 academic self balking at my own concerns. It is frequent for scholars who write about film, as Vivian Sobchack notes, to leave their viewing experience out of their work, to forget the visceral impact of spectatorship and turn their response to film into an account that sidelines that first full-bodied encounter.[7] While my questions to my friend were asked prior to a possible viewing experience at a cinema, they point to a related separation between the kinds of things I usually write about and those I will talk about beyond the context of my work. In my research and teaching, and even as the objects of attention in my writing over the years fall frequently into the categories of documentary and art house cinema, I hold that any film is worthy of attention and worth seeing on the big screen, and yet here I was questioning this when deciding whether or not to go to the cinema. Financial value and value judgment—threaded through with worries about transmitting or contracting the virus—are thoroughly knotted together in all this with consideration of ethics and what film is good for, but registering this entanglement brings me to a productive point where these questions of value reach their limit and can begin to be unraveled.

INVALUABLE FILM: FROM AN ECONOMY TO AN ECOLOGY OF SPECTATORSHIP

The changes in how growing numbers of people have accessed film as a result of the coronavirus can be related back to Eskilsson's point about the pandemic serving to accelerate the formation of a new movie landscape or ecosystem. In this shifting terrain and the financial inequalities that accompany it, my own interest in the good and value of film leads me to ask what it could mean truly to recognize film as *invaluable* to everyone's altered lives. Designating film as invaluable points to it continuing to be a fundamental part of contemporary life in cinemas and at home, even though life is different from what it was pre-Covid-19 and may remain that way for some years, if not permanently. But, as a category, the invaluable is also what cannot be delimited or pinned down in terms of value, because it indicates, literally, what is priceless. In this respect, the exorbitance of this category carries something of the Levinasian ethical dimension with it and is aligned with the good that belongs to neither Being nor totality. Attending to the combined senses of the invaluable—film as indispensable and valuable beyond measure—makes any discussion of the question of value necessarily more interrogative than a definitive categorization of films according to selective value judgments that lay the foundations of goodness and ethical or moral worth. And in financial terms, it is suggestive of the possibility of rethinking the accessibility of film outside of restrictive economic models, which is both necessary and timely: it could open exploration of a free-flowing ecology rather than an economy of film spectatorship as a more ethical impetus for the times ahead.

The Covid-19 pandemic has shone a light on the urgency and the stakes of thinking interconnectedness that have long been emphasized in ecological theory. Timothy Morton talks of the viral and virulent way in which one thing infects something else when defining what he terms "the ecological thought."[8] This seems grimly apt for a virus that allegedly traveled from nonhuman animals to humans and also decimated economies. Admittedly, this is the very darkest kind of connectedness, and we have witnessed its horror through hundreds of thousands of deaths in different countries, in addition to the aforementioned effects on the film industry and so many other sectors. The question going forward is what needs to change in order to rethink connectedness once the virus abates and economies recover in the decades to come.

As I have been writing this piece, my concern has been to look to a post–Covid-19 era or, at least, an era in which Covid-19 is manageable everywhere. The desire to "get back to normal" served as a mantra for many at the outset of the pandemic, but so did a diametrically opposed wish on the part of many others *not* simply to go back to the way things were. Some of this latter desire is related to environmental problems that were lessened somewhat during the first UK lockdown: reduced pollution due to fewer cars and planes circulating, increased audibility of birdsong in otherwise eerily quiet cities, and so on. Following on from this, it is the possibility of looking beyond narrow economic interests that can drive change going forward in the context of film spectatorship. Of course, it was not just film scholars who wanted cinemas to survive and for large audiences to return for collective viewing. The economy of film and other sectors depends on this, and nobody would want to stand in the way of recovery, least of all the film scholar passionate about films screened in cinemas as well as in the home. But to make film more accessible to even more people without increasing the environmental problems that the pandemic lessened would be a move from an economy to an ecology of viewing, and from value to recognizing something invaluable for everyone. This kind of change would give everyone a choice whether or not to engage with film, freed from the paywall of affordability.

Crucially, this would also take us from an ethics of spectatorship relevant predominantly to the economically privileged to one open to all and therefore more deserving of its name. This is not to say that everyone should be watching film or to imply that people can only have a good life with film in it. It is, however, to leverage the moral imperative in the service of equitable access to film so that everyone can choose the place they afford it in their own lives unencumbered by financial limitations. Clearly, there are far more vital things than film to distribute more fairly and widely the world over, let alone countrywide. But in the years to come, it is not beyond the realm of possibility to conceive of supportive and sustainable ways of widening access to film for all, in the home and in cinemas. In fact, a long time prior to the pandemic, sporadic initiatives to make cinema more affordable were already in place in several venues across the United Kingdom. One—the Cube in Bristol, a single-screen art house cinema run by volunteers since the late 1990s—described its move to price things cheaply as an ethical rather than a business decision.[9] Many other independent cinemas have priced things cheaper still or made screenings free. More recently, in the online context, the feminist film journal *Another Gaze* launched a free worldwide streaming platform in March 2021—"Another Screen"—which is funded by donations. The lengthy period of emergence from a time of crisis seems a pertinent moment to think about how such ventures can be expanded further so that opportunities to view film cheaply or preferably without cost become far more pervasive.

The easing of each successive lockdown in the United Kingdom brought with it a loosening of restrictions, and one of the things that I looked forward to each time was the reopening of cinemas. In case you were wondering, the film that I debated seeing back in September 2020 was Christopher Nolan's *Tenet*. I did go to the cinema in the end, and I'm not sorry that I paid the money and made the trip—mask firmly in place, hands sticky from excessive sanitizing, and distanced from the few others in the auditorium space by what felt like a country mile. I was happy to follow such safety measures. But I would be even happier to pay for my future tickets at the cinema and for streaming subscriptions in my home if I knew that part of that money, or some other initiative, were facilitating sustainable access to film for those spectators still excluded by prohibitive costs. That really would be good.

NOTES

1. Tomas Eskilsson, *The Pandemic and Cinema: The Present and the Future*, October 2020, 2, https://filmivast.com/updated-edition-of-the-pandemic-and-cinema-by-tomas-eskilsson/. Accessed February 11, 2021.

2. Simon Critchley and Todd May, "This Is Not *The Good Place:* How Do We Make It Better?," *New York Times* online discussion for *The Stone,* chaired by Peter Catapano, Sunday, May 3, 2020.

3. Emmanuel Levinas, *Totality and Infinity: An Essay on Exteriority* [1961], trans. Alphonso Lingis (Pittsburgh: Duquesne University Press, 1969); and Emmanuel Levinas, *Otherwise than Being or Beyond Essence* [1974], trans. Alphonso Lingis (Pittsburgh: Duquesne University Press, 2004).

4. Sarah Cooper, *Selfless Cinema? Ethics and French Documentary* (Oxford: Legenda, 2006); and Sarah Cooper, ed., "The Occluded Relation: Levinas and Cinema," special issue, *Film-Philosophy* 11, no. 2 (2007).

5. See Luc Dardenne, *Au dos de nos images* (Paris: Seuil, 2005); and Luc Dardenne, *Au dos de nos images II, 2005–2014* (Paris: Seuil, 2015).

6. For an example of such scholarship, see Edward Lamberti, *Performing Ethics through Film Style: Levinas with the Dardenne Brothers, Barbet Schroeder, and Paul Schrader* (Edinburgh: Edinburgh University Press, 2019).

7. Vivian Sobchack, "What My Fingers Knew: The Cinesthetic Subject or Vision in the Flesh," in *Carnal Thoughts: Embodiment and Moving Image Culture* (Berkeley: University of California Press, 2004), 53–84, at 53.

8. Timothy Morton, *The Ecological Thought* (Cambridge, MA: Harvard University Press, 2010), 2.

9. Rachael Swindale, "Want to Save Money at the Movies? Here's the Full Picture," *The Guardian,* June 8, 2019, https://www.theguardian.com/money/2019/jun/08/want-to-save-money-at-the-movies-heres-the-full-picture. Accessed February 13, 2021.

4

... Stabilities and Mobilities

On the Generic Values of Emplacements, Displacements, and Outplacements

TIMOTHY CORRIGAN

In 2017, Jordan Peele's *Get Out* provoked a public controversy when it was nominated for a Golden Globe Award as the Best Picture Comedy rather than as the Best Picture Drama. More than a little annoyed by the classification of a film with a searing social message about the fear and victimization under the surface of contemporary race relations, Peele responded to the nomination by tweeting that he considered the film a documentary.[1] According to Peele:

> The problem is, it's not a movie that can really be put into a genre box .... Originally, I set out to make a horror movie. I ended up showing it to people and hearing [that] ... it doesn't even feel like horror .... I think the issue here is that the movie subverts the idea of all genres .... Call it what you want, but the movie is an expression of my truth, my experience, the experiences of a lot of black people, and minorities. Anyone who feels like the other. Any conversation that limits what it can be is putting it in a box.[2]

Indeed, *Get Out* might even be described as a metageneric critique of genre that narrates how Chris (Daniel Kaluuya), the protagonist, manages to escape and break out of a seemingly genteel house of horrors in a fashion that parallels the film's attempt to break out of that generic box. Based on a nightmare of repetition, it is an eerie tale about a wealthy white community that hopes to recover lost youth by grotesquely recycling mostly aging white minds into young black bodies. "Getting out," then, describes a barely articulated plea to Chris, by one of these recycled bodies, urging him to physically escape a house that

FIGURE 5. Outplaced and on the road in Chloé Zhao's *Nomadland* (2020).

once promised to be a home but has now become a house of horrors that aims to violently absorb him into its nightmarish white space. That plea might, in turn, be seen as paralleling Peele's self-reflexive call for textual escape from those generic boxes as homes and a return to his and others' experiential world and its histories, a world which constantly troubles even the most classical of genres.[3]

GENERIC HOMES: EMPLACEMENTS

Film genres have regularly been associated with cultural values in one way or another. Besides their economic value for movie producers and distributors, genres become reflections of particular ideological positions whereby the tropes and narrative structures of genre films may depict certain figurations of race, class, economics, gender, and even larger perspectives on the "spirit of an age." More obliquely, the construction of time and space in film genres can itself reflect certain cultural ways of seeing and organizing the world as a way of understanding and valuing that world, such as with the long shots of Westerns or the theatrical mise-en-scènes of musicals. By situating spectators within specific and repeated generic patterns of repetition and difference, the production and reception of film genres become fundamentally repeated rituals that reflect, engage, or redefine cultural beliefs, traumas, desires, and crises. In this sense, genres are always time-and-place bound rituals that align and realign audience expectations, values, and desires to fit a changing world, and their power and importance accordingly appear most visibly in the evolving mobility of a genre as it travels through history and around the globe, rather than in a static prescriptive model that defines the ideal shape of a particular genre. Most clearly exemplified in "local genres," such as the *Heimat* films of Germany or the *jidai-geki* films of Japan, but also present in the popularity of certain genres in particular periods of history, such as the musicals in the 1930s, genres traditionally offer audiences a recognizable and projected place in their cultural geography or historical moment, an emplacement in a cinematic home that provides some version of aesthetic and communal security and stability.

John Ford's Western *Stagecoach* (1939) illustrates how these cinematic emplacements represent the enactment and containment of specific historical and cultural values. For most, the film represents that most classical of genres, the Western, whose narrative and iconic conventions map its most prominent features, including the wandering cowboy, the Ringo Kid (John Wayne), panoramic landscapes of the American West, and the narrative conquest of a Western wilderness in order to establish a new homestead.[4] Across these formal figures, the film reinscribes key values within an American ideology that is under enormous pressures in 1939: in the still turbulent wake of the Great Depression at home and against the impending global chaos of World War II, *Stagecoach* confirms—across a desert frontier and the threat of both Native Americans (outside) and corrupt Americans (inside)—the power of heroic individualism to rescue the democratic space of a heterogeneous community (a stagecoach transporting a thieving banker, a woman of ill repute, an alcoholic doctor, and other stereotypes). In the end, the film and its mythic underpinning transform a violent desert into a garden home for the now-redeemed Ringo and Dallas (Claire Trevor) as they ride off into a newly secured freedom.[5] As a ritualistic repetition of the formal stabilities found in other Westerns, *Stagecoach* reconstructs and reaffirms those traditional values about heterosexual romance, the hierarchies of race, and the quest for a stable home within a 1939 landscape of a nation and world in crisis. For audiences of this and other classical genres, there's no place like home as a sanctuary for traditional values.

MOBILE HOMES: DISPLACEMENTS

Rooted in the formal and organizational parameters of repeated and differentiated icons, conventions, and narrative formulas, film genres are, in short, negotiations that can not only stabilize values but also destabilize ways of perceiving the world and the changing values implicit in those perceptions, sometimes reinforcing and sometimes challenging the myths, narratives, and images that a genre circulates through a cultural and technological community experience at the movies. If classic genres tend to emplace audiences in mainstream cultural values and social securities, other genres frequently displace those positions, often again as they are associated with the image and metaphor of the home.

One period when that framework of the generic home suffers massive stress and pressure occurs through the 1940s and World War II, after which genres often become a measure of that stress, requiring dramatic reevaluations and reinventions that reflect changing needs and desires, and repositioning the classical home through the anxious lens of exile and alienation. The emergence and centrality of new genres such as film noir and the road movie indicate these cultural shifts in which restless spectators increasingly find their place outside traditional generic values, a place where those values become revised negotiations with history and culture through new filmic structures and icons that now ritualize the traumatic wakes of the 1940s and 1950s. Usually these renegotiations function according to a vaguely binary logic: while classical generic films work to position and secure audiences within the narrative teleology of all that a conventional home represents or promises, many postwar genres aim to deconstruct or expose the fragility of those homes and their promises and give way to more explicit investigations of other values reconfigured in genre. From the 1940s through the 1960s, these generic renegotiations inform a spectrum of genres that expand through displaced and revisionist unveilings of myths and figures behind, for example, Westerns such as Ford's *The Man Who Shot Liberty Valance* (1962), where politicians displace independent cowboys, and where the exposed myths of individual bravery and conquest displace the facts of history. In the cynical words of the local newspaper editor in that Ford film, "This is the West, sir. When the legend becomes fact, print the legend."

Across this historical and cultural shift, Ford's 1956 *The Searchers* thus pairs and counterpoints incisively his prewar *Stagecoach* to offer a generic revision of how the world has changed for movie makers and movie audiences after the violent upheavals of World War II. In this postwar Western, the earlier John Wayne as Ringo, a rebel with a clear cause and destination, has become John Wayne as Ethan, an embittered and traumatized Civil War veteran who wanders the plains without the hope or desire for a home. In the opening shots, Ethan arrives through a classical Western long shot at the homestead on the range of his brother Aaron (Walter Coy), but shortly after he discovers that home burned and their daughters Lucy (Pippa Scott) and Debbie (Lana Wood) kidnapped by the Comanches. After finding the dead body of Lucy, he continues his search to find Debbie and presumably restore her to a home and family. Yet, Ethan's quest appears increasingly motivated by a profound alienation and a racist hatred bent on violent revenge and destruction. At a climactic moment in the film, however, Ethan turns away from murdering Debbie (now played by Natalie Wood), whom he believes has been sexually and racially compromised by a Comanche warrior, and instead returns her to the adapted family and reconstituted home of the Jorgensens. Ethan, though, can only turn his back on this partial and awkward reconciliation, in a parting long shot that confirms he will wander, forever mobile, always displaced outside the frame, and never able to find the comfort and stability of home.

A HOUSE IS NOT A HOME: OUTPLACEMENTS

As a measure of a largely recent—and for me most interesting—shift in generic and cultural value, the modern descendent of the Western has become the road movie. While horses and stagecoaches once crossed movie frontiers to discover Western homesteads or to displace those homes with restless and unsettled postwar quests, the contemporary road movie more fully translates those quests into the mobile homes of automobiles, motorcycles, and trucks, quests now with no certain destinations or even the anxious nostalgia of postwar Westerns. From Arthur Penn's 1967 *Bonnie and Clyde* through Wim Wenders's 1984 *Paris, Texas,* the traditional generic value of spectatorial emplacement into metaphoric homes, or the postwar displacement of those homes into a restless mobility, now maps identities and cultures along an open road, a directionless space which in the impoverished landscapes of the 2000s increasingly appears—somewhat ironically—with potentially new possibilities and values. Unlike Ford's two Western road movies, for me, many of those generic Western road movies have discovered strangely new destinations and values that may be best suggested by the notion of outplacement.

Technically, "outplacement" is a socioeconomic term that describes a suspended state or place in which a person retrains for new employment after having lost a job. This is a term and position especially appropriate and resonant for the broken economies of the 2000s, defined by the catastrophic effects of the 2008 economic collapse of the housing market in the United States and the growing homeless crisis of the contemporary underclass. Within this historical context, outplacement, then, suggests the new economic and sociological territories explored by contemporary road movies as reflections of emerging values centered on a crisis of identity, home, and economics. Within this crisis, these films often follow Ethan's dark wanderings, yet many of them now open an outplaced space with hints of transition and possibility.

Represented by a variety of films, from Agnès Varda's 2000 *The Gleaners and I/Les Glaneurs et la glaneuse* to Andrea Arnold's 2016 *American Honey*, this generic mutation across its Western road-movie heritage appears most concisely in two recent films by Chloé Zhao: the 2017 Western *The Rider*, which becomes the prelude to her 2020 road movie, *Nomadland*. In the first film, a former rodeo star, Brady (Brady Blackburn), has suffered a devastating head injury and struggles with his longing to return to his career and profession, while barely holding together what remains of an impoverished family with a spendthrift and alcoholic father and a younger autistic sister. Placed within the vibrant open vistas of South Dakota and supported by a cast of untrained actors (intentionally outside the frame of a Hollywood performative aura), the film drifts—in every sense—through a world of financial and physical destitution, in which homes and families appear mostly as the residue and remains of a now-crippled society and economics, and where a tentative compassion for a larger world becomes the only compensation for the loss of cowboy heroism and individuality. At the conclusion, outplaced physically, financially, and emotionally, Brady forsakes his nostalgic dream to return to rodeo riding in a shot/counter shot with his father and sister, a suspended moment suggesting a future without any clear direction or security except for the possibility of a fragile home based in mutual caring and hope.

In the second film, the Wild West has become a "nomadland," where economically outplaced workers occasionally pick up part-time employment in Amazon warehouses, the economic emblem of the 2000s, and where these disenfranchised and disaffected road warriors wander through different Western RV camps, while making temporary bonds and friendships. Significantly, this new Western loner is a woman—in this case, Fern (Frances McDormand)—who is disburdened of a lost or broken male heritage and reconstructs family with friendships that are always moving "down the road." At one point, she returns briefly to her former and now-abandoned empty housing complex, originally built as part of a large factory that later went bankrupt. She then drives off in her van, a vehicle carefully outfitted with items from the home she has lost. In these new Western spaces, concerned acquaintances tell her they are worried that she is "homeless," and her response indicates the new potentials she embodies as part of this recent generic variation: as a sign of the times, she insists she is not homeless, only houseless, a critical social and figurative distinction that also suggests a different generic value. That iconic anchor of the Western road movie, the house as home, is now merely a house, replaced by the wide-open door of a new kind of home, opening not on a narrative logic of the generic security or alienation, but as a vista on the world outside it where the socioeconomics of self must now fully rethink and reengage a place in that world.

Still based in industrial and formal repetitions of film genre, this third variety of generic engagements that I am calling "outplacements" neither *emplaces* spectators nor *displaces* perspectives and values, but instead pushes and extends generic formulas and conventions outside the walls of the genre and into the realm of lived social experience, a place where generic structures and destinations may only point to those extrafilmic experiences and the necessarily new values associated with them. This variation shows how especially contemporary genres mark the limits of a genre to respond to the changing social and ethical pressures informing them. Within the climate and crises of recent decades, genres frequently hesitate before, or resist, their own historical closure.[6] In this way, generic repetitions gesture toward the interstices in their recyclings and become the salient vehicles for revealing a world beyond the genre as a yet-unseen potential and possibility.

GETTING OUT

Over the last few decades, my own critical thinking has tended in precisely this direction: toward generic films that foreground the historical and cultural fissures within genres as a provocation to viewers to rethink and remeasure their inherited and evolving values and ethics, to open them up to a lived world beyond that of the cinematic world. One of the reasons that *Get Out* and its critical reception interests me is that my own work and writing has always, across different topics, gravitated to those films that attempt to open that box of genre: how Rainer Werner Fassbinder's films transform melodrama into a vista on postwar German society; how contemporary road movies deconstruct the masculine narcissism that had fueled that genre through the 1950s and 1960s; or how essay films rethink epistolary forms and travel genres.[7] What links these earlier arguments and *Get Out* is an insistence on a dialogic spectator who must bring these films off the screen of art and entertainment and reconfigure their generic trouble as a social and intellectual road sign to the world outside the cinema and within histories that generic cinema can barely contain.[8]

I've previously argued that contemporary movie genres, specifically, have often tended to mix and match traditional genres as a way to negotiate the cultural excess on their borders. They frequently collapse their generic conventions and formulas not as an oppositional structure but, in a way, to point to a world they fail to contain, a world they cannot adequately represent (what I once referred to as the "hysteria" of contemporary genre). In 1991, I wrote about the exhilarating collapse of the road-movie genre, as the contemporary descendant of the Western, whose conventions and formulas have often become "a rusty collage of postmodern cultural debris." In the open space that remains, "the debris of generic history now has the potential of becoming the generic cure," where we might select "across an expanded galaxy of images, other roads, other generic rituals, and other subjectivities with which to try to formulate different histories within other generic economies."[9]

Get Out is obviously neither a Western nor a road movie. Its generic instabilities, as well as its thematic and titular warning, do, however, place it productively outside the typical enclosures associated with genres and within the openings explored by other contemporary genres. Coincidentally or strategically, the film tested two endings. The final comedic ending now in distribution has the protagonist Chris rescued by his TSA friend, who arrives on the road where Chris has just killed the woman who seduced him into her suburban house of racial violence, while the unused and dark alternative ending has Chris arrested and jailed by police who arrive at the scene. On this road away from the home that pursues him, somewhere between comedy and horror, the two endings of the film seem to acknowledge a critically uncertain place where, especially for American minorities, generic expectations, icons, and formulas no longer suffice, and where, like an old house as home, generic boxes collapse before the truth of lived experience.

NOTES

1. That Peele was previously best known as a partner in the comedy team Key & Peele might indicate another example of the common debate about the relationship or conflict between auteurist critical models and generic critical models.

2. Quoted in Eric Kohn, "Jordan Peele Challenges Golden Globes Classifying 'Get Out' as a Comedy: 'What Are You Laughing At?,'" *IndieWire*, November 15, 2017, https://www.indiewire.com/2017/11/jordan-peele-response-get-out-golden-globes-comedy-1201897841/. Accessed October 29, 2021.

3. This shift strikes me as paralleling a similar argument made by Una Chaudhuri about the "geopathology" of modern drama as "a series of ruptures and displacements in various orders of location, from the micro- to the microspatial, from home to nature, with intermediary space concepts such as neighborhood, hometown, community, and country ranged in between." Una Chaudhuri, *Staging Place: The Geography of Modern Drama* (Ann Arbor: University of Michigan Press, 1997), 55.

4. André Bazin has famously called *Stagecoach* "the classic perfection" of "the ideal balance of social myth, historical reconstruction, psychological truth, and the traditional theme of the western *mise-en-scène*." *What Is Cinema?*, vol. 2, trans. Hugh Gray (Berkeley: University of California Press, 1971), 149.

5. That this home will be located in Mexico might suggest that even in this classical resolution there are the tremors of a nationalistic insecurity.

6. Despite my emphasis on the contemporary context for this generic variation, examples can be found throughout film history, with notable examples such as Luis Buñuel's bitingly satiric dismantling of the travelogue in his *Land Without Bread/Las Hurdes, tierra sin pan* (1933).

7. See Timothy Corrigan, *New German Film: The Displaced Image* (Bloomington: Indiana University Press, 1994); *A Cinema Without Walls: Movies and Culture After Vietnam* (New York: Routledge, 1991); and *The Essay Film: From Montaigne, After Marker* (New York: Oxford University Press, 2011).

8. This generic and spectatorial shift to "a world outside" relates, it seems to me, to the contemporary movement of film distribution and reception to streaming sites, where the regulatory structures built on a studio system are increasingly being restructured by increasingly diverse audiences.

9. Timothy Corrigan, "Genre, Gender, and Hysteria: The Road Movie in Outer Space," in *A Cinema Without Walls*, 159, 160.

PART TWO

Empathic Goods

5

... Lies, Loops, or Liberation

On the Dis/Obedience of Feeling More

MICHELE AARON

At the end of 2014, the United Kingdom's leading cinema company, Cineworld, launched a major rebrand—the Unmissables campaign—to lure people back to the "unique experience" it offered.[1] At its center was a 90-second film promoting cinema spectatorship and their new "unlimited" membership card. The ad is basically a slow-mo medley of near-caricatural, and mostly face-based, expressions of the "raw emotion" of viewing film.[2] Wide-eyed audience members of all ages and races enact various emoji-like gestures of bodily response: laughter, shock, amazement, delight, despair. There are close-ups of the bristling of hair, the contraction of a pupil, a gulp. Not just the body but bonds are in play, too—inevitably between the viewer and the screen but, more conspicuously, the familial and romantic: a child's fingers tighten around a father's hand; a woman nestles into her partner's side.

It is not the semiotic, ideological, economic, or even recursive registers of this film about film viewing that interests me here—though there is plenty to say about them—or, strictly, the seduction of the normative moving image. No, for my purposes, what this ad writ large—literally so in its final frames—was the value of being moved by the moving image. This value becomes financial—its pricelessness assigned an abstract fee: "Every Film. Every Feeling. One Price"—but, like the affordances of the membership card, it is a value without limits. The next and last frame return us to the company's logo, enhanced by the words that will thread through their ongoing marketing: "Feel More."

FIGURE 6. Mike Hoolboom's short film *Scrapbook* (2015), discussed later in this essay as a counterpoint to mainstream cinema.

This, Cineworld tells us, is what film viewing is good for: *feeling* or, better yet, feeling *more*.[3] And I am inclined to agree, at least broadly. In favoring the term the moving image in my work, I mean not to demote sound but to privilege film's emotivity, to emphasize its impact upon us. But the thing is, for me, this is not feeling for feeling's sake or film for film's sake: I am compelled by neither the intrinsic value of the moving image (whether as art or otherwise), nor the intrinsic value of the spectator's "shuddering" (whether as Kracauer's "unseeing" or, more altered, "conscious observer").[4] For me, the feelings generated by film move beyond the closed circuit of cinema, or self, that is so often, and problematically, celebrated. As such, film-feelings serve a purpose, a key—if disavowed—sociopolitical purpose in the world, and in world-making, and have always done so. What I mean by this is not only that film is an ethical realm—that it brings us into an affective relation with others, that it makes us feel for and with others in a way that re/scripts that relation—or that it is invaluable politically, that the structures, and commerce, of feelings that it depends upon and trades in are both ideological and normative. No, what I mean by this is that this thoroughly modern medium must be understood as one more ordering of things in the "colonial matrix of power";[5] that inherent to film, to its good or its bad—and certainly its theorization as such—is an epistemological obedience to a system of thinking, of feeling, of valuing, that is, at best, corrupt and, at worst, deathly.

Ok. Pause. Rewind. I got carried away there and spilled the beans too soon (even as I'm late to the party). So let me back up a little.

THE GEOPOLITICS OF FEELING

Film is an ethical realm. Through it we feel *for* but, more importantly, *with* others. In this feeling-with, we reach toward and connect to their vulnerability. This reaching toward, and connection, is, or rather must be, without return. If it is to avoid being unethical, our feelings for/with others must not be folded back upon, or trained to, our own interests. Such a move, echoing again in "being moved," vitalizes our obligation to the other, to doing right by them. In writing this Levinas-infused formulation of the good of film in early 2021, these words feel particularly live in relation to the world—in the time of a pandemic, "we all" have been asked to protect others, to live out our everyday ethical duty—and familiarly hollow in relation to film. I've spent the last decade or so straining for a better way of describing this dynamic between screen and self, contending with the power imbalance at the core of spectatorship and pursuing the potential of film to connect us and effect, rather than simply affect or aspire to affect, change as a result. My increasing commitment to this potential of film—which included starting a social-justice film festival (https://screeningrights.com/) to extend audiences for and critical debate on important international works—remains checked, and chastened, by the solipsistic thrall of so many socially conscious examples and by the similarly self-referential, and occasionally self-reverential, echo chamber of an already converted audience. Where the salving and saving of the privileged (Western/Northern/elite) spectator, and of this spectator alone—which characterizes so much spectatorship—may not be performed by the human rights–oriented film itself, it often seems to be revitalized, in its own way, in the good people to whom it preaches, whose main action of solidarity may well be their attendance. The unavoidable "I" at the center of "ethical" fuels the constant return to closed circuits of self and "cinema"—here as the collective experience of film—and spectatorship, and to the film-feelings of my opening gambit. This isn't exactly Levinas's fault, his hugely influential work, after all, refuses "to reduce alterity to the self-same."[6] Yet, the problems found with it by one of his major inheritors, the Latin American philosopher Enrique Dussel, prove highly relevant to the issues raised here.

Indebted to Levinas, and the primacy and pluralism of his ethics, Dussel nevertheless identifies Levinas's work as Eurocentric. In one of Dussel's earliest books, one of many not yet translated into English, he is outspoken about this. He states that despite Levinas's experiences of the Holocaust, he "had not suffered Europe in its [colonial] totality and Levinas's reference point continued to be Europe in itself."[7] While Levinasian ethics have enormous value for Dussel and Latin American philosophy, this problem of the "geopolitics of knowledge"—but also of the related passivity that Levinas ascribed to both the "other" and "the woman"—provide for us the bigger picture, the beans, that I spilled above.[8]

At the beginning of his 1977 treatise on the "historico-ideological genesis" and geopolitics of philosophy, *Philosophy of Liberation,* Dussel writes: "Before the *ego cogito* there is an *ego conquiro;* 'I conquer' is the practical foundation of 'I think.'"[9] Modernity—which for Dussel like others, starts in 1492—is inseparable from coloniality, its "darker side."[10] For Walter Mignolo, and the Modernity/(de)Coloniality collective, the alienated and oppressed peoples of the periphery—who were produced, Dussel argued, by colonialism—will only be liberated or rather "healed" through delinking, or "desprendimiento" as Aníbal Quijano called it in 1992, from this pervasive and naturalized system of domination.[11] All aspects of life at the periphery (economics, governance, institutions) were/are colonized, but it is the control over "knowledge ... and beings (subjectivity)" and "senses and perception" that resonate for our purposes especially.[12] As such, Mignolo argues: "'Delinking' is then necessary because there is no way out of the coloniality of power from within Western (Greek and Latin) categories of thought."[13] This "no way out" is key here not because of the potential hopelessness and accompanying complacency implied by this seemingly inescapable and often invisible power, but because of the radical praxes it obtains in its wake. For Mignolo, delinking requires epistemological disobedience first and foremost. It also requires a different approach to being and to sensing: it is not only (Western/colonial) knowledge that must be delinked from, but (Western/colonial) aesthetics that "have played a key role in configuring a canon, a normativity that enabled the disdain and the rejection of other forms of aesthetic practices."[14] Instead of modern aesthetics then, he instates as its opposite and its undoing, "decolonial aesthesis," and as such prioritizes an alternative way of "sensing and perceiving."[15] Art and culture assume a pivotal role in decolonial healing as necessary sites for aesthesic expression by those of the periphery. And they are sites for "re-existence" rather than resistance, for resistance "implies that you accept the rules of the game imposed upon you, and you resist. Re-existence means that you delink from the rules imposed upon you, you create your own rules communally and, therefore you re-exist affirming yourself as a human being."[16]

This "no way out" reverberates, too, in what Fred Moten describes as the fugitivity of radical Blackness that emerges in response to antiblack modernity.[17] Indeed, there is an incredibly rich, if rarely mined, correspondence between his and his colleagues' work and that of the Latin American figures. Both speak powerfully to the emancipatory energy, the transformative potential, of the arts for/from the peripheralized or "undercommons," despite a wall between them.[18] Moten's emphasis on "refusal" chimes with delinking: Saidiya Hartman's "critical fabulation" with re-existence.[19] But it is the common emphasis on an alternative sensorium—what Moten and Stefano Harney would call hapticality—that is particularly valuable here for our rethinking of the value of film-feelings.[20]

How, then, are we to understand film and film studies as (part of, product of, perpetuating) a naturalized, pervasive but disavowed system of domination? Even more important, how can we find film's "good" if film is inherently aligned with this system and expert at disavowal? Finally, for now, how might film, but especially the typically less creative practice of film theory, provide ways of delinking and aesthesically/haptically re-existing? Film's role in/as systems of domination is well-trodden—if enclosed and overgrown—terrain. While its "patriarchal unconscious" was oh-so-seminally recognized in the early 1970s, its connection to a wider imperialist unconscious (for imperialism is patriarchal) is of greater concern. Most striking, given Dussel's statement above, is Robert Stam and Louise Spence's remark in 1983 that the camera makes of us "armchair conquistadores," so that our "self-image" and our "sense of power" depends upon its othering and objectification of "the inhabitants of the Third World."[21] Unlike for Dussel, this othering and objectification is always about both race and gender and thus, as bell hooks has kept having to remind us, is always about "imperial white supremacist capitalist patriarchal values."[22] In other words, the very structures, and often content, of cinema, as well as the subjectivity it served, were colonial in nature: little wonder perhaps, given how its "beginnings . . . coincided with the giddy heights of the imperial project."[23] And "cinema" continued/continues to be so: in their groundbreaking *Unthinking Eurocentrism* in 1994, Stam and Ella Shohat would trace Western film's enduring "imperial imaginary."[24] In my own work, and after Achille Mbembe, I've characterized contemporary mainstream film as necropolitical, as using death—or rather who dies and how they die—to (re)enforce these "values" or this "imaginary" or sovereign power.[25] Only rare examples could, in their ethicality, evade film's deathly logic.

It is not my aim here to rehearse the myriad ways in which this "imaginary" remains current or cloaked, contested or countered, by films and film studies—by Third Cinema and national or regional cinemas from around the world, and by feminist, Black, Indigenous, queer, postcolonial, and intercultural work, for example. What I want to do, instead, is to stay close to the idea of an enduring epistemological obedience, and, with it, of the selfsame circuits or looping back of knowledge, aesthetics, and feelings as that which continues to define and limit our discipline and its ethics. The latter becomes "not evidence of a theory of liberation, but rather of 'law and order' criticism," as Teshome Gabriel called it, back in 1986.[26] It feels beyond urgent that we look again at how we just keep saying the same things or saying different things but in the same way and changing little. We keep sharpening our tools and making them gleam, but the house doesn't fall. Moten and Harney put the university in the dock for sustaining the artifice of innovation.[27] So I want to stay close to the idea of "a way out" too. What would an exit from this holding pattern look like?

WAYS OUT

David Martin-Jones has recently suggested, via Dussel and Gilles Deleuze, a way out of the modernity/coloniality bind *through* film, and it seems to be an antisolipsistic or anti-self-centered ethics that paves the way. His "ethics of hesitation" emerges from our encounter with the submerged truths or "lost pasts" of history found in a world of cinemas. Rather than enabling the spectator to hegemonically or Eurocentrically incorporate the lost past "as prosthetic or post memory," such a pluriversal film experience instead "provides the viewer with the chance to hesitate, and potentially to recognize *the relative centrality of their own place in world history*."[28] The spectator is able to pause and think again, aware now—potentially—of the coloniality/power imbalance of the world and their own complicitous place within it. However, what is good about film still seems to be how it can make us (the Western/Northern/elite spectator) better people. What is more, this sense of an only potential recognition, of only a chance for hesitation, however "empower[ing]," feels a bit too . . . well, hesitant or restrained in the wake of Mignolo, Moten, and Hartman's more radical, utopian, ambitions.[29] Something way more wayward or wild or promiscuous, and definitely queer, is required: the "terms of the conversation" need to change and not just the content.[30]

And so I turn to the short film *Scrapbook* (2015).[31] Made, or rather remade, by the Canadian filmmaker Mike Hoolboom, it provides a fascinating response to the ideas I have been grappling with here, and, as I hope will become clear, a counterpoint to the Cineworld ad with which I opened. Revisiting and adding to footage shot back in 1966 by Hoolboom's friend (and former teacher) Jeffrey Paull, *Scrapbook* takes us to the Broadview Developmental Center in Ohio, a home for autistic children. As a first screen of written text tells us, Paull "was part of a collective portrait project where residents worked in the darkroom, taking and developing pictures of each other, in order to re-see themselves." Hoolboom locates one of these residents "fifty years on," Donna Washington, who agrees to watch and rewatch the original footage and share her feelings about it. Recorded and edited, these become the voice-over for the film, though read by an actress at Washington's request, for, as she puts it, "actresses are more real." The German composer and sound artist Stephan Mathieu provides a mostly abstract, at times dissonant and at times calming, soundtrack. I name all these players not to honor detail but to emphasize assemblage.

Scrapbook shares with us the sitting and moving, eating and interacting, to-camera smiles and offscreen stares, of the young people inside Broadview. They are engaged or oblivious, casual or keen. There is no "capturing" or vérité going on here, no constructing of spectacle, sympathy, pathology, or vulnerability, or any other term in the lexicon of film or ethics, for Paull, and his camera, are clearly friends of the residents. And he's more "audiovisual healer" than Wiseman.[32] The black-and-white silent images are grainy, occasionally canted or overexposed. Some feel still; others are all movement. They contain individuals or groups. Like the young people, the frames and shots and sounds vary, and all are different. There is a convergence early on. "It's you" are the first words of the voice-over, as Washington sees herself as a young girl on the screen, looking into the camera, then coloring in the letter "p" of what becomes legible as "SCRAP." She's making a scrapbook. Washington reads into and out of the image as the start of many first-person/third-person blended self-narrations: "She's holding down the [first] letter. So she can spell the word crap. She's having a little crap." It starts with a joke (on authorship among other things), and one easily missed if it wasn't made clear. Immediately, Washington, younger and older, knows more than convention—the convention of misreading disability—dictates. The scrapbook takes shape and depends upon undoing normate and normative expectations of both people and film.[33]

There will be many more convergences between voice-over and image. In a typical way, Washington's words add meaning to what we see and vice versa: she speaks of laughing and we see someone laughing. But her perspective, her neurodivergent feelings about and sense of the world, is matched, I'd suggest, aesthesically, in the filmmaking. Washington says: "I don't look at a face. I disappear into it. And then, where is lonely? Lonely is gone. When you get absorbed in a sweater. In the gap between someone's teeth. There's no lonely." These words accompany a seamless series of vertical tracking shots up the body of one then another of the gathered group, from wooden floor to white ceiling. This flow over or through the young people, this restless journey over a singular body into another, synchronizes somehow with Washington's blurred sense of alienation and togetherness, of self and other. While I want to avoid an overread of Washington's wisdom—we want no seer here, no sound bite on her extraordinariness in this short piece—the film is profoundly moving in its implicit and expansive ethicality: "What Jeff showed me with his camera, is that you don't have to get stuck in someone else's face. . . . And then we realized we're all part of the same face. And I didn't have to be afraid of that. And he didn't have to be afraid of that." Washington's often painful and overwhelming reach toward others reveals the pitfalls and wonder of connection or friendship. She doesn't feel more, she feels "too much," and yet the mutuality of her relationship with Paull, with this "sad young man who was always smiling," is key. It undoes or, better yet, disengages from, the power imbalance between filmmaker and subject and between the neurodivergent and presumed neurotypical individual, and reveals the humility, openness, and care on both sides. Indeed, it undoes "sides": the binaries or boundaries or order that keep all systems (of domination) in place.

Scrapbook presents an alternative register of being and feeling and sensing, but also of ordering and organizing meaning in film. It operates outside of the "tightly regulated schema of character, behavior, desire, and intent" that underwrites its common forms: in this way, it is freed not only from "the geometry of film" but also from its "mental apparatus," and both, as Steven Eastwood reminds us, are neurotypical and integral to the modernity and normativity of the medium.[34] Janet Harbord, in a fascinating article which pointed me to *Scrapbook*, suggests that autism's "instructive quality" is to allow "us," the presumably neurotypical viewers, to realize "the narrow cast of visual codification that conditions cinema."[35] Film, or rather film theory, proves self-enlightening still. With *Scrapbook* however, the antiniche and unorthodox codifications, or better yet "registers," of the film matter most.[36] Through them, we—all viewers—are liberated from the matrix of power that underwrites spectatorship and film.

Like the Cineworld ad, *Scrapbook* is full of faces and gestures, and is about looking at them. Where, in the ad, the audience members sit rapt in onanistic emotion and devotion to the screen, the world of *Scrapbook* presents their reverse: the ad's—feeling more's—darker side upon which it depends. The Cineworld ad in its magisterial normativity disavows many things but, most important, it disavows *Scrapbook*. Harbord sets the primal scene through early medical films, but it is a scene without limits, without ends: "[a]s a standard language of cinematic gesture stabilized, it produced dialectically and in mirror form an unintelligible body, the body of the autistic child, that defies communicative injunction."[37] *Scrapbook* is that "autistic film assemblage" of Eastwood's proposition that might prove "emancipatory" and "deterritorializ[ing]."[38] But, as I hope to have shown, it is more than the dominance of the neurotypical body that is at stake here.

Scrapbook, then, operates outside of systems of domination; it operates as epistemological disobedience to the knowing, sensing, and subjectivity that is naturalized, pervasive, and disavowed elsewhere. In its beauty and self-consciousness, its reach and reach and reach toward others, it provides a state of aesthesic re-existence for the neurodivergent individuals in the film and for all those viewing it. It operates outside these systems of domination, but I don't mean fully outside: there is no fully outside. Washington is living in an institution in the film, after all, and more to the point, Hoolboom has been much applauded and awarded for his work. The issue of privileging a Western/Northern/elite film remains, regardless of Hoolboom's undercommon credentials.[39] But I don't mean to privilege it, or sidestep this issue, I mean to share the relief and joy and anguish of *Scrapbook*'s world-making. I mean to relish its break with the alienating traditions of history and representation and theory and emotions, with our endless self-fortification through film, with being afraid. And I mean to relish the respite it offers as the dis/obedience of feeling more, as an "insurgent feel."[40]

NOTES

1. Seb Joseph, "Cineworld Unveils Biggest Campaign to Capture 'Raw Emotion' of Cinema," November 7, 2014, https://www.marketingweek.com

/cineworld-unveils-biggest-campaign-to-capture-raw-emotion-of-cinema/. Accessed February 14, 2021.

2. Joseph, "Cineworld."

3. Due to the standardized layout of the volume, the image from *Scrapbook* has to appear at the top of the second page of the essay. Note, however, that the film will only be discussed later as an *alternative* to the normative pleasures of mainstream film.

4. Siegfried Kracauer, *The Theory of Film: The Redemption of Physical Reality* (Oxford: Oxford University Press, 1960), 58.

5. Walter Mignolo and Rolando Vazquez, "Decolonial AestheSis: Colonial Wounds/Decolonial Healing," *SocialText* (2013), https://socialtextjournal.org/periscope_article/decolonial-aesthesis-colonial-woundsdecolonial-healings/. Accessed February 18, 2021.

6. Sarah Cooper, *Selfless Cinema? Ethics and French Documentary* (Oxford: Legenda, 2005), 8.

7. Enrique Dussel and D. E. Guillot, *Liberación latinoamericana y Emmanuel Levinas* (Buenos Aires: Editorial Bonum, 1975), 8. Translated by and cited in Walter Mignolo, "Dussel's Philosophy of Liberation: Ethics and the Geopolitics of Knowledge," in *Thinking from the Underside of History: Enrique Dussel's Philosophy of Liberation* (Oxford: Rowman and Littlefield, 2000), 29 (brackets in original).

8. Walter Mignolo, "Epistemic Disobedience and the Decolonial Option: A Manifesto," *Transmodernity: Journal of Peripheral Cultural Production of the Luso-Hispanic World* 1, no. 2 (2011): 44–66, at 59. Mignolo will continue to criticize Agamben, too, as another key figure in Western ethical thinking whose "reflections are important, but they are late, regional, and limited." For Moten, Agamben's emphasis on "bare-life" is overused, fetishized even; see Fred Moten, "The Case of Blackness," *Criticism* 50, no. 2 (Spring 2008): 177–218, at 216n6.

9. Enrique Dussel, *Philosophy of Liberation* (Eugene, OR: Wipf and Stock, 2003 [1985]), 1 and 3.

10. Walter Mignolo, *The Darker Side of Western Modernity: Global Futures, Decolonial Options* (Durham, NC: Duke University Press, 2011).

11. Mignolo and Vazquez, "Decolonial AestheSis"; Aníbal Quijano, "Colonialidad y modernidad/racionalidad" (1989), repr. in *Los conquistados: 1492 y la poblacién indígena de las Américas,* ed. Heraclio Bonilla (Santafé de Bogotá, Colombia: Tercer Mundo Editores, 1992), 437–448.

12. Mignolo and Vazquez, "Decolonial AestheSis."

13. Mignolo, "Epistemic Disobedience," 45.

14. Mignolo and Vazquez, "Decolonial AestheSis."

15. Mignolo and Vazquez, "Decolonial AestheSis."

16. Mignolo, "Foreword," in *Decolonizing Sexualities: Transnational Perspectives, Critical Interventions,* ed. Sandeep Bakshi, Suhraiya Jivraj, and Silvia Posocco (Oxford: Counterpress, 2016), viii.

17. See Fred Moten, *Stolen Life: Consent Not to Be a Single Being* (Durham, NC: Duke University Press, 2018).

18. For a discussion of Dussel's patriarchal Eurocentrism, among other issues, see Laura E. Pérez, "Enrique Dussel's Etica de la liberación, U.S. Women

of Color Decolonizing Practices, and Coalitionary Politics amidst Difference," *Qui Parle: Critical Humanities and Social Sciences* 18, no. 2 (Spring–Summer 2010): 121–146.

19. Fred Moten and Stefano Harney, *The Undercommons: Fugitive Planning and Black Study* (Wivenhoe, NY: Minor Compositions, 2013); and Saidiya Hartman, "Venus in Two Acts," *Small Axe* 12, no. 2 (2008): 1–14, at 11.

20. Moten and Harney, *Undercommons*, 97.

21. Robert Stam and Louise Spence, "Colonialism, Racism, and Representation," *Screen* 24, no. 2 (1983): 2–20, at 4.

22. hooks refers to this throughout her writing, from *Killing Rage: Ending Racism* (New York: Holt, 1995) to *Writing Beyond Race: Living Theory and Practice* (New York: Routledge, 2012). My gratitude goes to Karl Schoonover for reminding me that hook's presence should be felt.

23. Robert Stam and Ella Shohat, "The Imperial Imaginary," in *Unthinking Eurocentrism: Multiculturalism and the Media* (London: Routledge, 1994), 4.

24. Stam and Shohat, "Imaginary," 4.

25. Michele Aaron, *Death and the Moving Image: Ideology, Iconography, and I* (Edinburgh: Edinburgh University Press, 2014); and Achille Mbembe, "Necropolitics," *Public Culture* 15, no. 1 (2003): 11–40.

26. Teshome Gabriel, "Colonialism and 'Law and Order' Criticism," *Screen* 27, nos. 3–4 (May-August 1986): 140–148, at 147.

27. Moten and Harney, *Undercommons*, 97.

28. David Martin-Jones, *Cinema Against Doublethink: Ethical Encounters with the Lost Pasts of World History* (London: Routledge, 2019), 10 and 2 (original emphasis).

29. Martin-Jones, *Cinema*, 9.

30. Mignolo, *Darker Side*, 92. My flurry of descriptors here reference Hartman's *Wayward Lives, Beautiful Experiments: Intimate Histories of Social Upheaval* (New York: Norton, 2019); Jack Halberstam's preface to *The Undercommons* and *Wild Things: The Disorder of Desire* (Durham, NC: Duke University Press, 2020); and Karl Schoonover and Rosalind Galt, *Queer Cinema in the World* (Durham, NC: Duke University Press, 2016), 14.

31. Hoolboom has made *Scrapbook* available on Vimeo: https://vimeo.com/132500065. Accessed February 14, 2021.

32. Paull is described as such on Hoolboom's webpage for the film: http://mikehoolboom.com/?p=17624. Accessed February 14, 2021. *Scrapbook* has been compared to Frederick Wiseman's controversial and unethical *Titicut Follies* (1967).

33. For more on the term "normate," see Rosemarie Garland Thomson, *Extraordinary Bodies: Figuring Physical Disability in American Culture and Literature* (New York: Columbia University Press, 2017 [1997]), 8.

34. Steven Eastwood, "Cinemautism," *Screen Bodies* 1, no. 1 (2016): 18, 16, 19.

35. Janet Harbord, "The Autistic Gesture: Film as Neurological Training," *NECSUS: European Journal of Media Studies* 8, no. 2 (2019): 129–148, at 145.

36. Karl Schoonover and Rosalind Galt favor "register" as a term because it "references cinema's mediation of experience, mobilizing intimacies, affects, and sensations." *Queer Cinema*, 212.

37. Harbord, "Autistic," 134.
38. Eastwood, "Cinemautism," 28.
39. For a discussion of Hoolboom's queer work, see Thomas Waugh, "Mike Hoolboom and the Second Generation of AIDS Films in Canada," in *North of Everywhere: English-Canadian Cinema Since 1980*, ed. Jerry White and William Beard (Edmonton: University of Alberta Press, 2002), 416–429; and Julianne Pidduck, "New Queer Cinema and Experimental Video," in *New Queer Cinema: A Critical Reader*, ed. Michele Aaron (Edinburgh: Edinburgh University Press, 2004), 80–98.
40. Moten and Harney, *Undercommons*, 98.

... Public Engagement

On Postcolonial African Cinema's Critical Value

LITHEKO MODISANE

In this reflective essay, I propose that the good of film is best tested against its potential to challenge dominant values through mobilization of public engagements on the issues that films raise, even if unanticipated by filmmakers themselves. Such engagements are sites of destabilizing fixed ideas about what is good in society. Film's potential to catalyze public critical engagements is a strength, and therefore one of its values. The essay relies on key observations made in my work on the publicness of films.[1] I begin with some remarks on the distinctive qualities of film, which, I argue, constitute its basic attributes and value when considered from the viewer's perspective. This is followed by reflections on the ethical premises of widely divergent fictional films—colonial films such as *De Voortrekkers* (1916, dir. Harold Shaw) and *Rose of Rhodesia* (1918, dir. Harold Shaw), and postcolonial ones like *Xala* (1975, dir. Ousmane Sembène), *Cry Freedom* (1987, dir. Richard Attenborough), *Mapantsula* (1988, dir. Oliver Schmitz), *Karmen Geï* (2001, dir. Joseph Gaï Ramaka), and *The Wound/Inxeba* (2016, dir. John Trengove). In the last part, I test the good of such films against narratives of their publicness. The running thread in the essay is that all films are normatively ethically oriented, albeit in different ways. However, it is not in their staging of the good that the value of film can be located. Rather, it is in their catalyzing of public engagements that the good of film is realized.

The question "what film is good for" is deceptively simple. In a global culture saturated with moving images, it may also seem antiquated.

FIGURE 7. El Hadji Beye (Thierno Leye) is chastised by Oumi (Younousse Sèye), one of his wives, in *Xala* (1975, Ousmane Sembène).

We inhabit screen worlds that mediate the material world and abstract ideas to us. Roughly 130 years of cinema have bequeathed to the world moving images and images that move us deeply. As a novel cultural form in the early twentieth century, cinema was often treated with contempt and relegated to the lowest of expressive forms. Elite opinion considered its ethical value and aesthetic pretensions to be nonexistent or inferior to the classical arts—that it was to a significant extent a proletarian form, and not always highbrow leisure, compounded its low status as an art form of note. Even the Frankfurt School philosophers Adorno and Horkheimer entertained the thesis of artistic inferiority of film and its consumerist ethos.[2] Nonetheless, the question of its ethical value—that is, its contribution to humanistic ideals—haunts our times. And it cannot be answered with a monosyllable.

Insofar as films can be said to be concerned with moral choices, in their aesthetics, character designs, narrative resolutions, and even outright advocacy in nonnarrative genres, they are articles of ethical interest. To be sure, ethical propositions that films present are directed at viewers for whom they are assumed to be good. Without viewers, the premise for propositions falls away. The success or failure of capturing viewer attention and even impressing certain ideas upon them depends on whether and how films match their resources to the sensorial disposition of the viewer. In other words, the activation of vicarious sensibility in the viewer, which may lead to identification with characters, viewpoints, or simply excite pleasure, is the basic measure of the success of the appeal of films. The dynamism of filmic signification has the potential to enthrall the viewer or disgust or mobilize her into action. Therefore, the ways in which films exploit their attributes ultimately determine the realization of their value.

And yet, while filmic signification may seem to prescribe ethical codes, this does not conclusively constitute the ethical value of films. Colonial films—that is, films made in colonial settings and that positively reproduce colonial sensibilities—powerfully illuminate this observation.

COLONIAL FILM: ETHICAL DEAD ENDS

If indeed film has ethical value, for whom would a good film be good? Under what conditions of life can film be deemed to be good? These questions may seem unwarranted, even unhelpful, but a consideration of conditions for goodness in society is key to reflecting upon an art form and practice that persists within and *not* outside contexts of its realization. After all, several theorists have considered film as externalized human consciousness—an alliance of the human and technology. As a provocation, I will mostly situate my reflection on film within the historical contexts of colonialism and postcolonialism, including the apartheid and postapartheid eras.

Being dehumanizing systems, colonialism and apartheid constituted the colonized as the Other, denied them equality, and in doing so enabled nonethical relations with them. Paradoxically, these were based on supposed ethical principles. The systems also affected the making, representation, and distribution of films. These present limit cases in the consideration of the ethical value of film. Were ethics to assume a world in which agents coexist on an equal level, in whom resides the potential for mutual recognition of their humanity, it would seem illogical to imagine ethics in an unequal society. Yet, in colonial and apartheid South Africa the absence of equality for *all* did not mean its absence for *some*. This suggests "ethical" premises for an exclusionary commonwealth.

As is widely acknowledged, colonial film was complicit in signifying colonial subjects as Other, and therefore incapable of imagining genuine relationality between colonial masters (the Same) and the Other—that is, relationality on equal terms. However, this was not accompanied by an absence of ethical considerations. Incidentally, in his reading of the colonial South African film *Rose of Rhodesia*, Yiva Habel appreciates the relevance of what he calls an "imperial ethics of care—a softer rhetoric of 'the white man's burden'—in order to 'civilize' subject peoples," as well as an "ethics of mutual care"—an advocacy of solidarity between white masters and Black subjects.³ Briefly, the film is about the theft of a diamond from a mine and its recovery. It also revolves around the threat and withdrawal of an anti-colonial rebellion by the local Chief Ushakapilla (Chief Kentani), thanks to the generous reward of the return of his ancestral lands by the colonizers. The execution of the film's ethics consisted in narratives of racial reconciliation, and loyalty to colonial authority. The acceptance of colonial servitude is a staple of colonial films and manifests in the form of histrionic supplication to the white master and acting at his behest by avenging him against fellow Africans. In *De Voortrekkers,* the figure of Sobhuza (Archibald Zonzo Goba) avenges the killing of Piet Retief (Dick Cruikshanks) and the Trekkers at Bloukrans by Dingaan (Tom Zulu), the Zulu king, ostensibly also avenging his earlier defeat and humiliation by Dingaan.⁴

The likes of Ushakapilla and Sobhuza's contrition and oaths of colonial allegiance are indicative of the ethics of colonial visions of society, however twisted their logics may be. Yet, the main ethical claims of such films are reflected in the signification of racial difference. Made a mere fourteen years after the South African War, or "Anglo-Boer War," *De Voortrekkers* deftly transposed the history of the conflict leading both to the Great Trek and the war itself onto racially redefined relations: "The trek is presented as a foreordained act of national righteousness, a way of establishing a new Jerusalem in the African veld of which the Union of South Africa will be the logical outcome."⁵ Motivated as it was by both political contingencies post–Vereeniging Treaty (1902), the use of British money in the making of the film, and the racially exclusionary designs of the two republics, the reconciliatory tone reconfigured whiteness by evacuating the Portuguese from claims to it and diverted historical conflict elsewhere.⁶ In achieving this, a double displacement of Portuguese and Zulus as the villains in a war for a "pure" white and Christian civilization is instated in the film.⁷

The identifiable ethics in the film are therefore predicated on reconciliation. Accordingly, in *De Voortrekkers,* similar to *The Birth of a Nation* (1915, dir. D.W. Griffith), a vision of society is laid out of mutual and equal recognition based on racial background, shared values, and figurations of the human community as white (Afrikaner and British). That the films were in principle predicated upon racial Othering appears to have been a decisive choice and yet was a prerequisite for foregrounding the moral premise of an ostensibly genuine human society. The circulation of *De Voortrekkers* mirrored its ideological and, automatically, ethically imagined outcomes. The film was shown in events curated precisely for Afrikaner nationalistic events. As Carli Coetzee puts it, it is a film that

> for many years in the twentieth century was screened annually on 16 December as part of the commemorations for the central battle between Boer emigrants and Zulu ("the Battle of Blood River"—now known as the Ncume River Battle) depicted in the film, its screening enacting and reinforcing a closed Afrikaner identity for its viewers. . . . *De Voortrekkers* depicts racial violence, and its reception histories are profoundly racialized.[8]

Given how illogical it is to imagine sound ethical relations in conditions of systematic inequality, films such as *De Voortrekkers* throw into sharp relief the difficulty in associating ethical claims in film with the good of such films. The ethics of colonial films present a complicated and complex problem. They advance the right of self-preservation of colonial society, but one that is contingent upon questionable views of the colonized: either as constitutive of servitude or ontologically absent. Though highly problematic, colonial films lay claim to goodness, but their ethical optics narrowed, rather than widened, the receptivity and public engagement of their claims. The shift from colonial to postcolonial ecologies of film production presents different contexts in which the ethical value of film can be engaged.

POSTCOLONIAL FILMS: ETHICAL ENGAGEMENTS

The histories of filmmaking in the African postindependence era, and in the apartheid and postapartheid eras in South Africa, display instances of heightened controversy around certain critical films. Such moments are characterized by state overreach, and even threats of violence or death. Banning and censorship for purported ethical or moral reasons—fear of political agitation, moral turpitude, and legislative transgression—characterize the public lives of such films. The controversy characterized by the banning of these films and sometimes heavily bifurcated public opinion avails them to examination of their ethical statuses. Such controversy can itself constitute the realization of the good of film. This is made even more urgent by films preoccupied with "taboo" subjects or politically inexpedient content.

Anti-colonial politics informed many African films after 1960. They point, in part, to a critical preoccupation with the social ethics of colonial and postcolonial societies. Even if they don't address the colonial issues directly, they attempt to recoup the precolonial era with the aim of extricating African epistemes from Eurocentric ones. Ousmane Sembène's *Xala* is an acerbic critique of the comprador bourgeoisie in postcolonial Senegal, and its facilitation of neocolonialist and anti-African attitudes. It adopts an allegorical mode in the form of African businessmen who conduct a hostile takeover from French businessmen of a chamber of commerce in an unnamed African country. However, they continue to act as guardians of French interests and do not serve African businesses and citizens. *Xala* was subjected to cuts in Senegal because of its disavowal of the corrupt postcolonial elite. Such reactions are signifiers of ethical contestations presented in censorial robes, and of the film's challenge of dominant ethical codes.

South Africa also has a fair share of controversial moments when the making of a film or its screening is followed by bans and discomfort in particular sections of society. The post-Sharpeville and post-1976 closing of political activity in South Africa compounded the problem, as films that challenged the state and dominant ideas could not be made freely. When they were made, it was surreptitious, as in the case of *Dilemma* (1962, dir. Henning Carlsen) and *Mapantsula*.

Cry Freedom and *Mapantsula* constituted moments in which the ethical question itself came into view. Not only were these films interrogating a particular political order, but they were also revealing the unethical malpractices of oppression. Both films were banned or allowed to be viewed only in designated venues.

Sir Richard Attenborough's *Cry Freedom,* which is ostensibly about the life and death of the Black Consciousness Movement leader and anti-apartheid activist Steven Bantu Biko (Denzel Washington), was initially also banned in South Africa. The film confronted the apartheid state with issues that were disallowed public airing—in the main, the philosophy of the Black Consciousness Movement and the death in detention of Biko. The state's clichéd public relations response—namely, that the film would violate the Internal Security Act—was couched in ethical hyperboles. Although *Cry Freedom* did not do well at the US box office, it garnered critical acclaim in the United States.[9] Surprisingly, the South African Publication Appeals Board allowed it to be shown uncut in 1988, a few months after it was screened overseas.[10] Peter Godwin and Eric Marsden of London's *Sunday Times* reasoned that this was a move aimed at "denying the producers the chance to advertise it as 'the film the South African government banned.'"[11] Yet seven hours after it was slated for release, the government overturned the board's decision and removed its posters and copies from movie theaters, ostensibly because it threatened public safety.[12] The drama surrounding the screening of the film—played out both in the film's reflection of violence, the display of the state's schizophrenic responses to the film's showing, and its resonance with audiences—indirectly surfaces the ethical imperative of the film. *Cry Freedom* was controversial enough to cause some Japanese companies to divest from South Africa.[13] However, the film remained controversial on another level, marring its legitimacy with ethical ructions: Biko's associates were wary of the film even before it was released because of its exaggeration of Biko's friendship with Donald Woods (played by Kevin Kline in the film) and lack of assurances about the part that Wood's character would play in the film. They denied Attenborough's claim of cooperation with them.[14]

Mapantsula, on the other hand, follows the exploits of a pickpocket called Panic (Thomas Mogotlane), whose accidental arrest on suspicion of involvement in illegal political activity transforms into a parallel narrative recalling his petty criminality, sexism, and betrayal of his fellows to the police. The government, in the form of the South African censorship board, claimed that *Mapantsula* would excite, among younger and impressionable Blacks, political attitudes against the state and white communities.[15] From an ethical perspective, *Mapantsula* and *Xala* are interesting in their staging of characters who are presented with moral choices. In *Xala*, El Hadji Beye (Thierno Leye) must make a choice between ethics of sound leadership and corrupt self-empowerment. In *Mapantsula*, Panic must either join the anti-apartheid struggle or continue to sell out the anti-apartheid activists. Such characters are examples of how films hold the potential to reverse certain unethical attitudes at the same time as they present their own ethical claims.

However, the public life of a film like *Mapantsula* has shown that the ethical choices are alive at the point of the viewer's encounter and engagement with it too. In my work, I have shown how *Mapantsula* gave rise to diverse critical opinions based on the character of Panic, whose ambiguity was equally rejected *and* celebrated by different activists of the African National Congress (ANC) in camps of the organization's armed wing (Umkhonto we Sizwe) outside South Africa.[16] In particular, the ensuing debate between two activists, Thando Zuma and Ralph Mzamo, illuminated the ethical contribution of the film not as a mere proselytizer of ethical conduct but as an invitation to consider ethical choices in the fight against apartheid.

THE ETHICS OF SEXUALITY, GENDER, AND RELIGION

Other African films—such as *Karmen Geï* and *Inxeba*—address contemporary postcolonial challenges such as gender, religion, and sexuality. Here I will focus on the free expression of LGBTQI+ sexualities in Africa. The Senegalese film *Karmen Geï*, the first African adaptation of Georges Bizet's opera *Carmen,* is the story of a bisexual woman and leader of a criminal gang who resists the sexual pursuit of a female prison warden. Her provocative dances to the beats of Senegalese music form part of her defiance of ordinary heteronormative orders, state authority, and inhibited representations of sexuality in African cinema. As Steven Nelson informs us, "On a radio program, Serigne Moustapha Diakhate, host of a religious radio program and high-ranking Mouride cleric, issued a fatwa against the film, although his information on the production was gained by reading the Senegalese scandal sheet *Mouers.*"[17] He was supported by his devout followers, who protested the showing of the film and threatened its director Joseph Gaï Ramaka and the film star Djeïnaba Diop Gaï with violence. Shortly thereafter the film was banned, in large part due to protests. The film was never shown in Senegal again. The vitriol against *Karmen Geï* and its banning manifests the undercutting of the ethical force of the film by shutting down public reckoning with the issues it raised. Yet, the controversy birthed public debates around religious freedom and freedom of speech.[18]

In the same vein as *Karmen Geï,* the South African film *Inxeba* deals with male homosexuality against the background of *ulwaluko,* the *rite de passage* from boyhood to manhood of AmaXhosa people. It follows a love triangle between an initiate and two supervisors of an initiation school. Culturally, the school is supposed to be hidden from public view and is sustained by cultural codes of secrecy. "Historically women and children were prohibited from observing men during the period of seclusion, as well as other aspects of the *ulwaluko* school," Carli Coetzee notes.[19] Though the practice is heavily archived in photography and film, it was not until its showing in *Inxeba* that it drew wide public attention to its portrayal on film.[20]

The release of the film was preceded by protests by the Man and Boy Foundation and the Congress of Traditional Leaders in South Africa. The organizations argued that the film misrepresented the ritual and identified scenes of explicit sex in a culturally sacred context.[21] Some cinemas in the Eastern and Western Cape provinces canceled the opening of the film due to protests.[22]

The South African Film and Publication Board successfully restricted *Inxeba* to specialist cinemas for reasons of explicit sex. It is notable that, while the banning was draped in robes of moral supremacy, the film pushed boundaries of the right to articulate dissent. From an ethical perspective, *Inxeba* is layered, both with regard to its making and subject matter. It addresses a deeply cultural issue at the same time as it challenges the supposedly singular idea of masculinity associated with it. However, the film's direction by a white filmmaker complicated the engagement that *Inxeba* sought to construct. The implication here was that a white man had no cultural legitimacy over African culture and that he therefore had no right to direct the film.

The ethical claims of a film, especially when they are based on a critique of dominant societal values, are often contingent upon their censorship or outright bans. In all instances of heightened reaction to a film, all sides involved lay claim to ethical standards as premise of their positions. All entertain views of what is a good film. These claims are, however, not to be confused with the ultimate question of the good of film *qua* film; they are not synonymous with the good of film as a form. Yet, they do lead in some contorted and unpredictable way to an answer, satisfactory or not. The controversy wrought by *Inxeba* pushed the boundaries of public engagement in a way that draws attention to the ethical dimension of film as a catalyst of an unpleasant *but necessary* reckoning with the fault lines of cultural values. In such instances, film becomes an ethical object thanks to its forging of a particular way of thinking about practices and values attached to them. It is in such tensions, majorly wrought by differences and inequalities, that the ethical value of film can be located. Certain films have ethical value, both because they challenge our ideas in resonant ways and because of staging productive tensions in their wake, which are responsible for reflection on what is good in and for society. Others, such as *De Voortrekkers*, provoke ethical questions precisely because of their ethical deficiencies. While all films may be ethical objects, only particular films succeed in critically staging their ethical value through presentation of ethical dilemmas, interests, and activation of engagement that sometimes unfold in the form of controversy. This is especially so in formerly colonized zones, where the issue of inequalities continues to assume critical dimensions.

NOTES

1. Litheko Modisane, *South Africa's Renegade Reels: The Making and Public Lives of Black Centered Films* (New York: Palgrave Macmillan, 2013).
2. For arguments on the aesthetic worth of film, see Roger Scruton, *The Politics of Culture and Other Essays* (Manchester: Carcanet Press, 1981).
3. Yiva Habel, "Hollywood Histrionics: Performing 'Africa' in *The Rose of Rhodesia*," *Screening the Past* 25 (2009), http://www.screeningthepast.com/issue-25-special-issue-colonial-africa-on-the-silent-screen-recovering-the-rose-of-rhodesia-1918/hollywood-histrionics-performing-%E2%80%9Cafrica%E2%80%9D-in%C2%A0the-rose-of-rhodesia/. Accessed October 8, 2021.
4. Hannes Van Zyl, "*De Voortrekkers* (1916): Some Stereotypes and Narrative Conventions," *Critical Arts* 1, no. 1 (1980): 24–31, at 26. The Voortrekkers were Dutch descendants who exiled themselves from British rule in the Cape colony and founded independent republics in the South African interior.
5. Lucia Saks, "A Tale of Two Nations: South Africa, *De Voortrekkers*, and *Come See the Bioscope*," *Ilha do Desterro: A Journal of English Language Literatures in English and Cultural Studies* 61 (2011): 137–188, at 155–157.
6. The Treaty of Vereeniging ended the Anglo-Boer War between the British and Boers. It heralded reconciliatory overtures between the two nations. The Portuguese were maligned in the film, likely because Portugal fought alongside the British during the war.
7. Saks, "A Tale of Two Nations," 156.
8. Carli Coetzee, "All Tickets Please, or How Cinema Histories of South Africa Can Stop Re-Enacting the Racialized Past," *Journal of Southern African Studies* 39, no. 3 (2013): 721–726, at 721–722.
9. Ivor Davis, "Critics Hail Attenborough's Biko Film," *The Times,* October 22, 1987, https://go.gale.com/ps/i.do?p=AONE&u=unict&id=GALE|A117560031&v=2.1&it=r&sid=bookmark-AONE&asid=6ab7e5af. Accessed October 8, 2021.
10. Peter Godwin and Eric Marsden, "Spectrum: Revealed—The Real Biko," *Sunday Times,* November 29, 1987, https://go.gale.com/ps/i.do?p=AONE&u=unict&id=GALE|A117718519&v=2.1&it=r&sid=bookmark-AONE&asid=cf921dbb. Accessed October 8, 2021.
11. Godwin and Marsden, "Spectrum: Revealed."
12. "S. Africa Seizes 'Cry Freedom,' Calling the Film Dangerous," *Los Angeles Times,* July 31, 1988, https://www.latimes.com/archives/la-xpm-1988-07-31-mn-10702-story.html. Accessed October 8, 2021.
13. "Japan and South Africa: No, but We Saw the Film," *The Economist,* April 2, 1988.
14. Donald Woods (1933–2001) was a South African anti-apartheid journalist and a friend of Bantu Biko.
15. Modisane, *Renegade Reels,* 105.
16. Modisane, *Renegade Reels,* 113–115.
17. Steven Nelson, "*Karmen Geï,* Sex, the State, and Censorship in Dakar," *African Arts* 44, no. 1 (2011): 74–81, at 76.
18. Mari Maasilta, "Transnational Senegalese Cinema Between Nationalism and Globalisation," *Glocal Times* 2, no. 5 (2006): n.p.

19. Carli Coetzee, *Written under the Skin: Blood and Intergenerational Memory in South Africa* (Johannesburg: Wits University Press, 2019), 144.

20. *Inxeba* was co-written by the novelist Thando Mgqolozana, Malusi Bengu, and John Trengove. *Inxeba* won numerous awards locally and abroad. It was also short-listed for an Oscar in the Best Foreign Language Film category. See Iavan Pijoos, "Screening of *Inxeba (The Wound)* Suspended Due to Protests," *News 24*, February 2, 2018. https://www.news24.com/news24/SouthAfrica/News/screening-of-inxeba-the-wound-suspended-due-to-protests-20180202. Accessed October 8, 2021.

21. Lindile Sifile, "Pledge to Halt Opening Screenings of '*Inxeba*,'" *IOL*, February 1, 2018, https://www.iol.co.za/the-star/news/pledge-to-halt-opening-screenings-of-inxeba-13045263. Accessed October 8, 2021.

22. Pijoos, "Screening of *Inxeba*."

7

... Shedding Light on Abject Lives

On Global Cinema as Ethical Art

SEUNG-HOON JEONG

Scene 1. Igor (Jérémie Renier), a Belgian teenager, walks with an African woman, Assita (Assita Ouedraogo), who will take the train for Italy to hopefully join her cousin and wait for her missing husband there. But in the underpass to the train station, Igor tells her that her husband got fatally injured when hiding from the inspectors of undocumented labor and died because his father, a smuggler of illegal immigrants, covered up this accident and buried him with Igor's reluctant help. Tormented with guilt, Igor left home and took care of Assita and her baby as he promised to do right before her husband's death. Now facing the truth of what happened to her husband, Assita silently turns around and helplessly walks back. Igor follows and walks along with her though they have nowhere to go. We are left immobile, watching their backs disappearing slowly into the endless-looking underpass in this last scene of La Promesse *(1996) by the Dardenne brothers.*

Scene 2. Sumida (Sometani Shōta), a Japanese teenager, walks with his girlfriend Shazawa (Nikaidō Fumi), who was heartbroken by his disappearance but relieved by his emergence from the lake where he seemingly drowned himself. The 2011 Fukushima disaster devasted his life: his mother left home with her lover, his alcoholic father became a gambler in debt, and a yakuza beat Sumida to retrieve money lent to his father. One day, Sumida's father bitterly wished Sumida were dead so that he could get his hands on the insurance money; an angry Sumida was driven to patricide. Tormented with guilt, Sumida tried to restart his life as a punisher of social evils, such as wanton murder, in vain. Now stopping short of suicide, he heads over to the police to turn himself in. Shazawa walks beside him. Though abused by her parents, too, she has always taken care of him, dreaming of living with him. They begin to run, crying and shouting over and over, "Don't give up, Sumida!" Sono Sion's Himizu *(2011) ends while we accompany them in the endless-looking ruins of Japan.*

FIGURE 8. Igor (Jérémie Renier) and Assita (Assita Ouedraogo) in *La Promesse* (1996, Jean-Pierre and Luc Dardenne).

These two similar endings are left open in the middle of an action, so we cannot imagine what will happen to those miserable characters. They just walk together on the road with no promise of a better future but still enduring their fate. What they share is nothing but the experience of being marginalized and degraded to the bottom of human life at the edge of a malignant global system and a crumbling post-catastrophic society. However, this shared "precarity" makes their contingent relationships all the more "precious," as they have nothing more to lose but their being, as such, to give each other like a gift. They show no political power to change the world but some ethical agency to take care of humanity crushed in the same world. I would say they embody an ethics of "walking side by side," an alternative ethics in global cinema regardless of whether it hails from the West or the East. But alternative to what? Let me briefly map the historical and discursive context in which to answer this question and locate the significance of this alternative.

THE ETHICAL PARADIGM OF THE GLOBAL SYSTEM

I formulate global cinema as always reflecting the ethical dilemma and potential of today's humanity in the age of globalization. This age, as often said, started with the so-called end of history, the Fukuyamaist version of Hegelian history driven by political ideologies that dialectically reconfigure the world order. Politics in its proper, traditional, or common sense involves the conflict between people's antagonistic standpoints on their community and their passionate actions for radical change. The end of the Cold War signaled the completion of this political history, opening a victorious single planetary market system with no alternative. Liberal democracy here began to serve as the humanizing cosmetics of neoliberal capitalism, while its traditional "big causes to die for," such as freedom and equality, gradually turned into ethical "default values" to be taken for granted in the name of human rights. The "Others," regardless of their race, ethnicity, gender, or religion, were to be ideally tolerated and respected in all-encompassing global rainbow communities. No wonder multiculturalism became the post-historical, post-ideological zeitgeist combined with identity politics, in which the pursuit of "political correctness" already implied the ethical articulation of politics.

This post-political ethics of tolerance and respect, however, has been the main target of leftist philosophers. For Alain Badiou, it updates yet decomposes Levinasian ethics of near-divine alterity ("Altogether-Other") into the ethics of secular relative differences or victimized cultural Others, whose human rights the multiculturalist embraces with a warm heart but often a presupposed distance.[1] The Others should not challenge this multiculturalist's status as the subject who has power to let them in. In fact, I add, tolerance is a dubious concept presuming the boundary between tolerable and intolerable and the hierarchy between its subject and object. In the tolerant subject's humanitarian defense of cultural relativism lies a condescending attitude toward its object; according to Badiou, this is the "self-satisfied egoism of the affluent West" with "pity for victims."[2] This egoism takes an aggressive turn whenever threatened, as shown in the French citizens' self-defensive slogan "Je suis Charlie" upon the *Charlie Hebdo* attacks. Badiou argues this exposes their double stance toward the Muslims supporting the French economy.[3] Multiculturalism might then be a postcolonial disguise for Europe's colonial legacy.

Likewise, the multiculturalist's patronizing gesture is suspected of refining racism. No longer an old-fashioned racist who says "I am superior to you," a post-racial liberal says "I respect your culture." Yet, as Slavoj Žižek notes, this respect still asserts his "privileged *empty point of universality*" from which to impose an important condition: "insofar as you respect my culture without bothering me."[4] (Similarly, doesn't the nice rich man warn his poor driver, "Don't cross the line!" in Bong Joon-ho's *Parasite* [2019]?) Multiculturalism, thus, works as a euphemism for cultural indifference, a form of "social distancing" from cultural Others or limited tolerance for benign cultures, such as is manifested through world music, dance, and cuisine without the Real of their alterity, which is often fantasized as too patriarchal, dangerous, or primitive to accept. To rephrase Žižek, multiculturalism deprives the Other of its toxic *jouissance* to celebrate its pleasurable wisdom, charming customs, or exotic commodities to safely enjoy just like all sorts of "X minus its harmful kernel": decaffeinated coffee, nicotine-free cigarettes, and so on. We consume cultural differences like orientalist simulacra in global markets, whether in a metropolitan food court or the New Age industry. Updating Fredric Jameson's postmodernism, to Žižek, multiculturalism thus works as "the cultural logic of multinational capitalism."

This double-sided globalization—including tolerable diversity and excluding excessive Otherness—underlies the ethical paradigm of the global system. In Jacques Rancière's terms, the global "consensus" on capitalist multiculturalism brings about "the ethical turn of politics" by evacuating the dialectic "dissensus" between conflicting parties or positions and the political redistribution of "the sensible," the process of the excluded people, invisible or voiceless, to be seen or heard in the symbolic order.[5] This political struggle gives way to the doctrine of consensual lawmaking that includes but ever reduces more different Others into a single, seemingly equal people. Here, the excluded are treated as either vulnerable Others to accept or threatening Others to reject. Human rights are then less politically pursued by dissident subjects than ethically assumed as either the absolute right of the victimized Other to save through humanitarian intervention or the self-protective right of the system to fight the fundamentalist Other who terrorizes it. Politics is then doubly ethicized: while the *soft* ethics of cosmopolitan hospitality becomes mainstreamed, the *hard* ethics of "infinite justice" is rationalized to defeat its "axis of evil" for the sake of security.[6]

Suffice it to recall the two historic falls that each defined a decade. If the fall of the Berlin Wall spread the soft-ethical dream of utopian globalism through the 1990s, the fall of the World Trade Center debunked its universality via the terroristic return of the excluded Other and triggered the 2000s hard-ethical counterterror operations. The system of glorious globalization turned out to have inevitably generated remnants or by-products that could not be part of it. Hence, a new radical antagonism emerged not between the system's inner different groups but between the whole system and its immanently produced outside. These two ends aim to destroy each other outside the law in the name of their own God, respectively, bringing no political resolution but endless hard-ethical retaliation, the vicious cycle of terror and counterterror. In sum, we are stuck in a self-contradictory yet nondialectic global system: the softer it is, the harder are both the attacks on it and its security measures; the more expansive the pity and sympathy, the more explosive the hate and apathy; and the more connection, the more contagion. Even a local incident can quickly impact a global network like a pandemic, as seen in the domino effects of not only terrorist attacks but also debt crises, nuclear disasters, climate anomalies, and viral diseases. No longer exceptional, such global catastrophes are now experienced as our life's "new normal."

ALTERNATIVE ETHICS IN GLOBAL CINEMA

Global cinema reflects this post-political world and life by dramatizing various cases of the excluded Other. Let me further conceptualize this Other, drawing on Julia Kristeva's idea of the *abject:* something disgusting or threatening, like bodily waste and corpses, that the subject rejects or expels for self-protection or ego formation. No longer part of "me" but not yet a "thing," the abject lingers between subject and object, self and other, life and death. This ambivalent psychoanalytic notion has been critically expanded to the "social abject": people cast out of their community or denied integration into a new community and whose social subjectivity is thus temporarily suspended.[7] Globally generated immigrants or refugees and the homeless, jobless, or any sorts of outcasts experience "abjection," being deprived of basic rights or legal protection. These global "noncitizens" experience either soft-ethical compassion or hard-ethical discrimination, often debased to either useful, exploitable Others or repulsive harmful enemies. They are easily targeted by all types of "sovereign" violence, from homophobia to genocide. I here mean by "sovereignty" the supralegal power of the subject/community to suspend the normal law and declare the state of exception or emergency, in which even killing the abject is not a criminal act but unpunishable just as, in Agambenian biopolitics, the sovereign can kill the *homo sacer* like an animal or "bare life" outside the law.[8] Sovereignty embodies this law's self-transcending potential, including the abject in the juridical order only via exclusion. The legal subject-object relation in soft ethics turns into the extralegal sovereign-abject relation in hard ethics, but these are two sides of the same coin, the global system.

In cinema, however, the abject do not remain bare lives as mere passive victims but always activate *agency:* the causative force to act to achieve a goal provisionally. Many films follow what I call "the narrative of double death" in this regard: protagonists first undergo the "symbolic death" of abjection, losing their identity, memory, family, or country due to a traumatic event or disaster, but then they become a sort of agent struggling to fulfill a mission—to restore their subjectivity or community, or even to take revenge or destroy the world—until ending up with success/failure or "real death." Such "abject agents" traverse global cinema across different genres and styles, representing or evoking global phenomena in diverse local settings. They are showcased in a wide spectrum of the French cinema post–*La Haine* (1995, dir. Mathieu Kassovitz) between soft-ethical multiculturalism and hard-ethical terrorism in films such as *The Class* (2008, dir. Laurent Cantet) and *Hadewijch* (2009, dir. Bruno Dumont). They are enslaved into the capitalist system like "dogs" or turned into "thieves" of capital, floating around East Asia in Korean films such as *The Journals of Musan* (2010, dir. Park Jung-bum) and *The Thieves/Dodukdeul* (2012, dir. Choi Dong-hoon). They appear as professional secret agents undergoing abjection in Hollywood, from blockbuster franchises like the Bond and Bourne series to mind-game films such as *Source Code* (2011, dir. Duncan Jones) and *Ghost in the Shell* (2017, dir. Rupert Sanders). The "cinema of catastrophe" in its broadest sense is full of abject agents striving for dominion, survival, or life's value in the face of "glocal" catastrophes, wherever they are, from *Dogville* (2003, dir. Lars von Trier) to *Timbuktu* (2014, dir. Abderrahmane Sissako).

Yet, the global mechanism of sovereignty and abjection remains unchanged, whether abject agents retrieve their normalcy, die (self-sacrificially) in doing so, or even turn into terrorists. Sometimes the screen displays the apocalyptic demolition of the world to reject the status quo radically. Still, the spectacle of catastrophe also betrays a failure to imagine a better, alternative, or utopian world. The hard-ethical punishment of humanity in the disaster genre is rather a visual symptom of impossible political change.

In this ethical dead end, let me bring back the alternative ethics I suggested via *La Promesse* and *Himizu*. What counts here is that Igor and Shazawa traverse the same egalitarian ground of "abjecthood" as Assita and Sumida. Only at this common bottom of all beings could we believe in the potential sanctity of being, the sacredness of human life as yet to be realized above bare life. Those teenagers' becoming-abject thus implies ethics at its most fundamental. It practices neither the soft ethics of unselfish charitable love for the abject Other nor the hard ethics of (suicidal) terrorism or rage against the world. Instead, it experiments with an alternative way out of this doubly ethical paradigm.

Moreover, Igor and Shazawa do not give something out of pity to the other but give themselves away by becoming an abject just like the other. This existential gift is not recognized or paid back as a gift by the giver or givee—it thus evokes Jacques Derrida's "pure gift" that deconstructs the capitalist economy of gift as exchange, the give-and-take calculation. Igor-as-gift, in particular, is based on unpayable indebtedness to Assita's dead husband. An ethical debt impossible to repay generates an ethical gift impossible to return. His becoming-abject-as-gift forms solidarity with the stranger in this way, outside his patriarchal, colonial, neoliberal world. It is noteworthy that he confesses the truth without facing her while "losing face" by facing his guilt. He made the promise to the face of her dying husband, the Levinasian "face of the other" incarnating the ethical commandment "You shall not kill," but he let him die, making him a "faceless" Other. In Žižek's view, the core of the "neighbor" lies not in their familiar face but the traumatic Real behind it that defamiliarizes one's relationship with him/her, and which evokes or reanimates something terrible that makes one guilty.[9] Igor's promise binds him to the faceless but unforgettable Third as such a neighbor who is beyond the face-to-face relation between Igor and his father and beyond a mere friend/enemy dichotomy.

This Third, if from the Third World, does not represent a cultural difference to assimilate or eliminate but the same abjecthood to embrace and overcome at once. Igor's "indifference" to Assita's exotic, often irrational ethnic culture implies no multiculturalist distancing but "the ethics of sameness."[10] True Otherness is not necessarily mediated by its collective identity and located behind the cultural barrier yet to be crossed. One can connect with the Other immediately in a common human struggle just as those abject couples walk together on the same ground for a new ethical relationship: not the face-to-face interpellation between two in Levinas, but the side-by-side accompaniment with the faceless Third. There is no utopia but only "atopia" here, or rather, the "atopian" movement of losing one's *topos*/place for stable identity or being abjected from one place to another. But this movement enables the abject to become an agent of gift-giving at its purest. Such abject agents interconnect and accompany each other across social, ethnic, racial, and even ontological differences between man, animal, and cyborg, as seen in *Shoplifters/Manbiki Kazoku* (2018, dir. Kore-eda Hirokazu), *Children of Men* (2006, dir. Alfonso Cuarón), *Life of Pi*

(2012, dir. Ang Lee), *Blade Runner 2049* (2017, dir. Denis Villeneuve), and the like. They form a temporary alternative family or network at the periphery of the global system without blood ties or collective identities, and perform atopian gift-giving based on their commonality without community, identity without pity, and solidarity without unity.

Hence, I say, "atopian ethics." It is an existentialist ethics about an inevitable mode of *amor fati,* namely, loving the fate of self-abjection or self-determination to stand by the abject Other as if or even if that is the only freedom to choose of one's will. It is not reducible to such ethical models as Kierkegaard's religious singularity, Levinas's facial duality, and Kant's imperative universality. The intrusion of an abject Third opens the closed self-Other or subject-object dyad as the base of Levinasian ethics. Still, this opening does not lead to a triad, that is, a society where multiple people need political justice for living together. In atopian ethics, solidarity between the abject, no matter how many, does not grow into political collectivity or form any stable community. Instead, what works is the atopian dynamics of the precarious yet precious gift-giving relation between a changeable two that is impossible in the existing regime of biopolitical and ethical relations. Of course, we do not know what would happen if we took an atopian walk side by side with the abject. What we know is that we would have nothing but the will to love our unknown fate.[11]

ETHICAL VALUES OF CINEMA AS ART

Let me further explore the fundamental relation between cinema "and" ethics via global cinema's atopian ethics. As Thomas Elsaesser suggests, the ontological and aesthetic questions that have penetrated film studies in its photographic and digital periods ("What is cinema?" and "Where is cinema?") should be followed by an ethical question in a postclassical, postmedia, posthuman era: "What is/was cinema good for?"[12] Let's then ask: what is cinema good for in our post-political age? In a nutshell, it is good for highlighting what both politics and post-politics miss or even dismiss. Politics is always based on collectivity, involving people's organization, maintenance, and change of their communities. It makes, preserves, and reforms the law that represents the generality of rules, norms, and universal imperatives. As a political ideal, even Kant's cosmopolitanism (without a world government) was also envisioned to create an orderly cosmic world regulated by principles and laws. It can be seen as a "Habermasian program" of world citizenship based on "conditional hospitality," holding the right to invite the Others governed by the economy of sovereignty and jurisdiction.[13] Doesn't this vision sound like the post-political soft ethics with all the problems we discussed? We could pursue this cosmopolitanism only by continually having it face and redraw its limits, especially "in the face of a stranger."[14] In other words, however utopian the world may be, it would inevitably need the sovereign law to govern itself as a peaceful whole while producing and encountering someone outside it. Yet, in close-ups from most films, what we see is not a political project or multitude but this individual's singular life.

In global cinema, such individuals appear as living symptoms of the global system. Often becoming or accompanying an abject neighbor, they embody what this system's law cannot represent: particular justice, unique situations, liminal experience, incalculable exchange, and unconditional responsibility without which there cannot be ethics per se. But their ethics is not Antigone's terroristic, self-destructive desire to go extremely against the law. Instead, they wander like walking atopia, settling in no place, seemingly ideal, yet keeping open the impossible promise of utopia. This ongoing "edging" to an "unpromised" land on the edge of the world performs existential *amor fati*, enabling them to embrace their abject being as such and as a gift. Here is the artistic potential of cinema. It can reflect harsh realities and social contradictions but not bring political solutions or radical changes. Instead, it can shed light on abject lives generated unavoidably in any system, even if utopian, and let them speak in distinct ethical ways that are irreducible to collective identity formations or the Rancièrian political redistribution of the sensible. That is, cinema, if not a political practice, can be an ethical art that questions the political order but always in concrete situations, draws attention to politically unresolvable ethical dilemmas, and gropes for new ethical directions away from established politics and ethics.

In fact, many socially conscious films are criticized for lacking a collective political vision, reducing structural problems to personal issues, or dramatizing fictive solutions led by individual heroes. While this criticism has been valid, alternative films have depicted a revolutionary class with no central character since Sergei Eisenstein's *Strike* (1925). Dziga Vertov radicalized this approach in the documentary genre, which has since been much better suited for directly presenting political reality. Likewise, political modernism in the 1960s and 1970s emerged through discontent with narrative cinema's "institutional mode of representation" (Noël Burch): illusionistic, reactionary, capitalist, patriarchal, and phallocentric.¹⁵ The ideological critique of cinema was then driven by the political desire for Brechtian or more experimental alternative modes, as seen in film practice (from the French New Wave to Third Cinema) and theory (Burch, Laura Mulvey, and Jean-Louis Comolli, among others). This cinematic politics takes on ethics in Serge Daney's famous critique of *Kapo* (1960, dir. Gillo Pontecorvo).¹⁶ For him, the film's tracking shot toward the electrocution of a Nazi camp inmate on a barbed-wire fence beautifies death so dramatically in the way of representing the unrepresentable so cheesily. In fact, Daney's lengthy essay is an updated elaboration of Jacques Rivette's short review of *Kapo* from 1961, titled "On Abjection."¹⁷ However, the word "abjection" never appears in the text and only vaguely indicates Rivette's contempt for the very tracking shot as a sort of "death porn." I mean to say, it has nothing to do with Kristeva's abjection.

Global cinema, in my framework, pursues no such antirepresentational ethical aesthetics but antihegemonic ethics within the represented diegesis. It does not confine us in the modernist impasse of elitist experimentalism but confronts us with abject Others in ways we would otherwise not encounter in today's real world. The ethics of global cinema is the ethics of the abject in this world. The abject are reductively typified as global news items in reality. Still, on screen, we palpably experience their singular existence and our potential abjection at once, thereby virtually walking side by side with them. This contingent solidarity, if not politicized, is crucial as the ground of potential social relations. Indeed, almost all narrative films center on protagonists and have limitations in staging a whole class or a social structure. But by the same token, films unfold narratives of individuals who symptomatically embody systemic inconsistencies and thus urge us to critique them existentially while raising unthought questions or possibilities that could not be answered or performed in any hegemonic collective logic. This artistic potential makes cinema ethical and, further, philosophical. Whether or not cinema itself does philosophy, a question often asked in film-philosophy circles, might be the wrong question here. It is already philosophical, inspiring our thoughts on what is unthinkable in reality.¹⁸

NOTES

1. Alain Badiou, *Ethics: An Essay on the Understanding of Evil* (London: Verso, 2012).
2. Badiou, *Ethics*, 3–7.

3. Badiou, "The Red Flag and the Tricolore," Verso Books (blog), February 2005, https://www.versobooks.com/blogs/1833-the-red-flag-and-the-tricolore-by-alain-badiou. Accessed November 2, 2021.

4. Slavoj Žižek, "Multiculturalism, or, the Cultural Logic of Multination Capitalism," *New Left Review* 225 (1997): 28–51, at 44. The single quotation marks refer to my own emphasis or phrasing.

5. Jacques Rancière, "The Ethical Turn of Aesthetics and Politics," in *Aesthetics and Its Discontents* (Cambridge: Polity Press, 2004), 109–132, at 115–118, 127–128.

6. For my elaboration on this double ethics, see Seung-hoon Jeong, "Introduction—Global East Asian Cinema: Abjection and Agency," *Studies in the Humanities* 44–45, nos. 1–2 (2019): ii-vi. This Introduction also introduces my formulation of global cinema in light of the double ethics.

7. Imogen Tyler, *Revolting Subjects: Social Abjection and Resistance in Neoliberal Britain* (London: Zed Books, 2013).

8. Giorgio Agamben, *Homo Sacer: Sovereign Power and Bare Life* (Stanford, CA: Stanford University Press, 1998).

9. Slavoj Žižek, "Neighbors and Other Monsters: A Plea for Ethical Violence," in Slavoj Žižek, Eric L. Santner, and Kenneth Reinhard, *The Neighbor: Three Inquiries in Political Theology* (Chicago: University of Chicago Press, 2013), 134–190, at 140–141.

10. Badiou, *Ethics*, 27.

11. I have discussed abjection and agency in some of my other essays, including, most substantially, my aforementioned article (see note 6, above). The paragraphs in this section on *La Promesse* and atopian gift/neighbor ethics are partly based on and revised from my lengthy analysis of the film and *The Edge of Heaven* in Jeong, "From 'Face-to-Face' to 'Side-by-Side': The Abject Neighbor in European Cinema," *Northern Lights: Film and Media Studies Yearbook* 18, no. 1 (2020): 53–67.

12. Thomas Elsaesser, *Film History as Media Archaeology: Tracking Digital Cinema* (Amsterdam: Amsterdam University Press, 2016), 21–26.

13. Jürgen Habermas and Jacques Derrida, *Philosophy in a Time of Terror: Dialogues with Jürgen Habermas and Jacques Derrida*, ed. Giovan Borradori (Chicago: University of Chicago Press, 2003), 163.

14. Habermas and Derrida, *Philosophy in a Time of Terror*, 163.

15. Noël Burch, *Life to Those Shadows* (Berkeley: University of California Press, 1990), 1–5.

16. Serge Daney, *Postcards from the Cinema*, trans. Paul Douglas Grant (Oxford: Berg, 2007), 17–38.

17. Jacques Rivette, "On Abjection," *Cahiers du Cinéma* 120 (June 1961): 54–55.

18. This last section is slightly revised from the last section of my latest book, *Biopolitical Ethics in Global Cinema* (New York: Oxford University Press, 2023), 299–302. The book also incorporates my pieces mentioned in notes 6 and 11, with changes.

8

... Empathy
On Its Limitations and Liabilities

MALCOLM TURVEY

One common answer to the question "What is film good for?" is that it is good at eliciting empathy for fictional characters. Another, related answer is that by affording us manifold opportunities to empathize deeply with characters, film can cultivate and refine our capacity for empathy. It can thereby enhance our ability to empathize with others in the real world and perhaps make it more likely we will show concern for, help, or in other ways behave morally toward them. This "optimistic" view, as the philosopher Gregory Currie calls it, of the relation among film, empathy, and morality can be found in theories of fiction more broadly.[1] The philosopher Martha Nussbaum, for example, has argued that what she calls human compassion, and the attendant desire to help others, is dependent on the "ability to imagine what it is like to be in [a] person's place (what we usually call *empathy*)."[2] Literature and other narrative arts, due to the "intense concern with the fate of characters" they promote through their vivid depiction of individual suffering, "cultivate" our capacity for "compassionate imagination" and are therefore "essential for civic participation and awareness."[3]

Film, however, is said by some to be especially good at fostering empathy due to its ability, through the close-up and other techniques, to exhibit and draw attention to details of the facial expressions and bodily behaviors of characters, which can trigger more automatic, "subpersonal" empathic responses such as emotional contagion and mimicry.[4] Film can also, according to the philosopher Robert Sinnerbrink,

FIGURE 9. Flora Cameron (Mae Marsh) in *The Birth of a Nation* (1915, D. W. Griffith).

"cultivate our moral perception" by affording us occasions to empathize with the often conflicting perspectives of a variety of characters in complex ethical situations.[5] As the film theorist Murray Smith puts it, film, and fiction in general, stretches and refines our capacity for empathy by expanding our opportunities for exercising it well beyond those we encounter in our own lives and intensifying our experience of it.[6] Currie has summarized this optimistic picture as follows: "A thought that has captured attention across the literary, philosophical, and psychological disciplines is this: fiction refines and enlarges our empathic sensitivities to morally charged situations, exposing us to exemplars—imaginary ones—of demanding, complex situations beyond those we are likely to encounter in daily life, expanding the circle of those we care about and our ability to help them."[7]

In this essay, I will challenge the assumption that film's empathy-enlarging ability, if it exists, is a virtue because it augments our capacity for empathy in the real world, thereby perhaps making it more likely that we will behave morally toward others. I call this an assumption because it is rarely explicitly articulated in theories of fiction, film, and empathy. However, I suspect this assumption is widespread, because theorists hardly ever acknowledge, let alone take into consideration, evidence that fiction-elicited empathy can have immoral or amoral outcomes. And they tend to celebrate fiction and film's empathy-expanding power without qualification. They seem to take for granted, in other words, that empathy leads to moral behavior, and that fiction-enhanced empathy must therefore be a moral good. But a number of philosophers and moral psychologists have argued that the relation between empathy and morality is not nearly as straightforward, or as unproblematic, as this optimistic view assumes. Not only is empathy not necessary for morality, they claim, but it can interfere with or undermine it.[8] If this is the case, we should question whether film's putative empathy-expanding power is as laudable as proponents of the optimistic view seem to suppose. In the first section of this essay, I point to empirical evidence indicating that empathic experiences occasioned by fictions might impede rather than enhance morality by giving rise to "empathy-avoidance," "burnout," and "self-licensing" behaviors. In the second section, I examine some of the moral biases and limitations of empathy and speculate as to how they might be activated by film and other forms of fiction. Finally, I conclude by suggesting that, given empathy's moral liabilities, we shouldn't value fiction's ability to "expand" empathy *tout court*. Instead, we should embrace its capacity to promote what I call "considered empathy," that is, empathy constrained and corrected by reason.

EMPATHY AVOIDANCE AND FICTION

It has become de rigueur in discussions of empathy to point out that the term has many different meanings, including sympathy, compassion, or concern for another, as well as mind reading, imagining what it would be like to be in another's shoes or imagining being them. In what follows, by empathy I mean what is often referred to as "affective empathy," in which, in responding to another's affective state, I come to experience that state too, thereby feeling something similar to what they feel.

It is easy to see why many assume that empathy in this affective sense is central to morality or leads to potentially moral behavior such as helping others. According to the self-interested or "egoistic" explanation of the empathy-helping relation, if you are suffering and I empathize with and feel your pain, your pain becomes my pain, and I am therefore more likely to help you alleviate your pain so that mine lessens too. Notice, however, that this explanation does not necessarily show that helping behavior is moral. My motivation to help you lessen your agony is purely selfish according to this explanation, because it is through diminishing your pain that I ease my own. Moreover, as the moral psychologist Paul Bloom points out, if my goal is to alleviate my own distress there is an easier way to do so, which is to avoid empathizing with someone in pain altogether.[9] Indeed, as Bloom reports, people often eschew the misery of others because they don't want to empathize with their pain and thereby experience the discomfort of that pain themselves. For instance, they cross the street to avoid encountering homeless people or turn off the television when news reports depict human wretchedness.

Although it is rarely acknowledged, I conjecture that the same "empathy-avoidance behavior" can occur in response to fictions. If we anticipate that we are likely to be exposed to the suffering of others in a fiction, especially those we already find sympathetic, we might well shun the fiction in order to circumvent the potentially unpleasant experience of empathizing with and feeling its characters' pain. I know in my own case that I sometimes have to force myself to see films, such as *12 Years a Slave* (2013, dir. Steve McQueen), in which I might empathize with highly sympathetic characters suffering intensely, and that I occasionally succumb to the temptation to avoid doing so. I suspect I am not alone. Those who subscribe to the optimistic picture of the relation among film, empathy, and morality tend to assume that film's empathy-eliciting power is always a desideratum. They overlook the possibility that this ability might have the consequence of encouraging people to avoid watching films in the first place, including morally worthy ones such as *12 Years a Slave*. There could be many viewers who regularly eschew films and other fictions about human suffering precisely because they don't want to put themselves through the unpleasant experience of empathizing with this suffering, especially if they have their own problems to contend with, have suffered in a similar way to the characters, or fear that they could suffer a similar fate. This might be considered selfish behavior, and undoubtedly in some cases it is. But it isn't necessarily so. I might be highly sympathetic, for instance, to the plight of modern-day slaves, and donate money and in other ways attempt to bring human trafficking to an end precisely because I can imagine how awful it must be for its victims. I don't need a film or another fiction to show me. Either way, it is an important empirical question how often empathy-avoidance behavior occurs in response to fictions, and one that friends of the optimistic view tend to overlook.

Bloom points to another vital area of empirical research that might have a bearing on the issue of empathy avoidance and fiction, which has to do with the phenomenon of empathic "burnout" or "distress." Far from increasing helping and other forms of potentially moral behavior, researchers such as Tania Singer have reported that the intense, repeated sharing of other people's pain through empathy can result in stress, avoidance, withdrawal from helping, and negative health outcomes, especially among those in the helping professions such as doctors and therapists.[10] Studies have also shown more positive outcomes when people are trained to adopt an attitude of compassion—in which one is concerned about the suffering of another but doesn't share their feelings—rather than empathy.[11] In the context of fiction, this research suggests that repeat exposure to graphic, empathy-provoking representations of human suffering might be too much for most of us to bear, and that we perhaps "regulate" the extent to which we consume such fictions, just as members of the helping professions must regulate the degree to which they feel empathy for their patients.[12] Some of us might, for example, alternate between watching a film such as *12 Years a Slave* and indulging in light-hearted comedies, or only occasionally see films about human misery. It could also be the case that if we consume too many such fictions, we will have less empathy to spare in the real world due to empathy fatigue. In one study, those experimental subjects who had read the most fictional novels in the prior year experienced the least empathetic concern for protagonists during the study.[13] Again, the point is that film's capacity to foster empathy isn't always morally advantageous. Too much empathizing can lead to withdrawal from and avoidance of other people's pain rather than the wish to alleviate it.

Currie has drawn attention to another area of fascinating research that raises questions about the optimistic view. Recent psychological work on what is called "self-licensing" appears to show that "prior behavior enhances a sense of self-worth which in turn gives people the feeling of being licensed to behave less well or less sensibly thereafter."[14] Studies indicate that if we do a good deed in the morning, we tend to feel virtuous (we have done our good deed for the day!) and are less likely to do a good deed in the afternoon or might even do bad ones. If true, it might be the case that empathizing with a suffering character in a fiction makes us feel worthy to the point that we are less likely to empathize with somebody suffering in the real world. Far from enlarging our capacity for empathy, fiction could shrink it. Currie acknowledges that there isn't much empirical evidence yet for the existence of this countervailing tendency. However, he also points out that the empirical evidence for the optimistic view is similarly thin. Studies that purport to provide evidence that consuming fictions is correlated with increased performance on empathy tasks tend to show only marginal and short-term improvement on these tasks, and some studies show none at all.[15]

SHOULD EMPATHY BE "CULTIVATED"?

So far, I have pointed to empirical evidence suggesting that film's empathic power might result in various kinds of empathy avoidance or suppression. Proponents of the optimistic view could acknowledge that such behavior perhaps occurs sometimes, yet still insist that, on balance, film's putative empathy-enhancing capacity is a virtue. When we do consume fictions, filmic or otherwise, our aptitude for empathy is extended, which can potentially make us more moral in the real world. However, there are reasons to question whether empathy is worth cultivating in the first place.

Most obviously, fictions can solicit empathy for morally flawed if not evil characters. In *The Birth of a Nation* (1915, dir. D. W. Griffith), film's empathy-eliciting power is used in the service of an ideology of white victimization, supremacy, and revenge that is repellent, as when medium shots and other techniques infamously encourage us to empathize with Flora, a white woman, who jumps to her death rather than be raped by Gus, a Black man (played by Walter Long, a white actor, in blackface). There is circumstantial evidence that such scenes lead to helping behavior in the real world, given the resurgence of the Ku Klux Klan after the film's release.[16] Arguably, some white people who saw the film empathized with the "suffering" of Southern whites at the hands of emancipated Black people during Reconstruction that the film vividly depicted, and as a result sought to help their real-life counterparts by joining the Klan and committing acts of violence and terrorism against Black people.[17] Whether or not this is exactly how the film affected its white audiences, this example shows that there is nothing intrinsically moral about empathizing with another person and coming to their aid.

C. Daniel Batson is the researcher who has probably done the most to establish empirically that there is a connection between empathy and altruism (which he defines as acting to increase another's welfare). In multiple experiments, he has tried to show that empathy motivates experimental subjects to help others even when there are no rewards for them, thereby contesting the "egoistic," selfish explanation of empathy and altruism mentioned earlier.[18] Yet, Batson acknowledges that "empathy-induced altruism is neither moral nor immoral; it is amoral. Sometimes it will encourage people to act in accord with their moral principles; at other times to violate them."[19] To take another example, while most of us condemn violence and cruelty, we find it easy to empathize with the victims of heinous atrocities—Holocaust survivors, for instance—to the point that we might endorse if not participate in sometimes extreme violence toward the perpetrators of these crimes. Meanwhile, fictions can exploit such empathic bloodlust. The films of Quentin Tarantino, for instance, often indulge in what Carl Plantinga aptly calls revenge scenarios, encouraging us to empathize with their protagonists' hatred toward Nazis and racists, and to cheer them on as they brutally exact their revenge on these and other evildoers.[20]

Examples like *The Birth of a Nation* also raise difficult questions about whether it's a virtue for film to augment our capacity for empathy by extending it to immoral characters and allowing us to feel their feelings intensely. While there has been much discussion of the phenomenon of "sympathy for the devil," friends of the optimistic view rarely consider the moral complexities of "empathy for the devil," of "cultivating" empathy using evil and other morally flawed characters, instead tending to focus on morally worthy or uplifting examples of fiction. Is our empathic ability "refined" if we empathize with the white supremacists in *The Birth of a Nation* and thereby experience their feelings of grievance, aggression, and hatred toward Black people? The answer to this question is doubtless a complex one, but friends of the optimistic view rarely address it.

Proponents of the optimistic view could argue that, to be sure, there are some cases in which empathy perhaps brings us too close to white supremacists and other evildoers, and sometimes this might have unfortunate real-world consequences. However, they could still insist that, in the majority of cases, empathy enhancement through fiction is bound to be a virtue given the crucial role empathy plays in morality. However, it is precisely this role that some experimental psychologists and philosophers have questioned. As we have seen, empathy is by no means necessary for morality. I can morally disapprove of the unequal global distribution of Covid-19 vaccines because I think it unfairly deprives people in poorer countries of the opportunity to be vaccinated. I don't need to first empathize with a particular person who has been robbed of the chance to receive the vaccine in order to arrive at this moral judgment. In general, as the philosopher Jesse Prinz has argued, we make moral judgments all the time in the absence of empathy. Empathy is also not necessary, he has claimed, for moral development or conduct.[21]

More important, experimental research suggests that empathy suffers from significant moral limitations, some of which Prinz and Bloom have helpfully summarized.[22] Studies indicate that when we empathize with someone such as a child who is suffering from an illness, we are more likely to move them to the front of a queue for treatment even if it's unfair on others who are equally or more deserving. Bloom sees such preferential treatment as an example of what is called the "identifiable victim effect," our tendency to help a particular, identifiable person who is suffering rather than a larger group of people equally or more in need, and for this reason he calls empathy "innumerate": "if our concern is driven by thoughts of the suffering of specific individuals, then it sets up a perverse situation in which the suffering of one can matter more than the suffering of a thousand."[23] Empathy is also subject to biases such as *physical attractiveness and "cuteness":* we find it easier to empathize with those we perceive to be physically appealing than those we find ugly or disgusting; *in-group biases:* studies show that we are more likely to empathize with members of our own racial or ethnic group, or other groups to which we belong; *proximity effects:* acts of political or racial violence, or natural disasters, are more likely to elicit our empathy for their victims if they occur in our own region or country even though far worse may be happening farther away; *salience effects:* perceptible, temporally circumscribed, localized events, such as shootings and natural disasters, trigger our empathic responses more readily than do more temporally and spatially diffuse, less perceptible ones, such as diseases and structural issues like poverty. It is for reasons such as these that Bloom and Prinz proclaim themselves to be "against empathy." For both, empathy is a poor moral guide.

FILM, FICTION, AND "CONSIDERED EMPATHY"

We do not have to adopt Prinz's and Bloom's extreme anti-empathy stance to recognize that consuming films and other forms of fiction might well magnify some of these less desirable features and effects of empathy. For example, fictions often partake of the "identifiable victim effect," focusing our attention on the suffering of one or two individuals at the expense of the many. And films are notorious for using "cuteness" and other forms of physical attractiveness to solicit empathy. They also tend to be much better at addressing "salient" forms of suffering (when did any of us last see a fiction film about the scourge of malaria, or the profound impact of access to early childhood education on inequality?), and it goes without saying that many reinforce in-group and proximity biases. Indeed, it could be the case that in "expanding" our capacity for empathy, some fictions and films make us *less* moral by "cultivating" these biases and limitations, thereby reinforcing them.

Nor do we have to agree with Prinz's and Bloom's conclusions to acknowledge that the empirical research they have drawn attention to challenges the optimistic view of the relation among cinema, empathy, and morality by suggesting that empathy is, at best, "amoral" because it results in both morally desirable and undesirable outcomes. If this is the case, then what is needed for morality isn't empathy alone but, as Currie puts it, "discriminating" or "intelligent" empathy, or empathy constrained and corrected by reason and reflection.[24] Rather than assuming that empathy and the helping behavior it can give rise to is always the morally correct response to another's suffering, we should question whether this is the case. Fortunately, film can prompt such reflective or what I call "considered empathy," as when in *M* (1931, dir. Fritz Lang) our empathy for the mothers of the children murdered by Hans Beckert and our desire to see him punished is subsequently thrown into question by Beckert's own testimony at his mock trial, in which Beckert makes his misery excruciatingly evident. *M* prods us to interrogate our empathic allegiance with the mothers and our bloodlust toward Beckert, and encourages us to reflect on broader issues of justice and punishment, thereby providing a powerful example of film's ability to promote "considered empathy." It might even affect how we morally evaluate and react to real-world examples of child-killers and their victims by making us less likely to rush to judgment. As this example suggests, by "considered empathy" I mean a response to one or more characters in a fiction in which, even if the characters in question are suffering and we are highly sympathetic toward them, as is the case with the mothers of Beckert's victims, we weigh whether we *should* empathize with them given factors such as the effects of their actions on others, how morally justified these might be, and the context in which they occur. But whether most films and fictions "cultivate" such "considered empathy" is another matter entirely.[25]

NOTES

1. Gregory Currie, *Imagining and Knowing: The Shape of Fiction* (Oxford: Oxford University Press, 2020), 199.

2. Martha Nussbaum, *Cultivating Humanity: A Classical Defense of Reform in Liberal Education* (Cambridge, MA: Harvard University Press, 1997), 91.

3. Nussbaum, *Cultivating Humanity*, 90, 97.

4. See Carl Plantinga, "The Scene of Empathy and the Human Face on Film," in *Passionate Views: Film, Cognition and Emotion*, ed. Carl Plantinga

and Greg M. Smith (Baltimore, MD: Johns Hopkins University Press, 1999), 239–256.

5. Robert Sinnerbrink, *Cinematic Ethics: Exploring Ethical Experience through Film* (London: Routledge, 2016), 102.

6. Murray Smith, *Film, Art and the Third Culture: A Naturalized Aesthetics of Film* (Oxford: Oxford University Press, 2017), 191–193.

7. Currie, *Imagining and Knowing*, 199.

8. See, e.g., Jesse Prinz, "Against Empathy," *The Southern Journal of Philosophy* 49, no. 1 (2011): 214–33; and Paul Bloom, *Against Empathy: The Case for Rational Compassion* (New York: HarperCollins, 2016).

9. Bloom, *Against Empathy*, 73–75.

10. Tania Singer and Olga M. Klimecki, "Empathy and Compassion," *Current Biology* 24, no. 18 (2014): R875–R878.

11. Olga M. Klimecki, Susanne Leiberg, Matthieu Ricard, and Tania Singer, "Differential Pattern of Functional Brain Plasticity after Compassion and Empathy Training," *Social Cognitive and Affective Neuroscience* 9, no. 6 (June 2014): 873–879.

12. Robert Eres and Pascal Molenberghs, "The Influence of Group Membership on the Neural Correlates Involved in Empathy," *Frontiers in Human Neuroscience* 7, no. 176 (2013): 1–6.

13. Caspar J. van Lissa, Marco Caracciolo, Thom van Duuren, and Bram van Leuveren, "Difficult Empathy: The Effect of Narrative Perspective on Readers' Engagement with a First-Person Narrator," *Diegesis* 5, no. 1 (2016): 43–63, at 54.

14. Currie, *Imagining and Knowing*, 211.

15. Currie, *Imagining and Knowing*, 207–209.

16. Desmond Ang has recently shown that racial violence and Klan membership rose significantly in those counties in the United States where the film was shown relative to those where it wasn't, and that the counties where it was shown continue to experience higher rates of hate crimes and hate groups a century later. See "The Birth of a Nation: Media and Racial Hate," HKS Faculty Research Working Paper Series RWP20-038 (November 2020).

17. In his memoir about his infiltration of the Klan in Colorado, which was adapted into the film *BlacKkKlansman* (2018, dir. Spike Lee), the former Black police officer Ron Stallworth reports that the Klan was still using *The Birth of a Nation* as a propaganda and recruitment tool in the 1970s. See Stallworth, *Black Klansman: A Memoir* (New York: Flatiron, 2014), 82.

18. For an overview, see C. Daniel Batson, *Altruism in Humans* (Oxford: Oxford University Press, 2011).

19. C. Daniel Batson, "Empathy-Induced Altruism and Morality: No Necessary Connection," in *Empathy and Morality,* ed. Heidi L. Maibom (Oxford: Oxford University Press, 2014), 41–58, at 47.

20. Carl Plantinga, *Screen Stories: Emotion and the Ethics of Engagement* (Oxford: Oxford University Press, 2018), 231–248.

21. Jesse Prinz, "Is Empathy Necessary for Morality?," in *Empathy: Philosophical and Psychological Perspectives,* ed. Amy Coplan and Peter Goldie (Oxford: Oxford University Press, 2011), 211–229, at 213–221.

22. Prinz, "Is Empathy Necessary for Morality?," 225–227; Bloom, *Against Empathy,* chap. 3.

23. Bloom, *Against Empathy,* 88–89.

24. Currie, *Imagining and Knowing,* 204, 217.

25. Thanks to Martin Rossouw and Julian Hanich for their helpful comments on an earlier draft of this essay.

9

... Political Impact

On the Societal Vibrancy of Film

JENS EDER

Every day, citizens of late modern societies watch hours of moving images, which contribute in many ways to their political thoughts and actions. The dangers involved are widely discussed: most films affirm hegemonic discourses, and quite a few spread propaganda, disinformation, and discrimination. Yet, films can also have significant positive effects—or "impact"—on politics. This essay focuses on such effects and how we can make the political impact of films altogether better.

What "better" means in the context of politics—that is, social coordination under conditions of unavoidable conflict—is, of course, highly controversial.[1] But that just makes political evaluation more interesting. I follow Adi Ophir's thesis that the avoidance of "superfluous evils," of concrete experiences of suffering and loss, should be at the center of ethics and politics.[2] Realizing political values such as justice or equality should thus be related to alleviating suffering and avoiding loss. The political—and aesthetic—evaluation of films depends on such ethical criteria and on their contributions to political practices and power relations.[3] Films can make visible evils that have been invisible before and can give viewers a sense of what certain kinds of suffering feel like. They can show ways to avoid the creation of suffering and loss, and how to create better futures instead. They can deepen political knowledge, stimulate interest in political participation, and produce altruistic action and other desirable effects. In all those respects, they call for changes—of laws, institutions, and practices concerning all political fields, such as

FIGURE 10. Camila Freitas's documentary *Landless* (2019).

the economy, the environment, work, social welfare, migration, or media. In so doing, films act as important complements of other discourses, such as political journalism.

This essay argues that it is entirely possible to increase the proportion of films and practices that actively engage with political values, shape social change, disrupt dysfunctional habits and open up new experiences. Focusing on contemporary films that are explicitly political and aim to reduce suffering for groups outside social power centers, the essay starts with some evidence showing that moving images do, indeed, have political impact. This raises the question of how such impact can be explained and how it depends on filmic forms. The results will allow us to compare conflicting strategies of political filmmaking and their impact.

DO FILMS ACTUALLY HAVE POLITICAL IMPACT, AND IF YES, HOW?

A wealth of contemporary examples indicates that a broad range of films across various media, genres, and styles have political effects.[4] Some are fictional: the Hollywood blockbuster *Avatar* (2009, dir. James Cameron) activated initiatives on the protection of Indigenous communities in the Amazon, as well as protests in other regions ("Avatar activism").[5] The social realist film *I, Daniel Blake* (2016, dir. Ken Loach) stimulated parliamentary debates about the welfare system in the United Kingdom.[6] Educational programs like *Sesame Street* (1969–, PBS) teach global young audiences values like tolerance.[7] The nonfiction field is equally diverse: "strategic impact documentaries" like *The Invisible War* (2012, dir. Kirby Dick) drive campaigns with specific political aims.[8] Popular documentaries like *Capitalism: A Love Story* (2009, dir. Michael Moore) use all rhetorical registers to win over larger audiences. Expressive documentaries like *The Act of Killing* (2012, dir. Joshua Oppenheimer, Christine Cynn, and Anonymous) use narrative perspective-taking to stimulate debates, in this case about the mass murder of alleged communists in Indonesia. Experimental films such as *Havarie* (2016, dir. Philip Scheffner), which harrowingly depicts the encounter of a refugee boat and a cruise ship, haunt the art world. Videos on social media reach millions, spark protests in countries from Syria (Abounaddara) to Russia (Navalny) to the United States (#BlackLivesMatter), and take various new forms—think of Belarusian witness videos, explainer animation like *Wealth Inequality in America* (2012, Politizane), vloggers like Rezo in Germany, mobilization videos by NGOs like Greenpeace, or the audiovisual investigations of Forensic Architecture.[9] The list could be continued (although cases from the Global South are as yet underrepresented in the literature). The following will not examine the differences between those fictional and nonfictional forms, but emphasize their common relationships to politics and ethics: as diverse as these films are, they are all produced or distributed with the intention to counteract "superfluous evils," alleviate suffering, and promote social or humanitarian values that are considered to be neglected or disregarded.

Beyond anecdotal reports, a growing body of empirical studies provides evidence for significant effects, which can be direct, local, and short-term, or indirect, global, and long-term. Most of that evidence comes from three sources:

(a) Media psychologists measure changes in viewers' attitudes before and after watching a movie. They found, for example, that *The Day After Tomorrow* (2004, dir. Roland Emmerich) increased the readiness for climate protection, *Black Panther* (2018, dir. Ryan Coogler) raised "concerns for social justice," and *The Hunger Games* (2012, dir. Gary Ross) heightened "belief in the justifiability of radical political action."[10]

(b) Social science researchers use qualitative and quantitative methods to examine "entertainment education." Most focus on fictional television programs in developing countries, such as the animated series *Meena* (1991–, UNICEF), which empowered girls in South

Asia. Others have demonstrated the agenda-setting impact of documentaries, such as *The Blue Planet* (2001/2017, BBC) concerning plastic pollution.[11]

(c) On the practitioner side, foundations like Doc Society and production companies like Participant Media conduct case studies of documentaries or "social impact entertainment" whose effects are strategically planned and monitored.[12] Some of those films stimulated debates (e.g., *Citizenfour* [2014, dir. Laura Poitras]), others influenced regulations (e.g., *GasLand* [2010, dir. Josh Fox]).[13] Online user engagement is an important indicator in such cases, and of course even more so with web videos.

The fact *that* many films actually generate political impact, also quite directly, is well established, then. This raises the question of *how* they do so, which is answered quite differently by diverse disciplines. Film theory has so far focused on single films evoking specific experiences of individual viewers during reception. It is a long way, however, from changing fleeting individual experiences to changing political institutions. Practice-led guides recognize that and distinguish between several stages of impact.[14] Drawing on their models, I suggest that impact develops across at least three dimensions:

(a) *Mental depth:* from making viewers aware of a political issue to evoking emotional involvement to shaping political attitudes and identities as a basis of behavior (e.g., intentions to vote).

(b) *Social organization:* from influencing individuals (e.g., lawmakers) to small communities (e.g., at a union's film screening) to larger groups and whole societies.

(c) *Temporal duration:* from triggering transient events (like protests) to implementing more stable practices and discourses to establishing permanent laws and institutions.

To speak of "political impact" means more than just influencing thoughts and emotions of individual viewers during reception. It can mean, for instance, to make powerful individuals change institutional structures or to anchor emotions of protest in social groups, or to shape lasting affect structures, "imagined communities," or "social imaginaries" through processes such as "social learning" or "cultivation."[15] Such collective and cumulative effects arise when many viewers watch many different films and interact with each other—and with opinion leaders, opponents, and other media—before or after viewing. Audiences are fragmented and interrelated: they clash with each other in comments on web videos or in discussions organized by unions or universities. Moreover, film production itself already has an impact on filmmakers, their protagonists, and allied or adversarial communities.[16] Examples are the documentaries *Landless/Chão* (2019, dir. Camila Freitas), a participatory production with landless activists in Brazil, or *Thank You for the Rain* (2017, dir. Julia Dahr), which contributed to founding farmer self-help groups in Kenya.[17]

Film's political impact is thus more complex and diverse than most film theories or empirical studies suggest. Like any media effects, it is mostly social, cumulative, indirect, and transactional.[18] We might visualize it like a dynamic, constantly changing network with countless nodes and connections between mostly local impact events. The political vibrancy of this network originates not only from a few blockbusters but also from countless smaller films with limited audiences—like most that made an impression on my own political thinking, such as *Let's Make Money* (2008, dir. Erwin Wagenhofer), *Work Hard Play Hard* (2011, dir. Carmen Losmann), or *Democracy: Im Rausch der Daten* (2015, dir. David Bernet). The effects of such individual films merge into the network and cumulatively produce deep, lasting impact over time.

THE IMPORTANCE OF FILM FORM

To stress the social complexity of impact is not to say that film reception and the specific form and content of individual films are not important—on the contrary, their power to move viewers is at the very heart of the social processes that unfold around them. Aesthetics and politics, feeling and thinking are inseparable in viewers' experiences. Elsewhere, I have outlined how four layers of experiences—sensory-affective perception of audiovisual forms, apprehension of represented worlds and events, understanding of overarching meanings, and reflection on the communicative situation of filmmaking and viewing—work together to elicit political emotions that in conditions of conflict diverge more from level to level.[19] Films offer paradigm scenarios, symbols, and messages carrying emotions, which form persistent affect structures or are transferred via memory and imagination to actual situations. Political emotions drive political action.[20] Outrage leads to protesting, compassion to supporting people in need, hope to building organizations, hate to attacking opponents, guilt to attempting redemption, or pride to empowering the powerless. Less obvious affects include epistemic emotions like the satisfaction of understanding a political situation, or existential feelings of how it feels to be in this situation.

Filmmakers have developed various aesthetic, narrative, and rhetorical strategies to evoke political emotions and communicate political values. Here's a tentative list:

(a) Engage in "critical worldbuilding."[21] Foreground disregarded world structures that are politically relevant (*Work Hard Play Hard*), or invent alternatives to current realities. Show dystopian or utopian futures and the ways that lead to them.

(b) Frame political problems and conflicts by depicting and evaluating their crucial issues, their sources, those responsible, and possible solutions (*An Inconvenient Truth* [2006, dir. Davis Guggenheim]).[22] Disclose and explain hidden reasons and causes of political problems.

(c) Develop a political argument by supporting a thesis with empirical evidence, logical reasoning, and audiovisual rhetoric (*Under the Dome* [2015, dir. Chai Jing]).[23]

(d) Establish intense embodied relationships to characters and align viewers with the moral and political conflicts of observers, helpers, or protagonists in complex situations or dilemmas (*The Look of Silence* [2014, dir. Joshua Oppenheimer]; many of the above films).

(e) Tell a story with protagonists and antagonists that represent different political values or positions, and convey a message through evaluating and solving their conflict (*Avatar, Meena*).

(f) Show political protagonists as admirable heroes or sympathetic characters who fight for a shared cause (*The Look of Silence, Black Panther*).[24]

(g) Build positive "parasocial contact" with characters belonging to discriminated or marginalized groups and elicit sympathy, empathy, and compassion with the suffering (*I, Daniel Blake; Most Shocking Second a Day Video* [2014, Save the Children]).[25]

(h) Give voice to members of socially disadvantaged and disenfranchised groups, stressing their agency and empowerment (*Landless*).[26]

(i) Elicit moral outrage about perpetrators (and maybe at the same time, show their perspectives) (*The Act of Killing*).

(j) Leave the story unresolved and open up a space for the viewers as possible co-protagonists in future developments (mobilization videos).

(k) Develop the story or argument from the perspective of the seeking, not the knowing. Involve the audience in a search for political knowledge and in the weighing of arguments, which keeps curiosity and suspense alive (*Democracy: Im Rausch der Daten*).

(l) Deconstruct or subvert political narratives. Show the present situation in a critical light using social realism, satire, or melodrama. Tell a metaphorical tale, an allegory, or parable that makes viewers infer correspondences to reality (*Parasite/Gisaengchung* [2019, dir. Bong Joon-ho]).

(m) Use an audiovisual style that evokes a sensuous, affective stance toward the political issue: ranging, for instance, from cold rationality to engaged analysis to corporeal intensity of compassion or outrage (*Havarie;* compare films about the financial crisis like *Let's Make Money* or *Capitalism: A Love Story*).

(n) Show the audience that you are trustworthy because you are on their side, possess expert knowledge, or offer a nonpartisan argument based on shared values (*Under the Dome*).

This incomplete list already indicates that the aesthetics and rhetorics of political film comprise a huge variety of forms beyond classical storytelling, which may aim at more adequate representation, deconstruction of stereotypes, formal irritation, or self-reflection.[27] The list also indicates that the often sweeping opposition between conventional and unconventional film forms seems too undifferentiated and ultimately misleading. While storytelling dominates in feature films, other moving images, such as web videos, more often choose explanatory forms or rhetorical argumentation. Elements from those forms may also be mixed, leading to various hybrids and new structures, as in *Most Shocking Second a Day Video* or *I Do Not Care If We Go Down in History as Barbarians/Îmi este indiferent dacă în istorie vom intra ca barbari* (2019, dir. Radu Jude). Even the framework of storytelling already allows for an enormous variety of building worlds, casting characters, taking perspectives, framing conflicts, developing plots, and ending stories or leaving them open.

Films aiming at social change need this aesthetic variety also because they meet psychological obstacles as well as epistemic and ethical challenges. From the spectators' perspective, political change usually demands effort, sacrifice (e.g., abandoning privileges), and overcoming crucial barriers, such as the perceived distance of persons and events, paralyzing impressions of doom, dissonances to everyday habits, denial of unsettling facts, and defense against identity threats.[28] Persuasion research lists further psychological obstacles from confirmation bias to reactance and empathy fatigue.[29]

Taken together, these obstacles give political films a disadvantage in an attention economy, where they compete against PR or entertaining fantasies of consumption. Moreover, the evaluation of political films follows demanding criteria. In contrast to propaganda (understood as epistemically flawed political persuasion coming from powerful groups), they have to meet *epistemic* criteria of factual truth and truthfulness, *ethical* criteria of respecting the concerns of their protagonists and viewers, and corresponding *aesthetic* criteria.[30]

Political ethics and epistemology suggest an aesthetics that is affective but at the same time attentive to the distribution of affect, and which is striking and convincing but avoids manipulative overpowering, aims at transparency, and offers spaces for reflection. Such criteria are not met easily: political aesthetics is in a permanent tension or precarious balance between simplicity, affectivity, and determination, on the one hand, and complexity, sobriety, and critical reflection, on the other. When should films strengthen or rather test political convictions? When should they be true to a complex reality or rather simplify it to reach larger audiences? When should they be aesthetically accessible or unwieldy? When should they be hopeful or fearful, utopian or dystopian?

THE CONFLICT BETWEEN "REFORMIST"
AND "RADICAL" APPROACHES

Such questions are a constant source of conflict between two tendencies of political filmmaking and theorizing that may be called "reformist" or "radical." Of course, many would not agree with these terms, and they cannot be strictly separated, but rather refer to poles of a continuum. Nevertheless, they indicate useful ideal types, which allow politics, aesthetics, and ethics to be brought into pointed but productive connections with each other and also shape many filmmakers' discussions and practices.

Typical "reformist" films appeal to public values they consider as commonsensical, such as the "European values" of the European Union or the human rights and global goals of the United Nations, including peace, social cohesion, equity, and well-being.[31] To implement such values, reformist films seek local, incremental changes within existing political and economic systems. Often, they are supported by supranational agencies for the "creative industries," by such national bodies as the Arts Council England, public service broadcasters, streaming services, large NGOs, social enterprises, or even major film studios. With their assistance, different types of films are created: "socially conscious" mainstream movies like *Black Panther*, "social issue documentaries" like *The Invisible War*, "entertainment education" programs like *Meena*, fundraising videos like the *Most Shocking Second a Day Video*, and other kinds of social impact entertainment or social marketing. Narratively and aesthetically, most of these films use tried-and-tested forms of emotional storytelling or rhetoric to address large audiences or precisely defined target groups.

In contrast, typical "radical" films focus on more controversial values, such as distributive justice or migrants' rights.[32] While reformist films aim at "social innovation," radical films aim at more fundamental "social change"—also of larger political and economic structures. To achieve it, they don't shy away from mobilizing civil resistance and sometimes even violent conflict. Radical films are often produced, distributed, or supported by activists, unions, artist groups, marginalized communities, or associations like the Radical Film Network. Again, there are various types, for instance, "popular activist" documentaries like *Under the Dome;* political art films, like *Havarie;* protest videos, like those of the Fridays for Future movement; participatory films created in cooperation with local communities, like *Landless;* and other kinds of films made by political groups or committed individuals. Often such films take overtly rhetorical, provocative, experimental, or "authentically raw" forms, combining political and aesthetic "radicality."

The frequently harsh debates between "radical" and "reformist" approaches seem to be based in their deontological versus utilitarian ethics. "Radicals" typically accuse "reformists" of compromising ethical, epistemic, or aesthetic principles and reject more conventional films even if they criticize political grievances.[33] "Reformists" counter by pointing to the greater reach and measurable impact of their strategic films, claiming that classical forms are more effective because they evoke more intense emotions in larger audiences.[34] The studies mentioned above seem to support that stance. Most films with measurable impact use rather classical storytelling; and experiments indicate that storytelling and entertainment enhance persuasion, because they reduce resistance to political messages.[35] "Reformist" filmmakers therefore try to overcome the obstacles mentioned above by making their films as accessible and emotional as possible. During production, they cooperate closely with NGOs, journalists, and possible publics, and during distribution, they organize targeted campaigns, screenings for politicians, and discussions with audiences.

In contrast, "radical" filmmakers focus more rigorously on principles and on their own community as imagined audience. They often claim that the reformist approach conflicts with originality, authenticity, and transparency; that it tends to manipulation, simplification, and intellectual confinement; and that its political demands are too opportunistic. They criticize its didactic, paternalistic, or ethnocentric stance; the influence of donors; or campaigns gone wrong. Moreover, they argue that the effects of "radical" films have hardly been investigated so far: even if "radical" films reach only smaller subcultural or intellectual groups, those groups might be particularly important political agents. And maybe harsh criticism of grievances and those responsible is sometimes more effective than spreading a general awareness of the problem?

This fierce debate is at the same time important and problematic. It is important because it points to relevant limitations and dangers of both approaches. It is problematic because the opponents often take dogmatic stances and work against each other, losing sight of their shared goals and values. Between and beyond the extreme poles of "radical" and "reformist" are many film forms positively shaping and realizing political values. To exclusively favor one of the poles would therefore be counterproductive: we need the whole variety of films to support social change. Political films could do more good if factions were not so divided, if a greater diversity of film forms were sought, and if film practice worked more deliberately toward that end. Of course, this concerns not the personal perspective of individual filmmakers who might very productively adopt a rigorously radical or reformist stance but the general political perspective. As outlined above, the complexity of impact processes already suggests that successfully communicating and realizing political values requires a variety of different filmic forms and practices: simple and complex, analytical and emotional, conventional and innovative, elitist and populist, polarizing and integrative films of all genres. Dogmatic favoritism of a certain kind of film aesthetics seems counterproductive. In the context of polarized neoliberal societies, sprawling "image wars," fragmented publics, and differentiated media discourses, we need a variety of films and strategies to achieve social change. To try and foster this variety is a mutual responsibility for funding institutions, television editors, film producers, festival juries, critics, and, ultimately, viewers.

NOTES

1. Cf. Matt Sleat, "What Is a Political Value? Political Philosophy and Fidelity to Reality," *Social Philosophy and Policy* 33, nos. 1–2 (2016): 252–272.
2. Adi Ophir, *The Order of Evils: Toward an Ontology of Morals* (New York: Zone Books, 2005).
3. Cf. Mette Hjort, "The Ethics of Filmmaking: How the Genetic History of Works Affects Their Value," in *Truth in Visual Media: Aesthetics, Ethics, and Politics*, ed. Marguerite La Caze and Ted Nannicelli (Edinburgh: Edinburgh University Press, forthcoming).
4. Cf. Yannis Tzioumakis and Claire Molloy, eds., *The Routledge Companion to Cinema and Politics* (New York: Routledge, 2016).
5. Henry Jenkins, "Avatar Activism and Beyond," in *Confessions of an Aca-Fan,* http://henryjenkins.org/blog/2010/09/avatar_activism_and_beyond.html. Accessed March 9, 2021.
6. Alex Ritman, "How Ken Loach's Cannes-Winning 'I, Daniel Blake' Sparked a Political Movement," *The Hollywood Reporter,* https://www.hollywoodreporter.com/news/how-ken-loach-s-cannes-winner-i-daniel-blake-sparked-a-political-movement-955618. Accessed March 9, 2021.
7. Charlotte F. Cole and June H. Lee, eds., *The Sesame Effect: The Global Impact of the Longest Street in the World* (New York: Routledge, 2016).
8. Kate Nash and John Corner, "Strategic Impact Documentary: Contexts of Production and Social Intervention," *European Journal of Communication* 31, no. 3 (2016): 227–242.
9. Chris Tedjasukmana and Jens Eder, "Video Activism on the Social Web," in *Contemporary Radical Film Culture: Networks, Organizations, and Activists,* ed. Steve Presence, Mike Wayne, and Jack Newsinger (London: Routledge, 2020), 41–52.
10. Fritz Reusswig, Julia Schwarzkopf, and Philipp Pohlenz, *Double Impact: The Climate Blockbuster "The Day After Tomorrow" and Its Impact on the German Cinema Public,* PIK Report 92 (Potsdam Institute for Climate Impact Research, 2004); Guan Soon Khoo and Erin Ash, "Moved to Justice: The Effects of Socially Conscious Films on Social Justice Concerns," *Mass Communication and Society* 24, no. 1 (2021): 106–129; Calvert W. Jones and Celia Paris, "It's the End of the World and They Know It: How Dystopian Fiction Shapes Political Attitudes," *Perspectives on Politics* 16, no. 4 (2018): 969–989; Meghan S. Sanders et al., "Entertainment Media and Social Consciousness," in *The Oxford Handbook of Entertainment Theory,* ed. Peter Vorderer and Christoph Klimmt (Oxford: Oxford University Press, 2021), 781–798.
11. Arvind Singhal and Everett M. Rogers, "A Theoretical Agenda for Entertainment-Education," *Communication Theory* 12, no. 2 (2002): 117–135; Jen-

nifer Males and Peter Van Aelst, "Did *The Blue Planet* Set the Agenda for Plastic Pollution? An Explorative Study on the Influence of a Documentary on the Public, Media, and Political Agendas," *Environmental Communication* 15, no. 1 (2021): 40–54.

12. The Doc Society, "Case Studies," n.d., *The Impact Field Guide & Toolkit*, https://impactguide.org/library/. Accessed February 2, 2021; Peter Bisanz, "The State of SIE," https://thestateofsie.com/the-state-of-social-impact-entertainment-sie-report-introduction-peter-bisanz/. Accessed February 5, 2021.

13. Caty Borum Chattoo, *Story Movements: How Documentaries Empower People and Inspire Social Change* (New York: Oxford University Press, 2020).

14. E.g., Learning for Action, "Deepening Engagement for Lasting Impact: A Framework for Measuring Media Performance and Results," 2013, Bill and Melinda Gates Foundation, https://cmsimpact.org/wp-content/uploads/2016/01/Deepening-Engagement-for-Lasting-Impact-Resoucres-reports.pdf. Accessed February 9, 2021; The Doc Society, n.d., *The Impact Field Guide & Toolkit*, https://impactguide.org. Accessed February 2, 2021.

15. Cf. Singhal and Rogers, "A Theoretical Agenda for Entertainment-Education"; Benedict Anderson, *Imagined Communities* (London: Verso, 2006); Charles Taylor, *Modern Social Imaginaries* (Durham, NC: Duke University Press, 2004); Wyatt Moss-Wellington, *Narrative Humanism: Kindness and Complexity in Fiction and Film* (Edinburgh: Edinburgh University Press, 2019).

16. Angela J. Aguayo, *Documentary Resistance: Social Change and Participatory Media* (New York: Oxford University Press, 2019).

17. Elisabet Cerqueira da Conceição, Camila Freitas, Luiz Enrique Gomes de Moura, and Paola Sartoretto, "Our Collective Narrative Was Being Constructed in the Film Production: A Conversation at the Crossroads Between Militants, Media Production, and Research," *Commons* 9, no. 2 (2020): 186–210.

18. Patti M. Valkenburg, Jochen Peter, and Joseph B. Walther, "Media Effects: Theory and Research," *Annual Review of Psychology* 67, no. 1 (2016): 315–338.

19. Jens Eder, "Collateral Emotions: Political Web Videos and Divergent Audience Responses," in *Cognitive Theory and Documentary Film*, ed. Catalin Brylla and Mette Kramer (London: Palgrave Macmillan, 2018), 183–203.

20. James M. Jasper, *The Emotions of Protest* (Chicago: University of Chicago Press, 2018).

21. Jeff Vance Martin and Gretchen Sneegas, "Critical Worldbuilding: Toward a Geographical Engagement with Imagined Worlds," *Literary Geographies* 6, no. 1 (2020): 15–23.

22. David Snow et al., "The Emergence, Development, and Future of the Framing Perspective: 25+ Years since 'Frame Alignment,'" *Mobilization: An International Quarterly* 19, no. 1 (2014): 23–46.

23. Willem Hesling, "Documentary Film and Rhetorical Analysis," in *Image—Reality—Spectator: Essays on Documentary Film and Television*, ed. Willem de Greef and Willem Hesling (Leuven: Acco, 1989), 101–131.

24. Sarah Kozloff, "Empathy and the Cinema of Engagement: Reevaluating the Politics of Film," *Projections* 7, no. 2 (2013): 1–40.

25. Edward Schiappa, Peter B. Gregg, and Dean E. Hewes, "The Parasocial Contact Hypothesis," *Communication Monographs* 72, no. 1 (2005): 92–115.

26. Aguayo, *Documentary Resistance*.

27. Cf. Robert Stam, *Keywords in Subversive Film/Media Aesthetics* (Chichester: Wiley Blackwell, 2015).

28. Per Espen Stoknes, *What We Think About When We Try Not to Think About Global Warming: Toward a New Psychology of Climate Action* (White River Junction: Chelsea Green, 2015), 82.

29. Nick Cooney, *Change of Heart: What Psychology Can Teach Us About Spreading Social Change* (New York: Lantern Books, 2011).

30. Cf. Sheryl Tuttle Ross, "Propaganda and the Moving Image," in *The Palgrave Handbook of the Philosophy of Film and Motion Pictures*, ed. Noël Carroll, Laura T. Di Summa, and Shawn Loht (Cham: Palgrave Macmillan, 2019), 757–780; Bill Nichols, *Speaking Truths with Film: Evidence, Ethics, Politics in Documentary* (Oakland: University of California Press, 2016).

31. Borum Chattoo, *Story Movements;* Mette Hjort, "The Public Value of Film: Moving Images, Health and Well-being," *Journal of Scandinavian Cinema* 9, no. 1 (2019): 7–23.

32. Steve Presence, Mike Wayne, and Jack Newsinger, eds., *Contemporary Radical Film Culture: Networks, Organisations, and Activists* (London: Routledge, 2020).

33. E.g., Sherry B. Ortner, "Social Impact Without Social Justice: Film and Politics in the Neoliberal Landscape," *American Ethnologist* 44, no. 3 (2017): 528–539.

34. E.g., Kozloff, "Empathy and the Cinema of Engagement."

35. Cf. Kaitlin S. Fitzgerald and Melanie C. Green, "Narrative Persuasion: Effects of Transporting Stories on Attitudes, Beliefs, and Behaviors," in *Narrative Absorption,* ed. Frank Hakemulder, Moniek M. Kuijpers, Ed S. Tan, Katalin Bálint, and Miruna M. Doicaru (Amsterdam: John Benjamins, 2017), 49–68; Anne Bartsch and Frank M. Schneider, "Entertainment and Politics Revisited: How Non-Escapist Forms of Entertainment Can Stimulate Political Interest and Information Seeking," *Journal of Communication* 64, no. 3 (2014): 369–396.

PART THREE

Sensitive Goods

10

... Moral Reflection

On the Reflective Afterlife of Screen Stories

CARL PLANTINGA AND GARRETT STRPKO

One source of the value of screen stories (narratives produced to be viewed on television, film, or other screens) is their capacity to elicit moral reflection. The word "moral" might cause alarm among some, as it could be taken to signal a retreat from political and social issues and a refocus on personal behaviors.[1] Moral issues as we discuss them, however, have to do with justice, equality, and respect for other individuals, among other things. The personal and the political are not so easily separated. All political and ideological positions are linked to moral beliefs and intuitions. Morality goes hand in hand with spirituality, politics, and all aspects of our lives in community. Morality and moral systems are a pervasive and ineluctable feature of human life. We can hope that in some cases, moral reflection leads to moral learning, though nothing guarantees that outcome.

One potential benefit of stories on screens, then, would be to generate moral reflection. How could a film accomplish this? An example might help here. One could point to *The Silence of the Lambs* (1991, dir. Jonathan Demme) for, among other things, its compelling representation of what it might be like to be a young woman in a professional setting dominated by men. FBI ingénue Clarice Starling (Jodie Foster) is the object of the male gaze of many of the men she comes in contact with, from fellow agents and trainees, to police officers not used to seeing female agents, to the men that hit on her, to a sociopathic cannibal and a serial killer. Seeing this film may lead viewers to reflect on the

FIGURE 11. FBI agent Clarice Starling (Jodie Foster) in *The Silence of the Lambs* (1991, Jonathan Demme).

experience of women in patriarchal institutions. This is a moral issue because it relates to an ethics of care.

Nothing ensures that *The Silence of the Lambs* will encourage such moral reflection. Neither the film itself nor the institutions and practices we identify below guarantees such an outcome. But films can provide the kind of experience that elicits reflection for many viewers, and various institutions have the capacity to contextualize and focus the viewer on the ethical dimensions of screen stories, opening up space for a possible moral understanding.

It should be said that if *The Silence of the Lambs* is good for eliciting moral reflection about female experience in patriarchy, this is certainly not the only public good it offers. We can find other reasons to value *The Silence of the Lambs,* for example, its excellence as a work of art or its demonstrated capacity to strongly move viewers. Neither does finding some good in the film in one respect preclude reasons for ethical criticism in another. For example, *The Silence of the Lambs* features an arguably harmful portrayal of the apparently transsexual serial killer Jame Gumb, or Buffalo Bill (Ted Levine), as a pernicious stereotype.[2]

Suppose, then, that we agree that some films, under some conditions, and for some audiences, can elicit valuable moral reflection and perhaps even understanding. By moral "understanding" we mean something beyond merely holding propositional beliefs. As Christoph Baumberger puts it, understanding is wholistic and "considerably more ambitious than acquiring knowledge." Understanding involves grasping how moral truths relate to each other, being able to use that information, and knowing what questions to ask to fill in gaps.[3] Understanding patriarchy or transphobia is more of an achievement than merely knowing something about it.

If it is the case that films can elicit moral understanding, there is no reason to think that this process occurs solely *during* a viewing. In fact, the screen story may function as a prompt for *later* moral reflection. We might call this phenomenon, after the philosopher Peter Kivy, the "reflective afterlife" of a work of art.[4] Kivy, who is writing primarily about literature, notes the "gappy" nature of reading. Long pauses between reading sessions lend themselves to reflection. Moreover, he argues, unlike listening to "absolute music," or in other words, music without lyrics, part of literary appreciation entails reflection about the themes dealt with in the work.

Although watching a film in the theater is more time-bound than reading a novel, filmic appreciation might also be said to entail reflection on the moral issues the film raises *after* the screening has ended. Additionally, literary "gappiness" could be said to apply to streamed serial dramas. Watching the 38-episode series *Borgen* (2010–2022) on Netflix provides plenty of time for reflection about the moral and political issues faced by the Danish Prime Minister Birgitte Nyborg (Sidse Babett Knudsen).

In relation to some of our viewing, however, there may at times be no reflective afterlife at all, or it may be brief and superficial. We may watch a film and then promptly forget about it. Or we file it into our mental pantheon with a quick evaluation such as "great" or "terrible" or "forgettable" and do not consider the thematic issues it raises. Some of these possible responses have to do with the features of the film itself. The history of film theory is replete with discussion of the formal features of film that may or may not encourage critical spectatorship.[5] In both content and form, some films call for moral reflection while others seemingly do not. Moreover, the physical conditions in which we view a film, and who we view it with, may encourage or discourage reflection.[6]

The activity of moral reflection also has to do with viewers themselves; some viewers notice moral themes more than others. Janet Staiger has claimed that viewers diverge widely in their responses to films, often "using" a film for personal or group purposes or to work through a personal or social issue. In her book *Interpreting Films*, for example, she notes the widely divergent responses to D. W. Griffith's *The Birth of a Nation* (1915), both at the time of its release and through subsequent decades.[7]

MORAL RHETORIC IN NARRATIVE FILM

A screen story's moral content is rarely transparent or universally appreciated. In reflecting on a film, viewers will differ about what moral themes they find to be salient or even what those themes are. Still, many films have more or less clear rhetorical projects, in the sense that they promote certain beliefs and attitudes. Narrative films are often rhetorical in whole or in part.[8]

Of course, films can be ambiguous in their thematic implications, and not all films clearly promote definite perspectives or propositional beliefs. One of the intriguing characteristics of Terrence Malick's *The Thin Red Line* (1998), for example, is its juxtaposition of the horrors of war with the startling beauty of nature. The film seems to put a contradiction before us. Is the world a pit of suffering and cruelty, a landscape of immense beauty, or somehow both? And even when films do promote simple, clear ideas, it is not as though the thematic implications of a film are presented as propositional assertions.

Taking this potential ambiguity into account, how do narrative films rhetorically communicate ideas about moral issues? We believe they do so in at least three ways. First, ideas are communicated through characters, as characters may be presented as virtuous or evil. In *The Silence of the Lambs,* audiences tend to admire the sympathetic protagonist Clarice Starling for her courage and ingenuity in dealing with the sinister cannibal Hannibal Lecter (Anthony Hopkins).

Second, a narrative film is a kind of example. As Noël Carroll notes, an entire film narrative can serve as an example of how a situation might unfold or how it ought to be dealt with.[9] *12 Years a Slave* (2013, dir. Steve McQueen) shows what it might be like for a free man to be kidnapped and put into slavery, enumerating various perspectives on slavery among the slaveholders and the devastating ways in which the institution of slavery devalues and dehumanizes people. When such narrative examples are repeated over and over, as they are in the various modes and genres of film and television production, we can call them "narrative paradigm scenarios."[10]

Third, narrative film communicates ideas through enthymemes. In other words, as Carroll writes, while films are not formal arguments, they nonetheless "presuppose ideas which the audience fills in in order for the narrative to be intelligible."[11] For instance, a film like *Saving Private Ryan* (1998, dir. Steven Spielberg) presents battle scenes with gruesome realism to invoke the idea that war is horrific. To make sense of the plight of the soldiers depicted in the film, audiences need to come to this conclusion on their own. Thus, an enthymeme has the phenomenology of something supplied by the viewer, though it is strongly prompted (in many cases) by the narrative.

These three ways are shared with literature, theater, and other forms of narrative art. What is unique or characteristic about the means by which screen stories elicit moral reflection? To fully answer this question is beyond the scope of this chapter. However, we could point to how stories on screens reach mass audiences and also appeal to the senses and elicit affects such as emotions and moods in characteristic ways.[12] Yet, even within a single medium such as film, various styles and genres provide remarkably different spectator experiences, such that generalizations about medium specificity must be handled with care.

In all three of the ways listed previously, then, films take thematic positions and possibly encourage moral reflection—through character, example, and enthymeme. Moral reflection often depends on the degree to which the viewer engages in the act of interpretation. Interpretation is not the sole activity of postfilm reflection; reflection, as we see it, may extend to all sorts of ruminations that cannot be defined as interpretation proper, for example, relating the events of a film to one's own life. But interpretation is certainly central. It can fill in many of the enthymematic gaps, discover previously unnoticed implications and ambiguities, fine-tune our responses, and clarify how we respond to a screen story differently than other viewers. Interpretation can be a social activity and is encouraged by various institutional practices, as will be detailed below.

INSTITUTIONS OF REFLECTION

Moral reflection on a film often occurs on an informal basis. A group of friends may see a film together and discuss its implications later over drinks or dinner. Such friends engage in "coduction," as Wayne Booth puts it, a process by which the meaning and value of a narrative develops over time through conversation and the give-and-take of opinion and insight that occurs in community.[13] But coduction can also be encouraged by the practices of various institutions, such as academia, professional criticism, and through social media interaction. In this section, we will discuss in depth how the practices of both formal and informal institutions can encourage reflection in film and media viewers.

Academia at all levels promotes moral reflection. Film and media courses train students to formally and thematically analyze screen stories. As pedagogical leaders, teachers screen films and may subsequently encourage and guide student reflection toward moral dimensions, equipping students with tools for interpretation and filling in enthymematic gaps through discussion. For instance, academic discourse may prepare students to engage with a host of morally significant social justice issues in film, such as the politics of representation and reception. Likewise, scholars contribute to ongoing critical conversations in the form of academic publishing, which helps identify issues of moral significance in the field and contemplate solutions.

The various academic disciplines differ in the *way* that moral issues are brought into the discussion. While in the United States, at least, film and media studies have until recently been reluctant to use the term "moral" in lieu of "political" or "ideological," discourse in philosophy has long engaged in discussion of ethics and morality. Films are used to examine diverse moral issues and have the advantage of forging connections between philosophy and popular culture.[14] We've seen discussions of the morality of memory in *Eternal Sunshine of the Spotless Mind* (2004, Michel Gondry), for example, or ethical issues having to do with the representation of race in films.[15]

At earlier levels of education, as well, teachers can use films to explore morality and ethics. Teachwithmovies.org is a website that specializes in providing teachers with lesson plans for a wide number of feature films, and includes a section for films with an emphasis on moral and ethical issues.[16] For example, a high school biology classroom might watch *Gattaca* (1997, dir. Andrew Niccol) to set up a discussion about the ethical implications of genetic engineering.

In fact, various websites from diverse perspectives are devoted to the promotion of films as prompts for moral reflection. One example is "What's the Big Idea?", a site created by the philosopher Tom Wartenberg (also a contributor to this volume) and filmmaker Julie Akaret that seeks to introduce philosophy to middle school students, focusing on practical moral/ethical situations that they typically encounter, such as bullying, lying, and environmental ethics.[17] The classroom settings of academia encourage a kind of guided coduction by directing the lines of questioning that follow a viewing.

Another potential source of moral reflection is professional film and television criticism. How can criticism encourage moral reflection? The primary business of popular film criticism is evaluation. Viewers, however, also sometimes read or watch criticism as a way to better understand what they've already seen. In this context, a critic may discuss the moral dimensions we've mentioned of character, narrative example, or enthymeme, and/or evaluate whether the film transgresses moral boundaries.

Take, for instance, the famed critic Roger Ebert's original review of David Lynch's *Blue Velvet* (1986). Ebert points to the enthymematic implication of the film, "that beneath the surface of Small Town, U.S.A., passions run dark and dangerous."[18] Yet, he also claims that this implication does not justify how the film juxtaposes episodes of voyeuristic and degrading sexual violence with satirically idyllic scenes of small-town America.[19] Ebert condemns the film as a moral failure, comparing Lynch's having made the film to the actions of its evil antagonist Frank Booth (Dennis Hopper).[20]

Additionally, moral ambiguity has taken root as a major theme of many popular television shows featuring anti-hero protagonists.[21] Award-winning and trendsetting shows such as *Mad Men* (2007–2015, AMC) and *Breaking Bad* (2008–2013, AMC) chart the course of seasons-long arcs of moral development or decay. This leaves ample room for critics to evaluate the moral dimension of character, often in explicit terms. For example, Jeff Jensen of *Entertainment Weekly* reviewed the finale of *Breaking Bad* by specifically exploring what he calls its "moral vision."[22] A review of multiple Emmy award–winner *Mad Men* from the *Huffington Post* frames the series as a "morality tale."[23] What these approaches have in common—whether it's Roger Ebert's moral outrage at a film like *Blue Velvet* or reflections on the moral visions of popular television series—is that they provide lay viewers with a space to encounter and ponder the moral themes reflected in film and media through character, example, and enthymeme.

Contemporary culture has also seen a growth in fan culture, or fandom, another potential source of moral reflection about screen stories. This growth is demonstrated by increasingly large fan conventions, the development of fan-worthy multimedia franchises, and professional and amateur criticism focused entirely on fan-heavy franchises such as *Star Wars* or *Marvel*. Karen E. Dill-Shackelford and Cynthia Vinney, in their book *Finding Truth in Fiction*, claim that "fandom, particularly fandom for complex drama, may be largely about the search for meaning, the clarification of values, and the quest to hone our skills and understanding."[24] The more obsessive engagement of fan culture with media texts picks up where common professional criticism ends.

This is readily apparent at Comic-Con, a series of international conventions originally dedicated to comic books that have now grown to draw fans of every type of popular media available. A common practice at Comic-Con is to showcase panels dedicated to specific shows, films, or franchises, made up of actors, directors, and other creatives. Comic-Con panels (and similar panels at other fan-based conventions such as *Star Wars* Celebration) allow a unique opportunity for fans to hear directly from creators about their work. This opens up an interesting avenue for creators to initiate moral reflection about their work for fans. One instance of this occurred at a lauded panel on HBO's series *Westworld* (2016–2022) at San Diego Comic-Con in 2019.[25] The series follows a futuristic theme park in which guests can live inside a Western, with artificially intelligent characters based on classic tropes populating the world. The setting is ample ground for the show to explore moral and philosophical themes related to technology and artificial intelligence. These themes came to the forefront in the panel, hosted by the New York University professor Amy Webb,[26] that gave creators of *Westworld* a chance to share their thoughts on themes such as humanism, artificial intelligence, and determinism versus free will. Through this sort of discussion, creators can elicit moral reflection among dutiful fans by encouraging interpretations of their work.

Another way to assess the relationship between moral reflection and fan culture is to consider fan fiction, a major staple of fan culture. Fan fiction is any fictional writing by a fan that takes the world of the work as its setting. Fan fiction can range from serious to satirical, brief to epic, and allows fans to reflect on the world of their fandom. What are some ways that fan fiction can encourage moral reflection? For one, fan fiction allows fans to extend the parasocial relationships they form with characters. One might tell the same story from the point of view of a villain to generate moral sympathy for them. In fan fiction that uses characters from the work, fans may express desires for those characters that carry moral weight and lead to fictional situations with moral implications.

An example of this would be the phenomenon of "shipping," in which a fan hopes for or projects a romantic relationship between two characters (who are not in a romantic relationship within the original work), such as Captain Kirk and Spock in the original *Star Trek* series (1966–1969, NBC).[27] A work of fan fiction that "ships" two characters might express moral satisfaction or approval by rooting for them to be "rewarded" with a romantic relationship. On the other hand, fan fiction may also brutalize or punish a character, thus passing moral judgment on them. Fan fiction need not necessarily deal with characters from the original work, however. It can also explore and critique the moral vision of a given world. For instance, a fan could write a story about a morally ambiguous situation that takes place in a world usually regarded as morally clear, such as *Star Wars*. Such a reinterpretation critiques the work as a moral exemplar. The practice of fan fiction can therefore encourage reflection on the moral dimensions of character and example.

For fans and lay viewers alike, the work of coduction is increasingly performed on social media. Various platforms provide different means of discussion and engagement. On Facebook, users can join groups dedicated to specific films or franchises, sharing related articles and posts. On Twitter, loosely connected networks of followers center around opinion leaders such as professional critics and film directors to discuss and interpret film and television. One of the most discussion-heavy social media platforms—and therefore the most conducive to coduction—is Reddit. Reddit is divided up into groups called "subreddits," where users can virtually gather to discuss and share content related to their interests, including media works and franchises. Here users can post questions or comments with which the rest of the community can engage in discussion.

Questions involving specifically moral reflection usually appear some time after a work has been released, perhaps even years. This gives time for viewers to digest and reflect on it themselves before opening up discussion to the group, an important difference from in-person coduction. This reflection often falls back on the dimension of character, with questions such as "What is this characters' moral vision?" "How would you rank the characters by various moral criteria?" Prompts such as these encourage the work of informal coduction in social media spaces.

Another increasingly important social media platform for moral reflection is YouTube, on which critics and filmmakers offer their analyses and perspectives on films and television. One example (among hundreds) is *Folding Ideas*, a YouTube media analysis and cultural criticism channel headed by Dan Olson that analyzes, for example, the ethics of propaganda in *Triumph of the Will* (with, at the time of this writing, 446,000 views), and in another episode, toxic masculinity in *Fight Club* (with over 500,000 views).[28]

For all these institutions, however, the work of coduction and moral reflection still rests heavily on informal discussion among peers. We must presume that there is a great deal of moral reflection that is more or less undocumented. Traditional film clubs, from student organizations on a university campus to public advocacy organizations to film nights at religious institutions, provide plentiful spaces for viewers to intentionally gather to view and discuss a screen story. So do various online film clubs that have become more popular during the Covid-19 pandemic.[29] This promotion of moral reflection, negotiation, and understanding is just one of many potential benefits of film and television narrative. And it occurs not merely in relation to the films themselves, but as embedded in the constantly changing social and institutional practices of a culture.

NOTES

1. The film theorist Robert Stam, e.g., has called the use of the word "moral" instead of "ideological," "disastrous." See his *Film Theory: An Introduction* (Oxford: Blackwell, 2000), 45. For a discussion of his thinking and these anxieties, see Carl Plantinga, *Screen Stories: Emotion and the Ethics of Engagement* (Oxford: Oxford University Press, 2018), 135–139.

2. In response to criticisms about *The Silence of the Lambs* from GLAAD (the Gay and Lesbian Alliance Against Defamation), the director Jonathan Demme is said to have made *Philadelphia* (1993) as a kind of penance. See Plantinga, *Screen Stories*, 88.

3. Christoph Baumberger, "Art and Understanding: In Defence of Aesthetic Cognitivism," in *Bilder Sehen: Perspektiven der Bildwissenschaft,* ed. Christoph Wagner, Marc Greenlee, Rainer Hammwöhner, Bernd Körber, and Christian Wolff (Regensburg: Schnell und Steiner, 2011), 41–67, at 47.

4. See the chapter "The Laboratory of Fictional Truth," in Peter Kivy, *Philosophies of the Arts: An Essay in Differences* (Cambridge: Cambridge University Press, 1997), 120–139.

5. For an overview, see Stam, *Film Theory,* esp. 64–71, 92–102, 140–157, 169–178, 267–291.

6. See, e.g., Julian Hanich, *The Audience Effect: On the Collective Cinema Experience* (Edinburgh: Edinburgh University Press, 2018).

7. Janet Staiger, *Interpreting Films: Studies in the Historical Reception of American Cinema* (Princeton: Princeton University Press, 1992). On *The Birth of a Nation,* see 139–153; on Judy Garland and gay fans, see 154–177. See also Staiger's *Perverse Spectators: The Practices of Film Reception* (New York: New York University Press, 2000), which features a chapter on the various cultural meanings of *The Silence of the Lambs,* 161–178.

8. For a discussion of the rhetorical nature of narrative film, see Plantinga, *Screen Stories,* 35–54.

9. Noël Carroll, "Film, Rhetoric, and Ideology," in *Theorizing the Moving Image* (Cambridge: Cambridge University Press, 1996), 280.

10. Plantinga, *Screen Stories,* 231–235.

11. Carroll, "Film, Rhetoric, and Ideology," 281.

12. See Plantinga, *Screen Stories,* and also his *Moving Viewers: American Film and the Spectator's Experience* (Berkeley: University of California Press, 2009).

13. Wayne Booth, *The Company We Keep: An Ethics of Fiction* (Berkeley: University of California Press, 1988), 70–74.

14. Kati T. Berg, "Teaching Ethics with the Help of Hollywood," *Ethical News* 12, no. 4 (2009): 5.

15. Christopher Grau, "*Eternal Sunshine of the Spotless Mind* and the Morality of Memory," in *Thinking Through Cinema: Film as Philosophy*, ed. Murray Smith and Thomas E. Wartenberg (Malden: Blackwell Publishing, 2006), 119–133; Dan Flory, *Philosophy, Black Film, Film Noir* (University Park: Pennsylvania State University Press, 2008).

16. "Teach With Movies," http://teachwithmovies.org/. Accessed November 6, 2020.

17. http://whatsthebigideaprogram.com/. Accessed November 3, 2021.

18. Roger Ebert, "Blue Velvet," *Chicago Sun-Times,* September 1986, https://www.rogerebert.com/reviews/blue-velvet-1986. Accessed November 3, 2021.

19. Ebert, "Blue Velvet."

20. Ebert, "Blue Velvet."

21. See, e.g., Emily Nussbaum, "The Great Divide: Norman Lear, Archie Bunker, and the Rise of the Bad Fan," *The New Yorker,* April 2014, 64–67. See also Margrethe Bruun Vaage, *The Antihero in American Television* (New York: Routledge, 2016).

22. Jeff Jensen, "Brilliant or Cynical? Struggling with Moral Vision of 'Breaking Bad,'" *Entertainment Weekly,* September 30, 2013, https://ew.com/article/2013/09/30/breaking-bad-brilliant-cynical-finale/. Accessed November 3, 2021.

23. Marilyn Sewell, "Mad Men: A Morality Tale," *The Huffington Post,* December 6, 2017, https://www.huffpost.com/entry/mad-men-a-morality-tale_b_7314360. Accessed November 3, 2021.

24. Karen E. Dill-Shackleford and Cynthia Vinney, *Finding Truth in Fiction: What Fan Culture Gets Right—And Why It's Good to Get Lost in a Story* (New York: Oxford University Press, 2020), 8.

25. Jevon Phillips, "Meet the 'Westworld' Panel Moderator Who Showed Comic-Con How It's Done," *Los Angeles Times,* July 24, 2019, https://www.latimes.com/entertainment-arts/tv/story/2019-07-24/comic-con-2019-westworld-hbo-futurist. Accessed November 3, 2021.

26. Phillips, "Meet the 'Westworld' Panel Moderator."

27. Henry Jenkins, "How to Watch a Fan-Vid," Henryjenkins.org, September 17, 2006, http://henryjenkins.org/2006/09/how_to_watch_a_fanvid.html. Accessed November 3, 2021.

28. https://www.youtube.com/c/FoldingIdeas/featured. Accessed November 3, 2021.

29. Zoe Whitfield, "Four Online Film Clubs Perfect for Lockdown," April 9, 2020, https://i-d.vice.com/en_uk/article/akwmkb/4-online-film-clubs-lockdown. Accessed November 16, 2020.

11

... Challenge and Discomfort

On Situated Elitist Pleasures in Art and Indie Film

GEOFF KING

Watching films can be considered to be "good" for viewers in many different ways. These range from what might very broadly be termed "escapist" pleasures, which have often been treated with suspicion from certain critical positions, to the value found in works of art or independent cinema that challenge the viewer or offer experiences of pronounced discomfort.[1] An opposition might be constructed between sources of pleasure and sources of challenge, although the latter might offer pleasures of its own to suitably oriented audiences (and any such opposition risks oversimplifying a complex and inevitably contentious field of debate). The valorization of art and indie cinema is often predicated on an implicit (or sometimes more explicit) *de*valuation of the qualities associated with work of a mainstream-commercial orientation. The good of art and indie film is also one that tends to exist for a constituency that is both limited and relatively privileged. Its enjoyment is generally an elitist phenomenon, primarily involving certain sectors of the middle and upper-middle classes.[2] This does not mean we cannot argue for the significance of this good. It would seem unfair, in the interests of correcting an undoubted imbalance in prevailing cultural hierarchies of value, to deny the merits of an elitist good or pleasure to those for which it is designed, or deny a relatively privileged group—to which many film scholars, such as myself, are likely to belong—any right to their own sources of value. Any claims made for such films need to be proportionate and situated, however, rather than excessive and

FIGURE 12. Uncomfortable incestuous sexual activity in *Dogtooth* (2009, Yorgos Lanthimos).

generalized. This is one of the key arguments I make in *Positioning Art Cinema: Film and Cultural Value* (2019), against a number of existing tendencies within the academic and broader cultural valuation of art cinema.

Claims made on behalf of art and indie film are often greatly overstated. Some forms of art cinema have been claimed to have transformational power, both those with overt political agendas and otherwise, which seems highly questionable (partly, but far from only, because of their limited reach). The values inherent within such films are also often implied to be broad, general, and universal, rather than rooted in both particular historical-cultural complexes and the taste preferences of particular, limited constituencies.[3] These qualifications are important if we are to understand phenomena such as art and independent cinema as involving *specific* regimes and practices of cultural production, consumption, and valuation, rather than as sources of cultural good that can be considered in a vacuum. None of this is, again, to deny any good to such works, but rather to locate them within particular social contexts. I am arguing here for an approach to film that draws on the domains of sociology and cultural studies, in this respect, rather than the sometimes more abstracting territories of philosophy or ethics.

FROM DISTINCTION MARKING TO INTERESTINGNESS

What, then, is the value of art and indie film for its particular likely audiences? This can be considered in at least two dimensions. One of the values of such products is the role they can play in the operation of sociocultural distinction-marking practices, along the lines most influentially outlined by Pierre Bourdieu.[4] Value can inhere in the mere fact that consumption of one type of product, conventionally positioned as of superior status in prevailing, institutionalized hierarchies, can give the consumer a sense of personal superiority over those who only view films designed for a much larger, popular audience. I can recognize an element of this complex—a kind of smug satisfaction—in the exercise of, and reflection on, my own viewing preferences. We can also look, however, at more specific qualities found and appreciated in works of art and indie cinema.

If pleasure based on distinction marking is partly defined in negative terms—Bourdieu famously argues that taste for certain things is often rooted in *dis*taste for others—it is possible also to identify more positive sources of good, pleasure, or value at the textual level, even if these might also often be valorized implicitly or explicitly in relation to negatively valued perceived opposites (the "subtle" restraint of some forms of art and indie film, for example, that enables a sense of nuanced discrimination on the part of the viewer, as opposed to the heavy-handedness often associated with the Hollywood blockbuster).

One subset of art and indie films that can be approached in this way, and is my principal point of reference in this chapter, is what I term the "cinema of discomfort."[5] This involves features that offer uncomfortable or awkward experiences, although short of the most violently assaultive or transgressive examples of art cinema found in some of the work of figures such as Catherine Breillat, Claire Denis, Lars von Trier, and Gaspar Noé.[6] Space prevents going into detail about the textual qualities of such work here (my main examples are films directed by Todd Solondz, Ulrich Seidl, Yorgos Lanthimos, Athina Rachel Tsangari, Roy Andersson, Ruben Östlund, Joanna Hogg, Maren Ade, and Rick Alverson), but a defining feature of many is to present material that is discomforting both in its content—including characteristically uncomfortable sexual encounters—and its audiovisual style of presentation. The latter includes a tendency to deny any clear signaling of how such difficult material is intended to be interpreted in emotional or moral terms, sometimes through formal distancing strategies of the kind described by Jeffrey Sconce as "blank" style.[7] A frequent basis of valorization of films of this kind, and for art and indie cinema more generally, is that it is "thought-provoking" or challenging in a more general way (terms of the kind used in many of the positive online viewer responses surveyed in my book on the subject). Viewers express themselves as finding some form of pleasure or value in the work on this basis, often predicated on positioning themselves as being able to meet such a challenge (sometimes, but not always, accompanied by the articulation of distinction-marking gestures in negative reference to other films or viewers).

The basis of appreciation established here can be understood with a framework offered by Todd Berliner in relation to Hollywood cinema.[8] Drawing on approaches from cognitive psychology, Berliner considers the "processing fluency" required to take pleasure from different varieties within the studio tradition, an approach that can be extended to include the fields of art and indie film.[9] Studio films are typically designed to be easy to process for viewers with any familiarity with the medium, as is necessary to reach large global audiences, although this does not mean that they lack any challenge at all. Two central sources of pleasure-good identified here are "pleasingness" and "interestingness."[10] The former offers "hedonic value," the basis of which includes a desire for immediate recognition and easy understanding (to this we might add pleasures resulting from qualities such as intensity and abundance, identified in the case of the Hollywood musical by Richard Dyer and applicable more widely to large-scale mainstream cinema).[11] Interestingness appeals to a desire for cognitive challenge, the arousal of thinking and comprehension.[12] This might also extend into the provocation of thoughts about ethical, sociopolitical, or cultural-aesthetic issues, major sources of the customary valuation of work from the art and indie sectors. In Hollywood, Berliner suggests, the usual aim is to provide maximum pleasingness combined with a moderate degree of interestingness. If these terms have some similarity with more traditional and questionably universalistic approaches to aesthetics, such as that of Kant, in which high art is viewed as requiring reflective thought and the popular is associated with the production of pleasing emotional bodily responses, it is notable here that elements of each are seen as being involved in the consumption of mainstream, popular work.

In Berliner's account, to increase the level of interesting challenge beyond a certain point is to risk decreasing the pleasure quotient for most viewers. They "start to become overwhelmed, and their pleasure diminishes and eventually turns into displeasure."[13] Such a challenge can offer its own satisfactions to those who are suitably oriented, however, in the realm where "an object grows less pleasing and increasingly interesting."[14] This approach offers a useful way to elucidate the otherwise rather blandly general notion that works of art and indie cinema might be judged to be more "interesting," to certain viewers, than the tendencies of the most commercially mainstream. The interest potentially provoked by more challenging films can be a source not just of coolly rational engagement but qualities such as excitement and exhilaration. This is particularly the case, Berliner suggests, when viewers are experiencing material that lies toward the far end of, but not beyond, their coping potential. Such a conclusion is supported by some of the viewer responses I have examined to the cinema of discomfort, as is a sense of some forms of discomfort pushing to a point at which viewers become uncertain how to react.[15]

Berliner expresses a positively evaluative appreciation of that which is defined in this way to be interesting, on the basis that this is a source potentially of more sustained and enduring appeal (a dimension applicable to other examples, such as films that gain cult status). In the stronger variants found in art and indie film, however, such an appeal remains likely to be socioculturally specific, quite narrowly so, rather than a general basis on which to ascribe notions of quality or value, a dimension not addressed in Berliner's account. This is not to say that evaluative judgments cannot be made about how effectively any individual examples might mobilize particular qualities, but to locate this as involving specific, acquired bases of appreciation (for a useful discussion of these issues in relation to complex television, see Jason Mittell's work on the subject).[16]

DISCOMFORT AND EXHILARATION

The sense of exhilaration identified by Berliner suggests that a source of pleasurable good can be found in discomforting material that goes beyond the realm of the cognitive and the intellectual. A bodily dimension of engagement also seems sometimes to be implied, in reactions expressed in phrases such as "skin-crawling" or "cringe-making." Such terms imply an aversive repulsion rather than what would usually be understood to be a source of pleasure, but a form of the latter seems in some cases to result from the heightened level of engagement involved. Such content has the potential to exert a fascination on the part of the viewer, a desire to keep watching that which would usually be hidden or conventionally unacceptable material, or the kind of simultaneous pull between the repulsive and the fascinating identified by Julian Hanich in instances of cinematic disgust.[17]

An engagement beyond the cognitive/intellectual can also be experienced in the sensuous, "poetic," expressive, or impressionistic qualities of some varieties of art or indie cinema, which might offer sources of valued pleasure closer in kind to some of those often associated with Hollywood-type productions, including the intensity or sensuous abundance identified by Dyer. Berliner's approach is useful in its identification of overlaps between the potential grounds of appeal of more and less mainstream varieties of cinema, both of which might be expected to include cognitive and sensory-emotional dimensions of their own kind. If those who possess more "expert" knowledge and experience of the arts tend to prefer more challenging works than those with fewer such resources—another way of framing the dimension of cultural capital central to Bourdieu—this is not necessarily a case of the former desiring to work harder than the latter, Berliner suggests. A greater challenge might be required by experts for them to receive much the same level of stimulation that easier experiences would offer to the less expert viewer. The key issue for Berliner is the relationship between the challenge and the "coping potential" of the viewer in any particular case.[18]

Comfort and a degree of the familiar and expected can be found within that which is discomforting or challenging, up to a point, for those already conversant with such material. This seems a useful way further to relativize and situate all these potential viewing experiences across a cinematic spectrum that includes a wide range and potential combination of approaches. Some viewers of the cinema of discomfort seem to value experiences that go beyond this point, however, although responses in such cases can be variable. Some positively relish the viewing of material that leaves them seemingly genuinely disconcerted and not sure exactly how to process what they have watched, while others express more mixed and uncertain responses. This is the case with some of the online responses I examine to highly discomforting sexual and other material in *Palindromes* (2003, dir. Todd Solondz) and *Dogtooth/ Kynodontas* (2009, dir. Yorgos Lanthimos), to cite just two examples.

It seems possible, as I argue in *The Cinema of Discomfort,* for a certain kind of good to inhere for some viewers in being pushed into places that provoke strong if uncertain feelings, even if this can be combined with more negative emotions. This might be seen as a kind of testing of the viewer within the relative safety of the bounds of the cinematic. If the cognitive dimension can include a requirement to untangle or resolve matters of narrative or meaning to a greater extent than is the norm in more mainstream, conventional work, a similar challenge can be posed by the cinema of discomfort, and some other forms of art or indie film, at the level of uncertain emotional responses. The two might also be combined, in cases in which viewers gain the opportunity to mobilize distinction-marking cultural capital or cognitive interest while remaining unsettled in their emotional responses and sometimes challenged in their ability to resolve their overall attitude toward the material.

NO UNSITUATED BASIS OF VALUATION

There might remain a temptation for some of us—myself included—to value this kind of willingness to accept challenge more highly than the (probably much more widespread) position from which it would likely be rejected, whether the challenge is cognitive, emotional, or any combination of the two. There is no basis for any unsituated, objective judgment, however. No variety of cinema is essentially more worthwhile than any other, in any ungrounded manner. None of us might be sufficiently free from the grasp of our own cultural matrices (our habitus, to use Bourdieu's term) to be entirely convinced of this at the "gut" level of our personally and socially acquired taste preferences, which cannot easily be shaken off. Their persistence is testimony to the strength of such cultural constructs, however, rather than representing the presence of anything that should be understood as objective, neutral, or universal.

One way to address this issue is suggested by a combination of the work of Bourdieu and that of another sociological theorist of taste cultures, Herbert Gans.[19] Cultures that are accorded "higher" status in prevailing regimes of value can be seen as *"better or at least more comprehensive and more informative than the lower ones,"* Gans suggests, although he strongly qualifies this point.[20] As a result of their publics being better educated, "these cultures can cover more spheres of life and encompass more ideas and symbols than the other cultures." This judgment only applies, however, as Gans argues, if we fail to take into account the *actual* publics that choose one culture or another, according to their own very varied and unequal social backgrounds. As Bourdieu puts it, a universal basis of aesthetic judgment could only exist if the underlying social conditions—including upbringing and education—were themselves equally and universally distributed, as they are clearly very far from being.[21]

We might also question more broadly the value attributed to the "thought-provoking" basis on which art and indie film are often valorized, even if this has been challenged by perspectives that focus on more physically embodied encounters with cinema of this kind or more generally, such as those offered by Vivian Sobchack and Martine Beugnet, although accounts of this kind still tend to involve an intellectualization of whatever process or meaning is said to be involved.[22] A wider celebration of cognitive challenge, and the ability to meet it, can be seen to be implicated in a "western" imperial/colonial context that is almost impossible to escape for any of us working within this complex, an epistemological regime identified by Walter Mignolo as the "dark side" of the entire project of western modernity.[23] The point is not that we should expect to be able to step free of such foundational regimes, the bases of which are local and specific but that have claimed a universality historically and geographically imposed through the often violent elimination of rival cultures, but that we should at least recognize their limitations. In Mignolo's formulation, no notion of objectivity that is not placed in parenthesis, and recognized as only one of many possible approaches, is safe from a slide ultimately into totalitarianism. He does not suggest that no value can be found in western modernity, but rather that this has to be measured against the global-scale damage wrought by its dark side and the rival claims of other cultural perspectives.

A condition in which there is a perceived absence of any generally prevailing norms—a widespread diagnosis in many accounts of modernity, whether in the broad context of post-Enlightenment secularization or more recent neoliberal-individualist challenges to forms of social solidarity—is the basis on which Siegfried Kracauer made his classic appeal for the distinctive value of film.[24] The medium is valorized here on the grounds that it is uniquely equipped to capture a sense of material reality, a quality offered as an alternative to abstraction of either the liberal-rational or religious varieties. It is hard to see this as anything other than one of many such cases of special pleading, however, of a kind often found in valorizations of art cinema in particular: a tendency to take certain potentialities of film, in particular uses, as supposed evidence of both its essence and a unique capacity to offer a transformative experience to the viewer. For an example of the latter, see the use of Kracauer and the frequent suspect in such discourses, Gilles Deleuze, in the valorization of the Berlin School movement offered by Marco Abel.[25]

None of this is to deny that we can identify legitimate sources of good in any type of film, including art and indie cinema; just that this needs to be done in a qualified, proximate, and situated manner. Claims of a greater ability to capture a sense of certain kinds of material reality, often the harsh social reality faced by those on the margins of society, can reasonably be made of varieties of art and indie cinema that build on the heritage established by the Italian neorealist tradition and its many successors around the world. Other forms of art or independent film can be read as offering implicit critique of the prevalence of neoliberal conditions of existence for more or less privileged sectors of society. Both kinds of approaches can be found in work associated with what became known as New Argentine Cinema, from the late 1990s, to cite just once of many critically celebrated global examples.[26] Any of these might be valued by those coming from a left perspective that I would share, or sometimes questioned for any perceived shortcomings by that measure. Such engagements do not relate to any "essence" of cinema, however, on the basis of which the good attributed to any particular practice can be given any privileged grounding.[27] The "good of film experience" that Kracauer seeks to identify seems better expressed as a range of potential *goods:* always in need of pluralization and to be argued for on particular grounds, and likely to be differently valued from different positions, among which no ultimately objective or unsituated basis exists for arbitration.[28]

NOTES

1. I use the terms "art" and "independent" (or "indie") film here largely interchangeably, although the latter tends to refer to films from the American independent sector that circulate through similar channels to those of art cinema from around the world. For a more extensive discussion of overlaps and points of difference between the two, see Geoff King, *Positioning Art Cinema: Film and Cultural Value* (London: I. B. Tauris, 2019), 59–78.

2. See, e.g., Michael Newman, *Indie: An American Film Culture* (New York: Columbia University Press, 2011) for such a reading of the position of American indie film.

3. On the broader historical bases of what have become sedimented assumptions about the value of "higher" art, see Larry Shiner, *The Invention of Art: A Cultural History* (Chicago: University of Chicago Press, 2001), which I discuss at greater length in King, *Positioning Art Cinema,* 49–50.

4. Pierre Bourdieu, *Distinction: A Social Critique of the Judgment of Taste* (London: Routledge, 1984).

5. Geoff King, *The Cinema of Discomfort: Disquieting, Awkward, and Uncomfortable Experiences in Contemporary Art and Indie Film* (New York: Bloomsbury, 2021).

6. On the latter, see Nikolaj Lübecker, *The Feel-Bad Film* (Edinburgh: Edinburgh University Press, 2015), and Asbjørn Grønstad, *Screening the Unwatchable* (Houndmills: Palgrave Macmillan, 2012).

7. Jeffrey Sconce, "Irony, Nihilism and the American 'Smart' Film," *Screen* 43, no. 4 (2002): 349–369.

8. Todd Berliner, *Hollywood Aesthetic: Pleasure in American Cinema* (Oxford: Oxford University Press, 2017).

9. Berliner, *Hollywood Aesthetic,* 16–17.

10. Berliner, *Hollywood Aesthetic*, 26–28.
11. Richard Dyer, "Entertainment and Utopia," in Dyer, *Only Entertainment* (London: Routledge, 2002), 17–34.
12. Berliner, *Hollywood Aesthetic*, 27.
13. Berliner, *Hollywood Aesthetic*, 26.
14. Berliner, *Hollywood Aesthetic*, 28.
15. King, *Cinema of Discomfort*.
16. Jason Mittell, *Complex TV: The Poetics of Contemporary Television Storytelling* (New York: New York University Press, 2015).
17. Julian Hanich, "Dis/liking Disgust: The Revulsion Experience at the Movies," *New Review of Film and Television Studies* 7, no. 3 (2009): 293–309.
18. Berliner, *Hollywood Aesthetic*, 28.
19. Herbert Gans, *Popular Culture and High Culture: An Analysis and Evaluation of Taste* (New York: Basic Books, 1999), which I cite in *Positioning Art Cinema*.
20. Gans, *Popular Culture and High Culture*, 167 (original emphasis).
21. Pierre Bourdieu, "The Scholastic Point of View," in Bourdieu, *Practical Reason: On the Theory of Action* (Cambridge: Polity Press, 2001): 127–140, at 135.
22. Vivian Sobchack, *Carnal Thoughts: Embodiment and Moving Image Culture* (Berkeley: University of California Press, 2001); and Martine Beugnet, *Cinema and Sensation: French Film and the Art of Transgression* (Edinburgh: Edinburgh University Press, 2007).
23. Walter Mignolo, *The Darker Side of Western Modernity* (Durham, NC: Duke University Press, 2011).
24. Siegfried Kracauer, *Theory of Film: The Redemption of Physical Reality* (Princeton: Princeton University Press, 1960). Examples of numerous accounts of contemporary "late" modernity in such terms include Zygmunt Bauman, *Liquid Modernity* (Cambridge: Polity Press, 2012); Anthony Giddens, *Runaway World: How Globalization Is Reshaping Our Lives* (New York: Routledge, 2003); and Ulrich Beck, *World at Risk* (Cambridge: Polity Press, 2009).
25. Marco Abel, *The Counter-Cinema of the Berlin School* (Rochester, NY: Camden House, 2013). I discuss such issues more generally at greater length in *Positioning Art Cinema*.
26. See, e.g., Joanna Page, *Crisis and Capitalism in Contemporary Argentine Cinema* (Durham, NC: Duke University Press, 2009).
27. For a critique of similarly excessive claims made by some academic advocates of "slow" cinema, see King, *Positioning Art Cinema*, 105–139.
28. Kracauer, *Theory of Film*, 285.

12

. . . Heterocosmic Connections

On the Many Worlds and World Values of Cinema

DANIEL YACAVONE

Film worlds theory, as it may be termed, has recently emerged as a rich area of multidisciplinary inquiry. Over the past decade and a half, theorists and philosophers have addressed cinematic world-making from aesthetic, affective, narratological, technological, ecocritical, existential-phenomenological, hermeneutic, and sociocultural perspectives.[1] From a higher-level vantage point of what these explorations have in common, narrative films have, or are, "worlds" in three primary senses: *fictional* (rather than factual); *virtual* (rather than actual); and *artifactual/aesthetic,* that is, intentionally and artistically created (rather than natural). Accordingly, films possess certain transmedial functions and values belonging to these world types, but also those that arise from their powerful combination in cinema. In this essay, I will offer some general observations on these worlds and associated salutary uses and values. The latter, as falling into several overlapping categories, doubtlessly intersect with those discussed elsewhere in this volume under the heading of the axiological *good* that cinema provides. My hope is that their (re-)framing in the global terms of worlds, environments, and atmospheres offers a distinctive and productive take on the topic.

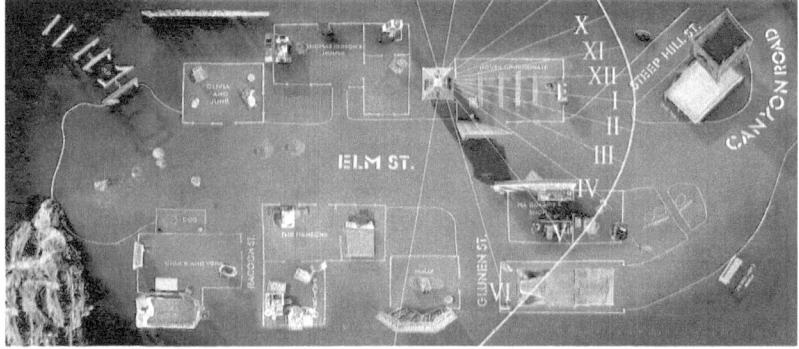

FIGURE 13. An aerial view of the schematic world of *Dogville* (2003, Lars von Trier).

FICTIONAL AND VIRTUAL WORLDS,
FUNCTIONS, AND VALUES

The fictional worlds of films encompass the places, characters, and events they present or refer to, as comprising the stories films tell and as extrapolated from them. These worlds vary greatly in denoted scope, detail, and presentation—from a full-blown perceptual illusionism characteristic of mainstream cinema to alternative conveyances, such as the schematic, Brechtian-influenced staging of *Dogville* (2003, dir. Lars von Trier). They have been more specifically understood as "diegetic worlds" in contrast with nondiegetic features of films (i.e., those existing outside of the world that characters know and inhabit, such as musical scores), and as story worlds (*fabula*) in contrast with plot and style.[2] In depicting groups of people, or other conscious beings, the fictional worlds of films are also social worlds. By the same token, they are subjective "life worlds" of their inhabitants' experiences, including what it feels like to be and act within them.[3]

Strictly speaking, the denoted worlds of films exist in the minds of spectators, who actualize and expand them in their imagination based upon the relevant information the cinematic work provides.[4] And certain basic functions and positive values of the fictional worlds of films are the direct result of this *imagined*, rather than only imaginary, status. Kendall Walton aptly identifies a number of these in his seminal analysis of the games of imaginative "make-believe" we play with fictions more generally. Together with their oft-suggested potential for individual and collective psychological catharsis, when imaginary realms are embedded within artworks—including, and perhaps especially, perceptually concrete ones such as films—they possess "a kind of objective integrity worthy of the real world and making their exploration an adventure of discovery and surprise."[5] The novelty, autonomy, and structured objectivity of fictional work worlds, as well as our collective subcontracting of their construction to professional creators (by which we accrue the "benefits of any special talent and insight they may bring to the task") are a common denominator of narrative cinema as entertainment, art, industry, and culture.[6] And, crucially, unlike our private worlds of dreams and fantasies, the experience of films' fictional worlds is a communal one. We share it with others who also participate in, and imaginatively inhabit, these worlds. Consequently, they provide common points of interpersonal and cultural reference, identification, and debate.

You and I encounter the same, unchanging fictional worlds of *Rules of the Game/La Règle du jeu* (1939, dir. Jean Renoir) and *Blade Runner* (1982, dir. Ridley Scott), themselves objective realities, while our respective experiences of them, and of the cinematic works presenting them, are different. Some of this first-person difference, and central features of cinematic form and experience, are captured in certain established understandings of *virtual realities,* or *worlds,* and *aesthetic worlds.*

Marie-Laure Ryan, a prominent theorist of narrative worlds, has reflected upon fundamental features that virtual-reality simulations share with familiar absorptive experiences of literary narratives and cinema, as likely the "most immersive of all media." Following the ideas of earlier writers on art and virtuality, she locates this commonality in the participant's self-aware immersion in unique, self-enclosed environments.[7] With their "own space and time," these are "in" the actual world (e.g., through the physical works or technological apparatuses that provide them), but not "of" it.[8] Instead, they are "dynamic simulations" of alternative "modes of being" under different conditions and forms of space, time, causality, perception, and memory as invariable structures of human experience. Corresponding with Gilles Deleuze's and Pierre Lévy's shared Bergsonian conception of virtuality (as "potentiality"), and its transformative capacities, such virtual domains allow their creators and, ideally, immersed experiencers, to rethink and reconfigure the actual.[9] With respect to cinema, specifically, some eight decades prior to Ryan's analysis, the psychologist and early film theorist Hugo Münsterberg argued from his broadly Kantian perspective that films present worlds "freed from the physical forms of space, time and causality."[10] He further maintained that this shedding of the "weight of the massive outer world" as no less than a triumph of "mind over matter" is the source of cinema's greatest psychological and artistic value.[11]

Such grand metaphysical claims for cinema's sui generis nature and transcendent power aside, films, as afforded by basic properties of moving-image media (analog and digital) and their creative uses, undoubtedly provide audiences with highly immersive perceptual and imaginative experiences that not only replicate ordinary, three-dimensional ones in various respects but also significantly diverge from them.[12] In their totality, these comprise experiential environments, or worlds. Whereas some are of a relatively more familiar, "user-friendly" kind associated with classical Hollywood-style cinema, numerous art films (such as the aforementioned *Dogville*) and postclassical Hollywood works, for instance, create more novel, defamiliarizing spatiotemporal environments and relationships. In this respect, and like many experimental films, they more actively challenge our perceptual-cognitive and affective faculties, and thereby sharpen and broaden them. This is apart from the profoundly open questions of if and how such global cinematic structures may additionally serve as useful models and impetus for the above-mentioned new ways of organizing our mental, social, and ethical lives (as also part of the utopian vision of the modernist cinematic avant-garde of the 1920s), and, in the process, aid in restoring a lost "belief in the world," that is, this actual world, as a place of stable identity and purposeful action, in Deleuze's much-discussed postmodern speculation.[13]

CINEMA'S AESTHETIC WORLDS

Ryan's account of the virtual worlds of narrative works, and their value, is a response to the immersive capacities and future potentials of twenty-first-century digital media. Yet her appeal in this context to the presentational forms of art as alternative spatiotemporal structures (of experience), through which all representations are filtered and transformed, stands in a long *anti-mimetic* tradition of reflection on artworks as worlds. This tradition dates from the mid-eighteenth century and continues through post-Kantian aesthetic thought in Romantic, formalist, expression-based, and phenomenological modes, and has certain echoes in European film theory from Münsterberg and Rudolf Arnheim, to Jean Mitry and Deleuze.[14] Among the earliest and most influential articulations of this perspective is that of Alexander Baumgarten, the founder of modern philosophical aesthetics, who describes artistic production as the "heterocosmic" creation of experiential realms at a pronounced remove from the natural world and its conditions.[15] The product of the same perception-centered, "esthetico-logical" thought, as distinct from abstract reason, which characterizes their experience, these autonomous aesthetic worlds possess their own "causal laws," organic-like holism, inner teleology, and a "poetic truth" that transcends direct, literal correspondence to what exists outside their confines.[16] For Baumgarten, as for subsequent thinkers and theorist-practitioners (including J. R. R. Tolkien), such work worlds—as equally if not more deserving of the world description than fictional worlds—are not primarily constituted by representational and fictional content. Instead, they are a matter of a work's purposefully organized form(s) and related feeling, including as vehicles for the artistic presentation of a subject and the "progressive revelation of its [the work's] particular theme."[17]

While the three types of worlds described may exist apart from the others in various media, they are no more exclusive in theory than in practice. Elsewhere I have attempted to accommodate the *fictional, virtual,* and *aesthetic* worlds of narrative films within an overarching conceptual framework. Briefly, this is based on a primary distinction I have drawn between the *world-in* and the *world-of* films.[18] The imagined/imaginary *world-in* is the world of the narrative fiction previously described. The *world-of,* in contrast, or what might aptly be termed a film's "cinepoetic" world, as a virtual and aesthetic reality with its own space and time, includes how the *world-in* is conveyed through cinematic means. Unlike the latter, the *world-of* has a perceptual and presentational rather than representational mode of existence. To take a basic example, when a mutinous sailor raises his arm multiple times in succession in order to smash a plate, in a famous montage sequence in Sergei Eisenstein's *Battleship Potemkin/Bronenosets Potyomkin* (1925), this repetition is a feature of the presentational *world-of* the film, as distinct from the fictional world, in which, and as grasped by viewers, the action occurs only once. As experientially entwined as the *world-in* and the *world-of* are, with the latter the only manifestation of the former in its perceptual specificity, for a host of reasons (beyond the scope of the present discussion), like the diegetic and nondiegetic, they are nonetheless logically and "ontologically" distinct. Moreover, spectators often experience them as essentially different.[19] Permanently conjoined in a film's creation, however, the *world-of* profoundly shapes the experience and meaning of the *world-in;* whereas the *world-in* confers narrative and conceptual significance to the creative and stylistic choices and their effects, which the *world-of* displays.

General and specific relations between the fictional *world-in* and the cinematic *world-of* films produce narrative, thematic, and stylistic meaning, together with affect and emotion. And a good deal of a cinematic work's artistic appreciation, as well as interpretation, entails some *focused awareness of, and reflection upon*, these relations. This likewise pertains to discussions of the ethical and moral dimensions of narrative films—their responsibilities, positive or harmful effects, et cetera—as linked to aesthetic ones, in which the *world-of* is taken to communicate something of an ethical or moral nature concerning the *world-in*, against the background of there being multiple cinematic ways to present a character or event, and to tell a story (an axiomatic assumption of both film semiotics and ethically centered film criticism). Such a conveyed perspective includes a film's and its makers' interpreted attitude toward the represented *world-in*, be it sincere or ironic. This broad normative dimension goes all the way down to the most basic creative choices in filmmaking, including as world-making. These pertain to *what* is and is not shown and heard, *when* it is, and *why* it is, in addition to *how* it is. And, of course, all humanly created worlds, including artistic and cinematic ones, are a matter of intentions, values, interpretations, and perspectives, as much as things (or their representations) and factual states of affairs.

FILM WORLDS AS REFLECTIVE/REFLEXIVE FORM AND EXPERIENCE

Among critical engagements with the *world-in* and *world-of* framework since its proposal, the Hegelian philosopher and film theorist Robert Pippin's adoption of it, including with a significant new inflection, speaks in illuminating fashion to a number of these points and to cinema's related goodness. Whereas my original explication focused on the represented *world-in* as a fictional-imaginary construct on the part of filmmakers and spectators, he emphasizes it as lived in and known by characters. Further, he analyzes the worlds in question and their relation within the context of films' and film genres' ruminations on ethical aspects of social and political life as prompting edifying reflections on the part of audiences. Pippin describes the "movie world" (*world-of*), as "a selection, highlighting, focusing, and, in its cinematic way, *commenting*" on the depicted world (*world-in*).[20] Tone, and a "mood suffused through" a film, akin to what I have articulated as global "film world feeling," is a significant part of this stylistically embedded commentary.[21] Thus, in writing about *Chinatown* (1974, dir. Roman Polanski) Pippin singles out the film's soundtrack, camera movement, and claustrophobic mise-en-scène, together with the particular "atmosphere of confusion and impotence" they help to create.[22] In addition to events of the plot, through these features and the atmosphere they generate spectators may grasp the moral ambiguity, corruption, and lawlessness of the filmmakers' depicted version of Chinatown as a place, and Los Angeles, more generally.[23] This includes as it is confusedly known—and, especially, felt—by characters, as their affective, as well as physical, environment. In these ways, perceived aspects of the *world-of* prompt us, as spectators, to not only intellectually recognize (the metaphor) that the lead character Jake's (Jack Nicholson) world and fate, vis-à-vis his "Chinatown," is also *our world*, condition, and fate. But, additionally, and to extend Pippin's argument in a more affective direction, through the presentational-stylistic *world-of*, we may also powerfully *feel* this exemplary connection (i.e., between the *world-in* and our actual world) and its existential weight. This process, by which the spectator affectively internalizes and, in contemporary theoretical parlance, "embodies" the cinematic work's aesthetic world makes its sociopolitical and ethical resonance in this and other cases especially personal, potent, and revelatory.[24]

In keeping with Hegel, for whom art is increasingly self-reflective, (pre-)philosophical thought in a concrete, sensory mode, but also notably similar to the earlier heterocosmic concept of artwork worlds, Pippin associates the *world-of*'s expressed commentary on the *world-in* (in any artistically "ambitious" film) with a higher-order "formal unity," "one organic purposive whole," and an "emerging, internal self-conception."[25] (Further describing it as "something like the 'point' of making and showing the film," he maintains that this is "unmistakably philosophical.")[26] Extrapolating from Pippin's observations, and as *Chinatown* exemplifies, both this reflection on a film's and its makers' part, and the spectator's full apprehension of it, necessarily entails thinking and feeling the depicted *world-in*, the cinematic *world-of*, and the actual world through the focusing prisms of the others.

If films in their world, or world-like, modalities have the potential to be aesthetic-rooted "reflective form" in Pippin's sense, they may also open a space for reflective and self-reflective experience, more generally. Münsterberg maintained in 1916 that much of the psychological captivation of the fictional "photoplay" lies in the perception of more things happening faster than in ordinary life, a feature that "heightens the feeling of vitality in the spectator."[27] Fostered by media technologies of instantaneous representation and communication, our inner and outer lives today seem to contain more events, occurring at a faster and mentally fatiguing rate, than those of any films. Thus, a major form of "vitality" some cinematic works provide is likely instead the result of an artistically organized and focused *reduction* of perceptual and imaginative experiences and their speed. While exclusive to no single film mode, style, or genre, this fact may partly underlie the much-discussed aesthetics of "slowness" and "contemplativeness" in contemporary art cinema—marked, as they are, by filmmakers' eschewal of spectacular thrills and immediate gratifications in the interest of maximizing what is captured in German as *Erfahrung* (in contrast with *Erlebnis*) as a relatively deeper type of experience, of a longer duration, from which the individual gains something more lasting.

Relatedly, at the more fundamental level of conscious awareness itself, the English polymath Raymond Tallis suggests that in the consciousness of art and "living with and within" works, such as great novels, we "truly experience our experiences" rather than simply having and passively undergoing them.[28] This lies in a true "connectedness," generally lacking in quotidian life, of each past and present moment of aesthetic experience, as corresponding to the structured unity (sometimes of a complex, dialectical kind) of the work's form and content. The co-emergent, temporally unfolding nature of both the *world-of* and the *world-in* films, through sequential images, and their composite aesthetic totality, also provides such a reflexive mental space and time to experience our conscious experience of them. In an era of alienated consciousness and an overabundance of disconnected sensory impressions and vast quantities of often qualitatively unstructured information—too large, and too fast-moving, to fully process, let alone reflect upon—it is not difficult to see how such higher-order, work-induced awareness may be among the deepest, most psychically replenishing values of artistically accomplished cinema.

WORLD CONNECTIONS AND CONVERGENCE

To tie together these observations, beyond basic entertainment and escapism, the functions and values of narrative films as worlds are, at base, a matter of many-layered connections, entanglements, and embeddings involving several distinct realities. These are, first, the connections between a film's fictional world (*world-in*) and cinematic-aesthetic world (*world-of*) as I, Pippin, and others, have described them. These embrace the variable relations, also central to cinematic narration (e.g., point of view), between characters' experience and knowledge of their worlds and the spectators' experience of them via the work's form and style. Second, it is a matter of relations of similarity and difference of these worlds separately and together to the *actual world* (or worlds, plural, in the form of the different historical worlds in which films are made and subsequently encountered). Along with it must be added the natural world, specifically, and the current "Anthropocene" environment, which is absorbed by the fictional and aesthetic worlds of films but in the form of its audiovisual presentation also stands out from them for attention in itself. All manner of beneficial aesthetic, existential, ethical, and political insights and awareness, cognitive as well as affective, may occur through these circuits. The same is true for connections forged between filmmakers and spectators in and through film worlds (*worlds-in* and *worlds-of*) as compelling vehicles for the conveyance of experiences, ideas, and feelings. Finally, cinematic worlds in these senses are interfaces for intersubjective communion and conversation among spectators and collective audiences, and generations of audiences, across time, place, and culture.

These connections, like the worlds they bring together, also entail each other in both filmmaking and viewing. A film's expressed reflection on the actual world is partly conveyed through its formal presentation of, and stylistic commentary upon, its fictional world. The relationship of filmmaker and spectator works through this channel, as well as through spectators' identification, empathy, and sympathy with and for characters and both their objective (i.e., public) and private worlds. Moreover, some films, such as *Contempt/Le Mépris* (1963, dir. Jean-Luc Godard), *The Purple Rose of Cairo* (1985, dir. Woody Allen), and *Adaptation* (2002, dir. Spike Jonze), draw explicit attention to these various world relations in cinema in self-reflexive and "commentative" ways.[29] In one long-standing reflexive trope, finding innovative expression in films like *Sherlock Jr.* (1924, dir. Buster Keaton) and *Mullholland Drive* (2001, dir. David Lynch), the virtual and parallel worlds of characters' dreams are metaphorically aligned with cinematic world-making and experience, including of a distinctly twenty-first-century, computer-aided variety, in the case of Christopher Nolan's perception-bending *Inception* (2010). Cinema seems to have an almost unlimited capacity not just to create worlds but, on a metalevel, to frame and reflect upon them, and encourage spectators to do the same.

In sum, films not only provide fictional, virtual, and aesthetic experiences, but (ideally) organize them into integrated, purposive wholes. They depict but also *create* worlds of different kinds and networks of relations among them. Along with whatever intrinsic value cinematic world creation and our experience thereof possesses, it subtends cinema's aesthetic, ethical, social, psychological, and philosophical capacities and benefits in some of the ways I have indicated. To meet a familiar objection: rather than an unwarranted, even ethically and politically dangerous detachment of a film's experience and meaning from reality construed as the actual world, emphasizing films as multiple autonomous worlds is to acknowledge the former's multiform presence in cinematic works. This is a presence not confined to a film's literal reference to the actual world, or its technological reproduction, but its recognized artistic transformation, complete with the awareness such defamiliarization engenders. At the same time, this ontological pluralism with respect to cinema insists on other salient features of aesthetic, virtual, and fictional worlds, and worlds more generally—including distance from the "real" or quotidian, boundedness, holism, qualitative singularity, irreducible affective atmospheres, enworlded human and nonhuman perspectives, and "ways of being" in an environment—that films, especially the greatest among them, exhibit. As I have elucidated in short compass, in addition to explaining why we theoretically and pre-theoretically alike think of and experience films as worlds unto themselves, these features speak to multiple facets of cinema's potential goodness.

NOTES

1. In addition to journal articles and studies of individual filmmakers, twenty-first-century books on cinema making significant use of a theoretical concept of *world* with these emphases include Daniel Frampton, *Filmosophy* (London: Wallflower, 2006); Adrian J. Ivakhiv, *Ecologies of the Moving Image: Cinema, Affect, Nature* (Waterloo, ON: Wilfrid Laurier University Press, 2013); Daniel Yacavone, *Film Worlds: A Philosophical Aesthetics of Cinema* (New York: Columbia University Press, 2015); Alberto Barraco, *Hermeneutics of the Film World: A Ricoeurian Method for Film Interpretation* (London: Palgrave, 2017); Adam O'Brien, *Film and the Natural Environment: Elements and Atmospheres* (London: Wallflower, 2018); Jennifer Fay, *Inhospitable World: Cinema in the Time of the Anthropocene* (Oxford: Oxford University Press, 2018); Robert Pippin, *Filmed Thought: Cinema as Reflective Form* (Chicago: University of Chicago Press, 2019); Claudia Breger, *Making Worlds: Affect and*

Collectivity in Contemporary European Cinema (New York: Columbia University Press, 2020); and Steffen Hven, *Enacting the Worlds of Cinema* (Oxford: Oxford University Press, 2022). Mark J. P. Wolf's *Building Imaginary Worlds: The Theory and History of Subcreation* (New York: Routledge, 2012), which touches on cinema in analyzing narrative and transmedial world-building, together with Alain Boillat's *Cinema as a Worldbuilding Machine in the Digital Era* (Indianapolis: Indiana University Press/John Libbey Publishing, 2022), should also be added to this by no means comprehensive list. An influential philosophical precedent and point of reference on the topic is Stanley Cavell's *The World Viewed: Reflections on the Ontology of Film* (New York: Viking Press, 1971), and, to a lesser extent, Nelson Goodman's more analytically oriented *Ways of Worldmaking* (Indianapolis: Hackett, 1978). I have transposed the latter to cinema in detail (see Yacavone, *Film Worlds*, 86–114).

2. See David Bordwell, *Narration in the Fiction Film* (Madison: University of Wisconsin Press, 1985), 48–62.

3. The represented worlds of films may also be construed as "possible worlds," in contrast with the world of empirical fact, as fictional worlds more generally have sometimes been theorized, including with reference to modal logic and its counterfactual worlds.

4. Bordwell, Christian Metz, and V. F. Perkins, among others, have stressed this core tenant of fictional worlds theory and analyzed the workings of cinematic story worlds as imaginative constructions. See Yacavone, *Film Worlds*, 11–35.

5. Kendall Walton, *Mimesis as Make-Believe* (Cambridge, MA: Harvard University Press, 1993), 68.

6. Walton, *Mimesis*, 67

7. Here Ryan builds upon Susanne K. Langer's philosophy of art as virtual experience. See Mary-Laure Ryan, *Narrative as Virtual Reality: Immersion and Interactivity in Literature and Electronic Media* (Baltimore, MD: Johns Hopkins University Press, 2001), 41–43. It is worth noting that many contemporary theorists and philosophers of "virtual reality" define it more restrictively as immersive, literally interactive, and computer-generated, therefore differentiating it from most films, as well as traditional artworks. See David Chalmers, "The Virtual and the Real," *Disputatio* 9 (2017): 309–352.

8. Ryan, *Narrative*, 42.

9. Ryan, *Narrative*, 42, 35. See Pierre Lévy, *Becoming Virtual: Reality in the Digital Age,* trans. Robert Bonono (New York: Plenum Trade, 1998), discussed in Ryan; and Gilles Deleuze, *Bergsonism*, trans. Hugh Tomlinson and Barbara Habberjam (New York: Zone, 1991) and Deleuze, *Cinema 2: The Time-Image,* trans. Hugh Tomlinson and Robert Galeta (Minneapolis: University of Minnesota Press, 1989), e.g., 68–83.

10. Hugo Münsterberg, *The Film: A Psychological Study* (New York: Dover, 1970 [1916]), 80. Münsterberg's pioneering work is best known in English as *The Photoplay: A Psychological Study.*

11. Münsterberg, *Film,* 95.

12. See Yacavone, "Film and the Phenomenology of Art: Reappraising Merleau-Ponty on Cinema as Form, Medium, and Expression," *New Literary History* 47, no. 1 (2016): 59–185.

13. See, e.g., Deleuze, *Cinema 2*, 172.
14. Yacavone, *Film Worlds*, 3–35ff.
15. See M.H. Abrams, "From Addison to Kant: Modern Aesthetics and the Exemplary Art," in *Doing Things with Texts*, ed. Michael Fisher (New York: Norton, 1989), 159–187, at 174–178; and Yacavone, *Film Worlds*, 8–10.
16. Abrams, "From Addison to Kant," 178.
17. Abrams, "From Addison to Kant," 178.
18. Yacavone, *Film Worlds*, 30–35. This distinction is partly indebted to Mikel Dufrenne's concepts of the represented and expressed worlds of artworks, and their relation. See *The Phenomenology of Aesthetic Experience* (Evanston, IL: Northwestern University Press, 1973), 166–190.
19. On this point, see Yacavone, *Film Worlds*, 11–35.
20. Pippin, *Filmed Thought*, 8n6.
21. Yacavone, *Film Worlds*, 169–170 and 196–201.
22. Pippin, *Filmed Thought*, 113.
23. For more on aesthetic atmosphere in films, see Hven, *Enacting the Worlds of Cinema*, and, including from an existential-phenomenological perspective, my discussion of "cineaesthetic atmospheres" in *Film Worlds*, 190–227.
24. My thanks to Dominic Lash, who analyzes Pippin's take on the suggested *world-in* and *world-of* distinction in these and other ways, and in the context of Pippin's larger theoretical and philosophical project, in *Robert Pippin and Film: Politics, Ethics, and Psychology after Modernism* (London: Bloomsbury, 2022).
25. Pippin, *Filmed Thought*, 8.
26. Pippin, *Filmed Thought*, 8.
27. Münsterberg, *Film*, 94.
28. Raymond Tallis, "Art (and Philosophy) and the Ultimate Aims of Human Life," *Philosophy Now* 57 (2006): 7–9, at 8.
29. Metz, *Impersonal Enunciation, or The Place of Film* (New York: Columbia University Press), e.g., 53–54.

13

... Depth of Experience

On Early Phenomenology and the Value of Boredom in the Cinema

CHRISTIAN FERENCZ-FLATZ

FILM AS ART

The early debates on film as art (involving Rudolf Arnheim, Günther Anders, etc.) have long faded into obsolescence. This essay doesn't aim to revisit these debates. Instead, it focuses on one of their aspects, namely, the distinction between the alleged superficiality of film and the profundity of genuine art, in order to draw some inferences from their *phenomenological* treatment that hold contemporary relevance about cinema's ability to provide experiential depth.

Early cultural critics frequently depicted film as facile entertainment, in contrast to the weighty importance of high art. Film, they argued, only appealed to the base instincts of the uneducated masses and did not require intellectual effort or concentration. While film offered intense thrills and excitements, it was unable to leave a lasting impression. I have shown elsewhere that one can find such clichés in the writings of many early phenomenologists working in the interwar period as well.[1] What is more interesting than these perfunctory assessments of the cinema, however, are the attempts by authors such as Moritz Geiger or Oskar Becker to ground them in a more solid phenomenological analysis of *experiential depth*. In the following, I show that by inquiring into what it means to speak about depth with regard to aesthetic experiences, early phenomenologists established a framework that can still be useful not for an idle dismissal of film but for understanding a

Depth of Experience | 151

FIGURE 14. Slow time in *Blissfully Yours* (2002, Apichatpong Weerasethakul).

contemporary phenomenon like slow cinema, associated with directors like Tsai Ming-liang, Lav Diaz, and Béla Tarr.

EARLY PHENOMENOLOGY

What strikes the reader of early phenomenological accounts of superficial and profound art is their persistent attempt to ground them in a discussion of the superficiality and depth of the corresponding *experience*. The most direct analysis to this extent is Geiger's 1927 essay "Oberflächen- und Tiefenwirkungen der Kunst" ("Superficial and profound effects of art"), which phenomenologically determines the true scope of aesthetic experience by contrasting it with both traditional aesthetics and contemporary psychologies of art. While traditional aesthetics only takes undisputed masterpieces as its reference and conflates their reception with religious or metaphysical experiences, psychologies of art usually blur the distinction between the aesthetic and everyday experiences like play.[2] In contrast to both, Geiger's phenomenological account is interested in working out the distinctive nature of aesthetic experience. By focusing especially on reductive psychological approaches to the aesthetic, Geiger shows that their blurring of the distinction between aesthetic and everyday experiences is only justified if one refers to the superficial effects of artworks, like amusement, pleasure, or sentimentality, while ignoring their deeper ones, like profound upheaval or bliss. In Geiger's view, only the latter are truly distinctive for the aesthetic, whereas the former characterize the reception of lower productions like the burlesque, cabaret, dime novels, or dance music.

Geiger's short essay only cursorily grounds this distinction by associating superficial art with the "vital" sphere of the subject, while the more profound art forms involve the self.[3] However, in an earlier essay from 1913, "Beiträge zu einer Phänomenologie des ästhetischen Genusses" ("Contributions to a phenomenology of aesthetic pleasure"), Geiger developed a more extended argument. By delineating the question of experiential *depth* from quantitative *intensity,* he identified in that essay five criteria for determining when an experience is to be considered deep:

(a) when the experience involves the ego (in contrast to when it doesn't);

(b) when the ego participates in it more fully (in contrast to when it is more unengaged);

(c) when the experience touches the ego in the most profound layers of its being (in contrast to when it remains unaffected at its core);

(d) when the experience pervades consciousness more fully (in contrast to mere foreground experiences, which can be accompanied by other background experiences); and

(e) when the experience is characterized by a specific weight, that is, when it is more serious and has an intrinsic importance (in contrast to frivolous experiences).[4]

According to Geiger, these criteria apply primarily to high art; experiences like amusement, sentimentality, and superficial pleasure do not meet these criteria, so he denies them recognition as truly aesthetic. In an essay from about the same time, Becker, his fellow phenomenologist, terms such superficial experiences *aesthetoid,* rather than aesthetic, and adds examples like erotic excitement, horror, and suspense, as illustrated in detective dramas.[5] In ascribing such experiences to the periphery of subjective experience, both authors evoke a layered architectonics of the human subject, which is largely shared by early phenomenology. A telling example can be found in Max Scheler's groundwork, *Formalism in Ethics,* which first coined the notion of the "vital," also employed by

Geiger. Scheler establishes a hierarchy of values, ranging from the pleasurable to the holy, with vital values positioned below the spiritual values of the personal subject. In his view, there is a connection between the height of a value and the depth of the satisfaction it produces, such that simple joy is frequently accompanied by an in-depth dissatisfaction of the spiritual person, an observation frequently illustrated with reference to "superficial" sexual intercourse.[6] According to Geiger, such a sexual encounter often remains shallow and disengages the profound I, in contrast to love, which should be an experientially "deeper" experience.[7]

While there is little mention of film in these texts, their descriptions are consistent with the usual disparagement of cinema in the cultural criticism of the time, which also pervades other writings of the aforementioned phenomenologists. According to this view, the cinematic medium is fundamentally shallow, because its titillations, thrills, erotic incitements, et cetera only touch upon the vital sphere, while leaving the deeper layers of the personal subject untouched or dissatisfied. The result, they argue, is a deep feeling of spiritual void, which accompanies contemporary entertainment, in general, and cinema, in particular.

CHALLENGING DEPTH

There were various means to counter this argument during the interwar period. One way was to challenge the hierarchy of depth and surface values. This was Siegfried Kracauer's strategy in his well-known essay "Cult of Distraction" (1926). According to Kracauer, the categories normally opposed by cultural critics to contemporary superficial life—like "personality," "interiority," or meaningfulness—and the naive affirmation of cultural values associated with depth, are historically bound to become ideologically suspect. This is because their original foundations have been shaken with the social and technological upheavals of the twentieth century, such that works of art defining themselves in reference to such values most frequently only serve to repress truly urgent matters of contemporary life by promoting a bookish agenda of authentic interiority. While the latter only serves as an escapist defense mechanism against the pressing issues of social change, the avowed superficiality of contemporary entertainment, which abandons highbrow claims of true art, could hold a superior moral value.[8] Following this argument, cinema can be regarded as a potentially more honest artistic endeavor insofar as it denounces the outdated model of aesthetic depth and seriousness altogether.

A different way to challenge the argument is to reconsider the categories of "deep" and "superficial" when describing subjective experience. In their treatment of these categories, the phenomenologists quoted above follow a Cartesian view of consciousness, which leaves little room for unconscious experience, its sediments, and impulses. According to their architectonics of the human subject, depth is measured exclusively by way of proximity to the conscious I, conceived as a unitary and unproblematic pole of its lived experiences. But how does depth change scope once the entire range of un- and subconscious lived experiences is included, and how does this affect our understanding of the cinema and its shallowness? A consideration of these questions can be found in Walter Benjamin.[9] According to him, an experience is only truly assimilated by the subject, becoming an object for authentic recollection, if it is not lived through in conscious awareness in the first place. This is because, according to Benjamin's reading of Proust via Freud, conscious experience only allows its superficial registration, making it available for voluntary recollection but preventing it from leaving a more profound and lasting mark, which could only occur unawares. In Benjamin's view, the notion of "shock" is defined here as an impression that runs the risk of traumatizing the subject if it were to be received off guard, but which can be warded off by its conscious, superficial reception.

This interpretation reverses Geiger's analysis by defining superficial experience according to the same criteria he uses to determine experiential depth. Consequently, the alleged superficiality of the cinema becomes ambivalent. On the one hand, it is seen as a valuable and necessary feature that determines the superior social use of the cinema, that of helping us exercise the "apperceptions" needed in our contemporary intercourse with a world that could otherwise cause trauma.[10] On the other hand, Benjamin's reflections also open the path for questioning a possible experiential depth of the cinema in entirely different terms. Accordingly, true depth would only pertain to films that still manage to touch their viewers despite the defensive mechanism of cinematic reception, intended to keep shock at bay. This does not occur by surpassing that mechanism, that is by overstimulation, but rather by discreetly undermining it.

DEPTH AND BOREDOM

A further alternative is put forth by Heidegger in his lecture course *The Fundamental Concepts of Metaphysics* (1929/1930), another significant contribution to the early phenomenological discussions of experiential depth. While not engaging any of the aforementioned phenomenologists, the lecture and especially its ample discussion of boredom puts a similar understanding of depth and superficiality into play. Heidegger begins his analysis by considering a trivial example of what he terms "superficial boredom": waiting for a train in a desolate station.[11] In his view, boredom is here not readily accessible as an affect to be dissected by means of introspection, but instead it is primarily given in our struggle to escape it, namely, in our effort to find some distraction. Thus, a phenomenology of boredom should approach its object by focusing on the complex dynamics between distraction and boredom, and in so doing Heidegger arrives at the two main characteristics of boredom: "being held in limbo" and "being left empty." In contrast to "superficial boredom," which involves "becoming bored by" (something), he also develops two further forms of boredom, namely "being bored with" (a specific situation) and "profound boredom."

Heidegger illustrates the second form of boredom, "becoming bored with," with the example of a merry social evening, whereby one is absorbed and present, but later concedes in all honesty that they were actually bored. He explicitly terms such boredom as "deeper" than the first form discussed, while his criteria for determining this difference are in perfect agreement with the aforementioned early phenomenological considerations. Just like Scheler, Heidegger sees the second form of boredom as a superficial enjoyment, marked by a latent profound dissatisfaction. Just like Geiger, he determines the difference in depth between profound and superficial boredom by showing that: (a) the former originates in the subject (as "Dasein"), while the latter is provoked by an external event; (b) the former pervades the entire situation and doesn't merely relate to a single object; and (c) the former is existentially more serious and significant than the latter.[12] These structural analogies to the early phenomenological accounts of experiential depth are only nuanced by the fact that, with his third form of "profound boredom," wherein all objects and possibilities of action fall prey to devaluation, Heidegger departs from traditional representations of personal subjectivity by stipulating as its "subject" an anonymous *Dasein* determined by temporal horizontality.

Of course, there are various ways to fit the cinema into Heidegger's framework. First, one could consider films in general as a mere diversion for casting off superficial boredom, and this is indeed the view of most early phenomenologists. Second, one could regard the film itself as a possible object of superficial boredom, in response to which one can mobilize various entertainments, such as second-screen interactions. Third, one could see watching a film as an engrossing satisfaction, secretly eaten away at by the deeper dissatisfaction of the second form of "being bored with." Finally, one could try and relate the cinema to the third form of "profound boredom." This last is what previous attempts to engage Heidegger's reflections from a film-scholarly perspective have tried to do. To this extent, both Richard Misek and Chiara Quaranta specifically focus on films associated with "slow cinema."[13] In contrast to fast-paced entertainment movies, such films, they contend, use an aesthetic of the slow, empty, and discordant to engender a different experience of perceptual time. In doing so, they allow accommodating viewers to experience profound boredom. This example and its interpretation lend themselves to some considerations with regard to experiential depth, which I will try to identify in five short observations (a–e).

EXPERIENTIAL DEPTH IN SLOW CINEMA

(a) For Heidegger, the three forms of boredom do not simply pass into one another.[14] Nonetheless, profound boredom offers the existential foundation for the others, while the intermediary, second form of boredom appears to morph into any of the other two provided there is "a corresponding transposition of man's existence . . . either toward the surface and into the realm of his busy activities, or into the dimension of . . . existing proper."[15] Thus, when one immerses oneself fully into surface entertainment, latent boredom—which is only kept dormant by successful diversion—easily turns into superficial boredom whenever that entertainment fails to maintain our attention. Similarly, the second form of boredom only needs to be brought out of latency and adopted existentially in order to allow for a full-fledged profound boredom to develop. These considerations shed an interesting light on the experience of slow cinema films like those of Apichatpong Weerasethakul, which cannot be plainly associated with either of the aforementioned forms of boredom per se. On the contrary, when describing their experience, one should first of all work out its specific fluidity and vacillation: the viewer may start off by being superficially bored, share some moments of engrossing contemplative satisfaction, do a lot of self-forgetful mind-wandering, and eventually arrive at a stable, all-embracing, profound boredom.

(b) When analyzing superficial boredom, Heidegger hypothesizes what makes waiting for a delayed train in a destitute station boring. The situation deviates from the "ideal time" of using a station, when one arrives shortly before departure to take advantage of its unhindered and immediate functionality.[16] This description could also offer a hint for the analysis of cinematographic boredom. Thus, the "ideal time" of cinematic narration would be one wherein the dramatic expectations of each scene are immediately fulfilled—or at least ceaselessly fed, for instance, in an ongoing intentionality of suspense—by its subsequent development. Instead, this mechanism is principally brought to a halt in slow cinema. In nonresponsively abandoning the dramatic intentions awoken by their narrative elements, they let the expectations of their viewers bounce off like inanimate objects. As such, they are at the opposite end of the superficially captivating art discussed by early phenomenologists.

(c) Fumbling with one's phone while watching a film can be seen as a distraction that hinders deeper concentration or as a chance to engage in second-screen interactivity. In either case, its consideration complicates the relationship between (superficial) boredom and entertainment. For if a film is at core a pastime for a free afternoon, that is, an entertaining way of escaping profound boredom, fumbling with the phone is an entertainment in the second degree, in relation to which the film itself becomes the object of boredom. One could argue that this impedes the reception of the film, but this is not the point for Heidegger. The main problem is that such a divertissement only hinders boredom to gain depth. According to Heidegger, the latter would occur if "we are not opposed to [boredom], if we do not always react to protect ourselves, if instead we make room for it."[17] Slow cinema does little to oppose boredom, and thus it appears to be in the interest of both an existentially more profound experience and a more pertinent reception for the spectators to abstain from resisting boredom while watching the film. However, such an attitude may be at odds with the ideal of committed and attentive viewership.

(d) According to both Misek and Quaranta, slow cinema stimulates the viewers to engage in their own reflections and ruminations. In so doing, they allow their minds to wander and thus deflect from the film. This point was discussed extensively by Julian Hanich, whose typology of mind-wandering in the cinema considers five criteria: the ability to retain control over one's experience; the degree of attention to the film; the power held by the film over the spectator; the degree of withdrawal into the private sphere; and the qualification of the experience as an intrusion or an enrichment of the film.[18] Accordingly, slow cinema, for Hanich, intentionally *allows* the viewer's attention to drift and is *enriched* by daydreaming. However, it is clear that drifting off can occur in the cinema either along the lines of superficial boredom or its profound version. In the first case, the film is merely a failed entertainment, which should be replaced by a more gripping one, if only a mental divertissement. Mind-wandering thus becomes a way of escaping boredom into the superficial realm of everyday concerns. Alternatively, profound boredom—whereby all beings recede into indifference and no longer provide existential possibilities for the subject[19]—also entails giving up on the film, which can no longer withstand such indifference.

Despite their resemblance, these two forms of deflection have opposing valuations of watching the film. In the first case, sticking to the film could open the path for an existentially more unhindered, deeper experience of boredom; in the latter, it means the opposite: resisting the deeper abandonment of profound boredom, which would also imply letting the film go. While it may be difficult at times to decide between the two, in the case of slow cinema the film itself is relevant for determining the experience of the viewer. For in not grabbing their attention, the film also projects indifference toward attending or not attending the film proper and thus meets profound boredom halfway. Apichatpong Weerasethakul's famous endorsement of viewers falling asleep during his films may be seen as substantiating this same indifferent reception, which could help induce profound boredom in that it doesn't just regard everything on screen as equally indifferent but also proves indifferent to the very distinction between watching and not watching the film. This assessment seems to contradict Geiger's final criterion of the intrinsic dignity of the aesthetic object, which he considers paramount for the evaluation of its depth. However, the fact that, in the case of slow cinema, the abandonment of the aesthetic object may achieve existential depth even while conforming to the innermost intention of that object also provides the true measure of its dignity: it gains in existential import paradoxically when it requires less attention.

(e) Both Misek and Quaranta, who apply Heidegger's framework to film, associate the second form of boredom mainly with the experience of enjoying a mainstream blockbuster. This is, however, a reductive reading of Heidegger that assimilates his views to those of Scheler or Geiger. According to this interpretation, cinematic entertainment would be implicitly devalued as a mere vital pleasure against the backdrop of the subject's more profound existential core and its corresponding values. Instead, Heidegger's account of the entertaining dinner party as illustrating the second form of boredom does not share in any of these overt negative valuations. On the contrary, Heidegger presents the dinner party as a situation that is not only entertaining but as intellectually stimulating and sparkling as the most captivating arthouse film, which one can enjoy fully and without intellectual guilt; it is only the self-forgetfulness of such enjoyment that is ultimately eaten away at by profound boredom. In other words, a work that surrenders to boredom, like slow cinema, *uniquely* counts as existentially deeper than most arthouse films, which may aim at higher aesthetic values and more intense satisfactions, but which nonetheless appear as shallow in light of profound boredom. For, if boredom is an affect that can be measured on a scale of experiential depth and superficiality, it is also a measure of experiential depth itself, to which slow cinema alone conforms.

THE AESTHETICALLY HOPELESS

According to Becker:

> One shouldn't misunderstand Kant's thesis that the enjoyment of beauty is "without interest" in the sense that the aesthetic experience lacks any interest. Nothing is further from the truth. For the complete lack of interest only characterizes boredom, which is, even more than the ugly, the actual counter-pole to beauty. It is, so to say, the aesthetically hopeless, as it is further away from beauty than the ugly, which is sometimes "interesting."[20]

In Becker's view, a true aesthetic experience both stimulates interest and breaks it. Therein it delineates itself from the gripping, thrilling, and engrossing productions of popular entertainment. Following this criterion, one could have made the case for accepting as "true art" various films that systematically tamper with the viewers' interest and hinder its immediate gratification, while still captivating their attention. In contrast to such an endeavor, I have here focused on slow cinema primarily because it explores the opposite end of this spectrum. In overtly embracing the "aesthetically hopeless," slow cinema does not merely illustrate one particular aesthetics of film but instead addresses a limit phenomenon of the aesthetic in general, shedding new light upon it. By playing upon profound boredom, slow cinema proves interesting not least in that it no longer allows the viewer to distinguish between the boredom induced by the diegesis as a mere aesthetic mood, a "fictional emotion" that can be appreciated aesthetically, and the real emotion experienced in the film theater, which undercuts aesthetic appreciation in ultimately also finding the film itself boring.[21]

NOTES

1. Christian Ferencz-Flatz, "Film in der frühen Phänomenologie," *Zeitschrift für Ästhetik und allgemeine Kunstwissenschaft* 61, no. 1 (2016): 119-136.
2. Moritz Geiger, "Oberflächen- und Tiefenwirkungen der Kunst," in *Proceedings of the Sixth International Congress of Philosophy*, ed. Edgar S. Brightman (Cambridge, MA: Harvard University Press, 1927), 462-468, at 463f.
3. Geiger, "Oberflächen- und Tiefenwirkungen," 465.
4. Moritz Geiger, "Beiträge zu einer Phänomenologie des ästhetischen Genusses," *Jahrbuch für Philosophie und phänomenologische Forschung* 1 (1913): 567-684, at 627.
5. Oskar Becker, "Von der Hinfälligkeit des Schönen und die Abenteuerlichkeit des Künstlers," *Jahrbuch für Philosophie und phänomenologische Forschung,* Ergänzungsband (1929): 27-52, at 33.
6. Max Scheler, *Formalism in Ethics and Non-Formal Ethics of Value: A New Attempt Toward the Foundation of an Ethical Personalism,* trans. Manfred Frings and Roger Funk (Evanston, IL: Northwestern University Press, 1973), 96f.
7. Geiger, "Beiträge," 623.
8. Siegfried Kracauer, "Cult of Distraction: On Berlin's Picture Palaces," in *The Mass Ornament: Weimar Essays* (Cambridge, MA: Harvard University Press, 1995), 323-328, at 326.
9. See Walter Benjamin, "On Some Motifs in Baudelaire," in *Illuminations,* ed. Hannah Arendt, trans. Harry Zorn (New York: Schocken, 1968), 155-200, at 160f.
10. Walter Benjamin, "The Work of Art in the Age of Mechanical Reproduction," in *Illuminations,* 217-252, at 240.
11. Martin Heidegger, *The Fundamental Concepts of Metaphysics: World, Finitude, Solitude,* trans. William McNeil and Nicholas Walker (Bloomington: Indiana University Press, 1995), 78f.

12. Heidegger, *Fundamental Concepts*, 127f.

13. Richard Misek, "Dead Time: Cinema, Heidegger, and Boredom," *Continuum: Journal of Media and Cultural Studies* 24, no. 5 (2010): 777–785; and Chiara Quaranta, "A Cinema of Boredom: Heidegger, Cinematic Time and Spectatorship," *Film-Philosophy* 24, no. 1 (2020): 1–21.

14. Heidegger, *Fundamental Concepts*, 156.

15. Heidegger, *Fundamental Concepts*, 157.

16. Heidegger, *Fundamental Concepts*, 105.

17. Heidegger, *Fundamental Concepts*, 82.

18. Julian Hanich, "When Viewers Drift Off: A Brief Phenomenology of Cinematic Daydreaming," in *The Structures of the Film Experience by Jean-Pierre Meunier: Historical Assessments and Phenomenological Expansions*, ed. Julian Hanich and Daniel Fairfax (Amsterdam: Amsterdam University Press, 2019), 336–352.

19. Heidegger, *Fundamental Concepts*, 138f.

20. Becker, "Von der Hinfälligkeit des Schönen," 33 (translation mine).

21. This work was supported by a grant of the Ministry of Research, Innovation and Digitization, CNCS/CCCDI—UEFISCDI, project number PN-III-P4-ID-PCE-2020-0791, within PNCDI III.

14

... Striking Beauty

On Recuperating the Beautiful in Cinema

JULIAN HANICH

But what precisely is wrong with creating a place of beauty in a bad world?
—Arthur C. Danto

AN OBSERVATION

Film is a beautiful art. It is far from the only beautiful art, and it is certainly not always beautiful. But sometimes it is also full of beauty. Let me underline this: while clearly a form of entertainment, a dream factory, a tool for moral or political interventions, the cinema also enables experiences of striking beauty.[1]

Viewers may feel enraptured by the *beauty of nature* in Terrence Malick's *Days of Heaven* (1978) or Jane Campion's *The Piano* (1993). They might be enchanted by the *artistic beauty* of the skillful lighting in Victor Erice's *The Spirit of the Beehive/El espíritu de la colmena* (1973), the splendid animation of *Spirited Away/Sen to Chihiro no Kamikakushi* (2002, dir. Hayao Miyazaki), or the elegant staging of two motorboats gliding smoothly through the night in Michael Mann's *Miami Vice* (2006). Not least, spectators may hold their breath when confronted with the *physical beauty* of Gong Li or Alain Delon, Audrey Hepburn or Denzel Washington, Adèle Haenel, Rock Hudson, or Elliott Page.[2]

Since we can best approach knowing what beauty is by evoking it elaborately, let me craft a few ekphrastic lines about an encounter that left me speechless with its visual and acoustic splendor. The instance occurs in the fifth of the five remarkable scenes that constitute the 74

FIGURE 15. Nie Yinniang (Shu Qi) prepares for a martial-arts fight in a birch-tree forest in Hou Hsiao-hsien's *The Assassin* (2015).

minutes of Abbas Kiarostami's *Five Dedicated to Ozu* (2003). Not only because of its darkness and its intricate soundscape does this scene stand in stark contrast to the previous four episodes. While the screen remains black at first, we hear dogs bark, crickets chirp, frogs croak cacophonically. Slowly, a white spot appears. It turns out to be the reflection of the moon on a pitch-black pond at night. The ripples of the water, caused by delicate winds, transform the mirror image into protean shapes of white. We witness the treatment of an arch-Romantic motif (the moon at night), but also a study in chiaroscuro, reminiscent of the early experiments by Walter Ruttmann, and a playful toying with our imagination of the unshown and unseen. Occasionally, we hear distant thunder rumble. And at one point the rain sets in. A series of lightning bolts, like flashes of a photo camera, illuminates the drizzling rainfall in the night. As in a flicker film, for split seconds the flashes reveal nothing less than a Jackson Pollock–like action painting snatched from nature. This is the beautiful magic of this film shot on digital video: it allows you to see paintings in motion, from Edward Hopper, Gerhard Richter, and Mark Rothko to J. M. W. Turner and Claude Monet, and at the same time makes the temporality of film a central concern. Later, the rain stops and the moon becomes visible again, this time surrounded and sometimes occluded by clouds in various shades of gray. Duck-rabbit–like, the images allow us to switch focus from the surface of the pond with its ripples and raindrops to the reflection of the celestial drama. At the end, and rounding off these splendid 27 minutes, a cock crows and a new day dawns. Birds start singing. Colors emerge. Light is born out of darkness on that peaceful pond.

A scene like this, I would claim, allows for a pleasurable *contemplation* of its beautiful cinematic appearance and at the same time sends out an existential *invitation* to inhabit its beautiful world. No doubt, then, beauty is a valuable experience of the cinema. And yet, in a way, it isn't.

AN OBJECTION

The history of thinking about film has been a story of growing suspicion toward the beautiful as an aesthetic category. Here, film critics and scholars have merely followed what has been called the "flight from beauty" (Roger Scruton) in the arts during the twentieth century more generally.[3] And it certainly doesn't help that beauty—or some perverted version of it—has migrated into the domains of commercials and advertisements, the fashion industry, industrial design, the beautification complex, and political propaganda.

To be sure, we can find occasional attempts in early and classical film theory to make room for the beautiful—there are traces in the writings of Georg Lukács, Hugo Münsterberg, Louis Delluc, Victor Oscar Freeburg, Jean Epstein, Germaine Dulac, Béla Balázs, and others.[4] Yet, from the 1930s onward, this changed drastically, despite scattered references in the writings of André Bazin, Éric Rohmer, and some avant-gardists like Jonas Mekas. The trend culminated in an outright antipathy towards the beautiful in political modernism, counter-cinema, and the avant-garde of the 1970s. Exemplary in this respect are two key texts of film studies. In her manifesto, "Visual Pleasure and Narrative Cinema," Laura Mulvey writes unambiguously: "It is said that analyzing pleasure, or beauty, destroys it. That is the intention of this article."[5] Likewise, it is obvious where Tom Gunning's sympathies lie when he writes in his much-cited essay "An Aesthetic of Astonishment: Early Film and the (In)Credulous Spectator" that "The aesthetic of attractions developed in fairly conscious opposition to an orthodox identification of viewing pleasure with the contemplation of beauty."[6] We also encounter a rejection of beauty in by-now canonical manifestos, such as Glauber Rocha's "An Aesthetics of Hunger" or Hito Steyerl's "In Defense of the Poor Image," and in many other texts as well. (James S. Williams even speaks of a "profound mistrust," even a "prohibition of beauty," in much postcolonial African cinema.)[7]

Don't get me wrong: I do not at all question the importance of these interventions in favor of a politically and socially engaged aesthetics—and consequently I do not intend to sound provocative or polemical. As beauty has not been an aesthetic category with any cachet in academic film studies and criticism, however, my aim is simply to create more awareness for the beautiful *in* film and the beauty *of* film as form. While in philosophy, aesthetics, and, to some degree, art history we have seen a renewed interest in the beautiful over the last two decades, and while Black authors from Toni Morrison and Achille Mbembe to Zadie Smith, Saidiya Hartman, and Christina Sharpe have found beauty a topic ready to rediscover, I cannot see the contours of a profound, let alone sustained, discussion of cinema's beauty in our discipline. As a matter of fact, the quantity of moments of filmic beauty is in *inverse proportion* to the quality of the theoretical interest in it. Doesn't Rohmer's observation, from as early as 1961, still hold true? "My colleagues at the daily or weekly papers, collaborators or not, friends or not of *Cahiers*, will ... not be shocked, I hope, if I am surprised to see them, especially lately, say little about the very notion of *beauty* in their criticism."[8]

I would venture to say that we have arrived at a point where—at the very least among cinephiles and art connoisseurs—*experiencing* a film as beautiful and uttering a *judgment* of beauty are both fraught with embarrassment. While critics are not shy to admit their veneration of F. W. Murnau's *Tabu* (1931) or Malick's *The New World* (2005), I cannot refute the sense that, for them, it's mixed with a drop of shame, as if they found it beautiful almost against their will and couldn't help thinking: "How can I admire a film that revels so naïvely in the beauty of nature and unabashedly glorifies the beauty of the human body?'"[9] Moreover, I am never really sure if it *really* goes without saying that the admiration for a film like Jean-Luc Godard's *Contempt/Le Mépris* (1963) *also* derives from the sheer beauty of some of its sun-flooded Mediterranean images, its strikingly beautiful male and female stars, and the beautifully sad music of Georges Delerue.

That's why films often have to be more than "merely" beautiful. We find this rhetoric of justification, to cite just one random example, in Geoff Andrew's remarks about *Five Dedicated to Ozu:* "[The film] is *also* a sublimely beautiful response to the natural world, taking its place alongside [Kiarostami's] earlier rural road-movies. But there's *more to it* than that. First, despite the lack of a story, the [five] films are *far more than just* pretty pictures."[10] For hundreds of years, beauty was art's ultimate goal. Today, beauty, if tolerated at all, is no longer enough.

At the very least, then, we should reclaim a sense of ease when asserting the beauty of cinema. For those who feel left alone, in the harsh winds of our contemporary anti-beauty climate, we need to build shelters. As the philosopher John Armstrong puts it, "We love the things we find beautiful but we are inarticulate when we try to communicate this love. This is a pity; and not only because we wish to let others know about the things we most like."[11] When it comes to films this seems all the more true: critics and scholars lack an articulate vocabulary and useful concepts, not least because we don't have a proper tradition in film aesthetics that has taught us to converse about the beautiful in film. In a way, we have to *learn* the language of beauty—maybe again, maybe for the first time. For one, we might usefully distinguish the beauty *in* film from the beauty *of* film: between the beautiful objects the film depicts and the beauty of the film's depicting, between *what* type of beauty is shown and *how* beauty is presented. Obviously, a film can show us a myriad of beautiful objects and events: beautiful people; beautiful landscapes; beautiful cities, neighborhoods, and buildings; beautiful dances and other forms of movements; and even beautiful acts of moral goodness. But films can also give us access to less-than-beautiful objects and events *in a beautiful way*. Thus, films can make us encounter beautiful things and they can show us things beautifully. (And, of course, they can also do both.)

Equally important seems to be a change of perspective toward beauty. With Richard Neer we can describe the task of the critic in Wittgenstein's terms: good critics are able to afford their readers what the Austrian philosopher called the *dawning* of an aspect, when all of a sudden we see another aspect of the same thing or when we see the same thing differently.[12] Recognition of beauty would involve seeing a film *as beautiful*—and not focusing on something else. Although film's beauty is so often right there, critics often don't grasp it because they look for—and hence *see*—something else. They are busy interpreting the meaning of a film, uncovering its ideology, or pointing out problems of representation, so that they remain untouched by its beauty. This sort of complaint is nothing new: Susan Sontag, David Bordwell, Hans Ulrich Gumbrecht, Rita Felski, and many others have launched critiques of the neglect of style, form, presence, and pleasure in art.[13] Yet, I fear, we have to add a lament about the disregard of beauty as well.

But are the tides perhaps already turning? We have witnessed the rise of slow cinema, which admits the very contemplation many consider essential for the experience of beauty; we encounter a widespread admiration of filmmakers such as Malick, Hou Hsiao-hsien, Todd Haynes, and Wong Kar-wai, whose works are often suffused with beauty; we find in film studies a renewed interest in both philosophical aesthetics and form; and isn't there, more concretely, a promising focus among film scholars on new aesthetic categories like the pretty, the precious, the cute, the wondrous, and the eerie, but also older categories such as the sublime and the ugly?[14]

AN ORIENTATION

Calling a film "beautiful'—exclaiming "Oh, that's such a beautiful film"—is something people do in everyday conversations, but what they mean is often different from what the *aesthetic category* of the beautiful comprises. Of course, what *that* implies has been a matter of some dispute for the last, say, two and a half thousand years. It goes without saying that I cannot provide a proper description of the experience of beauty in the scarce space at my disposal—this will have to wait for another occasion.[15] To arrive at a useful circumscription of beauty's terrain one would have to first fence it off from other aesthetic and emotion categories—be they *neighboring* categories (such as the pretty, kitsch, sublime, awe, fascination, wonder, to be moved) or *opposing* categories (like the ugly, grotesque, boring, excess). Moreover, with Jerrold Levinson I am convinced that the experience of beauty is not one but comes in different types.[16]

Yet, for a start, I want to suggest that experiences of beauty can have different inflections. As in my Kiarostami example above, they can lean toward a pleasurable *contemplation* of beautiful objects or events and bend toward an existential *invitation* to a beautiful world. This would make room for the intuition that a film's beauty can fully absorb us in the here and now, but it can also point us beyond itself and invite us to apprehend glimpses of a different and better life.[17]

The contemplative experience of beauty derives from and is tied up with the Kantian-Schopenhauerian tradition: when we experience something as beautiful we contemplate it without practical interests and desires, without thinking about its ulterior purposes—we are simply riveted by and devoted to the object in pure perception right now. When we perceive, say, beautiful nature in film in a contemplative mode, we concentrate on its myriad phenomenal ways of *appearing*—and nothing else.[18] As such, contemplation focuses on particulars, not generalities. It is always *this* individual natural object at *this* particular time in *this* specific appearance: how, in *Five Dedicated to Ozu, this* small white spot appears as the moon and reflects on *this* pitch-black pond; how the ripples of *this* water, caused by *these* delicate winds, play with the mirror images and shapeshift them; how *these* lightning bolts illuminate *this* drizzling rainfall in the night suddenly and wildly.

For Kant, beauty is famously characterized by a *dis*interested form of pleasure, which is—let's not repeat this oft-made mistake—entirely different from being *un*interested in and detached from the beautiful object: contemplating beauty can come with strong fascination and rapt attention. However, it is not haunted by any material, sexual, cognitive, or other kind of practical interest beyond our pleasurable perceptual interest in the here and now. As Elizabeth Prettejohn summarizes nicely, "we do not expect to gain anything from it—neither trivial gratification, nor the furtherance of our self-interest, nor even the satisfaction of having benefited other people or worthy causes."[19] In the contemplative mode our perception is free of values, passions, and desires—except for the momentary value of the beautiful, the passionate perceptual and bodily pleasure it brings, and the desire to continue savoring it. Importantly, this also implies that we do not search for meaning: the beautiful object is not regarded as a symbol or a sign that stands for something else.[20] The contemplative mode perceives the object as both senseless and eminently sensuous—which also implies that even though there is nothing to understand and interpret, there is a lot to *describe,* for ourselves and others. This does not mean that a hermeneutic mode is forever blocked. But in the contemplative mode, interpretations are temporarily suspended.

Some may call this *useless*, but others may underline the *freedom* that comes with beauty's riddance of all things practical and goal-oriented. In fact, the disinterestedness of the Kantian beauty is taken to an extreme by Schopenhauer, who considers the contemplation of beauty as a *liberation* from the struggles of the human will, an emancipation from the shackles of sexual lust and other bodily cravings.[21] Instead, beauty purges us of what otherwise might charm or tempt our will and thereby excite it by promising immediate satisfaction (hence beauty is a paradoxical immediate satisfaction *without* immediate satisfaction).

Many interpreters have taken Schopenhauer's anti-hedonist philosophy of beauty to reject pleasure and the body—and for good reason. But we don't have to follow Schopenhauer all the way into this bloodless territory. We can concede that experiencing beauty is calming, soothing, and pacifying, because we don't want anything from it other than contemplation, and we can still insist that this involves intense bodily pleasures. Confusing physiological arousal with intensity of experience would commit us to making a category mistake: every time I am watching Kenneth Anger's *Eaux d'artifice* (1953) I have a powerful pleasurable experience that is very intense, but with its soothing quality it does not arouse me physiologically—the only thing I want from the film is following its course.

And let's not forget that there is a long history of thinkers who believe that beauty can be tinged by pain—which has to do not least with its transient, ephemeral quality. Even though it's a deeply pleasurable experience, we know it won't last endlessly: it fades and perishes, often in no time. And isn't the temporal art form of film, which many commentators have described as unsuitable for contemplation, particularly relentless in this respect? Unlike architecture, painting, sculpture, or photography, film changes quickly and eats time insatiably. As Roland Barthes puts it, when watching a film "I am constrained to a continuous voracity."[22] It's true: a scene may blossom in full beauty for a moment—and has already withered in the next instant as the filmmakers decided to take it away from us. This transient quality may make you want to implore the *moment,* like Goethe's Faust, with a phrase every German high school student has memorized by heart: "Stay a while! You are so beautiful!" But, and here's the upside, film's forward flow is also full of promises: we never know when beauty might strike again. It can emerge, even erupt at any time.[23]

Now, next to this pleasurable *contemplation* of beauty, the beautiful can also be experienced as an existential *invitation* to catch glimpses of a different and better life. Here beauty, as a "promise of happiness" (Stendhal), augurs new joys: we apprehend the qualities of beautiful nature, architecture, design, human beings—simply the world as a whole in all its manifestations—as existential invitations to partake in their splendor. Experiencing something as beautiful thus not only implies a savoring of its appearances, as in the contemplative mode, but also a utopian desire to *be* there and *inhabit* that world.[24] We do not so much contemplate what *is appearing;* instead, beauty's invitation to happiness could be called a *pre-appearing.*

Seen from this perspective, beauty is the opposite of ugliness. In ugly nature, for instance, characteristics like hardship, despair, loneliness, emptiness, and senselessness prevail—it is excluding and repellent.[25] Whoever has been confronted with the hardships some human beings have to go through in Michael Glawogger's powerful documentary *Workingman's Death* (2005) may have an inkling of what an ugly life may be like; whoever has gone through the despair and loneliness in Lukas Moodysson's *Lilya 4-Ever* (2002), a harrowing portrait of post-Soviet malaise, knows what the term "ugliness" is meant to express. The beautiful, instead, is inviting and inclusive. The remote Swedish landscapes in Bo Widerberg's *Elvira Madigan* (1967) have this welcoming character to me: my Romantic self feels as if it wanted to be there and to live a decelerated life far away from the stressful city. In turn, my modern self feels enchanted by the splendid Roman apartments and villas in Paolo Sorrentino's *La Grande Bellezza*: set next to the Colosseum and enveloped by the pleasant warmth of Italian summer nights, they create a yearning for being a flaneur like Jep Gambardella (Toni Servillo) in a stressful city that is at the same time so beautiful.

John Armstrong, therefore, calls beauty a "happy apprehension of how life should be": "it puts us in touch with an aspect of ourselves that we value highly (our 'true home'), an aspect of existence in which, for a while, we feel that we are what we should be. An order of value is made apparent to us."[26] But here, again, we can immediately sense the potentially painful side of beauty, which makes it anything but perfect: "It's the impossibility of having a beautiful life that gives artistic beauty its particular impact and poignancy."[27] Thus, the pain in existentially inviting beauty has a different quality: it derives from an evocation of the good life that may remain forever unfulfilled.[28] In beauty, happiness is present *as a promise*, but, as a promise, it is also not yet here. That makes beauty so fascinating: it is a temporary antidote to a lack—but as an antidote it can make this lack itself tangible.

AN OBLIGATION

In her moving memoir "Beauty Is a Method," Christina Sharpe writes about her mother's insistence on beauty as an act of resistance against the ugliness of poverty and the violence against Black people she grew up with: "What is beauty made of? Attentiveness whenever possible to a kind of aesthetic that escaped violence whenever possible."[29] We can read her essay as an attempt to overcome the confines of a bleak world by admitting beauty in it: the beautiful allows us to break out and, as she puts it, "make new worlds." To emphasize this point, Sharpe uses a quote from Saidiya Hartman, in which the African American historian claims that beauty is "not a luxury" but "a way of creating possibility in the space of enclosure, . . . a transfiguration of the given." Without this transformative power of the beautiful, which takes us back to its utopian and compensating character, we would give up on a fundamentally human value. I hope it doesn't sound callous, even flippant if I draw on writers who, as Black women, articulate their thoughts on beauty from a positionality different than mine. I cite them to underline that experiencing beauty is a necessity in all corners of life, and restricting the beautiful to a "Western" or "bourgeois" worldview would be as patronizing as it would be empirically shortsighted. Beauty is a practice, Sharpe argues, that one needs to *do*. Beauty is also a value, I contend, that one needs to *admit*. In the cinema, just as much as everywhere else.

NOTES

Epigraph: Arthur C. Danto, *The Abuse of Beauty: Aesthetics and the Concept of Art* (Chicago: Open Court, 2003), 115.

1. For me, the moment of epiphany, when I began to be fully taken in by cinema's beauty, must have been the premiere of Terrence Malick's *The Thin Red Line* at the Berlin Film Festival in 1998. The celebrated return of Malick, whose oeuvre is easily the single most important interrogation of the beautiful in film, got me increasingly absorbed in a subsequent series of films that all either investigate or celebrate beauty in film, or often both. Here I am thinking of *American Beauty* (1999, dir. Sam Mendes), *In the Mood for Love* (2000, dir. Wong Kar-wai), *Crouching Tiger, Hidden Dragon* (2000, dir. Ang Lee), *Far From Heaven* (2002, dir. Todd Haynes), *Ferien* (2007, dir. Thomas Arslan), *A Single Man* (2009, dir. Tom Ford), *Uncle Boonmee Who Can Recall His Past Lives/Lung Boonmee raluek chat* (2010, dir. Apichatpong Weerasethakul), *Melancholia* (2011, dir. Lars von Trier), *Stranger by the Lake/L'Inconnu du lac* (2013, dir. Alain Guiraudie), *La Grande Bellezza* (2013, dir. Paolo Sorrentino), *Clouds of Sils-Maria* (2014, dir. Olivier Assayas), *Journey to the West/Xi You* (2014, dir. Tsai Ming-Liang), *The Assassin/Cìkè Niè Yinniáng* (2015, dir. Hou Hsiao-Hsien), *Moonlight* (2016, dir. Barry Jenkins), *Call Me by Your Name* (2017, dir. Luca Guadagnino), and *Portrait of a Lady on Fire/Portrait de la jeune fille en feu* (2019, dir. Céline Sciamma), to name but a few obvious ones.

2. My examples will inevitably raise eyebrows among readers whose senses and sensibilities are different from mine. Obviously, they are not a plea for universal acceptance or even a dictate that expects meek, uniform agreement. Rather, I hope they invite readers to find examples that match their own tastes more adequately.

3. Roger Scruton, *Beauty: A Very Brief Introduction* (Oxford: Oxford University Press, 2011), 144.

4. For a helpful overview, see Laura Marcus, "'A New Form of True Beauty': Aesthetics and Early Film Criticism," *Modernism/modernity* 13, no. 2 (2006): 267–289.

5. Laura Mulvey, "Visual Pleasure and Narrative Cinema," in *Visual and Other Pleasures* (Bloomington: Indiana University Press, 1989), 14–26, at 16.

6. Tom Gunning, "An Aesthetic of Astonishment: Early Film and the (In)Credulous Spectator," in *Viewing Positions: Ways of Seeing Film,* ed. Linda Williams (New Brunswick, NJ: Rutgers University Press, 1994), 114–133, at 124.

7. Glauber Rocha, "An Aesthetics of Hunger (1965)," in *On Cinema,* ed. Lucía Nagib, Ismail Xavier, Charlotte Smith, Stephanie Dennison, and Cecília Mello (London: I. B. Tauris, 2018), 41–45; Hito Steyerl, "In Defense of the Poor Image," *e-flux* 10 (2009), https://www.e-flux.com/journal/10/61362/in-defense-of-the-poor-image/. Accessed August 12, 2021; and James S. Williams, *Ethics and Aesthetics in Contemporary African Cinema: The Politics of Beauty* (London: Bloomsbury, 2019), pp. 8 and 3.

8. Éric Rohmer, "The Taste for Beauty," in *The Taste for Beauty,* trans. Carol Volk (Cambridge: Cambridge University Press, 1989), 70–80, at 70 (original emphasis).

9. For a nicely written account of a critic's struggle to admit the beauty of Malick's film, see Mark Cousins, "Praising *The New World,*" in *The Cinema of Terrence Malick: Poetic Visions of America,* ed. Hannah Patterson, 2nd ed. (London: Wallflower, 2007), 192–198.

10. Quoted from the BFI DVD booklet, 6 (emphasis added).

11. John Armstrong, *The Secret Power of Beauty: Why Happiness is in the Eye of the Beholder* (London: Penguin, 2004), 4.

12. Richard Neer, "Connoisseurship and the Stakes of Style," *Critical Inquiry* 32, no. 1 (2005): 1–26, at 16–18.

13. Susan Sontag, "Against Interpretation," in *Against Interpretation and Other Essays* (New York: Farrar, Straus, and Giroux, 1966 [1964]), 3–14; David Bordwell, *Making Meaning: Inference and Rhetoric in the Interpretation of Cinema* (Cambridge, MA: Harvard University Press, 1989); Hans Ulrich Gumbrecht, *Production of Presence: What Meaning Cannot Convey* (Stanford, CA: Stanford University Press, 2004); and Rita Felski, *The Limits of Critique* (Chicago: University of Chicago Press, 2015).

14. See, e.g., Rosalind Galt, *Pretty: Film and the Decorative Image* (New York: Columbia University Press, 2011); Lutz P. Koepnick, *The Long Take: Art Cinema and the Wondrous* (Minneapolis: University of Minnesota Press, 2017); Mark Fisher, *The Weird and the Eerie* (London: Repeater Books, 2016); and Nathan Carroll, ed., *The Cinematic Sublime: Negative Pleasures, Structuring Absences* (Bristol: Intellect, 2020). On wonder, see also the contributions of Catherine Wheatley and Jaimie Baron in this volume.

15. As will become clear, however, I am interested in a phenomenology-inflected understanding of beauty with an emphasis on the *viewer's experience*. For helpful overviews of various conceptions of beauty, see, e.g., Umberto Eco,

On Beauty: A History of a Western Idea, trans. Alastair McEwen (London: MacLehose Press, 2010 [2004]); and Crispin Sartwell, "Beauty," in *Stanford Encyclopedia of Philosophy*, ed. Edward N. Zalta (Winter 2017), https://plato.stanford.edu/archives/win2017/entries/beauty/. Accessed October 26, 2021.

16. Jerrold Levinson, "Beauty is Not One: The Irreducible Variety of Visual Beauty," in *The Aesthetic Mind: Philosophy and Psychology*, ed. Elisabeth Schellekens and Peter Goldie (Oxford: Oxford University Press, 2011), 190–207. Levinson proposes seven types of beauty: abstract, artifactual, artistic, natural, physical, moral, and accidental-everyday beauty.

17. This distinction is indebted to the work of two preeminent contemporary German philosophers of aesthetics: Martin Seel's *Eine Ästhetik der Natur* (Frankfurt am Main: Suhrkamp, 1991) and Christoph Menke's *Die Kraft der Kunst* (Berlin: Suhrkamp, 2013).

18. Seel, *Ästhetik der Natur*, 38ff.

19. Elizabeth Prettejohn, *Beauty and Art: 1750–2000* (Oxford: Oxford University Press, 2005), 43.

20. Seel, *Ästhetik der Natur*, 39.

21. Arthur Schopenhauer, *The World as Will and Presentation*, trans. Richard E. Aquila, vol. 1 (London: Routledge, 2016 [1819/44]).

22. Roland Barthes, *Camera Lucida: Reflections on Photography*, trans. Richard Howard (New York: Hill and Wang, 1981), 55.

23. Not least, watching a film on a laptop or Blu-ray player allows us to jump back and revisit what strikes us as particularly beautiful.

24. Seel, *Ästhetik der Natur*, 90.

25. Seel, *Ästhetik der Natur*, 94.

26. Armstrong, *Secret Power of Beauty*, 74.

27. Armstrong, *Secret Power of Beauty*, 85.

28. See also Theodor W. Adorno, *Aesthetic Theory*, trans. Robert Hullot-Kentor (London: Continuum, 1997), 82.

29. Christina Sharpe, "Beauty Is a Method," *e-flux* 105 (2019), https://www.e-flux.com/journal/105/303916/beauty-is-a-method. Accessed August 12, 2021.

PART FOUR

Reviving Goods

15

... Wondering Offscreen

*On Cinema's Transformations of
Our Relation to the Unseen*

JAIMIE BARON

I have a terrible memory for most films. Many I have forgotten almost as soon as the credits scroll by. For instance, I have seen most of the major superhero films, but I doubt I could recount the plots if my life were at stake. This is not to say I did not enjoy them; my brain simply discarded them as soon as their narratives were resolved. I am in my forties, so perhaps my brain is just full; my memory certainly is not what it used to be. Yet, I do not believe that is the only reason I fail to remember most films. Frequently, films give me the feeling I have already seen them even when I know I have not. This may be a consequence of the narrative predictability of many genre films; it may also be the difficulty of producing an audiovisual experience that is truly novel and therefore—at least for less impressionable viewers like me—memorable. I find photographs much easier to remember than moving images. The very fact that they do not move seems to make it possible for my mind to retain them. The experience of time and movement onscreen is rarely something I can replicate with my mind's eye. I remember many movies as stilled fragments rather than dynamic continuities. There are, however, exceptions: cinematic moments that are so remarkable that they persist in my memory as flow rather than arrest. I believe the memorability of certain film moments may have as much, if not more, to do with what is unseen than what actually appears onscreen. Here, I would like to consider what this has to do with the experience of wonder.

FIGURE 16. The disappearance of Josie (Tessa Thompson) in *Annihilation* (2018, Alex Garland).

The film and cultural theorist Siegfried Kracauer's account of his earliest experience of cinema gestures toward a relationship between cinematic memorability and what lies offscreen. At the end of the preface to his foundational *Theory of Film,* he recounts his very first cinematic encounter, which spurred him to write an essay titled "Film as the Discoverer of the Marvels of Everyday Life." He writes:

> And I remember, as if it were today, the marvels themselves. What thrilled me so deeply was an ordinary suburban street, filled with lights and shadows which transfigured it. Several trees stood about, and there was in the foreground a puddle reflecting invisible house facades and a piece of the sky. Then a breeze moved the shadows, and the facades with the sky below began to waver. The trembling upper world in the dirty puddle—this image has never left me.[1]

Kracauer's sense of marvel and thrill are, here, enabled by the seemingly simple act of pointing the camera at a puddle and allowing film and nature to transfigure the reflection of the offscreen "upper world" into an image that is for him, precisely, unforgettable.

This description speaks, in part, to the mnemonic power of the film frame and screen themselves. In an essay concerning memorability and film, Edward Casey puts forth two "preliminary conditions of the particular memorability of filmic images."[2] The first, he suggests, has to do with the isolation of the film screen in a darkened theater from its surroundings, the decontextualization of the image. "This is a decontextualization which permits the screen to stand out from its immediate environs: to become an entity in its own right, to be focused on for its own sake, and thus remembered as a thing framed in itself and by itself."[3]

By eliminating peripheral distractions, the cinematic screen becomes the site of intensified focus, which thereby enhances the potential memorability of its content. Kracauer refers to the way in which the lights and shadows transfigured an "ordinary suburban street," suggesting that in daily life he might not have looked twice at this "ordinary" scene. Hence, he implies that it was the film frame—and the additional frame of the puddle—that focused his attention on this unremarkable street with its lights and shadows and reflections, transforming it into a "marvel." This makes intuitive sense. So much of our daily perception is limited to those things that are necessary to accomplish our goals that only rarely do we really look at any one object for more than a few seconds at a time. Our eyes are constantly darting about, seeking new information. In the dark of a theater, we are suddenly given opportunity and permission to simply *look*, rather than look *for*. Casey notes, however, that not *all* films or film images are memorable, and suggests that a second condition of cinematic memorability is "surprise or the unexpected." He argues that the films we forget "fail to provide the unforeseen, the irregularities which offer points of attachment for subsequent remembering."[4] What is surprising and unexpected emerges, in Kracauer's description, primarily through duration. As the breeze moved the shadows in the puddle, the house facades and the sky below them began to waver. His attention gathered by the film frame, he was able to marvel at the mimetic and transformative capacities of a puddle.

WONDROUS TIME

Also striking to me, however, is that what Kracauer retained most clearly was something that did not actually appear onscreen. Rather, it was the reflected image of objects beyond the edges of the frame that stayed in his mind. In a related fashion, I sometimes "remember" not what I see onscreen but a cinematic moment or event that is temporally elided. There have been numerous instances when I am sure I remember seeing a certain image in a film that, upon watching it again, I find absent. Julian Hanich has written elegantly about various ways in which a film viewer can be encouraged to "perceive" and "remember" a film image (or sound) that was, in fact, omitted. He writes, "A conspicuous elision and a filmic evocation simultaneously set in motion the viewer's *sensual imagining* of the visual or aural kind. Their imagining fills in and enriches what the film's visuals or its soundtrack both conceal and allude to at the same time."[5]

I often—unwittingly—participate in such sensual imagining in my memories of films. For instance, in preparing to write this essay, I found myself dwelling on an image I remembered from *Annihilation* (2018, dir. Alex Garland). Based on a science fiction novel by Jeff VanderMeer, the film concerns an area in the US Pacific Northwest that has been engulfed in a "shimmer," which numerous investigators have entered and from which they have failed to return. A group of five female soldiers and scientists, including Lena (Natalie Portman), a cellular biology professor, and Josie (Tessa Thompson), a physicist, and led by Dr. Ventress (Jennifer Jason Leigh), go into the "shimmer" to try to learn more. Within this space, they find that all matter is being refracted and recombined, including the DNA of the animals and plants they encounter. Soon after, the characters' own DNA begins to mutate and their bodies to transform accordingly. The film as a whole is strikingly beautiful. Computer-generated images of hybrid plants and animals with unexpected forms, vibrant color combinations, and startling movements abound, producing a sense of a tangible yet alien world.

Yet, one image in particular haunted my memory. Nearing the end of film, after three of the five women have died or disappeared, Lena and Josie encounter a group of flowering trees that have taken on the approximate form of human bodies. Having recognized that her own DNA is in the process of being transfigured, Josie looks down at the stems starting to emerge from her wrists before she stands up and wanders away from Lena. She turns back to Lena in medium long shot to say, "Ventress wants to face it. You want to fight it. But I don't think I want either of those things." She walks away from the camera and from Lena, who stands up to follow her. The camera tracks smoothly forward as Josie walks farther away, then cuts to Lena rushing after her. Next, the camera cuts to a close-up of purple and white flowers, and in the background we see a pair of legs disappear behind another group of lush trees. In my memory, I watched Josie's arms sprout tendrils and flowers, her body transforming into a blossoming tree—like Daphne becoming a laurel to escape the advances of the god Apollo. When I watched the film again, however, I found that this image of transformation is, in fact, implied in the film but visually elided. Continuing to pursue Josie through the trees, Lena emerges in a field full of flowering humanoid trees, standing around like lost souls, but none of them is identifiable as Josie. Indeed, we never see Josie again in the film. Given that we do not actually witness Josie's transformation, it appears that my mind filled in the gap created by the ellipsis, and it is my own mental image I "remembered."

Beyond the particularly evocative way in which this ellipsis is structured, I would suggest that another part of what made me mentally produce this image is the lack of resolution of Josie's narrative. We do not, in fact, ever see or find out what happened to Josie; we never find out what she wanted or whether she attained it. Perhaps she became a tree or perhaps she continued to wander through the "shimmer" in some other form; the film refuses to offer certainty one way or the other. This lack of certainty—and perhaps the urge to resolve it—also seems to me to be linked to both memorability and the wondrous. In her book *Reclaiming Wonder*, which traces the idea of wonder throughout the history of Western philosophy, Genevieve Lloyd notes that wonder itself is defined by its elusiveness. She writes, "Lacking any clear location, it sometimes seems to be grasped only in a sense of something that has gone missing."[6] That memorable yet missing image in *Annihilation* continues to evoke for me a sense of wonder even though I now know that it does not exist.

There are many other missing cinematic images in my (in)experience that perform this evocation of unforgettable wonder. For instance, the endings of films that I remember best are not those that concluded with a passionate kiss or a tragic death, but rather those that end in ambiguity. For instance, the image of the wobbling spinning top at the end of *Inception* (2010, dir. Christopher Nolan), whose continued spinning or falling is linked to whether what we are seeing onscreen is diegetically "real," is indelible to me—not only because it led the entire audience with which I watched the film to groan in frustration, but also because it denied epistemological stability even as the lights came up. Similarly, *Paradise Now* (2005, dir. Hany Abu-Assad) ends with a shot of would-be suicide bomber Said sitting on a crowded Israeli bus, the camera tracking slowly toward his face until we can see only his eyes; the film then cuts to a blank white screen accompanied by silence. After we watched the film together, my companion insisted that the bomber had blown himself up. I noted that it was a fiction and that all we had seen was a blank white screen, so that the question of whether he had blown himself up or not was undecidable. My friend had, nevertheless, conjured this event in her mind from the white screen. In each of these cases, the denial of closure inscribed a missing image (or at least a missing event) into memory.

In addition to their lack of closure, however, what links these film moments is their foregrounded offer of an opening into implied but unseen temporalities, timelines that we do not experience directly but which we may conjure in our imaginations. This opening, in fact, inheres in Christian Metz's definition of diegesis as "the sum of a film's denotation: the narration itself, but also the fictional space and time dimensions implied in and by the narrative, and consequently the characters, the landscapes, the events, and other narrative elements, insofar as they are considered in their denoted aspect."[7] This sense of implied diegetic time that extends beyond the film offers a sense of other possibilities, of other beings living in time that we do not share with them. The famous final shot of *The Graduate* (1967, dir. Mike Nichols) in which Benjamin (Dustin Hoffman) and Elaine (Katharine Ross), having fled Elaine's wedding to another man, are sitting in the back of a moving bus, is particularly evocative of an unknown future. Over the course of the long take, their expressions move from elation to uncertainty. This is not a cliffhanger, a "to be continued . . . " that sets up a coming sequel but, rather, suggests a future to which we will not be privy. I have often wondered what happened to Benjamin and Elaine, even though I know that nothing actually did.

WONDROUS SPACE

Whereas an ellipsis "cuts out" time, a long take seems to do the opposite. Yet, ellipsis and duration can have related effects in terms of their incitement to wonder. As we look in time, something inevitably changes, whether the change takes place on the actual screen or in our perceptions—or both. As Lutz Koepnick has argued, long takes "tap into the durational to make us probe different attentional economies as much as to clear the ground for the promise of the wondrous, the experience of something that defies expectation."[8] The longer we look, the more we experience change. Indeed, the duration of a shot is often key to its memorability. (Accordingly, the rapid-fire editing of superhero movies may be part of the reason I have such trouble retaining them in memory.) Of course, it would seem obvious that the longer we look at something, the more we will remember it, but I want to suggest that certain long takes may make us "remember" more than we actually see; they may evoke a spatial and social context that extends beyond the frame of the film.

Often, it is this implied context—which I have not actually seen—that I "remember" best, possibly because, through duration, it begins to bleed into my own. In her book *How to Do Nothing,* the artist and theorist Jenny O'Dell suggests the need for us to take back our attention from the media economy generated by digital technologies and social media platforms that produce endless content without context. In Kracauer's description, by isolating its content and focusing our attention, the film image reveals to us the marvelous, which has been until now latent, unremarked. By contrast, the digital decontextualization O'Dell describes is of a different order; social media offers a rapid stream of content in which each image appears to contain a complete meaning, sufficient in itself without reference beyond its frame, and it is then quickly succeeded by another piece of decontextualized "news." The very speed at which these nuggets of content pass allows them to bypass our attempts to contextualize and thereby begin to understand them in relation to anything else. At this rate, we not only cannot process *what* is missing, but we cease to be aware that anything *is* missing. In this attention economy, there is no space for wonder. O'Dell notes, "Context is what appears when you hold your attention open for long enough; the longer you hold it, the more context appears."[9] In other words, attentional duration and contextual understanding are linked. O'Dell also observes that seeking context requires a certain humility, because "to seek context is already to acknowledge that you don't have the whole story."[10] Wonder implies such epistemological humility.

This sense of a context or story that exceeds my actual audiovisual perception is often based, for me, not only in duration but also in stillness. Indeed, the most memorable long takes for me are not those famed mobile shots like the opening of *Touch of Evil* (1958, dir. Orson Welles). (Although I do remember that shot well, partly because I have seen and taught it many times, my reaction to that shot is one of admiration for the skill involved in its production rather than of wonder.) Instead, they are the static long takes that go on seemingly too long. During such takes, I find that the offscreen space and time of the diegesis becomes increasingly present, pressing up against the borders of the spatiotemporal frame, despite their invisibility. Of course, I know intellectually that what lies beyond the frame of a fiction film is a full crew working on set to create the illusion of the diegetic offscreen. Yet, for all that, it is this diegetic offscreen—which exists only or primarily in my imagination—that often I retain. And while the idea of the wondrous often has a positive connotation, it can also be the basis for a political or social awareness and critique. Lloyd notes:

> Reclaiming wonder can also mean something more directly political: a concern with strategies of resistance to the circulation of spurious certainties,

which would have us ignore the crucial space between "knowing" and "not-knowing"—the space where what Arendt called "engaged thinking" can occur.[11]

This tension between knowing and not-knowing is echoed in the tension between onscreen and offscreen space, particularly through the use of ambient sound that implies continuity between what we can and cannot see. Through cinematic duration, a space in which "spurious certainties" give way to "engaged thinking" may emerge.

The director Steve McQueen is known for his long takes, but one shot from his 2013 film *12 Years a Slave* has stayed with me though I have seen the film only once several years ago: a long shot of the main character Solomon Northrup (Chiwetel Ejiofor) alive, with his hands tied, dangling from a noose so that only the tips of his toes reach the ground. This shot, of him struggling to hold some of his body weight on his toes so that he will not strangle to death, goes on for what feels like several minutes. There is no dialogue, only the ambient sound of the plantation and of Northrup struggling to breathe. The content of the shot is, of course, horrifying. Watching and listening to a person try to keep himself from strangling to death by balancing on his toes solicits a visceral embodied response. Despite my intellectual awareness that actor Ejiofor's life was not in actual danger, I nevertheless become intensely aware of my own breathing and its vulnerability to obstruction. Had this shot lasted only a few seconds, it might have passed into the category of voyeuristic spectacle. All too often, the enslavement of Black people in the United States is rendered onscreen as a horror, but its very representation elicits a certain thrill, a pleasure in feeling appalled. This shot did something else. As I waited and waited for the shot to end, I became suddenly aware of the space beyond the frame, the expanse of the Southern states and the millions of enslaved people who were just outside of my vision. In other words, over the course of however long that shot actually lasted (and I have intentionally decided not to check), the embodied horror of American slavery became overwhelming and, frankly, real to me in a way that I had not experienced previously. The many books I had read and films I had seen on the subject of slavery had given me a (false) sense of "knowing" about it. In contrast, by making me look for "too long," *12 Years a Slave* intensified my awareness of all I did not know, cannot know, will never know, and yet must confront about this horrific period in history. By the end of the shot, my spurious certainties had been dislodged. Indeed, the shot had ceased to simply "represent" and instead became a kind of portal, albeit a portal through which I could not enter.

WONDERING ABOUT OTHERS

All of the films discussed above are fictional (or, in the case of *12 Years a Slave*, fictionalized), so the implied temporalities and spatialities do not overlap with the historical world that we as viewers share. However, wondrous time and space—the implied time and space that evoke a sense of wonder—are deeply relevant to our experience of the real. Writing during the Covid-19 pandemic, staying in my home nearly all the time, I often started to wonder whether the rest of the world, the rest of humanity, was still really there. My various screens offered audiovisual access to other times and spaces, but fiction and nonfiction began to feel equally virtual. I sometimes had to remind myself that approximately seven billion people were all out there—breathing in and out (or trying to), conducting their lives as best they could under the circumstances. This sense of the presence of others "offscreen" but living in time and space is linked to the difference between "story" and "plot." The time of the story by definition extends beyond the plot. It includes all that is implied by the plot but which is not actually visible or audible onscreen. The pandemic has made me wonder much more intensely about the "story" occurring beyond the plot of my own life, what is elided and offscreen in relation to my own experience. In other words, our experience of the actual world is not so different from that of a cinematic diegesis. Most of the rest of the universe outside my house during the pandemic was, for me, implied. Other lives and experiences are, likewise, diegetic but not presented to my direct perception.

One of the greatest tragedies—but also potentialities—of the pandemic has been its revelation of the ways in which people who live in a given situation are, broadly speaking, unable to take in the facts of others' situations. Many of the people who have plenty of food are only vaguely aware that other families are starving. Those who have heat in winter shrug when they find out that families not so far away are freezing to death in their homes. Those who have been vaccinated against the virus may forget how many people still have no idea if and when they may receive this precious commodity. If film is good for anything, I believe in its power to evoke others' contexts of experience, not simply through identification but through that sense of diegetic space and time extending beyond the frame. In his investigation of the offscreen, Eyal

Peretz describes "a new thinking that the modern work of art activates by creating frames that unframe, thereby letting the dimension of the pure call [which eliminates identity and belonging] resonate and become present in our life, allowing us to have something in common."[12] Whether fiction or nonfiction, film can activate this "pure call," leading us to seriously imagine times and spaces that we do not ourselves inhabit, but for which we, as human beings, have an ethical responsibility toward those who do. Film, with its ellipses and offscreen spaces, opens a passage to wonder, which can extend beyond the fictional realm to the real. And if wondering and caring are not precisely the same thing, they are not entirely separate either.

Returning to memory: Victor Burgin writes of his own cinematic memories as "sequence-images" that "present a configuration—'lexical, sporadic'—that is more 'object' than narrative." He continues:

> What distinguishes the elements of such a configuration from their evanescent neighbors is that they seem somehow more "brilliant." In a psychoanalytic perspective this suggests that they have been attracted into the orbit of unconscious signifiers, and that it is from the displaced affect associated with the latter that the former derive their intensity. Nevertheless, for all that unconscious fantasy may have a role in its production, the sequence-image as such is neither daydream nor delusion. It is a *fact*—a transitory state of percepts of a "present moment" seized in their association with past affects and meanings.[13]

This sense of being "seized" by the "brilliance" of a cinematic moment is, in my view, not simply about summoning associations to our own pasts. That I may come to "remember" a fragment of another's experience with an intensity similar to that with which I (re)experience my own is an opening to a potentially radical form of empathy.

The pandemic has revealed the very fundamental, microscopic, and biological ways in which we are linked to other people—and animals—that we may never actually see or touch. Thus, thinking about actual, noncinematic space as a diegetic space suggests not only the implied space of the rest of the world, but an implicating space—a space in which we are all implicated. The words "imply" and "implicate" both stem from the Latin *implicāre*, which means "to entangle, involve, connect closely."[14] As we conjure the wondrous temporalities and spatialities beyond what we actually encounter, we are entangled in them. We are implicated. Thus, the cinematic evocation of wonder is not merely an invitation to fantasy. Rather, it is what may allow us to care about that which remains—like Kracauer's "trembling upper world" reflected in the puddle—always beyond the borders of our existential frame.

NOTES

1. Siegfried Kracauer, *Theory of Film: The Redemption of Physical Reality* (Princeton: Princeton University Press, 1997), li.

2. Edward Casey, "The Memorability of the Filmic Image," *Quarterly Review of Film and Video* 6, no. 3 (1981): 241–263, at 255.

3. Casey, "Memorability of the Filmic Image," 255.

4. Casey, "Memorability of the Filmic Image," 256.

5. Julian Hanich, "Omission, Suggestion, Completion: Film and the Imagination of the Spectator," *Screening the Past* 43 (April 2018), http://www.screeningthepast.com/issue-43-dossier-materialising-absence-in-film-and-media/omission-suggestion-completion-film-and-the-imagination-of-the-spectator/. Accessed November 3, 2021.

6. Genevieve Lloyd, *Reclaiming Wonder: After the Sublime* (Edinburgh: Edinburgh University Press, 2018), 207.

7. Christian Metz, *Film Language: A Semiotics of the Cinema* (Chicago: University of Chicago Press, 1990), 98.

8. Lutz Koepnick, *The Long Take: Art Cinema and the Wondrous* (Minneapolis: University of Minnesota Press, 2017), 1.

9. Jenny O'Dell, *How to Do Nothing: Resisting the Attention Economy* (Brooklyn, NY: Melville House, 2019), 155.

10. O'Dell, *How to Do Nothing,* 155.

11. Lloyd, *Reclaiming Wonder,* 13.

12. Eyal Peretz, *The Off-Screen: An Investigation of the Cinematic Frame* (Stanford, CA: Stanford University Press, 2017), 13.

13. Victor Burgin, *The Remembered Film* (London: Reaktion Books, 2004), 21.

14. "implicate, v.," *OED Online* (Oxford: Oxford University Press, December 2020).

16

... Coming to Wonder

On Cinema's Renewal of Vision

CATHERINE WHEATLEY

> The world will never starve for want of wonders; but only for want of wonder.
> —G. K. Chesterton

This essay begins with a mistake.

Or perhaps: it begins with a misreading.

Or perhaps: it begins by taking something out of context.

Or perhaps: it begins by seeing something differently (differently than it was intended to be seen, differently than it is ordinarily seen).

In Stanley Cavell's lecture "The Good of Film," first presented at the Center for Human Values, Princeton University, in 2001, Cavell outlines what he understands to be film's affinity with a certain conception of the good, one that has to do with transformation and Emersonian perfectionism. To put it very simply, for Cavell, films, or at least good films, work out ideas in Emersonian perfectionism—the striving to be the best self one can be—and in working through these ideas on screen they encourage the spectator to do the same. In the course of sketching out these ideas, and the origins of his interest in perfectionism, Cavell describes himself as "coming to wonder."[1] Upon first encountering it, I found this phrase particularly striking. What might it mean, I asked myself, to "come to wonder"? What might it mean in the context of film? Is Cavell describing here a sudden arrival at a moment of intellectual inquiry or aesthetic appreciation—an experience of being wonderstruck? Certainly, he seemed to me to be evoking a familiar experience, and one that resonated profoundly with my memories of watching certain scenes and moments.

FIGURE 17. A cinema scene from Gus Van Sant's short film *First Kiss* (2007).

In fact, Cavell was not coming to wonder. He was coming—after a typically long and meandering clause—to wonder *about* something (as it happens, he was wondering about a perceived religious fervor within the work of Wittgenstein, so nothing to do with film at all, really). He had not arrived at a place of wonder (*wonder*, the noun) but was rather engaged in the act of wondering (*to wonder*, the verb). And yet that phrase—"coming to wonder"—lingered in my mind, and I found myself continuing to wonder about wonder, about the ability of film to generate wonder in the spectator, and about the ethical and political stakes of that wonder. This essay offers some thoughts on what it might mean, then, to come to wonder at the cinema, and what good it might serve.

WONDER, FIRST

Philosophy, according to Plato, begins in wonder. Descartes sees wonder (*l'admiration*) as the "first of the passions." The phenomenologists Edmund Husserl and Maurice Merleau-Ponty draw a link between wonder and the phenomenological concept of the *epoché*—the setting aside of assumptions and beliefs about an object in order to consider the thing in itself—when they argue that by suspending judgment humankind is able "wonder before the world."[2] The feminist theorists Luce Irigaray, Sara Ahmed, and Bonnie Mann have argued in different ways that wonder is at the heart of how we might relate to others, allowing for the recognition of both difference (of others) and sameness (of ourselves to others) and thus bridging, at least to some extent, political and social divides. For Irigaray, wonder is "the moment of illumination—already and still contemplative—between the subject and the world."[3] Throughout the philosophical history of wonder, metaphors of the visual abound. Wonder *illuminates* the world, allowing us to see it in a different light. For Philip Fisher, wonder is first and foremost a relation to the visible world—"the outcome of the fact that we see the world"—and thus the visual arts have a privileged relationship to it.[4]

Film furnishes us with ample opportunities for wonder at the new and the strange. It is rife with novelties and first sights: from rockets landing on the moon, to dinosaurs looming into view, to never-seen-before places and creatures, and even animals that talk. Small wonder, then, that wonder has often been understood to be synonymous with astonishment (what Descartes calls *l'étonnement*) and to be yoked, in particular, to the science fiction genre.[5] One of the few film theorists to write about wonder outside the bounds of science fiction and SFX, Lutz Koepnick understands film's evocation of wonder as having to do not with the shock of the new but in terms of seeing the familiar differently. He argues that certain films have the power to "usher the visitor into a state of wonder," through the use of long-take cinematography, which forces us into an extended contemplation of the object or image onscreen. For Koepnick, wonder is connected to time, as the instant of wonder (the noun) gives way to the durational process of wondering (the verb). Wonder produces "curiosity" and "rapt attention."[6] Koepnick associates it with the body of film often referred to as slow cinema.

Like Koepnick, I am interested in wonder not as a first vision but as a revision: for this, it seems to me, is where its ethical import lies. It is my belief that anything at all can become an object of wonder when it is viewed under the right conditions. However, unlike Koepnick, I do not believe these conditions are the result of a particular film style but rather of film's inherent ability to frame the world for us.

"AS IF ANEW"

According to Wittgenstein, "the aspects of things that are most important for us are hidden because of their simplicity and familiarity": we see, but don't notice, what is always right in front of us. "The real foundations of their inquiry do not strike people at all. Unless that fact has at some time struck them.—And this means: we fail to be struck by what, once seen, is most striking and most powerful."[7] Ahmed understands wonder as arising from both an encounter with an unfamiliar object and one that is familiar but which has become ordinary. It is the latter case that Ahmed is more interested in: the phenomenon whereby the ordinary becomes extraordinary through wonder, appearing, in Ahmed's words, "as if anew."[8] Here, wonder is "an affective relation to the world," one that "expands our field of vision." It is "the precondition of the exposure of the subject to the world; we wonder when we are moved by that which we face."[9]

Wonder, thus, comes not only from seeing something new or strange, but also from seeing something differently: out of context, from a new angle, in a new light. The shift from seeing something new to seeing something differently matters in terms of film's privileged relationship to the aesthetics of wonder. Fisher contrasts the arts of the instant (architecture, sculpture, painting) with the arts of time (music, dance, and literature).[10] The arts of suddenness can engender wonder, he argues, because they are visual, and because they can be apprehended suddenly, unexpectedly, and at once. The arts of time, on the other hand, are incommensurate with an experience of wonder, because they rely on expectation of what will come next, of development or progression, often via the experience of narration or plot.

Film—which Fisher does not mention—straddles these two categories. An art of time made up of twenty-four images per second, each of which is filled with hundreds of tiny, sudden details, film does not just rely on plot. Sometimes, as in the case of experimental film, it does not have a plot at all. Film, unlike a novel, say, needs to fill in all the details of the scene, such that the ordinary is ever present (to borrow an image from Paul Willemen: a written scene can proceed very well without having to specify the pattern on the wallpaper, but a filmed scene cannot). Film is always, constantly, taking the material of everyday life and presenting it to us anew, and while this is sometimes in service of a story, often it is not. Sometimes things on film are *just there*. And sometimes, their presence is surprising in itself. Fisher describes just such an experience of wonder with regard to a passage from Vladimir Nabokov's *The Gift* (while, for Fisher, novels cannot give rise to wonder for their readers, they can describe its occurrence in their characters), in which the hero suddenly glimpses "a blindingly white parallelogram of sky being unloaded from [a] van—a dresser with mirror across which, *as across a cinema screen*, passed a flawlessly clear reflection of boughs sliding and swaying."[11] Fisher notes Nabokov's mention of the cinema screen but leaves it dangling, tantalizingly. And yet—what better evocation of cinema's power to reveal the ordinary world to us anew through its reframing might we find? We have all experienced, haven't we, the uncanny moment when we catch sight of ourselves in a mirror, or are presented with a photo or clip of ourselves, and for a moment see only a stranger before the picture dissolves into our own familiar yet unfamiliar features. Nabokov's mirror, like the cinema, expands this experience to other things, people, and objects.

Consider, then, Fisher's central example of the rainbow. Fisher, who is primarily interested not in the wonder of the ordinary but the wonder of the rare and unusual, claims that the rainbow is the quintessential experience of wonder because it appears to us instantaneously at times and places we cannot predict. But a rainbow's wonders go beyond the mere element of surprise: viewed from above, the rainbow appears not as an arch but a circle, an experience which is breathtaking because it does not fit with our expectations of how we expect a rainbow—any rainbow—to look. A new perspective yields new wonders. Fisher points out that in Plato, Iris (the rainbow) is the child of Thamus (the God of wonder).[12] It is surely no coincidence that the word "iris" also denotes the colored part of an eye, the organ of vision, as well as a cinematic shot masked in a circular form: a shot typically employed to gradually begin or end a scene, but often used, too, to call attention to an object or character, or to create an impression of looking through a small area like a keyhole. Looking, that is, differently.

With this glancing portrait of cinema's powers of reframing in mind, film might just emerge as the medium in which wonder is most pervasive. Wonder can be found in any film and all films, because what film does is show us the world from a perspective other than our own ordinary one. It can be found in any cinematic moment that generates a hushed "wow" as we find ourselves blinking at a familiar object or image or situation that suddenly appears *as if anew.* The pink seashell curve of an ear, shot in close-up. The foamy crest of a wave smacking against the shore, the light bouncing off it and flaring into the camera lens. The rough grain of carpet, the sparkling, velvet flocked wallpaper of a hotel bedroom. A white plastic bag, blowing in the wind. These are all everyday things; we might say boring, banal, or insignificant. Film can capture their beauty. But more than this, it can reframe them, render them *strange and beautiful,* despite the fact that we may have seen these objects, or objects like them, many times before. As such wonder is not antithetical to the ordinary or to expectation, but inherently bound up with both.

POETRY OF THE ORDINARY

In Cavell's article "The Thought of Movies," he argues:

> I understand it to be . . . a natural vision of film that every motion and gesture and station, in particular every human posture and gesture, however glancing, has its poetry, or you may say its lucidity. . . . Any of the arts will be drawn to this knowledge, this perception of the poetry of the ordinary, but film . . . democratizes the knowledge. . . . *It says that the perception of poetry is open to all*, regardless as it were of birth or talent, as the ability is to hold a camera on a subject, so that a failure to perceive, to persist in missing the subject, is ascribable only to ourselves, to failures of our character; as if to fail to guess the unseen in the seen, to fail to trace the implications of things—that is, to fail the perception that there is something to be guessed or traced, right or wrong—requires that we persistently coarsen and stupefy ourselves.[13]

In wonder, the ordinary is rendered strange. We see it "as if anew," in Ahmed's phrase. In this much, wonder has something in common with Bertolt Brecht's *Verfremdungseffekt* and Viktor Shklovsky's defamiliarization or *ostranenie*.[14] But there are key differences.

First, for Shklovsky defamiliarization is the preserve of poetry, which he distinguishes from ordinary language: "Poetic speech is *formed speech*," he writes. "Prose is ordinary speech—economical, easy, proper, the goddess of prose [*dea prosae*] is a goddess of the accurate, facile type, of the 'direct' expression of a child."[15] Wonder, on the other hand, allows us to see what Cavell calls "the poetry of the ordinary."[16]

Second, as Ahmed points out, wonder distinguishes itself affectively from other forms of what we might call "alienation devices" in its connotations of joy, innocence, and purity. Wonder is often associated with children, naivety, and even primitivism and foolishness. We might speak of "childlike wonder"; in London, the Science Museum's children's section is called the WonderLab, while the shoemaker Clarks runs a marketing campaign called Wonder of Wisdom, which comprises a series of cinematic short films that capture the defining moments of wonder in childhood that influenced the life and works of notable individuals. We can think, too, of the narrator of Montesquieu's *Lettres Persanes*, agape at the sophisticated wonders of the Western world; of Buddy, equally enamored of the human world as he careers around New York in *Elf* (2003, dir. Jon Favreau); or indeed the credulous Uncle Josh, trying to interact physically with the wondrous screened world in Edwin S. Porter's 1902 short *Uncle Josh at the Moving Picture Show*. It seems that often the "firstness" that Descartes attributes to wonder is understood as its opening onto more rational responses. Wonder is, in this reading, something we grow out of. Indeed, we might argue that Shklovsky and Brecht are precisely opposed to this pleasurable, captivating state, in which we are in thrall to the vision before us.

Both Ahmed and Mann recognize that wonder involves the possibility of what we might call a "willful naivety," but they draw contrasting conclusions. Mann argues that the phenomenological *epoché*'s suspension of judgment risks presenting ideologically constructed phenomena as natural or given.[17] Put otherwise, when we look at something "as if" for the first time, we turn a blind eye to social and cultural formations. Ahmed demurs. Far from an erasure of history, she argues, wonder "allows us to see the surfaces of the world as made, and as such opens up rather than suspends historicity."[18] That is, it is history itself that has become ordinary, taken for granted. "[T]o re-encounter objects as strange things is not to lose sight of the history, but to refuse to make them history by losing sight. Such wonder directed at those objects that we face, as well as those that are behind us, does not involve bracketing out the familiar, but allows the familiar to dance with life."[19]

Wonder radicalizes our relationship to both our past and our present, and through it our future: allowing us to see that things need not be as they are. What we think of as ordinary might become extraordinary, and vice versa. Unlike *ostranenie* or the *Verfremdungseffekt,* wonder does not shock, stun, or alienate.[20] Rather it emphasizes pleasure, proximity, and care. It opens onto hope. Wonder is "a world consciousness that can leave us shattered." But that shattering is also "what enables us to become alive to possibility."[21]

A PLACE OF WONDER

Cavell was not, as it transpires, especially interested in wonder in "The Good of Film." Or then again, perhaps he was. Ahmed describes her own experience of wonder in relation to feminism as "like moving out of false consciousness, though now I see that I was not moving into the truth as such, but just towards a way of understanding that explained things better."[22] Cavell, meanwhile, talks about reading Emerson as an exercise in "coming to oneself, as if one had been in a trance."[23] In this experience, which echoes Ahmed's own account of coming to wonder, Cavell moves from "loss to recovery . . . despair to interest."[24] This movement is analogized by the couples in the genre that Cavell describes as the Hollywood comedy of remarriage, a genre made up of films such as *The Philadelphia Story* (1940, dir. George Cukor), *His Girl Friday* (1940, dir. Howard Hawks), *Adam's Rib* (1949, dir. George Cukor), and *The Awful Truth* (1937, dir. Leo McCarey). These men and women have come to take their spouses and their domestic lives for granted. But over the course of the films that they inhabit, they come to view their other halves as if anew. One way in which they do this is by venturing out of their familiar domestic setup into what Cavell, after the literary historian Northrop Frye, refers to as "the green world." In practical terms, this is usually Connecticut. More abstractly, it is, according to Cavell, a place from which to shift perspective: "a place from which the ordinary world is broken into, out of which *beauty and isolation and* strangeness intertwine to reveal a glimpse of community and the possibility of change."[25]

The couples who enter the green world often revert there to a state of childhood. We see this most clearly in *Bringing Up Baby* (1938, dir. Howard Hawks), in which Katherine Hepburn and Cary Grant play at brothers and sisters, and mummies and daddies, and hide and seek, and dress-up, and as they do come to wonder at each other and eventually fall in love (again, Cavell might say). There is, admittedly, in the green world, a sense of purification: a return to innocence. But these characters must eventually return home, to the ordinary world. Their task now is to carry this sense of wonder with them while negotiating a domestic world that, through routine, social circumstances, and all sorts of conditions that encourage haste and sharpness and misunderstanding, hinders us seeing things anew. As Mann points out, it would be lovely to return to a time before knowledge and its responsibilities—"to be light again," but wonder "will not wash us clean."[26] Wonder is not a baptismal event. Still, in its wake we are able to see possibilities that were not previously visible to us. To paraphrase *The Awful Truth*'s Lucy Warriner (Irene Dunne), everything is the same but different.

The green world is not a place of transformation, then, but of revelation: it allows its visitors to grasp what is already there, before their eyes, visible but unseen. It is a place of wonder, in which the ordinary world can be reframed, made unfamiliar, revealed anew in its beauty and strangeness. It helps its visitors to notice things and to stop taking them for granted. And isn't this an apt description, too, of the cinema? One of the important discoveries of Cavell's book *The World Viewed* is the way in which film, by its very nature, calls our attention to parts of the world that we might otherwise overlook: film allows us to look "as if anew" at what is onscreen, in part by asking what might be unseen, unnoticed, or taken for granted.[27] So it is not such a great leap to suppose that the cinema might be, for its audience, a green world and a place of wonder. When we enter the cinema, do we not find ourselves coming to wonder? And when we leave it, isn't our vision renewed? Just like the green world, the cinema grants us, temporarily, "a wish not for power over creation . . . but a wish not to need power, not to have to bear its burdens," and just like Cavell's central couples, we, too, must eventually return to the world that we seem to have lost or neglected, through habit, familiarity, and inattention.[28] This world remains the same, but we might just be able to see it differently. And from here, the possibilities are endless.

As the philosophers knew well, wonder is only a beginning.

NOTES

Epigraph: Gilbert Keith Chesterton, *Tremendous Trifles* (1909), https://www.gutenberg.org/files/8092/8092-h/8092-h.htm. Accessed November 4, 2021.

1. Stanley Cavell, "The Good of Film," in *Cavell on Film,* ed. William Rothman (New York: SUNY Press, 2005), 333–348, at 336.

2. Maurice Merleau-Ponty, *The Phenomenology of Perception,* trans. Donald Landes (New York: Routledge, 2012 [1945]), 14.

3. Luce Irigaray, "Wonder: A Reading of Descartes' *The Passions of the Soul,*" trans. Caroline Burke and Gillian C. Gill, in *Feminist Interpretations of René Descartes,* ed. Susan Bordo (University Park: Pennsylvania University Press, 1999), 105–113, at 109.

4. Philip Fisher, *Wonder, the Rainbow, and the Aesthetics of Rare Experiences* (Cambridge, MA: Harvard University Press, 1998), 17.

5. See, e.g., Michele Pierson, *Special Effects: Still in Search of Wonder* (New York: Columbia University Press, 2002); and Vivian Sobchack, *Screening Space: The American Science Fiction Film* (New Brunswick, NJ: Rutgers University Press, 1997).

6. Lutz Koepnick, *The Long Take: Art Cinema and the Wondrous* (Minneapolis: University of Minnesota Press, 2017), 9.

7. Ludwig Wittgenstein, *Philosophical Investigations,* German text, with an English translation by G.E. M. Anscombe, P.M.S. Hacker, and Joachim Schulte, 4th ed. (Oxford: Wiley-Blackwell, 2009), 56.

8. Sara Ahmed, *The Cultural Politics of Emotion* (Edinburgh: Edinburgh University Press, 2014), 179.

9. Ahmed, *Cultural Politics,* 179.

10. Fisher, *Wonder, the Rainbow,* 21.

11. Fisher, *Wonder, the Rainbow,* 25 (emphasis mine).

12. Fisher, *Wonder, the Rainbow,* 10–11.

13. Stanley Cavell, "The Thought of Movies," in *Themes Out of School: Effects and Causes* (San Francisco: North Point Press, 1984), 14 (emphasis mine).

14. Bertolt Brecht, "On Chinese Acting," trans. Eric Bentley, *The Tulane Drama Review* 6, no. 1 (1961): 130–136; and Viktor Shklovsky, "Art as Technique," in *Literary Theory: An Anthology*, ed. Julie Rivkin and Michael Ryan (Malden, MA: Blackwell, 1998), 8–14.

15. Shklovsky, "Art as Technique," 13.

16. Cavell, "The Thought of Movies," 14.

17. Bonnie Mann, "Feminist Phenomenology and the Politics of Wonder," *Avant: Trends in Interdisciplinary Studies* 9, no. 2 (2018): 43–61.

18. Ahmed, *Cultural Politics*, 180.

19. Sara Ahmed, *Queer Phenomenology: Orientations, Objects, Others* (Durham, NC: Duke University Press, 2006), 164.

20. Tom Gunning resists this division between wonder and *ostranenie*, and across his writing often uses the terms awe, shock, awe, and astonishment interchangeably, expressing a preference for the last as a blanket term. My own sense—one that finds agreement in Ahmed and Fisher—is that wonder is a rather more gentle term. For more, see Annie van den Oever and Tom Gunning, "Viktor Shklovsky's *Ostrannenie* and the 'Hermeneutics of Wonder,'" *Early Popular Visual Culture* 18, no. 1 (2020): 15–28.

21. Ahmed, *Cultural Politics*, 179.

22. Ahmed, "Feminist Wonder," *feministkilljoys*, July 28, 2014, https://feministkilljoys.com/2014/07/28/feminist-wonder/. Accessed August 31, 2021.

23. Cavell, "Good of Film," 337.

24. Cavell, "Good of Film," 340.

25. Cavell, "Good of Film," 344 (emphasis mine).

26. Mann, "Feminist Phenomenology," 50.

27. Stanley Cavell, *The World Viewed* (Cambridge, MA: Harvard University Press, 1979).

28. Cavell, *World Viewed*, 40.

... Moral Improvement

On How Watching Films Might Make Us Better People

THOMAS E. WARTENBERG

Philosophers have been addressing the question of the relationship between film and ethics with increasing frequency in recent years. As part of the ongoing debate about the philosophical potential of film and related media, such as television and video games, philosophers have attempted to show that people who watch such media become morally better individuals.[1] The question that I would like to pose with this essay—can watching films improve us morally?—provides a means to assess the validity of this claim.

Psychologists have argued as far back as 1963 that watching aggressive behavior on film can cause children to act more aggressively.[2] As Vanessa LoBue reports in *Psychology Today*, preschoolers who were shown videos of adults violently interacting with an inflatable doll copied the aggressive behavior of the adults and even invented novel forms of violence to inflict on the doll.[3] This result has, of course, been supplemented with the recognition that watching gun violence on a screen can have even more deleterious effects. This suggests that, whatever the connection between watching films and moral behavior, it won't be a one-way street: going to the cinema is not going to guarantee that one emerges a better, morally improved, person.

Even if we can't connect film as an art form directly with increased moral awareness and/or activity, the question remains whether *certain* types of films can function to give us moral instruction and, hence, make us better people. That is the question I attempt to answer here.

FIGURE 18. Harry Lime (Orson Welles) in *The Third Man* (1949, Carol Reed).

CAVELL ON MORAL PERFECTIONISM

In a 2000 essay "The Good of Film," Stanley Cavell presented his answer to this question. Cavell chose this title in response to the request that he address the relationship between moral philosophy and film. Rather than attempt to respond to that question in its full generality, Cavell offers something more personal, namely, an account of how his own interest in the relationship between film and ethics developed. This explains why his essay focuses on the ethical perspective in two film genres he designates as the "Hollywood Comedy of Remarriage" and the "Melodrama of the Unknown Woman."[4] As he takes these two genres to develop the idea of *moral perfectionism*, a discussion of how the films show the importance of that idea demonstrates one form of the relationship between film and moral philosophy.

Before pursuing Cavell's line of thought, I want to focus on the title that Cavell gave his essay, "The Good of Film." The signification of that phrase is not obvious. A first attempt at unpacking it takes the good of film to mean "the value of film," or what good films can do from a moral perspective. This is, of course, a huge topic, for films can do good in many ways. One example of how films can do something morally valuable is by making their audiences aware of the plight of people that they probably had not considered previously. Luis Buñuel's *Los Olvidados* (1950) is an example of such a film, for it focuses on young native children living in the slums of Mexico City, a group of people to whom most film audiences had probably not devoted much thought. The film made its audience aware of how the young slum dwellers suffer and the tragic consequences.

Cavell himself understands "the good of film" differently. For him, it can be unpacked by means of the following question: "What does film as an artistic and cultural medium posit as the Good, the valuable, the useful?"[5] The question is whether there is a conception of the good that the medium of film somehow endorses or celebrates.

The two film genres Cavell has written about share a view of the good he calls moral or Emersonian perfectionism. At the core of this notion lies the idea that there is a better *self* available to us than the self we ordinarily are aware of in the course of living our lives. On Cavell's account, the films in these genres present their audiences with characters undergoing moral transformations. At the beginning of Frank Capra's wonderful Depression-era comedy *It Happened One Night* (1934), for example, Ellie Andrews (Claudette Colbert) stands in need of moral instruction, having lived an extremely sheltered life. Peter Warne (Clark Gable) provides that for Ellie, and she becomes a more mature, savvy person, thereby embodying the type of moral transformation Cavell sees these films as figuring.[6]

Cavell claims, then, that the films in these two genres depict a type of moral improvement undergone by some of the films' main characters. Yet can we conclude that audience members watching these films will themselves be transformed?

Cavell's interpretations of these films are notoriously difficult to follow. In an attempt to show that these films require the type of philosophical activity he expends on them, Cavell refers to philosophical ideas with which many filmgoers are unlikely to be acquainted. How are we to understand the impact that such films will have on their audiences if unpacking the meaning of the film requires, as Cavell suggests, awareness of the ideas of Kant, Kierkegaard, Nietzsche, Heidegger, and Emerson, among others?

Martin Rossouw has argued that audiences need to have a "preparatory ethics" to be able to receive the "message" contained in a philosophically significant film.[7] It's not just a matter of bracketing one's own beliefs in order to be able to listen to what the film is saying, though that is important, but being philosophically prepared to understand the film's message. The question is, how much does the audience need to know about ideas of philosophers from Kant to Heidegger to grasp that *It Happened One Night* is a dramatic rendering of the idea of moral perfectionism?

Consider a film viewer preparing to watch *It Happened One Night* by reading *The Critique of Pure Reason*. Yes, the blanket that Ellie and Peter hang between them to keep her reputation intact can be seen to have similarities to Kant's invocation of a split between the real world of noumena and the apparent world of phenomena, as Cavell suggests. But does a viewer need to know the Kantian reference to understand the film? Wouldn't this simply require too much of viewers?

My understanding of Cavell's position is that films like *It Happened One Night* present viewers with ideas that also animate such texts as *The Critique of Pure Reason*. Cavell is not arguing that viewers need to have prepared themselves for viewing the film by reading Kant, but that the film acquaints its audience with ideas similar to those found in the first *Critique*. The idea is that such films present "serious" ideas to their audiences. They are not just vehicles for light entertainment, "fluff," as the traditional category of screwball comedy would suggest.

Still, this doesn't answer the question we have been considering: does watching a film like *It Happened One Night* improve its audience, making them morally better people?

Here is one route to a negative answer to that question. If one accepts Noël Carroll's account of film audiences as seeking to answer questions posed by a film's narrative—what he dubs the "erotetic" theory of film narration—then one might think that the only effect that a film need have on an audience is that of resolving the intellectual puzzles its narrative poses.[8] As a result, one might doubt that audiences would come away from a film like *It Happened One Night* with anything other than a smile on their faces from a pleasant evening's entertainment.

SINNERBRINK ON CINETHICS

In his book *Cinematic Ethics: Exploring Ethical Experience through Film*, Robert Sinnerbrink presents a different perspective on the relationship between film and morality. Sinnerbrink claims that films have a complex relationship to ethics. He uses the term *cinempathy* to characterize this relationship, which he specifies as follows: "a cinematic/kinetic expression of the synergy between affective attunement, emotional engagement, and moral evaluation that captures more fully [than other terms] the ethical potential of the cinematic experience."[9] Sinnerbrink's introduction of this term stems from his belief that simply talking about empathy and sympathy fails to convey the multidimensional character of our ethical engagement with film.

Sinnerbrink uses a scene from the Academy Award–winning Iranian film *A Separation/Jodāi-e Nāder az Simin* (2011, dir. Asghar Farhadi) to explain his idea. He analyzes a scene in which all three members of the central family come into conflict. The issue is Simin's (Leila Hatami) desire to bring up her daughter Termeh (Sarina Farhadi) in a country that is not undergoing a conservative religious turn that portends strict controls on women. Nadar (Peyman Moadi), the *pater familias,* wishes to remain in Tehran to care for his ailing father. Even such a brief description makes it clear that the film is concerned with fundamental social tensions rife in Iranian society as it attempts to find a way to reconcile traditional practices with modern Western ones.

In this scene, Simin is planning to leave their home and wants Termeh to come with her. Nadar wants Termeh to remain with him, and she wants to keep the family intact. Sinnerbrink points out that the filmmakers deliberately alter the ways in which the characters are respectively shot during the scene—for example, close-up or more distantly, posed directly in front of the camera or shot from the side or rear—in order to get viewers to understand the perspective of *each* of the characters in alternation. The claim is that the film resists easy applications of "right" and "wrong" to the characters' stances, preferring to give us a more nuanced understanding of the tensions that have led to their disagreement.

In line with my previous discussion, we should think about the three aspects of a viewer's ethical engagement with *A Separation*. In terms of the preparatory ethics, first, it is important that viewers not think that they understand the conflicting forces at play in Iranian society so that they can appreciate how the film portrays the conflict upon which it focuses. The second aspect, the narrative itself, presents a number of ethical issues, in particular whether the father has an obligation to his daughter's welfare that overrides his obligations to his elderly father. This ethical conflict does not admit of an easy solution, for tradition and Westernization cannot be resolved in a simple manner. And the third aspect of the ethical engagement audiences have with films is their own moral improvement as a result of viewing a film. It is true that audience members will have some improved beliefs about Iranian society, compared at least to the stereotyped images presented in many Western accounts. But does this count as their *moral improvement?*

One could support this idea by pointing out that viewing a film like *A Separation* engages a range of ethical attitudes held by filmgoers. The film asks them to lay aside any assumptions they might have about what is the right thing to do in the complex situation depicted in the film. Viewers undergo a type of education, one in which they find themselves experiencing the reasonableness of different, conflicting views. Because we employ the same habits of feeling whether we are living our lives or watching a film, the film can help us be more sensitive to others' points of view, thereby making us more moral people.

So, Sinnerbrink provides one example of a film that can "improve people." But his argument depends upon Farhadi's use of a very specific cinematic style, one that does not privilege any character's point of view. Our more general concern about the possibility of moral improvement for film audiences still remains.

THE THIRD MAN AND MORAL TRANSFORMATION

To further address this issue, I turn to *The Third Man* (1949, dir. Carol Reed). The pulp-fiction author Holly Martins (Joseph Cotton) has arrived in Vienna at the invitation of his "best friend" Harry Lime (Orson Welles) only to discover that Lime has just been killed in a car accident. After the funeral, Martins is confronted with the claim of the British intelligence officer Major Calloway (Trevor Howard) that Lime is a major criminal in the Viennese underground. Expressing his loyalty to his friend, Martins accuses Calloway of being a crooked cop who is using Lime to cover up his own misdeeds.

During the course of the film, Martins's understanding of his situation will be transformed as he comes to realize that Calloway is an honest cop, Lime a bad guy, and himself a gullible bumbler playing at being a detective. Martin's ethical evolution requires him to shed his allegiance to Lime and cast a more critical eye on his supposed best friend. Martins's transformation is a process that takes place through the assistance of both Lime and Calloway: Lime, inadvertently when he shows himself to be an egoist only concerned with his own welfare, and Calloway, an honest cop who repeatedly acts with honesty and compassion, more intentionally, as he tries to convince Martins of Lime's evil actions and to protect him from the dangerous criminals with whom he has fallen in.

For my purposes here, it will be sufficient to limit our discussion to the final stage of Martins's ethical transformation. On the way to a train that he never manages to catch, Martins goes to a hospital with Calloway. In the children's ward, Martins witnesses firsthand the effects Lime's treachery—he sold diluted vials of penicillin used to treat children and others for encephalitis—had on his young victims. Once he has seen with his own eyes the deaths and suffering caused by Lime's actions, Martins is willing to be Calloway's "dumb duck decoy," as he puts it, for he realizes that he is the only one able to bring Lime to justice and that he has an obligation to do so despite his previous relationship with Lime. In order to be comfortable doing this, Martins has had to reject his belief that Lime was his best friend and come to see him more realistically.[10]

A philosophically sensitive audience watching this film will be aware of Martins's ethical transformation and its philosophical significance. They will see that Martins changes his evaluation of Lime's character, and that this allows him to act morally by assisting Calloway in bringing Lime to justice.

We have not so far addressed the question of whether an audience that has witnessed Martins's ethical transformation will be subject to an ethical makeover of their own. If we conceive of the audience along the lines of Carroll's account of erotetic narrative discussed earlier, then I don't see how that audience could be transformed, only entertained. But there is more to our situation as film audiences than Carroll allows, as we have seen in Sinnerbrink's discussion of *A Separation*. How do these ideas apply to *The Third Man?*

Martins's moral transformation involves him coming to perceive Lime's real character rather than continue to be misled by the "screen memories" he has of their relationship. In part, this happens during the famous Ferris wheel sequence that takes place at the Prater amusement park. As Lime and Martins ride the wheel, Lime inadvertently reveals his true nature. Not only has he sold out his lover, Anna Schmidt (Alida Valli), to the Russians, he is prepared to kill Martins if that is the only way to prevent his own arrest.

Martins's understanding of his supposed best friend has been transformed. He realizes that, even as a young man, Lime was only concerned with his own welfare. Realizing that Lime is capable of morally problematic actions, such as betraying his girlfriend, Anna, with whom Martins has fallen hopelessly in love, Martins recovers memories of his relationship with Lime that show Lime not to have been the best friend Martins remembered him being. In particular, he remembers how, when the two of them were in danger of being caught while on a prank, Lime had an escape plan for himself that left Martins holding the bag. His seeing Lime to be capable of treachery allows Martins to shed his idealized vision of his friend in favor of a more realistic one.

At the heart of Martins's transformation is his coming to a more adequate understanding of the ethical responsibilities he has to assist in the capture of his former "best friend." Similarly, viewers of the film also acquire this ethical knowledge, for they have witnessed Martins's moral transformation, in which he has revised his understanding of the characters of both Lime and Calloway, as well as how that affects his own moral obligations.

Still, this doesn't by itself provide us with grounds for claiming that the audience has undergone a similar transformation. They might learn something about moral obligations, but does it really make sense to claim that they have themselves undergone a moral transformation?

To fully address this issue, we need to explore the nature of *The Third Man* as a *film* more carefully. It has often been noted that *The Third Man* employs many of the techniques of film noir. One of these is structuring the narrative in such a way that the audience is unsure of how to interpret what is taking place. Relying on this, the film is able to intentionally deceive its audience, presenting it with an unreliable narrative.

From the beginning, the film depicts situations ambiguously, making space for alternative interpretations. When Calloway tells the drunken Martins that Lime is the worst criminal in Vienna, the audience initially doesn't know whether to believe him or to accept Martins's protestation that Lime is a great guy who might have gotten involved in some petty crimes, echoing a claim made by the unidentified narrator of the film's opening newsreel-like sequence about the moral climate of post–World War II Vienna. The audience is wary and uncertain, skeptical of both Calloway and Martins, and doesn't know exactly who or what to believe.

As the film progresses, the audience becomes aware that Calloway is telling the truth. This happens as it emerges that Lime is a master manipulator and criminal, though also a very appealing person. Indeed, one of the ethical insights the film provides its audience is that evil can be done by someone who appears very attractive rather than the warped human beings, such as *Othello*'s Iago, who are often taken to be paradigmatic villains. But in coming to see Lime in this way, and therefore coming to trust Calloway, there has been a transformation in the audience's interpretation of the film world and thus also a rejection of its previous skeptical stance.

Still, the film keeps tricking its viewers. There is a wonderful scene in which Martins gets into a taxi that speeds off and he—and the audience—think that he is being kidnapped by Lime's criminal gang.

It turns out the taxi is simply taking Martins to a lecture he had forgotten about, so that the ride is not the sinister occurrence it appeared to be. Like Martins, viewers have used a faulty framework to understand that incident, even if just moments later Martins is actually pursued by the very criminals he had anticipated sent the taxi for him.

Carroll's erotetic model goes some way to explaining the audience's reactions to this scene. When the taxi takes off and Martins seems to have been kidnapped, the narrative presents the audience with the question, "What is happening? Has Martins been kidnapped by Lime's henchmen?" And we think we know the answer. But when the taxi arrives at the club at which Martins is to give a talk, we realize that we were mistaken, so that our initial solution to the puzzle needs to be rejected. We might even enjoy the way that the film has tricked us, so that we become aware of the technique employed by the filmmakers. In acknowledging that we have been subject to deception, we also realize that film has the ability to trick us in this way, thereby acknowledging an important capacity of this medium.

But have we undergone an ethical transformation as the result of our awareness that we have jumped to a false conclusion? *The Third Man* might encourage such a transformation by getting the audience to revise its assumptions about film viewing and listening. The audience might reflect on the deceptions that the film engaged in and realize that these deceptions were possible only because of certain fundamental features of film viewing. This would result in a more self-conscious and reflective film audience.

There is another dimension to the recognition inspired by the audience's realization that they have been tricked by the film. Perhaps they will realize that, like Martins, they have been able to be duped precisely because of their reliance on stereotyped categories, such as jumping to the conclusion that a fast taxi ride must be a kidnapping. Aware of their tendency to make such problematic inferences, the audience may become more self-critical about how they think about difficult ethical situations and achieve a genuine if limited moral insight.

CONCLUSION

In this essay, I have not tried to present a comprehensive account of the relationship between film and morality. My goal has been more modest: to show that there are certain types of films that have the potential to affect their audiences in a manner that enhances their moral awareness and understanding. To that end, I have looked at three different accounts of films that have an ethical impact: Cavell's discussion of comedies of remarriage; Sinnerbrink's introduction of the notion of cinempathy; and my own interpretation of *The Third Man* as involving its audience in self-criticism of its viewing practices.

Each of these attempts highlights a different relationship between films and morality. Cavell emphasizes the manner in which the narratives of the films he considers posit an ethical transformation in their characters toward the position he dubs "moral perfectionism." Sinnerbrink emphasizes the multidimensional ethical experience audiences undergo while watching a film like *A Separation*. I consider how a film can get its audience to achieve a more sophisticated understanding of the activity of film viewing.

Whether the increased moral understanding claimed for viewers of these films actually results in a transformed ethical practice—their moral improvement—remains an open question for me. To some extent, this is an empirical question. Philosophers have not generally emphasized the relationship between their accounts of cinematic ethics and empirical research, but I think that the sort of research I cited at the outset of this essay, on the relationship between watching violent films and violent behavior in children, also needs to be done in relation to morality and the cinema. Hopefully, such research will help substantiate the claim that watching certain types of films can actually improve us as moral agents.

NOTES

1. Throughout, I use the terms "ethics" and "moral" as synonymous.
2. Albert Bandura, Dorothea Ross, and Sheila A. Ross, "Imitation of Film-Mediated Aggressive Models," *The Journal of Abnormal and Social Psychology* 66, no. 1 (1966): 3–11.
3. Vanessa LoBue, "Violent Media and Aggressive Behavior in Children," *Psychology Today,* January 8, 2018, https://www.psychologytoday.com/us/blog/the-baby-scientist/201801/violent-media-and-aggressive-behavior-in-children. Accessed April 3, 2019.
4. Stanley Cavell, "The Good of Film," in *Cavell on Film,* ed. William Rothman (Albany: SUNY Press, 2005 [2000]), 333–348. On the two Cavellian genres, see Stanley Cavell, *Pursuits of Happiness: The Hollywood Comedy of Remarriage* (Cambridge, MA: Harvard University Press, 1981); and *Contesting Tears: The Hollywood Melodrama of the Unknown Woman* (Chicago: University of Chicago Press, 1996).
5. Cavell, "Good of Film," 334.

6. There are some problems with Cavell's account of this film and others in the genre. In *It Happened One Night,* Peter is himself in need of an ethical transformation, for he is a show-off and a know-it-all. Ellie helps Peter realize this, in part because he falls in love with her and has to acknowledge his feelings and therefore his dependency on her to achieve a sense of well-being. Cavell doesn't acknowledge this aspect of the film, treating Peter as simply the agent of Ellie's transformation.

7. Martin P. Rossouw, *Transformational Ethics of Film: Thinking the Cinemakeover in the Film-Philosophy Debate* (Leiden: Brill, 2021), 187ff.

8. Noël Carroll, "Movies, Narration, and the Emotions," in *Philosophy and Film: Bridging Divides,* ed. Christina Rawls, Diana Neiva, and Steven Gouveia (London: Routledge, 2019), 209–221.

9. Robert Sinnerbrink, *Cinematic Ethics: Exploring Ethical Experience through Film* (London: Routledge, 2016), 95.

10. I should note that the ending of the film is ambiguous, because Martins seems just as benighted as he was at the beginning of the film as he stands, waiting for Anna to pass him by unseeing.

18

... Cinematic Ethics
On Film as Transformative Experience

ROBERT SINNERBRINK

FILM-PHILOSOPHY AND CINEMATIC ETHICS

Several theorists concerned with the relationship between film and philosophy have recently advanced a bold claim: that cinema can engage in philosophy in a manner comparable to, although differing from, philosophy itself. Inspired by Stanley Cavell and Gilles Deleuze, film philosophers claim that film and philosophy are closely related, sharing problems to which they respond in distinctive ways and thereby open up new possibilities of thought.[1] Thomas Wartenberg and Paisley Livingston have argued for a "moderate" version of the "film as philosophy" thesis (that films can illustrate ideas, stage thought experiments, or offer counterexamples), whereas others have proposed a "bolder" version (that film can do what philosophy does, challenge philosophical assumptions, or offer new paths for thinking).[2] Stephen Mulhall, for example, offers an influential version of "bold" film-philosophy, claiming that films can be "philosophy in action," which has sparked an ongoing debate over the very idea of "film as philosophy."[3]

A number of critics have criticized this approach.[4] The main point of contention has been Mulhall's statement that films can philosophize in "just the ways philosophers do," a claim that raises metaphilosophical questions regarding what we mean by "philosophy" and how it can or should be done.[5] As films do not engage in "reason-giving" practices, offer arguments, or avoid ambiguity, we cannot regard them as

FIGURE 19. Neil (Ben Affleck) and Marina (Olga Kurylenko) driving toward Mont-Saint-Michel in *To the Wonder* (2012, Terrence Malick).

properly philosophical.[6] In response, some philosophers have argued that some films can be described as "giving reasons" supporting a claim, as presenting (analogical) arguments in visual form, or as staging complex "thought experiments" with real philosophical and moral import.[7] For others, film prompts us to consider what counts as a "philosophical" contribution, and the media through which we can communicate such affective thinking, which is why we can bring film and philosophy together in a mutually illuminating encounter.[8]

Much recent work in this field has turned to film ethics or the ethical potential of cinema. We can understand certain kinds of cinema as engaging in ethical thinking, both expressing and soliciting varieties of ethical experience, hence prompting critical engagement. It can expose us to emotionally challenging forms of experience that invite a philosophical response. Indeed, cinema can be a medium with "a remarkable capacity to evoke ethically significant experience with the power to provoke philosophical thinking."[9] This approach is what I call "cinematic ethics": the idea of *film as a medium of ethical experience*.[10] From this point of view, cinematic ethics takes "an experiential approach to ethics, one that proceeds via the aesthetic experience, emotional engagement, and cognitive understanding that cinema so richly provides."[11]

The idea of cinematic ethics offers a way of understanding "the good of film": its potential to sharpen our moral perception, challenge our beliefs, and enhance our understanding of moral-social complexity. Cinematic ethics refers to the modification of horizons of meaning and reframing of morally relevant experiences and problems in ways that have the potential to alter our ways of thinking. In this way it can bring together the three important aspects of the cinema-ethics relationship: ethical content in narrative cinema, the ethics of cinematic representation (from filmmaker and spectator perspectives), and the ethics of cinema as symptomatic of broader cultural, social, and ideological perspectives. We can add to this the *aesthetic dimension* of cinema—the role of *aesthetic experience* in refining and focusing our attention and thus conveying meaning—as a way of evoking ethical experience that invites critical reflection. This would mean modifying claims concerning film as philosophy into a claim concerning "cinematic thinking": emphasizing the affective, "noncognitive" dimensions of the aesthetic experience cinema can afford, an aesthetic encounter prompting thought via cinematic means.[12] Cinematic experience can alter our ethical orientation, shift horizons of meaning, and reconfigure settled beliefs, in ways subsequently elaborated in theoretical terms. In this integrated manner, linking affective responses with cognitive reflection, both during and after our viewing of film, we can defend the ethical significance of cinematic experience.

ROSSOUW'S METATHEORETICAL CRITIQUE OF FILM-PHILOSOPHY

This ethical dimension is also at the center of Martin Rossouw's recent critique of film as philosophy.[13] Rossouw adopts a "metatheoretical" perspective, examining the theoretical assumptions that have shaped the film as philosophy debate. For Rossouw, film philosophers should reflect more upon their methodological approaches, their conceptions of philosophy and of film, which both ground the claim that films can contribute to philosophy. As Rossouw asks: "which assumptions about 'philosophy' . . . do we bring to the notion of films doing philosophy? What are the various paths along which we analyze and interpret films as philosophy? . . . Why do we want (or not want) films to 'do' philosophy in the first place?"[14] The latter question, for Rossouw, points to the underlying ethical motivation behind film-philosophy. He claims that film-philosophy implicitly "colludes with ethically significant conceptions about film," which means that anyone engaging with film as philosophy must deal with "film ethics."[15] This does not mean analyzing the "ethical content" of specific films so much as acknowledging the "metaphilosophical" claim that film philosophers bring an implicit ethical vision to bear on their philosophical engagement with cinema.

More specifically, Rossouw argues that film philosophers assume an unacknowledged "transformational ethics" that underpins their claims concerning film as philosophy. Film philosophers argue that films can contribute to philosophy via cinematic means, but underlying this is a commitment to film-philosophy as a means of achieving "personal transformation."[16] They assume that "films as philosophy offer viewers the prospect for some form of personal edification, whether this is to become more critical, wise, open, aware or (re)attuned."[17] In short, film philosophers assume an implicit "transformational ethics of film" that motivates their reflections on what film can achieve; but this is a ground, Rossouw contends, that remains unacknowledged and undertheorized in the film as philosophy debate.[18]

ROSSOUW'S OBJECTIONS TO FILM-PHILOSOPHY

Rossouw proposes four objections to film-philosophy in his metaphilosophical critique. I shall call these the "elitism," "idealism," "performative contradiction," and "imposition" objections, defining them briefly and offering responses to defend film-philosophy understood as cinematic ethics. The point is to defend the aesthetic experience of cinema as a *transformative experience* with moral-ethical potential and philosophical significance. We can thereby defend cinema as a source of transformative experiences that can foster ethical understanding.

Film-philosophy as exclusivist/elitist: The bold version of film-philosophy, according to Rossouw, suffers from "undue exclusivism" in not being available to all spectators or being too challenging for "untutored viewers."[19] Defenders of the "bold" version assume a philosophically expert viewer who draws on specialized background knowledge and a preparatory ethics. In this sense, it caters to an elite cadre of theorists and/or viewers: "they are the ones who are ethically prepared, the self-mastering viewers, the select few who manage to fashion the ordinary activity of film-going into an extraordinary event."[20] Despite its anti-elitist intentions, "bold" film-philosophy remains an "anti-egalitarian" mode of cinematic engagement.

It is not clear, however, what Rossouw means here by "exclusive" or "elitist." Does this mean that we prevent individuals from engaging with film philosophically? Or that assuming background philosophical knowledge is somehow unfair? In this regard, film-philosophy is no different from other forms of philosophy (e.g., ethics, epistemology, or metaphysics) that bring specialized knowledge to their inquiry. Bringing knowledge of Nietzsche's critique of utilitarianism to *Eternal Sunshine of the Spotless Mind* (2004, dir. Michel Gondry) is no more exclusionary or elitist than bringing it to Jeremy Bentham's *An Introduction to the Principles of Morals and Legislation* (1781). Philosophical reflection, by its very nature, assumes background knowledge in order to engage in argument or debate. Indeed, it is difficult to imagine a form of philosophical inquiry that presumes no background knowledge, expertise, or argumentative skill (as Rossouw admits). Nonetheless, it remains in principle open to all even if the nature of such inquiry and its specific techniques mean that it may not be appealing to all.

Film-philosophy as too idealistic: Citing film philosophers' claims that we should refrain from imposing presumed philosophical frameworks onto a film, Rossouw argues that this means film-philosophy demands that viewers suspend their theoretical prejudices but also assert philosophical or ethical claims on behalf of the film. The problem is that "urging a drastic abandoning of our philosophical beliefs about film," as Rossouw puts it, is too idealistic or demanding for any real-world engagement with a cinematic work.[21] "I struggle to see how such a cognitively open, assumption-free encounter with a film (or any other experience, event, text) could exist or be fostered," he writes.[22] Both the demand to "give up one's philosophical beliefs," and the philosophical-ethical claims made on this basis, are unrealistic and thus unlikely to be realizable in practice.[23]

Film-philosophy, however, is no more "idealistic" than other "aesthetic cognitivist" accounts of art having epistemic as well as moral-ethical significance and thus potentially transformative effects. As Nelson Goodman famously put this view (also held by philosophers such as Hegel), "the arts must be taken no less seriously as the sciences as modes of discovery, creation, and enlargement of knowledge in the broad sense of advancement of the understanding."[24] Although debate continues over aesthetic cognitivist accounts of art (that it can yield knowledge, understanding, or moral learning), cinema does not seem any more vulnerable to such skeptical critiques than other art forms.[25] Indeed, film philosophers have argued that there are specific ways in which cinema may be more apt for eliciting such moral insight thanks to its multimodal character and capacity to engage us emotionally and cognitively at once.[26] Is Rossouw's critique directed solely at film or also at other arts that claim to be transformative (e.g., literature)? If directed solely at cinema, why would it lack this capacity compared with other arts? If the transformative potential of cinema were illusory, what would be the point of making movies about characters who make moral choices, battle injustice, or develop morally throughout the narrative? What would be the point, for that matter, of criticizing the ideological dimensions of cinema with respect to representations of gender, "race"/ethnicity, class, colonialism, ecology, or political issues? These questions are pertinent because of our assumptions that art, including film, can be ethically (and perhaps politically) transformative.

Film-philosophy as (performatively) contradictory: Rossouw argues that (bold) film-philosophy is afflicted by a (performative) contradiction that arises because film philosophers claim to suspend their theoretical assumptions, yet they retain a belief in the philosophical significance of film. Indeed, they retain "a belief in film as such," thereby courting self-contradiction: "As I see it, the preparatory requirement to give up one's philosophical beliefs is not necessarily a contradiction; but the hypothetical act of *meeting* the requirement is a clear-cut performative contradiction."[27] Such an argument, however, relies on the premise that film philosophers should "give up" *all* their philosophical beliefs about film, which seems implausible for any kind of philosophical reflection. Film philosophers typically claim, rather, that we should approach a film and be receptive to its aesthetic qualities, cinematic features, and narrative complexities, refraining from the instrumental use of the film as merely illustrating a philosophical concept in ways that are implausibly reductive or that violate the integrity of the work.[28] This captures elements of any hermeneutic approach to art that acknowledges its aesthetic features, while also aiming to understand its philosophical meaning.

To continue, film-philosophy, according to Rossouw, presupposes a "preparatory ethics" through which practitioners prepare themselves in order to engage philosophically with film. The problem is that this preparatory ethics, for Rossouw, performs the philosophical work that film philosophers attribute *to the film,* claiming that (the encounter with) film is the "initiator" of this ethical experience. The underlying belief, responsible for both the preparatory ethics and claims that film is philosophical, is the idea that film conceals reservoirs of meaning that we can only access and express via complex hermeneutic work.[29] According to Rossouw, it is this "belief in film" as having a "knowingness"—harboring a deep meaning that requires assiduous interpretation to reveal—that lies at the heart of the preparatory ethics making possible the film as philosophy enterprise.[30]

The relationship between "preparatory ethics" and transformative ethical effects, however, is a "hermeneutic circle" that remains a condition of our engagement with art. We always bring partial background knowledge (hermeneutic "prejudices") to whatever we care to interpret and understand, and cannot grasp the whole at once prior to adopting piecemeal interpretations in light of our partial background knowledge. This is especially the case with works of art, which require some background understanding of cultural context, history of the art form, and even biography of the artist to enable interpretation and understanding of the work. As Arthur C. Danto and other philosophers point out, we often require a prior grasp of the "artworld"—or in this case, "cineworld"—in order to engage in the hermeneutic game that enables a proper engagement with modern art. Moreover, we can develop deeper understanding with subsequent interpretations, drawing on further background knowledge, new horizons of meaning, dialogue with others, and competing interpretations, while acknowledging that a "total" understanding of the work remains unavailable.

The same applies to the way we engage with cinema and to the practices of film-philosophy. We bring background knowledge and a motivation priming us toward the aesthetic experience of film, but this is simply part of the hermeneutic process of arriving at a more complex understanding with subsequent experiential encounters. Without entering debates concerning the "aesthetic attitude," we can always bring different attitudes to bear toward a work of art (aesthetic, instrumental, social, reflective, personal, historical, institutional, political, ideological, etc.), which include a desire to engage with the work ethically and philosophically. This is not a question-begging circularity but signals rather our participation in the hermeneutic circle that defines practices of interpretation and understanding. It is our experiential encounter with the work that prompts philosophical engagement (grounded in aesthetic experience), not the imposition of an ethical approach that "forces" us to see the film as philosophically significant. There is no more contradiction involved in bringing an ethical or philosophical approach to a film than doing so in relation to any other object of theoretical interest.

Film-philosophy as imposition: Rossouw's fourth objection concerns the problem of identifying the *initiative* for these claims concerning philosophical meaning, which are then *imposed* on the film without adequate justification. As he asks, "where lies the main initiative for the supposed self-transformation that follows from films doing philosophy? ... [W]ho initiates and sustains the cinemakeover—the film or the viewer?"[31] Rossouw argues that film philosophers, as philosophically committed, ethically prepared viewers, are the real source of philosophical or ethical meaning (and thus transformative power) attributable to a film: "Both the preparatory ethics of film as philosophy and the hermeneutics of overreading thus proceed from a supposed belief in the knowingness that films and related works possess."[32] Indeed, this prior belief, according to Rossouw, turns the film into a pretext for the activity of philosophical or ethical interpretation ("overreading"), which serves as the basis for any claims concerning its transformational potential. As he skeptically concludes: "Film can lay no special claim to transformational effects just because it happens to be (one of the many possible things) intended for such effects by someone with the necessary ethical attitude."[33]

In arguing that film philosophers claim to "let the film speak for itself" but then impose their own philosophical interpretations, Rossouw presents a false dilemma: the "initiative" for film-philosophy must lie either with the film itself or with the philosophical critic. What is missing in Rossouw's construal, however, is the *interplay* between the cinematic work and philosophical viewer: the work that invites a philosophical or ethical mode of response, whether by intentional design or aesthetic composition; and the viewer whose "beholder's share" includes a receptivity to the aesthetic experience of film and any philosophical or moral reflection it may inspire. Rossouw's critique overlooks, moreover, the role of *aesthetic experience* in the film-philosophy encounter. It is one's own aesthetic experience of art—the distinctively cinematic (ethical) experience that the work evokes—that serves as the experiential basis for the aforementioned "preparatory ethics" and subsequent claims concerning film as philosophy or cinematic ethics.

CINEMATIC ETHICS AS TRANSFORMATIVE EXPERIENCE

Leslie A. Paul has argued that there are some experiences that change or transform who we are in ways that we cannot predict or anticipate, altering the epistemic attitudes, cognitive decisions, moral preferences, and even the personal identity of the subject who undergoes them.[34] This means that we cannot always apply decision procedures, for example, to epistemic or moral claims in cases in which we require knowledge by acquaintance in order to know what an experience is like or how we should act in a given situation. Paul's "thought experiment" example is being a vampire, a state of being undead that one might be able to imagine but can have no real knowledge about unless one has somehow experienced being a vampire. More familiar examples of transformative experiences include having a child, suffering a life-changing illness, falling in love . . . and, perhaps, pursuing philosophy (as a way of life). I am not the same person I was thanks to the experiences I have undergone. I was not able to understand the nature of those changes, however, until I underwent those transformative experiences myself, unlike ordinary experiences that do not fundamentally alter who I am or what I take myself to be. Moreover, I cannot predict prior to having such an experience what it will be like or what outcomes it might yield.

Paul's claims concerning "transformative experiences" are an analytic version of the existential conception of freedom or possibility: the idea that experiences can be transformative in the sense that what we experience can alter who we are in ways that are unpredictable but life-changing. We might compare this idea of existential possibility with Hannah Arendt's idea of *natality*, where the defining feature of human action is the capacity to "begin anew," to introduce "newness" into the world through free thought and action.[35] Although Arendt's focus is politics, art is another locus of natality; cinematic art—along with cinematic experience—can have this potential for "natality" in ways that reveal who we are and what matters to us.

Paul's account focuses on the role of transformative experiences in relation to knowledge and (moral) decision-making procedures. What of existentially transformative experiences, which affect how we understand who we are or what we might become? We should restore an existential sense to transformative experiences that influence what possibilities present themselves to us as meaningful. Artworks, for example, offer aesthetic experiences that can transform not only who I think I am but also how the world reveals itself to me. They are occasions for reminding ourselves, but also for discovering, what we care about in life.

My claim is that art, including cinematic art, can provide transformative experiences (in certain cases and contexts). Philosophy, too, can be a transformative experience, transforming who I am thanks to my encounter with certain philosophical ideas, works, teachers, communities, or practices. If that is possible for philosophy, then why not for arts like film?[36] Indeed, there are many ways in which cinema can contribute to a transformative ethics. Films can provide "perspicuous presentations" (Wittgenstein) of situations or events that reframe what we understand about the world. They can provide a phenomenologically rich understanding of perspectives or experiences remote from one's own. They can reconfigure previously held beliefs or views that can transform our horizons of meaning. They can even provide existentially meaningful forms of experience that elicit care or concern for others, for nature, or for the world itself. These are four related ways in which we can describe cinematic experience as not only contributing to philosophy but as expressing a transformative ethics.[37]

On a more speculative note, we might understand the recent resurgence of interest in cinephilia as a cultural renovation of the idea of "philosophy as a way of life."[38] From this perspective, film-philosophy can be a way of shaping our existence ethically through thoughtful engagement with film. It could become a cultural practice defined by a love of cinema (and of philosophy), committed to the idea that cinema can reveal the world anew, wiping away, as André Bazin once wrote, "that spiritual dust and grime with which my eyes have covered it."[39] Cinema can reveal an aesthetically intensified experience of reality, expressing a love or care for existence—for nature and spirit—that includes whatever exceeds our habitual ways of knowing. It expresses an intensity or energy that can move us emotionally, cognitively, and morally. As Martin Seel argues, this intensity or capacity for moving us expresses the unique *ethos* of film, which is its capacity for transformative effects on the viewer: "cinema can disturb, rattle, play out, and thus question the configurations of our impulses, affects, and affinities in their opaque intertwining and interlocking with convictions and emotions of all kinds."[40] It can alter, rearrange, or reconfigure affective, emotional, and cognitive attitudes and beliefs, transforming ordinary experience into aesthetic experience with ethical significance and existential import. This is why film philosophers claim that cinema has the capacity to elicit transformative ethical experience.

NOTES

1. Stephen Mulhall, *On Film* (London: Routledge, 2002); Thomas E. Wartenberg, *Thinking on Screen: Film as Philosophy* (London: Routledge, 2007); and Robert Sinnerbrink, *New Philosophies of Film: Thinking Images* (London: Continuum, 2011).

2. Wartenberg, *Thinking on Screen*; Paisley Livingston, *Cinema, Philosophy, Bergman: On Film as Philosophy* (Oxford: Oxford University Press, 2009); Daniel Frampton, *Filmosophy* (London: Wallflower Press, 2006); Mulhall, *On Film*; and Sinnerbrink, *New Philosophies of Film*.

3. Mulhall, *On Film*, 4; Paisley Livingston, "Theses on Cinema as Philosophy," in *Thinking through Cinema: Film as Philosophy*, ed. Murray Smith and Thomas E. Wartenberg (Malden, MA: Blackwell, 2006), 11–18; and *Philosophy and Film: Bridging Divides*, ed. Christina Rawls, Diana Neiva, and Steven S. Gouveia (New York: Routledge, 2019).

4. Livingston, "Theses on Cinema as Philosophy"; Bruce Russell, "The Philosophical Limits of Film," in *Philosophy of Film and Motion Pictures: An Anthology*, ed. Noël Carroll and Jinhee Choi (Malden, MA: Blackwell, 2006), 387–390; and Murray Smith, "Film Art, Argument, and Ambiguity," in *Thinking through Cinema: Film as Philosophy*, ed. Smith and Thomas E. Wartenberg (Malden, MA: Blackwell, 2006), 33–42.

5. Mulhall, *On Film*, 4.

6. Livingston, "Theses on Cinema as Philosophy"; Russell, "Philosophical Limits of Film"; and Smith, "Film Art, Argument, and Ambiguity."

7. Aaron Smuts, "Film as Philosophy: In Defense of a Bold Thesis," *The Journal of Aesthetics and Art Criticism* 67, no. 4 (2009): 409–420; Wartenberg, *Thinking on Screen*; and Thomas Elsaesser, *European Cinema and Continental Philosophy: Film as Thought Experiment* (London York: Bloomsbury, 2019).

8. Frampton, *Filmosophy*; Sinnerbrink, *New Philosophies of Film*; and David Davies, "Philosophical Dimensions of Cinematic Experience," in *Philosophy and Film: Bridging Divides*, 135–156.

9. Robert Sinnerbrink and Lisa Trahair, "Film and/as Ethics," *SubStance* 45, no. 3 (2016): 3–15, at 6.

10. Robert Sinnerbrink, *Cinematic Ethics: Exploring Ethical Experience through Film* (New York: Routledge, 2016), 10–17.

11. Sinnerbrink, *Cinematic Ethics*, 9.

12. Robert Sinnerbrink, "Re-Enfranchising Film: Towards a Romantic Film-Philosophy," in *New Takes in Film-Philosophy*, ed. Havi Carel and Greg Tuck (London: Palgrave MacMillan, 2011), 25–47.

13. Martin P. Rossouw, *Transformational Ethics of Film: Thinking the Cinemakeover in the Film-Philosophy Debate* (Leiden: Brill, 2021).

14. Rossouw, *Transformational Ethics of Film*, 3.

15. Rossouw, *Transformational Ethics of Film*, 4.

16. Rossouw, *Transformational Ethics of Film*, 5.

17. Rossouw, *Transformational Ethics of Film*, 6.

18. Rossouw, *Transformational Ethics of Film*, 6.

19. Rossouw, *Transformational Ethics of Film*, 196.

20. Rossouw, *Transformational Ethics of Film*, 197.

21. Rossouw, *Transformational Ethics of Film*, 201.

22. Rossouw, *Transformational Ethics of Film*, 199.

23. Rossouw, *Transformational Ethics of Film*, 201.

24. Nelson Goodman, *Ways of Worldmaking* (London: The Harvester Press, 1978), 102.

25. See Gordon Graham, *Philosophy of the Arts: An Introduction to Aesthetics*, 3rd ed. (Abingdon: Routledge, 2005), 58–62ff, for an overview.

26. See Carl Plantinga, *Screen Stories: Emotion and the Ethics of Engagement* (Oxford: Oxford University Press, 2018); Sinnerbrink, *Cinematic Ethics*; and Jane Stadler, *Pulling Focus: Intersubjective Experience, Narrative Film, and Ethics* (London: Continuum, 2008).

27. Rossouw, *Transformational Ethics of Film*, 201

28. Sinnerbrink, "Re-Enfranchising Film"; and Mulhall, *On Film*.

29. Rossouw, *Transformational Ethics of Film*, 202.
30. Rossouw, *Transformational Ethics of Film*, 201–202.
31. Rossouw, *Transformational Ethics of Film*, 203.
32. Rossouw draws on Colin Davis's critique of "overreading": "Overreading refers to philosophical interpretations of literature and film that push—and often completely overrun—the boundaries of how we normally gather meaning from a work. (Both Cavell and Deleuze happen to belong to the 'canon' of overreaders that he [Davis] identifies and explores.)" Rossouw, *Transformational Ethics of Film*, 202.
33. Rossouw, *Transformational Ethics of Film*, 204–205.
34. Leslie A. Paul, "Précis of *Transformative Experience*," *Phenomenology and Philosophical Research* 91, no. 3 (November 2015): 760–765.
35. Hannah Arendt, *The Human Condition* (Chicago: University of Chicago Press, 1958).
36. A critic might argue that, if one accepts that art can be transformative, then it follows that cinema can be, too, so the real dispute is over the transformative character of art. As remarked, there is ongoing debate over aesthetic cognitivism as an approach to art as well as the idea of art changing behavior. I take it as evidence for art's transformative power, however, that art's moral-ethical as well as ideological-political character continues to be both promoted and debated, along with the fact that art remains subject to cultural censorship practices.
37. I discuss these aspects of transformative ethics in Terrence Malick's recent "Weightless Trilogy"—*To the Wonder* (2012), *Knight of Cups* (2015), and *Song to Song* (2017)—as offering Kierkegaardian aesthetic meditations on love, ethics, and religiosity. See Robert Sinnerbrink, *Terrence Malick: Filmmaker and Philosopher* (London: Bloomsbury, 2019), 161–206.
38. Pierre Hadot, "There Are Nowadays Professors of Philosophy but No Philosophers," trans. J. Aaron Simmons, *Journal of Speculative Realism* 19, no. 3 (2005): 229–237.
39. André Bazin, *What Is Cinema?*, trans. Hugh Gray, vol. 1 (Berkeley: University of California Press, 1976), 15.
40. Martin Seel, "The Ethos of Cinema," special issue, *Contemporary Aesthetics* 5 (2016), https://digitalcommons.risd.edu/liberalarts_contempaesthetics/vol0/iss5/3. Accessed July 22, 2022.

19

... Spiritual Exercises Before a Screen

On "Film as Philosophy" and Its Transformational Ethics

MARTIN P. ROSSOUW

TV BUDDHA

The pursuit of personal transformation is not restricted to the expert endeavors of mahatmas, mystics, and monks. People often also pursue their self-work and transformation through a number of rather ordinary, everyday practices: things like reading, journaling, listening to music, taking walks, spending time in nature, or perhaps having a running schedule like Forrest Gump. So what about *watching films?* This hypothetical instance of film spectatorship may go by many names. Michel Foucault would call it a "technology of the self."[1] I like to think of it as an instance of "transformational ethics."[2] But, to up the polemical ante, let me here follow the French philosopher Pierre Hadot and give it the synonymous, yet slightly more provocative label of a "spiritual exercise"—a procedure which "invites us to establish a relationship of the self to the self" with the aim of achieving "a profound transformation of the individual's mode of seeing and being."[3] Can we think of the act of going to the movies, of rewatching an old favorite on Blu-ray, of a weekend spent binge-watching Netflix, as *such* an exercise?

When it comes to the question of what film is good for (or, I should say, what it *can* be good for), the suggestion that film spectatorship may amount to a spiritual exercise is one well worth wrestling with. There is no denying the ubiquity and historical persistence with which personal transformation as a general value has always wooed humanity. This

FIGURE 20. Nam June Paik's video installation *TV Buddha* (1974), Collection Stedelijk Museum Amsterdam. © Nam June Paik Estate.

ubiquity is attested to as much by contemporary rituals of life coaching, psychological guidance, and mind-altering drugs as it is by arrays of spiritual exercises inspired by cultural and religious traditions across millennia. Nor is there any denying that aesthetic experience—its potential for consolations, cultivations, and purifying catharses, especially at the hand of "high art"—is frequently revered as a source of transformation in the manner of spiritual exercises. And yet while a litany of traditions and practices bespeak the value of personal transformation in all walks of life, dare I say that *gluing yourself to a movie screen* is not typically raised as an option to attain it, and it is certainly not a "spiritual exercise" that enjoys any widespread recognition.

At gut level, the idea of watching films as a spiritual exercise just has an oxymoronic sense of irony to it—a sense that I find exquisitely captured by Nam June Paik's well-known video sculpture artwork, *TV Buddha*. First produced in 1974, the basic premise in all of Paik's iterations of *TV Buddha* has remained the same: a smallish Buddha figure is placed before a television set, behind which is a video camera that records the Buddha looking at the screen, thus capturing the figure in a closed-circuit loop. Certainly, what the Buddha *could* be watching on his TV, and indeed *is* watching in this case, is a significant point to which I'll circle back. But, prior to that, I'm simply struck by the obvious disconnect between the *two things* in face-off here. It is not only a cultural disconnect between tradition and modernity, as commentators like to observe, but a spiritual disconnect: that such a *pious* figure is made to sit in meditative posture in front of a television, that most *pulpy* and *profane* of screen media. If anything, most spiritual exercises will rather involve an ascetic avoidance of such "screen time" for the sake of mindfulness and personal well-being. "Buddha" *plus* "TV" somehow doesn't add up to our conventional intuitions of what a spiritual exercise should be. It feels like an infringement of categories. Like comparing apples and oranges. Or confusing your mandalas with *The Mandalorian* (2019–, Disney+).

That said, for all the curiosity that might go with this idea of a spectatorial spiritual exercise, it *does* have a curious way of often popping up once you're on the lookout for it. One field where you certainly can expect to run into it is at the juncture of film and religious studies. An intriguing case in point is Francisca Cho's *Seeing Like the Buddha,* which proposes that films can take on the role played by Buddhist icons and images by not merely articulating Buddhist teachings but by ultimately *enacting* them—thus cultivating for viewers ways of being in the world that have previously only been sought through traditional contemplative practices.[4] Yet make no mistake: such evocations of the idea are not only the reserve of religious devotees. "What is interesting," as S. Brent Plate observes, "is how many secular film theorists [also, ultimately] *point toward* something like a practice of watching particular types of films, as if mimicking St Ignatius's spiritual exercises or a Buddhist Eightfold Path."[5] It is this "pointing" that has become the source of my own fascination: that a noninvested and seemingly unconcerned field might still implicitly point to ways in which watching film can be a spiritual exercise. And to feed my fascination I had to look no further than my disciplinary home base, film-philosophy, and what has come to be known as the "film as philosophy" debate.

"THE GOOD" OF FILM AS PHILOSOPHY

In its contemporary form, the film as philosophy debate has developed around the work of philosophers such as Stephen Mulhall, Thomas Wartenberg, and Robert Sinnerbrink, among others, building upon the earlier pathbreaking influences of Stanley Cavell and Gilles Deleuze.[6] The essential project of these philosophers is to establish how films might be said to do philosophy, or contribute to philosophical reflection, whether in the shape of cinematic arguments, thought experiments, or even films that are claimed to enact their own philosophically relevant modes of thought. In other words: you won't find any out-and-out talk about spiritual exercises here.

Even so, you need only to pose the question of *value* to see that a shadow of spiritual exercises has in fact been tiptoeing through the debate all along. Undoubtedly, by claiming that films can "do philosophy," or "think" in a cinematic way, the philosophers concerned adopt a position on "what film is good for," and in this way advance an implicit yet inevitably ethical, value-laden agenda. But the point is that when you level at the debate the question of the good of film, you get the *obvious* answer (e.g., "Well, 'doing philosophy' obviously suggests that film holds a potential cognitive value that can aid us in our intellectual pursuits"); but usually wrapped up in it also a rather *less obvious* answer, quietly unfolding in the debate like an intriguing sub-plot. And, for me, it's the sub-plot that steals the show: namely, that philosophers persistently also envision edifying *practical effects*—potential transformations of perceptions and experience—as the good of viewing films as philosophy. Considered as an exercise in valuation, the debate therefore seems just as concerned with the value of *personal transformation,* valuing films that do philosophy also for doing transformative things to us.[7] By casting various visions of how and why self-transformation may result from watching films, these philosophers are, in effect, having a crack at transformational ethics, a transformational ethics *of film,* even though they themselves wouldn't think of it in these terms. And seeing that *such* a transformational ethics posits film spectatorship as the enabling means or technique of self-transformation, the film as philosophy debate inadvertently also yields a picture of spectatorship as a spiritual exercise.

So, in what follows, and with TV Buddha as my guiding image, I pick out four moments indicative of how the film as philosophy debate conjures up the possibility of spiritual exercises before a screen. I must stress, however, that these film-based spiritual exercises are not "official releases" from the field, so to speak. Officially, these philosophers are busying themselves with the problem of film as philosophy; the nascent, still undertheorized spiritual exercises part of their project, more than a subplot even, is the unscripted drama that's only been transpiring in between and behind the scenes. Hence, I like to think of the cases below as a set of "sneak peeks" at an attraction yet to be fully recognized for what it is.

SPIRITUAL EXERCISES THROUGH FILM?
FOUR SNEAK PEEKS

Let's first off contemplate the scene of TV Buddha before his screen as an exercise in *self-examination*. Of course, in Paik's installation, he is looking at a recorded picture of himself. But to *really* look at himself, a number of film philosophers would say, TV Buddha may well do better to watch a blockbuster philosophical hit like Lana and Lilly Wachowski's *The Matrix* (1999) or David Fincher's *Fight Club* (1999). In the film as philosophy debate, such so-called "twist films" or "mind-game movies" are frequently approached as staging thought experiments, and in this sense are said to hold self-reflective value for their audiences.[8] Consider Thomas Wartenberg's well-known account of *The Matrix* as a philosophical thought experiment.[9] For Wartenberg, *The Matrix* "does" philosophy by doing the same done by classical skeptical thought experiments, and doing it in a valuably updated and immersive way. *The Matrix* thus not only illustrates an "unsettling [of] our established habits of belief and action in order to reestablish them on a firmer, more critically aware foundation," but it also makes us *participate* in the main protagonist's initial acceptance of a false reality and the ensuing removal thereof, thereby leading viewers like TV Buddha to question beliefs about their own (increasingly screen-mediated) reality.[10]

What's left unsaid in Wartenberg's account, however, is the deep roots that conventional philosophical thought experiments actually have in spiritual exercises. Wartenberg approaches *The Matrix* as a remediation of the so-called evil demon thought experiment. But this classical skeptical scenario from René Descartes' *Meditations*—a series of intellectual exercises extending over six days, with noted indebtedness to ancient disciplines such as Platonic *aversio* and Stoic assent—is itself steeped in associations with spiritual exercises.[11] And it certainly seems that the transformational underpinnings of thought experiments *as spiritual exercises* are part and parcel of their perceived value when remediated in film. The "film as thought experiment" functions for the likes of Wartenberg as something more than a dry academic exercise. There are definite existential stakes to knowing that your assumptions and unquestioned perceptions can be fallible; plus, viewers are afforded an introspective uncovering of such unquestioned beliefs in the interest of attaining greater autonomy and self-knowledge. In this respect—we have to admit—our TV Buddha watching *The Matrix* could easily be considered as engaged in a spiritual exercise, one, in fact, as old as the Socratic injunction to "Know Thyself."

For a second sneak peek, let us have TV Buddha tune in to TCM to watch the 1950 Billy Wilder film noir classic, *Sunset Boulevard*. Noël Carroll submits Wilder's tale about a forgotten, aged silent cinema star as one of his cases for the possibility of film as philosophy.[12] In short, Carroll argues that any film which can fulfill the task of reminding us of important but neglected truths should be seen as enabling philosophical contemplation, and in this sense "does" philosophy. But, clearly, "doing philosophy" here amounts to nothing other than a spiritual exercise: by Carroll's account, *Sunset Boulevard* essentially acts as a memento mori, less "Know Thyself" than "Remind Thyself"; an exercise in *recollection* that calls to mind for viewers the inevitability of our mortality with respect to the process of aging. As Carroll notes, the exercise is driven not only by the story of the fading Hollywood star, Norma Desmond (Gloria Swanson), but also by factors like Wilder's recourse to horror film stylistics, which adds cinematic substance to the theme of mortal aging.[13]

It's no coincidence that Carroll's implied spiritual exercise comes down to a contemplation of the troubling, "mortal themes" of our existence, themes that we are likely to neglect or suppress, like aging and death. This marks what is, in fact, a towering commonplace in the film as philosophy debate: films are most likely to be valued philosophically when they pose some manner of *challenge, resistance,* or *difficulty* for the viewer to contemplate. Ideally speaking, films should "provoke, incite, or force us to think."[14] More than mere contemplation, that is, philosophers tend to value films that elicit from viewers some form of *contemplative endurance:* experiences of difficult thinking and difficult things to think about.[15] And in Carroll's implied spiritual exercise, such endurance stems from being reminded of, and thus having to meditate on, the inevitability of death—which, come to think of it, really amounts to a *pre*-meditation of death.[16] The *premeditatio malorum*, the prestudy or previsualization of bad fortune, was a key spiritual exercise for the likes of Seneca and Marcus Aurelius, who prescribed that one should actively imagine potential evils or troubles lying ahead in order to train your reactions in preparation for when they really befall you. Say, that you might end up with a bullet in the back, dead, in a swimming pool. Or, more likely, that one day you *will* become grotesquely old and probably also forgotten. Either way, TV Buddha would do well to kick-start this exercise by watching *Sunset Boulevard.*

A third sneak peek. If Stanley Cavell had to mine Paik's *TV Buddha* for spiritual exercises, he would've no doubt wanted that TV to screen films like *It Happened One Night* (1934, dir. Frank Capra), *The Phila-*

delphia Story (1940, dir. George Cukor), or *His Girl Friday* (1940, dir. Howard Hawks).[17] But why make our Buddha binge on Hollywood remarriage comedies? For Cavell, this classic genre represents the epitome of films that busy themselves with *moral perfectionism*, the conjoined philosophical *and* ethical value that he thus attributes to remarriage comedies.[18] Of course, the version of perfectionism of interest to Cavell is distinctly "Emersonian" (after Ralph Waldo Emerson): a perfectionism without perfection; aimed at recovering our singular selves from the ordinary everyday; to "become who you are" in an ongoing process of becoming and a willingness to change. Perhaps the key ingredient to this process is what Cavell refers to as "the responsiveness to and examination of one soul by another."[19] That is to say, like many ancient philosophers, Cavell endorses the spiritual exercises of *friendship* and *dialogue*. The intervention of "the Friend" is indispensable to Cavell's outlook on personal transformation, as it is "the Friend" who inevitably guides one's progress of self-becoming through everyday instances of confrontation and conversation.[20] Hence this insatiable enthusiasm that Cavell has for the classic Hollywood remarriage comedy. For it is ultimately the presence of a demanding form of friendship—that with a marriage partner—that constitutes the remarriage comedy as such a captivating study of the Emersonian pursuit to "become yourself." As Cavell puts it, these films are obsessed with the idea of "becoming, or being changed into, a certain sort of person."[21] It is a process prompted as much by a marriage in crisis as it is by "undramatic, repetitive, daily confrontations . . . with respect to the reality, the separateness, of another."[22] And the process is primarily carried out by repeated passages of conversation between the couples concerned.

So let's call this the good that Cavell finds *in* these films, the fact that they stage the ordinary, everyday spiritual exercise of couples in conversation. But surely, it seems to me, Cavell suggests the same perfectionist exercises presented onscreen to also occur between the films and *us*—that the good *in* these films may equally prove to be the good *of* the remarriage comedies, their tangible value to us as viewers. This entails that the remarriage comedy in toto may function as "the Friend" who initiates its own series of confrontations and conversations with the viewer. They say three's a crowd, but one could go so far as saying that TV Buddha gets drawn into a triangulated dialogical exercise, one in which the remarriage-couple *together* comprises a "Friend" who reaches beyond the screen to form a second-order dialogue with their viewer.[23] As part of this dialogical constellation, the viewer should well expect a similar process of "responsiveness to and examination of one soul by another." And if you think that the act of watching golden rom-coms is too mundane for such a spiritual exercise to occur, know that for an Emersonian such as Cavell *that* is precisely the point. It is supposed to be as ordinary as a marriage.

For a fourth and final sneak peek, I should add that spiritual exercises are not limited to the sort of inward-turned "concentrations of the self" that we have considered so far. The flip side is that spiritual exercises are just as often characterized by what Hadot would call "expansions of the self."[24] This is indeed a wildly recurring motive in the film as philosophy debate: that films can also turn viewers "outwards," as it were, by offering them a means to alternative perspectives, new experiences, and breaking existing molds of the self. This expansionist motive in the debate correlates with one of the most common spiritual exercises of ancient philosophy: "contemplation of the world."[25] For the ancients, the value of contemplating the world relates to a transformation of literal *vision,* how the philosopher *sees* the world. For contemporary film philosophers, the value of contemplating the world *through film* relates to a transformation of the viewer's vision more broadly conceived— typically spoken of in terms of shifting *perspectives* and gaining *new ways of seeing*.[26]

So, presumably, TV Buddha would want to watch some Terrence Malick. Malick is frequently endorsed by philosophers (and critics, like Jon Baskin) as a filmmaker who foregrounds "perspective" and "problems of seeing," who challenges viewers "to see in a new way," and who educates our perceptions by making us work through and reconcile opposing points of view.[27] Most of these Malickian perspectival affordances are depicted in a manner reminiscent of the "reframing" exercises practiced by Greco-Roman philosophers. Take Robert Sinnerbrink's account of Malick's *The New World* (2005).[28] Sinnerbrink argues that the film is an ambitious attempt at staging for viewers, on top of the clashing cultural perspectives that it works through, the very perspective of *nature itself* as an acting subject. It's the stuff of Stoicism, powered by cinematics. Through Malick's evocative use of nature cinematography, rapturous editing, and music, that is, viewers are given an experiential foothold for adopting a frame of mind akin to what the Stoics called "the view from above" or "the view of the cosmos."[29] In Sinnerbrink's terms, *The New World* lets us experience a greater, even "impossible," perspective that eclipses opposing cultural perspectives by bringing us to see our deeper unity in and with nature.[30] And you don't even have to be the outdoorsy type. Quite a prospect for a Buddha with just a TV.

INFREQUENTLY ASKED QUESTIONS

As Michel Foucault would have it, the work of self-transformation may occur not only by one's "own means" but also "with the help of others."[31] Yet, surely these "others" need not be restricted only to other *people*. With the samples taken from film as philosophy above, I hope, it has become clear how our experience of *film* might emerge as such an "other"—an aid or even essential means—occasioning for viewers the kind of self-work that comprises a spiritual exercise. Admittedly, given the unofficial "sneak peek" status of the examples cited, the overall picture that we can glean from the debate will always be decidedly speculative and, thus, *incomplete*. Dealing with spiritual exercises as such is not the central mission of these philosophers. So we cannot expect them to spell out a "how-to" guide for practicing self-transformation through film, let alone to critically interrogate an idea that is basically a by-product of their debate. But this also means that there are by default pivotal questions about the prospect left unposed, questions that presumably point the way for *how* we ought to value films as spiritual exercises going forward.

One question concerns the potential communal dimensions of such spiritual exercises. Our Buddha is, of course, a solitary figure, alone before his TV—quite like the *singular* model "spectator" routinely assumed by philosophers as the recipient of film as philosophy's transformational solicitations. But how might his spiritual exercises be affected by the likely possibility of being in the company of fellow TV Buddhas? What Julian Hanich has labeled the "audience effect"—the influence of other people while watching a film—is no doubt an important part of this equation, and depending on the situation (and indeed also the *cinema situation*, ranging from the massive auditoria to intimate living room viewings) seems capable of enhancing *or* detracting from TV Buddha's transformational success.[32]

There are also decisive questions about the temporal dimension of spiritual exercises through film. What happens to the spiritual exercise once the film is over—is the exercise then over too? Oftentimes the film as philosophy debate seems to suggest that these spiritual exercises occur only *while* the film is playing. But in what ways may the exercise live on when the Buddha walks away from the screen? Any notion of watching films as a spiritual exercise will have to take into account our memories and imaginings of the film in the postviewing experience, and how these "afterimages" of film may offer a continuing means for the exercise that started during the screening.[33]

Another question related to temporality concerns the frequency of watching required. Would it not be necessary for our Buddha to resort to second viewings and even repeated viewings? To my mind, it is only through cultivation and active training that spiritual exercises can realistically bring about "transformation." And for that you need, well, *exercise*. You need some form of *repetition*. Yet there would probably be more to such repetition than simply rewatching old stuff. One option might be to look up films that feature prominently repeating motifs or cycles—such as reliving the same day with Bill Murray in *Groundhog Day* (1993, dir. Harold Ramis)—which may put us through our paces in a single sitting. On that premise, it is rather appropriate that we've been dealing with a *television* Buddha. For it does seem that the kind of repeated engagement dictated by television as medium (our serial engagements with a storyworld, a set of characters, or a collection of related films) foregrounds a genuine possibility of actually *practicing* (on a daily, weekly, or "seasonal" basis) one's spiritual exercises before a screen.

However, prior to any of these questions is still the issue of *why film*. Why single out *moving images*, regardless of whether they're on TV or cinema screens, as the enabling means for transformational ethics? Now I do think that there is something to be said for the immersion and experiential richness afforded by film, that "films can sometimes do some things better," as many film philosophers would point out.[34] And there's also something to be said, given the stop-start nature of reading or our dealings with interactive digital media, for how film screenings afford a "constituted time" experience, within which spectators can relinquish control and submit to the rhythms and process of a film from start to end.[35] But, seeing that spiritual exercises have long been with us *before* the screen (if I may pun my own title), I cannot but wonder whether film might still turn out to only be an incidental accessory—one of many possible substitutes—whose efficacy ultimately depends on the *person using it* for a spiritual exercise. It certainly is revealing how philosophers in the film as philosophy debate incessantly emphasize the need for a suitable attitude or frame of mind on the part of the viewer for films to have their desired philosophical and transformational effects.[36] I therefore find it poignant that our guiding image, the TV Buddha, is indeed staring at an image of *himself*. Spiritual exercises may well be something that film is good for. But it's the good intentions we bring before the screen that will probably make the difference.

NOTES

1. See, e.g., *Technologies of the Self: A Seminar with Michel Foucault*, ed. Luther H. Martin, Huck Gutman, and Patrick H. Hutton (Amherst: University of Massachusetts Press, 1988).

2. Martin P. Rossouw, *Transformational Ethics of Film: Thinking the Cinemakeover in the Film-Philosophy Debate* (Leiden: Brill, 2021).

3. Pierre Hadot, *Philosophy as a Way of Life: Spiritual Exercises from Socrates to Foucault* (Oxford: Blackwell, 1995), 83, 90. Also see Pierre Hadot, *What Is Ancient Philosophy?* (Cambridge, MA: Harvard University Press, 2002).

4. Francisca Cho, *Seeing Like the Buddha: Enlightenment through Film* (Albany: SUNY Press, 2017).

5. S. Brent Plate, *Religion and Film: Cinema and the Re-Creation of the World*, 2nd ed. (New York: Columbia University Press, 2017), 144 (emphasis mine).

6. For helpful introductions to the film as philosophy debate, see Murray Smith and Thomas Wartenberg, "Introduction," *Journal of Aesthetics and Art Criticism* 64, no. 1 (2006): 1–9; Thomas Wartenberg, "On the Possibility of Cinematic Philosophy," in *New Takes in Film-Philosophy*, ed. Havi Carel and Greg Tuck (Basingstoke: Palgrave Macmillan, 2011), 9–24; Robert Sinnerbrink, "Film-Philosophy," in *The Routledge Encyclopedia of Film Theory*, ed. Edward Branigan and Warren Buckland (London: Routledge, 2013), 207–213; and Diana Neiva, "Are There Definite Objections to Film as Philosophy? Metaphilosophical Considerations," in *Philosophy and Film: Bridging Divides*, ed. Christina Rawls, Diana Neiva, and Steven S. Gouveia (London: Routledge, 2019), 116–134. Also see Robert Sinnerbrink's essay in this volume.

7. Rossouw, *Transformational Ethics of Film*, 110–114.

8. On twist films, see George Wilson, "Transparency and Twist in Narrative Fiction Film," *Journal of Aesthetics and Art Criticism* 64, no. 1 (2006): 81–95. On mind-game films, see Thomas Elsaesser, "The Mind-Game Film," in *Puzzle Films: Complex Storytelling in Contemporary Cinema*, ed. Warren Buckland (Malden, MA: Wiley-Blackwell, 2009), 13–41.

9. Thomas Wartenberg, "Philosophy Screened: Experiencing *The Matrix*," *Midwest Studies in Philosophy* 27, no. 1 (2003): 139–152; and *Thinking on Screen: Film as Philosophy* (London: Routledge, 2007), 55–75.

10. Wartenberg, "Philosophy Screened," 145; and *Thinking on Screen*, 73–74.

11. See the chapters of John Cottingham and Theodor Kobusch in *Philosophy as a Way of Life: Ancients and Moderns—Essays in Honor of Pierre Hadot*, ed. Michael Chase, Stephen R. L. Clark, and Michael McGhee (Malden, MA: Wiley-Blackwell, 2013), 148–166 and 167–183. Also see Hadot, *What Is Ancient Philosophy?*, 265.

12. Noël Carroll, *Minerva's Night Out: Philosophy, Pop Culture, and Moving Pictures* (Malden, MA: Wiley-Blackwell, 2013), 161–182.

13. Carroll, *Minerva's Night Out*, 165–169.

14. Robert Sinnerbrink, *New Philosophies of Film: Thinking Images* (London: Continuum, 2011), 142.

15. Rossouw, *Transformational Ethics of Film*, 92–93.

16. See Hadot, *Philosophy as a Way of Life*, 85, 93–101; and *What Is Ancient Philosophy*, 136–137.

17. See Stanley Cavell, *Pursuits of Happiness: The Hollywood Comedy of Remarriage* (Cambridge, MA: Harvard University Press, 1981); and *Cities of Words: Pedagogical Letters on a Register of the Moral Life* (Cambridge, MA: The Belknap Press of Harvard University Press, 2004). For this brief reflection, however, I am limiting myself to Cavell's more condensed set of reflections in the essay "The Good of Film" in *Cavell on Film*, ed. William Rothman (Albany: SUNY Press, 2005 [2000]), 333–348.

18. Cavell, "Good of Film," 335–338.

19. Cavell, "Good of Film," 339.

20. Cavell, "Good of Film," 336; and *Cities of Words*, 27.

21. Cavell, "Good of Film," 338.

22. Cavell, "Good of Film," 340.

23. Rossouw, *Transformational Ethics of Film*, 185.

24. See Hadot, *Philosophy as a Way of Life*, 189–220.

25. See Hadot, *Philosophy as a Way of Life*, 251–263; and *What Is Ancient Philosophy*, 229–231.

26. See, e.g., Stephen Mulhall, *On Film*, 2nd ed. (London: Routledge, 2008), 136, 140–141.

27. Jon Baskin, "The Perspective of Terrence Malick," *The Point Magazine* 2, April 4, 2010, http://thepointmag.com/2010/criticism/the-perspective-of-terrence-malick. Accessed September 22, 2021.

28. Robert Sinnerbrink, "Song of the Earth: Cinematic Romanticism in Malick's *The New World*," in *Terrence Malick: Film and Philosophy*, ed. Thomas Deane Tucker and Stuart Kendall (London: Continuum, 2011), 179–196.

29. See Hadot, *Philosophy as a Way of Life*, 238–250; and *What Is Ancient Philosophy*, 206–207.

30. Sinnerbrink, "Song of the Earth," 190–192.

31. Michel Foucault, "Technologies of the Self," in *Technologies of the Self*, 16–49, at 18.

32. Julian Hanich, *The Audience Effect: On the Collective Cinema Experience* (Edinburgh: Edinburgh University Press, 2018). A few years ago, Hanich and I (with our friend Jakob Boer) actually experimented with a "Contemplative Cinema Club" at the University of Groningen. Although this endeavor on work nights was admittedly short-lived, it did at least confirm to us that the quiet-attentive company of colleagues *does* make one more determined to sit through demanding experimental/minimalist films such as *Hotel Monterey* (1973, dir. Chantal Akerman) and *Die große Stille/Into Great Silence* (2005, dir. Philip Gröning).

33. See Carl Plantinga and Garrett Strpko's essay in this volume for a helpful first step in thinking about the "reflective afterlives" of film, even if they deal with moral reflection and not spiritual exercises (nor film as philosophy) as such.

34. Damian Cox and Michael Levine, *Thinking through Film: Doing Philosophy, Watching Movies* (Chichester: Wiley-Blackwell, 2011), 11.

35. Daniel Fairfax, "The Experience of a Gaze Held in Time: Interview with Jacques Aumont," *Senses of Cinema* 83 (2017), https://www.sensesofcinema.com/2017/film-studies/jacques-aumont-interview/. Accessed July 30, 2021.

36. See Rossouw, *Transformational Ethics of Film*, 187–206.

PART FIVE

Communal Goods

20

. . . Remembrance and Reflection

On Social Justice Cinema in the #BlackLivesMatter Era

MARYANN ERIGHA LAWER

Since the year 2013, the rallying cry of #BlackLivesMatter has engaged millions of concerned citizens across the world on the social media platform Twitter and beyond. The phrase gained currency after a jury of five white women and one mixed-race woman rendered a not guilty verdict for George Zimmerman, the 28-year-old white man who shot and killed a 17-year-old Black teenage boy, Trayvon Martin, who was walking to his residence. In response to police shootings, killings, and—in some cases—outright murders, people took to the streets and social media to protest and organize for a socially just future. #BlackLivesMatter evolved from a social media hashtag to a full-fledged movement to bring attention to, and ultimately end, the injustice.

Still today, we can witness the tireless efforts and ubiquitous iconography of #BlackLivesMatter organizations. #BlackLivesMatter is declared from the mouths of activists, academics, politicians, and pastors; in schools, homes, places of business, and centers for worship. The phrase is inscribed in various fonts—from all caps to bold print—across T-shirts, lawn signs, and handmade placards. Collectively, the overarching goal and hope is a United States and global village that values Black life. Further aims are to promote a safe and socially just existence through a host of prescriptions—from ending police brutality to implementing a fair living wage.[1]

Filmmakers, too, have been inspired to participate in the Movement for Black Lives. Since #BlackLivesMatter became the chant heard

FIGURE 21. Oscar (Michael B. Jordan) and his daughter Tatiana (Ariana Neal) in *Fruitvale Station* (2013, Ryan Coogler).

'round the world, filmmakers have contributed to the conversation through the production of social justice–oriented #BlackLivesMatter movies. Here, it is crucial to distinguish between three specific yet interrelated genres. First, the *social problem film* is an old tradition that highlights social issues, a segment of which is embedded in the larger canon of African American cinema. Second, the *social justice film* is a contemporary extension of that tradition, broadly applicable to socially conscious films from across the globe that addresses inequality and related movements for societal change. Third, while also situated within the enduring social problem film tradition, *#BlackLivesMatter movies* are a distinct branch of social justice films located within the US context of the modern Black freedom struggle.

Within their multiple shared meanings, stories, and sentiments, #BlackLivesMatter films distinctly catapult audiences into the onscreen lives of characters whose experiences are immersed in the context of contemporary social justice issues. There is substantive meaning worthy for audiences to grasp while thrust into the throes of empathy. Movies in the social justice genre of #BlackLivesMatter films allow viewers to reflect upon persistent racism in the United States, compounded with its impact on individuals and communities, to remember the victims of police violence and imagine alternative possibilities for social life.

SOCIAL PROBLEM FILMS AND BLACK LIVES

The cultural theorist Stuart Hall observed that "when Blacks appear in the documentary/current affairs part of broadcasting, they are always attached to some 'immigrant issue': they have to be involved in some crises or drama to become visible actors in the media.... Blacks participate, then, in broadcasts defined by the media as 'black' problems: and they do so within constraints, given in the very professional definition of what constitutes 'good television,' by the producers themselves."[2] From Britain, where Hall made his observations, to the United States, Black subjects in media have existed in the space of social problem programs. The social problem film not only engages with what issues are constituted as social problems—conflicts about pollution, poverty, or terrorism, for example—but also can extend to entire people being depicted as problems. A centerpiece of African American cinema on social problems focuses on the long-standing issue of white racial violence against Black lives.

With immense frequency, the problem of white racial violence has been depicted in popular American movies. Of early African American filmmakers who tackled serious civil matters, Oscar Micheaux stands out prominently. Micheaux's films were among the first to grapple with white Americans' violent lynchings of Black Americans.[3] Years later, Sidney Poitier's image became synonymous with "the slap heard round the world"—the nickname describing the now-famous scene from *In the Heat of the Night* (1967, dir. Norman Jewison). In the movie, a detective (Poitier) is wrongfully arrested for a crime he did not commit, then assists the local police chief in solving the crime while battling white racism. The moniker refers to Poitier's emphasis on not being slapped by a white American in the movie, in the midst of the Civil Rights era no less, without returning the gesture. In the following decade, during the 1970s, white violence persisted onscreen as Blaxploitation films depicted white oppression battling Black resilience.

From the films of Oscar Micheaux through the "race movies" era of African American film production between the 1910s and 1950s, and beyond, the trend of social problem narratives centering on white racism continues today in contemporary films—and yet, the achievement of racial justice and the extension of basic humanity to all racial groups remains elusive in the culture.

Still, major studio films of contemporary times reflect upon race and racism in the civil rights era. To mention a few: *Pride* (2007, dir. Sunu Gonera) recounts the story of an all-Black swim team, *Hidden Figures* (2016, dir. Theodore Melfi) follows African American female mathematicians during the space race, the hotly debated *The Help* (2011, dir. Tate Taylor) depicts experiences of African American maids during the 1960s, and *Glory Road* (2006, dir. James Gartner) details the first all-Black basketball starting lineup to win an NCAA championship in 1966.[4] While these films present narratives of forward progress that suggest growing racial integration and inclusivity in majority white societies, the genre of #BlackLivesMatter social justice films, on the contrary, problematizes this utopian depiction of progress.

As centralizing concepts, genres contain multiple dimensions. Principally, genres signify collective meaning: they unite films with similar plots, settings, characters, themes, and storylines. While genres are formal categorizations, usually not conceived prior to their emergence, the precision with which they connect multiple films makes their presence and influence impossible to deny. Besides the many truths and revelations they bear for films, genres also tell audiences a considerable amount about cultural desires, fears, and emotions. Genres and subgenres reveal information about populations and communities: the gamut of their thoughts, interests, joys, emotions, and experiences. In some instances, the meanings within genre films have relevance for audiences with particular demographic or social characteristics, capturing group adherence to or avoidance of certain narratives.[5] Of especial importance is how and why genre categorizations emerge from moments or periods of cultural significance, intertwined with the sociopolitical moment of their production. Media artifacts can bring to light "matters of concern" that affect populations greatly and direct their collective energies to galvanize attention toward pertinent issues.[6] Thus, given all the varied meanings and substance that genres embody, the social problem film genre, here specifically concerning films about anti-Black racism in the United States, has emerged over time within African American film production and among non-Black filmmakers who make movies about African Americans. Subsequently, the emergent contemporary genre of social justice #BlackLivesMatter cinema captures and reflects the pulse of the moment characterizing the modern freedom struggle in the United States.

THE VALUE OF #BLACKLIVESMATTER MOVIES AS SOCIAL JUSTICE CINEMA

In the current moment, violent incidents resulting in deaths continue to capture the collective shock, frustration, and trauma of global onlookers. The year 2021 alone witnessed the trial of Derek Chauvin, a white Minneapolis police officer who murdered George Floyd, an African

American man. Chauvin knelt on Floyd's neck until he stopped breathing, and the world watched from video footage captured with a cell phone. On the same day that Chauvin was found guilty of murder, a white police officer named Nicholas Reardon from Columbus, Ohio, shot and killed Ma'Khia Bryant, a Black teenage girl—among other tragedies.

The tumultuous era's vocal sentiments of solidarity expressed through social media, protests, political rallies, teach-ins, and other venues parallel the artistic consciousness of filmmakers. As the Movement for Black Lives seeks racial and social justice through wide-ranging societal change, contemporary filmmakers mobilize cultural productions to confront issues of racial injustice and dramatize encounters with white racism, prejudice, and oppression.

A crucial branch of social justice cinema, the #BlackLivesMatter film genre interrogates issues of racism, police brutality, and quite often excruciatingly painful instances of white police violence against African American communities as a means to shape discourse and effect change. Three films that encompass much of the spirit of social justice cinema in the Movement for Black Lives era are *Fruitvale Station* (2013, dir. Ryan Coogler), *The Hate U Give* (2018, dir. George Tillman, Jr.), and *American Son* (2019, dir. Kenny Leon). Based on a true story, *Fruitvale Station* chronicles the last day in the life of Oscar Grant III (Michael B. Jordan). With friends, Oscar celebrates New Year's Day in the wee hours of the morning in 2009 when Johannes Mehserle, a first-generation white German immigrant and BART transit officer, shoots and kills him. *The Hate U Give* follows Starr Carter (Amandla Stenberg), a private-school student from an urban neighborhood who witnesses a white cop shoot and kill her childhood friend Khalil (Algee Smith). The film follows Starr as she copes with the shooting and ultimately musters up the courage to testify against the police officer who killed Khalil. Adapted from a stage play, *American Son* delves into the life of Kendra Ellis-Connor (Kerry Washington), a concerned mother who visits the local police station after her son Jamal has not come home one night and is unresponsive to her multiple attempts to reach him.

These films offer poignant reflections upon racism in the United States. Cultural producers' vivid portrayals illustrate systemic racial inequalities, honor the remembrance of victims, and necessitate pensive reflection among audiences. Moreover, the films illuminate the perspectives of victims of violence and their families and communities.

REFLECTIONS UPON RACISM

Viewers observe a normal day in the characters' lives, a day that could represent a single day in any of our lives as they engage in mundane activities. *Fruitvale Station* follows the last day in the life of twenty-two-year-old Oscar Grant III as he shops for groceries, visits his daughter, and celebrates with his friends on New Year's Eve. In *The Hate U Give*, while catching up with a dear friend, Khalil drives down an empty street and listens to music. He and Starr flirt innocently, exchange smiles, and tease one another about their tastes in music. In *American Son*, Jamal is a high school student who goes out one night on a drive with friends. These characters are ordinary people, in ordinary moments. Yet in each instance, that day becomes their last. Knowing this fact, viewers are attuned to remember and cling onto those seemingly minor details.

In *American Son*, Kendra Ellis-Connor is a concerned mother who is a mixture of emotions—nervous, frantic, worried—while she paces around a police-station waiting room, the setting of the film. Kendra's son left home in a hurry that night and has not yet returned, which is uncharacteristic of him; he is not answering his phone or replying to her text messages. She is hopeful that her missing son will come back home alive. The officer on duty, Paul Larkin (Jeremy Jordan) asks her: What friends was he with? Does he know them? For how long? What car does he drive? What is he wearing? The everyday minutiae become memorialized, scrutinized, extraordinary. The details become important to the extent that Trayvon Martin's memory in the public mind has become synonymous with a bag of Skittles and a bottle of iced tea.

While police brutality marks a central theme in the films, preceding each incident is a string of ordinary affairs. There is nothing unforgettable or even particularly interesting about driving a car or riding the subway on a given night. Rather, these commonplace actions constitute routine activities in which people regularly engage. Yet under the brunt of white racism, the quotidian too easily becomes disrupted. Permanently so. In a society plagued by white racial violence, otherwise ordinary, unremarkable moments carry an unjustified level of heightened precarity—such that African Americans partaking in innocuous, routine activities like barbecuing or bird-watching are not immune from attacks of white violence and harassment.[7] Characteristically mundane actions unnecessarily spiral into scandals about racism.[8] Accordingly, driving has become attributed with precarity in the meme "Driving While Black," iconically captured in the seminal 1948 text *The Negro*

Motorist Green Book, which charted places that were safe or unsafe for Black people to circumvent white violence while traveling across the United States.[9] In each film, the pervasiveness of the quotidian machinations of white racism is emphasized, exemplified by the recurring scene of the fateful encounter between the white police and the Black victim.

As a consequence of intergenerational white violence, many African American parents engage in conversation with their children at young ages about interactions with police. One such conversation is the "making it home" talk, in which mothers instruct their children, and specifically their sons, on how, if accosted, to interact with police in order to make it home safely.[10] *The Hate U Give* begins with such a message that young Starr has internalized by the time she is a teenager. Traffic stops and pedestrian stop-and-frisks, as modern slave patrols, happen with such alarming regularity and frequency in the lives and neighborhoods of Black youths like Khalil. In this manner, he finds no reason why he should not reach for his hairbrush and engage in a bit of self-grooming during what seems to be a routine encounter. Starr, who is shielded from such police encounters, though, insists that he should keep his hands visibly in sight in order to "make it home."

Social justice cinema provides audiences an opportunity to examine the enduring impact of systemic white racial violence in the United States, such as the resultant disparate life experiences and encounters with trauma of different racial groups.[11] Throughout films in the genre, the juxtaposition between Black and white is visually apparent. In *The Hate U Give,* Starr straddles two worlds: the predominantly white private school she attends features high ceilings and is brightly lit, unlike the majority Black school in her neighborhood, which is overcrowded with narrow hallways. In *Fruitvale Station,* the white men involved in the train altercation are quickly and quietly ushered away without incident. In stark contrast, the Black men are detained, handcuffed, and berated. Even further, one policeman goes as far as to shoot and kill Oscar Grant III.

In *American Son,* likewise, race drives the dramatic tension. Visually, the police station was constructed during the historical era of Jim Crow segregation and thus contains an old relic of two separate and unequal water fountains. Downtrodden and defeated, Kendra rests her elbow on the small water fountain—marked colored. In another scene the racial juxtaposition is present in Kendra's conversation with Officer Larkin.

Kendra: Do you have a Black son?

Officer Larkin: No ma'am. I have two young daughters. White daughters.

Kendra: Then let's skip the empathy tactics, ok, because believe me, you have no idea.

Officer Larkin: Fine. Whatever.

The gulf of life experiences between them forges an impasse in understanding and, in Kendra's mind, only engenders a pretense of empathy.

Furthermore, in a flashback, Kendra recalls her worst fear as a mother living in a society plagued by white racism. During her recollection, her white husband sleeps soundly in bed while she, worried about her child, awakens suddenly from a nightmare. As she stands in the doorway and peers in to check on her son, her mind wanders to imagery and remnants of white violence: lynchings, nightsticks, officers, badges, and acquittals. She tells her husband, who himself wears a badge, "And you were a little boy asleep on the other side of town dreaming of becoming one." Although Kendra seeks out the police for help, she is also keenly aware that they might rather become the source of grief and the bearers of tragic news.

REMEMBRANCE OF VICTIMS

Absence and void are as much a part of the genre of #BlackLivesMatter movies, with departed or soon-departing protagonists. *American Son* relies heavily upon "suggestive verbalizations" through the communication of evocative language to give imaginative presence to an absent character.[12] Jamal's presence fills the conversation within the police station and even the title of the movie, though he is missing on screen. Jamal is known to us only in the stories that his mother recounts, in the memories of his father, and in the impersonal description (age, weight, height, last-worn clothing) of a police report, in the same manner that offscreen pictures and stories of victims of police killings posthumously fill social media hashtags, feeds, and memes.

In the films, as in social life, skeptical looks, pregnant pauses, stigmatizing labels, and bitter accusations attempt to malign the absent victim's character. There is quite often a presumption of criminality and guilt rather than of innocence for Black boys.[13] After a white police officer kills Khalil, discussions about Khalil's past emerge, and people debate whether or not he has sold drugs. In another instance, Kendra explains bluntly: "You think our bourgeois son has no right to associate with other Black kids without stamping a presumption of guilt all over himself." In their wake, there is a tendency to malign the victims' character. Official records such as those found in ritualistic news reports assert the police as the authoritative voice, obscuring other accounts of events.[14]

The presumption of guilt sways the focus of discussion, taking precedence over the lost life or the excessive violence. The conversation in *American Son* veers to the content of a bumper sticker that reads: *SHOOT COPS with camera phones when they make a bust.* In *The Hate U Give,* debate ensues over whether Khalil was holding a gun or a hairbrush. Trivial objects become the undue focal points of contention, resulting in the subjugation of the victims and the diversion of social justice aims.

Film is good for ruminations about those gaping silences to be filled by empathy that are absent in media coverage of police killings. In this way, the cinematic gaze brings value in supplanting news rituals. Starr's persistence illuminates Khalil's authentic image and legacy. As a parent, Kendra desires that Jamal be understood as she remembers him and not how he is made out to be through the eyes of white racism and law enforcement. The title *American Son* centers Jamal's life as a matter of concern for all viewers. As if he were *our* son, our child, who deserves national attention. To recall President Barack Obama's words in a speech about race in America: "If I had a son, he would look like Trayvon." Jamal's invisibility helps to imagine him as anyone's child, to put any viewer in his mother's shoes. Film empowers the subjects to speak and, in other instances, enables their loved ones to speak for them.

THE STANDPOINT OF FAMILIES AND COMMUNITIES

Beyond empathy for victims of white racial violence, #BlackLives Matter films convey messages of empathy for loved ones who lose someone special, thus placing these films almost always in connection with drama, and on occasion melodrama. In *Fruitvale Station,* a wide view of the hospital captures family and relatives as they await news from doctors about Oscar's condition, mustering hope that he will recover. These depictions illustrate the continuing repercussions of police brutality that reverberate through communities.

Key scenes help audiences understand the frustration that loved ones experience when seeking truth, justice, and reconciliation. In *The Hate U Give*, Starr is deeply disturbed by the white police officer's killing of her friend Khalil. As she fully immerses herself in the cause of seeking justice for Khalil's premature death, her friendships with her white private schoolmates become strained.

A lack of transparency frustrates concerned women seeking out information. The thick blue wall obstructs Kendra's efforts to obtain any information on Jamal's whereabouts and health status. Yet, racial double standards abound, and the wall suddenly becomes porous when Kendra's white husband Scott Connor (Steven Pasquale) enters the room. Kendra is both stunned and incensed upon observing the instant rapport between the two white males as they engage in small talk. Like Kendra, Oscar's girlfriend and the mother of his child, Sophina (Melonie Diaz) cannot pass beyond the blue wall's barricades. After shots are audibly fired, Sophina's attempts to physically transgress the boundaries of yellow tape are blocked. These scenarios capture the frustration and divide between those men in uniform purported to protect and serve and those citizens awaiting that expectation to be fulfilled.

Furthermore, the emotions of injustice in the wake of lives lost are dramatized with the tears and groans of grieving women—Starr, Sophina, and Kendra. Starr mourns at the scene of the death and thereafter. Sophina is distraught at the hospital when the doctor returns with upsetting news. Kendra sobs as the lieutenant reads the official report of Jamal's final living moments. Their lives are forever changed by their loved one's premature absence.

Empathy for lost lives is achieved from different vantage points: from the victims and from their significant others, parents, friends, and community members. The films provide spaces to remember the victims of police killings as people with lives, goals, aspirations, and loved ones left behind, bringing to light nuanced viewpoints in the struggle for societal reformation. Additionally, *American Son* and *The Hate U Give* offer perspectives on empathy for police officers, interestingly communicating these messages through Black officers who are uninvolved with the incidents. Though as Lieutenant John Stokes (Eugene Lee, in *American Son*) and Starr's uncle Carlos (Common, in *The Hate U Give*) offer their outlook on events, both men embody a detached familiarity. While expressing condolences for the unfortunate tragedies, their very presence appeals to convolution, at a glance seemingly within the aggrieved community but upon closer inspection profoundly outside it.

CONCLUSION

Certainly #BlackLivesMatter movies and their filmmakers make urgent interventions in narratives about the modern freedom struggle. More than a dozen films can be counted as part of this genre, from Spike Lee's classic *Do the Right Thing* (1989) to more recent films, including *Queen and Slim* (2019, dir. Melina Matsoukas), *My Name Is Myeisha* (2018, dir. Gus Krieger), and *See You Yesterday* (2019, dir. Stefon Bristol). *Straight Outta Compton* (2015, dir. F. Gary Gray) further illustrates the merging of genres, in this instance fusing social justice cinema with the musical biopic.

In this contexture of genre, filmmakers embrace cinema as a medium of remembrance and reflection: simultaneously a space to dramatize and memorialize people and events and to express—visually, aurally, and artistically—the virtues, struggles, and emotions of a movement. By providing viewers with outlets for remembrance and reflection, #BlackLivesMatter–inspired social justice cinema offers multiple avenues for empathy. Of course, cinema alone cannot change society. Though, like Black Lives, films matter deeply.

Films lend vivid portraits for nuanced discussion of pressing issues at hand. Films provide important spaces to rise above the discourse of status quo white racism: the rehearsed and standardized journalistic discourses, the instances when police killings or murders become "officer-involved shootings" or "police-involved incidents"; the videotapes delayed or unreleased; the footage "missing" or obstructed; the tracks covered; the officers delicately placed on paid administrative leave or quietly transferred to remote precincts. Films are good for honoring people who have passed and fostering solidarity among people who are living. Films serve as points of reference for people desiring to be connected, learn, empathize, and possibly act. The value of social justice cinema as a genre, thus, stands in its power to inspire sustained action and radical change while immersed in the throes of racial empathy.

NOTES

1. Christopher J. Lebron, *The Making of Black Lives Matter: A Brief History of an Idea* (New York: Oxford University Press, 2017).

2. Stuart Hall, "Black Men, White Media," in *Selected Writings on Race and Difference,* ed. Stuart Hall, Paul Gilroy, and Ruth Wilson Gilmore (Durham, NC: Duke University Press, 2021 [1974]), 51–55, at 52.

3. Mark Reid, *Redefining Black Film* (Berkeley: University of California Press, 1993).

4. NCAA is the abbreviation for National Collegiate Athletic Association.

5. Jason Mittell, "Genre," in *Keywords in Media Studies,* ed. Laurie Ouellette and Jonathan Gray (New York: New York University Press, 2017), 81–83.

6. Herman Gray, "Race, Media, and the Cultivation of Concern," *Communication and Critical/Cultural Studies* 10, nos. 2–3 (2013): 253–258.

7. Apryl Williams, "Black Memes Matter: #LivingWhileBlack with Becky and Karen," *Social Media + Society* (October–December 2020): 1–14.

8. Maryann Erigha, "Race Scandals as Racial Projects," in *The Routledge Companion to Media and Scandal,* ed. Howard Tumber and Silvio Waisbord (New York: Routledge, 2019), 370–379, at 371.

9. Marcus Hunter and Zandria F. Robinson, *Chocolate Cities: The Black Map of American Life* (Oakland: University of California Press, 2018).

10. Shannon Malone Gonzalez, "Making It Home: An Intersectional Analysis of the Police Talk," *Gender and Society* 33, no. 3 (2019): 363–386, at 377.

11. Marcus Bell, "Criminalization of Blackness: Systemic Racism and the Reproduction of Racial Inequality in the US Criminal Justice System," in *Systemic Racism: Making Liberty, Justice, and Democracy Real,* ed. Ruth Thompson-Miller, Kimberly Ducey, and Joe R. Feagin (New York: Palgrave Macmillan, 2017), 163–183.

12. Julian Hanich, "Suggestive Verbalizations in Film: On Character Speech and Sensory Imagination," *New Review of Film and Television Studies* 20, no. 2 (2022): 145–168.

13. Carl Suddler, *Presumed Criminal: Black Youth and the Justice System in Postwar New York* (New York: New York University Press, 2019).

14. Paul J. Hirschfield and Daniella Simon, "Legitimating Police Violence: Newspaper Narratives of Deadly Force," *Theoretical Criminology* 14, no. 2 (2010): 55–182.

21

... Making Movie Generations

On the Cultural Work of Hollywood Remaking

KATHLEEN LOOCK

YET ANOTHER *GHOSTBUSTERS* MOVIE!

Due to the Covid-19 pandemic, the release of *Ghostbusters: Afterlife* (dir. Jason Reitman)—the latest addition to the *Ghostbusters* franchise—has been repeatedly delayed and is scheduled for November 2021 at the time of writing. Unlike the 2016 reboot *Ghostbusters: Answer the Call* (2016, dir. Paul Feig), which took a fresh, tongue-in-cheek approach to the franchise with its gender-swap premise, in-jokes, cameos, and fanboy villain, *Afterlife* functions as a direct sequel to the 1980s *Ghostbusters* (1984, dir. Ivan Reitman) and *Ghostbusters II* (1989, dir. Ivan Reitman). Judging from the tone, visual style, and retro aesthetic of the trailer, this movie is invested in the idea of legacy and infused with nostalgia for the 1980s. A single mother (Carrie Coon) and her two kids, Trevor (Finn Wolfhard) and Phoebe (Mckenna Grace), move to their late grandfather's farm in Oklahoma. When Trevor and Phoebe discover the iconic ECTO-1 vehicle, ghost traps, jumpsuits, and other strange equipment in the abandoned farm buildings, they realize that their grandfather was a Ghostbuster and eventually follow in his footsteps, hunting ghosts and saving the rural small town that has become their new home. The trailer contains numerous Easter Eggs and subtle callbacks to the past, but except for some footage from the first *Ghostbusters* movie and voice-over with a recontextualized line from Bill Murray's Peter Venkman ("Call it fate, call it luck, call it karma. I

FIGURE 22. Promotion image from the trailer of *Ghostbusters: Afterlife* (2021, Jason Reitman).

believe everything happens for a reason"), it does not feature any of the original cast members, who have committed to reprising their roles. Instead, *Afterlife* focuses on Trevor, Phoebe, and their new friends, who represent the next generation of Ghostbusters.

Following the fan backlash and disappointing box-office performance of *Answer the Call, Afterlife* returns to the familiar *Ghostbusters* material and emphasizes continuity through generational renewal. Or, put differently, *Afterlife* offers a politically conservative and controversial course correction for the franchise, strategically employing serialization as a method to connect past and present, to bring the 1980s into the new millennium, and to endow the "original" *Ghostbusters* with an almost mythical quality. The seriousness and pathos the trailer wants to convey are unexpected given the tone set by the first *Ghostbusters*. As one critic put it, "the trailer endeavors to create reverence for a very irreverent film, in which Dan Aykroyd gets his dick sucked by a ghost, among countless other indelible gags."[1] The growing popularity (and profitability) of *ongoing narratives* makes such radical, retrospective transformations possible (and, perhaps, necessary to continue the story in a way that balances nostalgia with present-day sensibilities). *Afterlife* summons nostalgia for something that never was, or at least not quite like what viewers would likely remember. Having kids follow in the footsteps of the 1980s Ghostbusters creates a powerful narrative premise that appeals to younger and older generations alike: whereas younger viewers can discover the Ghostbusters story along with Trevor and Phoebe, the setup also encourages older viewers to remember their childhood and to relive their own first encounter with the team of paranormal exterminators. In that regard, *Afterlife*'s sentimental attitude toward the past is profoundly evocative, tapping into the emotional connections that viewers build with their childhood media and making these connections shareable across generations.

Brimming with ideas about inheritance and heritage, about reproduction and continuity, the latest *Ghostbusters* movie raises pertinent questions about the cultural work of film and, more specifically, of what I call "Hollywood remaking." I use this term to describe Hollywood's long-standing practice of recycling popular storytelling material in the form of film remakes, sequels, and reboots. I argue that Hollywood remaking establishes complex connections between time, memory, and identity that are tightly bound up with ideas about cultural transmission, generational belonging, and nostalgia.[2] *Afterlife* is not only a prime example of Hollywood's penchant for creating and sustaining profitable brands through long-term narrative serialization and expanding storytelling universes, but also shows the nostalgia-tinted interplay between time, memory, and identity at work. It informs the plot and visual style of the movie as well as its production history: written and directed by independent filmmaker Jason Reitman, son of the director of *Ghostbusters* and *Ghostbusters II*, Ivan Reitman, *Afterlife* was quickly framed in generational terms. In interviews, Jason Reitman established his authorial power by foregrounding his own childhood memories of and fannish devotion to his father's *Ghostbusters* films as necessary credentials to direct the sequel: "I've always thought of myself as the first *Ghostbusters* fan, when I was a 6-year-old visiting the set," he told *Entertainment Weekly*, insisting that the experience shaped him and also made him wonder whether he would someday be making his own *Ghostbusters* movie.[3] Meanwhile, Ivan Reitman, who is one of the producers of *Afterlife*, was touched that his son wanted to join the family business, speaking of "a passing of the torch both inside and out."[4] The notion of legacy is central to the plot of this *Ghostbusters* movie and likewise established as a discursive element by the Reitman director duo, who effectively promote the franchise as a family heirloom that is handed down from father to son.

If the question is what films—in particular, film remakes, sequels, and reboots—are good for, then one possible answer is that they provide a sense of continuity, organize the passage of time both on a collective level and for individual viewers, and hold and sustain identificatory potential over the course of our lives. Hollywood remaking can prompt the formation of what I call "movie generations": mnemonic communities that share a "we-sense" based not only on the same historical, political, and societal experiences but also on historically situated media experiences. I argue that through the repetition and serial unfolding of narratives over extended periods of time, Hollywood remaking encourages the prolonged reception of and engagement with fictional characters and their storyworlds. Remaking draws on the cinematic past to build a repertoire of shared media texts that partakes in the shaping of selfhood and in the construction and maintenance of communal coherence. The persistent return of *Ghostbusters* or, to name other examples, *King Kong*, *Invasion of the Body Snatchers*, *Planet of the Apes*, and *Star Wars* over the course of many years and decades, invites viewers to travel back in time, to remember specific iterations in their historic moment, and to realize that they are not alone with their memories but belong to a group of people that has also lived and aged alongside the same popular media texts that remain relevant in the present and will likely continue to exist in the future. Taking cues from memory studies' work on the relationship between memory and media, as well as generation theory's interest in formative media experiences, I will explore "the good" that may be attached to Hollywood remaking in terms of time, memory, and identity.

TIME

Hollywood remaking produces continuity. Film remakes, sequels, and reboots always come to form part of *ongoing* narratives—irrespective of their own claims to novelty, originality, and status as stand-alone works of art. It does not matter whether the movies are explicitly serialized on the level of plot, because processing familiar material in new historical contexts renders the entirety of movies based on that material legible as *serial texts* that evolve over time. What is being continued, in other words, does not automatically have to involve the movies' sustained storyworlds and the narratives that unfold onscreen. Rather, the process of recontextualization goes hand in hand with a serial progression that manifests itself at one remove from the diegetic level. Frank Kelleter and I have proposed the term "second-order seriality" to describe the "ongoing narratives about (and through) ongoing narratives" that remaking produces.[5] They reach beyond the fictional worlds onscreen and inscribe movies into overarching accounts of

Hollywood's—and, by extension, the nation's as well as the viewers' own personal—history. As serially evolving narratives, they become sites of ongoing cultural work, expressing and shaping how a culture thinks about itself and how individuals position themselves within that culture. From this vantage point, Hollywood remaking is as much about producing time-bound media experiences that foster generational belonging as it is about transcending such temporal constraints.

Serial narratives that endlessly generate follow-up possibilities by translating repetition into difference, Kelleter writes, "play an important part in creating systemic trust in the improbable reality of their own—and hence their own culture's—persistence."[6] This means the continuation of stories we already know contains a promise of "infinite futurity" that extends to the culture at large and to its capitalist system of cultural production.[7] Hollywood remaking, too, "has a stabilizing function, as each new variation reinforces the entire system of cultural self-generation and furthers the culture's belief in its own existence and continuity."[8] Remaking builds trust that the constantly changing world in which we live nevertheless remains the world we know. What distinguishes the serial narratives that remaking produces from those in other serial media with regular daily or weekly rhythms (newspapers, radio, and television) is their extended duration, often over decades, and their stance toward the past. Hollywood remaking stresses continuity by weaving a historical thread around and through the cinematic past that reaches into the present and future. And in so doing, remaking also draws attention to the passage of time in a manner that foregrounds change. Each new version of an already familiar story stands in for a specific moment in terms of its cultural, social, and political dynamics, as well as its position in film history, which is defined by industry trends, technologies, performers, narrative structures, visual aesthetics, politics of representation, and, more generally, the medium's affordances and constraints at the time. In addition, Hollywood remaking can become deeply enmeshed in everyday life, where it organizes the passage of time along the viewers' lived experiences, different life stages, and overall aging processes.

Usually, it is a new film version that encourages audiences to recognize themselves as belonging to a generational community. For instance, a recent remaking cycle that brought movies and television shows from the 1980s back onto the big screen—including films such as *The Karate Kid* (2010, dir. Harald Zwart), *The A-Team* (2010, dir. Joe Carnahan), *Footloose* (2011, dir. Craig Brewer), and *21 Jump Street* (2012, dir. Phil

Lord and Chris Miller)—gave rise to nostalgic musings among film critics, who now remembered the "originals" as generation-defining cultural touchstones.[9] Because of the remaking process, the old movies emerged as memory prompts that could take viewers back in time to an idealized, collectively shared pop-cultural past that was, in effect, responsible for who they had become and how they understood themselves in the present. But this good admittedly comes as a double-edged sword, since viewers also experienced these new movies as "an effort to trammel the memories of an entire generation," in the words of one critic.[10] Hollywood remaking always explores possibilities of variation and continuation, introducing change that is never limited to the remake, sequel, or reboot at hand but retrospectively affects the meanings and memories of previous movies as well. The 2016 *Ghostbusters* reboot, *Answer the Call,* elicited similar, if more vehemently negative, reactions among mostly male-identifying fans. Their toxic, misogynistic, and racist discourse centered on the "ruined childhood" trope and a fannish sense of loss that drew attention to the ways in which films can become formative media objects that impact memory and trajectories of the self.

MEMORY

According to Marita Sturken, "memory establishes life's continuity; it gives meaning to the present, as each moment is constituted by the past. As the means by which we remember who we are, memory provides the very core of identity."[11] But memory is never only a matter of personal recollection; it is always socially produced and shaped by collective contexts. The concept of "cultural memory" describes how the individual and the collective interact to construct versions of a shared imagined past that can be transmitted from one generation to the next through objects, images, monuments, commemorative traditions, and institutions.[12] A wide array of media—including films—generate memories that link individuals to a collectively shared past and affect how we understand our own life story within the larger historical structures of a culture. I propose that media objects which are *not* concerned with the violent and traumatic experiences (e.g., World War I, the Holocaust, 9/11) that interest cultural memory studies can also fuel processes of individual and collective identity formation.

Memories shape identities and a sense of self during the course of our lives and, over time, popular culture—the movies and television shows we watch, the novels and comic books we read, the music we listen to, and the video games we play—becomes thoroughly entangled with these memories. Hollywood remaking produces media objects that store, circulate, and transfer memories and meanings and establishes a distinctive temporal relationship between movies and viewers. Through its combination of repetition and variation, remaking always conjures up the past, mediating memories on the diegetic level ("intertextual memory") but also in that more abstract sense, in which they invoke the real world and lived experiences outside the movies ("extratextual memory").

Intertextual memory refers to the fact that movies remember earlier versions of themselves and self-reflexively comment on the conditions of their own existence. It renders the films' own pasts visible (and relevant) for audiences. Film remakes contain traces of the past that refer viewers back to one or more previous renditions, sequels rely on the viewers' serial memory in order to continue a story, and the appeal of reboots is significantly enhanced when viewers recognize how the new movie differs from an older version. Intertextual memory involves a variety of memory prompts, ranging from the repetition of entire plots or plot elements to the restaging of iconic scenes, to the return of familiar actors in familiar roles to flashbacks, cameo appearances, and self-referential comments. In addition, such connections between movies are often foregrounded in the movies' paratexts, popular film criticism, and academic publications.

Extratextual memory describes how Hollywood remaking always draws attention to cinema's shifting media affordances, and how any reconfiguration of familiar fare carries meanings that extend beyond narrative and formal structures to a specific media-historical, cultural, and biographical moment with which the film is henceforth associated and in which it is forever recalled. Remaking always calls up memories and, in so doing, it can evoke nostalgia for specific films from the past; their moment in time; their historically located media technologies; and, ultimately, for that younger, carefree version of the self (the child). By triggering memories of previous films and their particular production and reception contexts, remaking encourages the formation of movie generations.

IDENTITY

My concept of movie generations takes German sociologist Karl Mannheim's "The Problem of Generations" ("Das Problem der Generationen," 1928) as its point of departure.[13] In his essay, Mannheim develops a theory of generational identities that stresses the importance of collectively shared memories. For Mannheim, generation-defining intellectual, social, and political events that are experienced during one's formative years shape how members of roughly the same age group construct who they are and how they locate themselves historically. They share a common *Zeitheimat* (W. G. Sebald): a nostalgically imagined "home in time" that fosters a sense of belonging and that one can always travel back to by taking a trip down memory lane. Despite his insistence that only memories based on firsthand experiences (e.g., the bodily experience of World War I) can produce generational units (*Generationseinheiten;* e.g., the war generation as a "lost" generation), Mannheim acknowledges that works of art (and their mediated memories) can become "vehicles of formative tendencies" and shape generational identities (e.g., Erich Maria Remarque's *All Quiet on the Western Front* as a generation-defining text that rhetorically produces the war generation as a "lost generation").[14]

As a medium-specific concept, "movie generations" combines these ideas with recent findings, which suggest that media experiences play a constitutive role in the process of generation-building because media representations, repertoires, and technologies, together with prevailing media-consumption cultures and audience practices, hold identificatory potential through which generational belonging can manifest itself.[15] Hollywood movies—specifically those that have repeatedly been remade, continued, expanded, and revised—have "group-forming potency" and provide insights into the mechanisms of generation-building, in particular the double logic of generationality and genealogy.[16] Sigrid Weigel makes this distinction, maintaining that generation is never only about contemporaries who share the same experiences (*generationality*).[17] Beyond this synchronic understanding, the cultural concept of generation also has a diachronic dimension that involves ideas about inheritance and heritage, cultural reproduction and transmission, and, eventually, the continuity of culture (*genealogy*). According to Astrid Erll, "generationality and the rhetoric of genealogy appear as flipsides of social identification. . . . [N]o generationality without its genealogical other" (e.g., the "lost generation" as unthinkable without "the old men," i.e., "the older generation of parents, teachers, and politicians" against which the young men who fought in World War I define themselves as a group).[18] The formation of movie generations similarly depends on both "contemporaneity and transmission."[19] Remaking enables movie generations to recognize themselves as such in the ways their movie version differs from previous or later installments, but also provides successive groups of viewers with points of access to a shared storytelling history and common repertoire.

Central to my thinking through Hollywood remaking in terms of memory and generation is Mannheim's notion of "fresh contact." He explains that, given the "continuous emergence of new participants in the cultural process," generational experience is constituted in the formative moment when individuals "come into contact anew with the accumulated heritage."[20] Hollywood remaking thoroughly complicates this idea of fresh contact because it does not simply preserve "timeless" classics and offers them up as a treasure trove of cultural heritage that can be handed down from one generation to the next. Rather, remaking is all about timeliness and serially evolving narratives that introduce novelty and additional layers of meaning as they repeat the already-seen. Of course, fresh contact necessarily implies that there are different vantage points in the process of generational renewal, because fresh contact "always means a changed relationship of distance from the object and a novel approach in assimilating, using, and developing the proffered material."[21]

With remaking, to be clear, fictional characters, storyworlds, and themes both maintain and renew their identificatory power across generations, yet the movies that continuously emerging new age groups encounter during their formative years never remain the same. Each movie generation has its own (usually favorite) movie version that creates a we-sense among group members. Remaking revives the memory of these formative media objects from the past each time Hollywood releases a new movie that is the version of fresh contact for the next generation of viewers. As a result, remakes, sequels, and reboots are inherently shareable media texts. These movies connect past and present as they simultaneously build on, bolster, and challenge the lasting legacy of material to which audiences—then and now—can relate. Bringing back *Ghostbusters*, *A Star Is Born*, *Jumanji*, *TRON*, or *Jurassic Park* at distinct historical moments effectively foregrounds how the years are passing and the times are changing. Each new iteration of these Hollywood movies shapes a movie generation and helps viewers to sustain a sense of self across different life stages—childhood, youth, adulthood, and late life.

CONCLUSION

Given that Hollywood remaking inevitably strives to balance continuity and change in order to attract and satisfy as large an audience as possible, it seems almost paradoxical that remakes, sequels, and reboots are now so often met with alarm and perceived as an outright threat by fans, tastemakers, and cultural gatekeepers. They formulate fears that remakes, sequels, and reboots will supersede their predecessors, interfere with their cultural legacies, and transform their meanings. In these contexts, Hollywood remaking is framed as an attack on childhood memories, as an intrusion into the subtle ways in which favorite movies can shape and confirm one's worldview and self-concept throughout life. Yet, such reactions ultimately foreground what film is good for. We are likely to form sentimental attachments to films that belong to (and eventually come to represent) a formative period in our lives, and Hollywood remaking both foregrounds and challenges such identificatory processes when it brings familiar characters, stories, and themes back onto the big screen. Film remakes, sequels, and reboots foster a we-sense through the formation and maintenance of movie generations and stabilize the interplay between time, memory, and identity. But they also perform cultural work in terms of revision and renewal by questioning and destabilizing ideologies that older versions offer their respective movie generations.

To promote the enduring relevance of certain characters and storyworlds over possible others is always also a political decision (not a merely economic one), and reactivating old movies and meanings invariably comes with a critical potential to reframe, rewrite, and revise the past so that familiar material is in keeping with current tastes and attitudes. While examples like *Ghostbusters* and the recent *Star Wars* sequels speak to a longing for continuity that goes hand in hand with a growing need for stable memories and meanings in an increasingly fragmented and disorienting world, they also draw attention to generational differences and lay bare the misogyny and racism of toxic fan practices. In these instances, Hollywood remaking becomes a productive force that invites reflections on how cultural transmission, generational belonging, and nostalgia normalize conservative politics, on the one hand, and create opportunities for progressive updates and revisions, on the other.

NOTES

1. Jeremy Gordon, "*Ghostbusters* Is the Future of the Culture Wars," *The Outline*, December 9, 2019, https://theoutline.com/post/8409/ghostbusters-reboot-trailer-stranger-things-paul-rudd-finn-wolfhard?zd=2&zi=znkj5pok. Accessed September 5, 2020.

2. I explore this connection in my forthcoming book *Hollywood Remaking* (Oakland: University of California Press, 2024) and in my research group "Hollywood Memories: Cinematic Remaking and the Construction of Global Movie Generations," funded by the German Research Foundation (DFG). We conduct empirical audience research to gain insights into cross-cultural and cross-generational memories, experiences, and attitudes regarding Hollywood films and remaking (https://hollywood-memories.com/).

3. Jason Reitman quoted in Anthony Breznican, "*Ghostbusters* Resurrected: Jason Reitman Will Direct a New Film Set in the Original Universe," *Entertainment Weekly*, January 15, 2019, https://ew.com/movies/2019/01/15/new-ghostbusters-movie-jason-reitman/. Accessed September 5, 2020.

4. Breznican, "*Ghostbusters* Resurrected."

5. Frank Kelleter and Kathleen Loock, "Hollywood Remaking as Second-Order Serialization," in *Media of Serial Narrative*, ed. Kelleter (Columbus: Ohio State University Press, 2017), 125–47, at 144.

6. Frank Kelleter, "Five Ways of Looking at Popular Seriality," in *Media of Serial Narrative*, 7–34, at 30.

7. Kelleter, "Five Ways of Looking," 30.

8. Frank Kelleter, "Toto, I Think We're in Oz Again (and Again and Again): Remakes and Popular Seriality," in *Film Remakes, Adaptations, and Fan Productions: Remake/Remodel*, ed. Kathleen Loock and Constantine Verevis (Basingstoke: Palgrave Macmillan, 2012), 19–44, at 38.

9. See Kathleen Loock, "Retro-Remaking: The 1980s Film Cycle in Contemporary Hollywood Cinema," in *Cycles, Sequels, Spin-Offs, Remakes, and Reboots: Multiplicities in Film and Television*, ed. Amanda Ann Klein and R. Barton Palmer (Austin: University of Texas Press, 2016), 277–298.

10. Guy Adams, "Hollywood Ate My Childhood: Why Film Remakes Are Desecrating Our Most Precious Memories," *The Independent*, July 22, 2010, http://www.independent.co.uk/arts-entertainment/films/features/hollywood-ate-my-childhood-why-film-remakes-are-desecrating-our-most-precious-memories-2032073.html. Accessed August 31, 2014.

11. Marita Sturken, *Tangled Memories: The Vietnam War, the AIDS Epidemic, and the Politics of Remembering* (Berkeley: University of California Press, 1997), 1.

12. Jan Assmann, "Communicative and Cultural Memory," in *Cultural Memory Studies: An International and Interdisciplinary Handbook*, ed. Astrid Erll and Ansgar Nünning (Berlin: De Gruyter, 2008), 109–118, at 110–111.

13. Karl Mannheim, "The Problem of Generations," in *Collected Works*, vol. 5: *Essays on the Sociology of Knowledge*, ed. Paul Kecskemeti (London: Routledge/Kegan Paul, 1952), 276–320.

14. Mannheim, "Problem of Generations," 305; cf. Astrid Erll, "Generation in Literary History: Three Constellations of Generationality, Genealogy, and Memory," *New Literary History* 45 (2014): 385–409, at 388–396.

15. Andra Siibak, Nicoletta Vittadini, and Galit Nimrod, "Generations as Media Audiences: An Introduction," *Participations: Journal of Audience and Reception Studies* 11, no. 2 (2014): 100–107; and Göran Bolin, *Media Genera-*

tions: Experience, Identity, and Mediatised Social Change (London: Routledge, 2017).

16. Mannheim, "Problem of Generations," 305.

17. Sigrid Weigel, "'Generation' as a Symbolic Form: On the Genealogical Discourse of Memory Since 1945," *The Germanic Review* 77, no. 4 (2002): 264–277.

18. Erll, "Generation," 396.

19. Erll, "Generation," 396.

20. Mannheim, "Problem of Generations," 293.

21. Mannheim, "Problem of Generations," 293.

22

. . . Reaching Unlettered Audiences

On Global Blockbuster Cinema and Its Oral Affinities

SHEILA J. NAYAR

Decades ago, Bengali filmmaker Satyajit Ray wrestled with the interpretive difficulty inherent in Jean Renoir's *The Rules of the Game/La Règle du jeu* (1939). "Although perfectly comprehensible on the surface," Ray conceded, it is still "a difficult and demanding film," constantly requiring the spectator to "read between the lines and, like all great works of art, one has to go back to it again and again to discover fresh nuances of meaning."[1] Based on Ray's description, we can infer some of the devices upon which *Rules* pivots: calculated ambiguity, polysemy, and, by virtue of the semantic density inherent in these, a need for audiences to be alert to the director *behind* the film (e.g., is Renoir employing symbolism here; is he being ironic?). How otherwise are spectators cognitively to read between the lines except through an isolated, intellectual mental decoding?

Now, imagine if those spectators not only did not apprehend French but were also *not literate*. Imagine, instead, that the audience comprised Bengali or English speakers who had never been inculcated into the culture of the written word.[2] Obviously, they would be incapable of reading the subtitles; but less obvious to many—including many film scholars—is that the movie would be asking them to engage with narrative devices that have expressly emerged out of our long-term engagement with *alphabetic literacy*. After all, it can hardly be only by accident that the "semiotic exchanges" (Christopher Collins) anticipated in engaging with Renoir's film—the polysemy and concerted ambiguity

FIGURE 23. Nebula (Karen Gillan) in *Avengers: Endgame* (2019, Anthony and Joe Russo).

that make it, as Ray says, so "difficult and demanding"—are virtually never part and parcel of storytelling shaped by *orature*.[3]

The Ugandan linguist Pio Zirimu coined the term "orature" to circumvent the inferiority often assigned to arts whose roots are grounded in oral tradition: in the spoken word as the primary medium of thought and expression.[4] For Ngũgĩ wa Thiong'o, Zirimu's concept is "tantalizing," because it "point[s] to an oral system of aesthetics that [does] not need validity from the literary."[5] Nor does Zirimu's neologism condescendingly insinuate illiteracy. Orature can be equally as sophisticated as literature—until, of course, literacy colonizes the globe, such that exclusively orate culture is sent into retirement and bequeathed a lesser status, whether as "traditional" or "mythical," or (more degradingly) as "uncritical" or "naively utopian."

Yet, stories that lean toward the traits aligned with orature continue to thrive, and nowhere more than in global blockbuster cinema. Indeed, what I plan to show here is how and, indeed, why a significant matrix of orate storytelling norms undergird the top-grossing global blockbusters of the last fifty years, including Hollywood's *Avengers: Endgame* (2019, dir. Anthony Russo and Joe Russo), *Avatar* (2009, dir. James Cameron), *Titanic* (1997, dir. James Cameron), and *Star Wars* (1977, dir. George Lucas), as well as China's *Wolf Warrior 2/Zhàn Láng 2* (2017, dir. Wu Jing) and India's *Baahuabli 2: The Conclusion* (2017, dir. S.S. Rajamouli).[6] Yes, these films may be negotiating decidedly (post)modern landscapes of urban architecture, fashion, the latest communication technologies, even alternately imagined futuristic worlds, and, yes, they may be tightly plotted in a manner that is indisputably a by-product of writing culture, but they also indisputably *eschew* the sorts of literately derived semiotic exchanges compelled by the likes of Renoir's films—or even Ray's.[7]

This is not intended as an inherent touting of spectaculars (which pretty much all these films are). Rather, it is a recognition that such films may be providing spectators who are not—or not yet—autonomous from the epistemically oral realm an access to stories that are otherwise denied them in a global culture largely circumscribed by the written word. In this sense, the very movies that some critics have derided for their "aural excessiveness," "fuzzy emotional content," and indulgence in "wantonly expansive, hyperbolic, even hysterical acts of cinema" may be doing *good*—or, at the least, a service—when it comes to audiences for whom literacy is not the precondition of modern existence.[8] Intriguingly, the previous descriptions are Vivian Sobchack's, regarding what critics "culturally trained to value asceticism, caution, and logic" recoil from when it comes to Hollywood's historical epics of yore—to which we might add (as she does) those films' reliance on "highly recognizable stars," rhetorical and material excess, lack of subtlety, and extravagance of action and place.[9]

While there are many reasons why literate individuals might likewise take to such epic blockbusters—for example, the awesome experience of spectacular immersion, a pleasurable slip into nostalgia, extrication from the cognitive "work," or atomizing negotiation that a literate aesthetics demands—I focus instead on how these films operate in a manner that provides epistemic agency for a body of spectators that is too often neglected in the critical milieu and for whom comparatively fewer storytelling resources contemporarily exist.[10]

MEMORY DEPENDENCY

There are film ethicists today who argue that, for the sake of engaging the mental faculties, films that subvert spectacle through "ethical ambiguity or moral dissonance" are the most constructive, given the philosophical challenges that they induce.[11] Such subversion is *not* in the interests of orature, however, given that intentionally interrupting, endangering, or eroding meaning's face value quashes memory dependency. Narrative in the oral milieu is shaped to foster its being retained, not to promote or demand interrogation. Survival of a narrative through time is the objective, which is why, in this context, semantic transparency is a *value,* not an aesthetic defect.

So, while the highly educated reviewer assessing a movie like *Titanic* might lament its reduction of "the human element of tragedy to a series of schematic caricatures," wherein "Jack is entirely true and brave; Rose is a misunderstood rich girl," and "Cal is a ruthless, sneering villain, straight out of Victorian melodrama," such face-value characterizations are the most *economical* means by which to render the story intelligible and, hence, easily registrable to the mind.[12] Of course, characters that are outsized and devoid of nuance, that are "flat, diagrammatic and simply profiled" (Geeta Kapur) tend to forestall realism, with that realism often doubly thwarted by those characters being played by *movie stars*—such that Jack is also always Leonardo DiCaprio, much as Leng Feng in *Wolf Warrior 2* correspondingly remains Wu Jing.[13] While this may give them what Sobchack calls an "'overdetermined' presence," consider the extent to which that assists in rendering such figures memorable.[14] The same works across franchise films like the *Avengers* series, given its heroes and villains traveling from one film to the next and, so, transporting with them a *pre*-known aura that, much like a talisman, reinforces their spell. And if their mode is "heroic"—bereft of the inner psyches or ambiguities of character that art cinema privileges—that, too, prevents their dissolution into a complexity that would impede decipherability and hence the narrative's memorability. If Homeric epic is any guide, a hero's currency may have less to do with heroism, in fact, than with his serving as a "technical convenience" in the service of knowledge's organization.[15] Even *Titanic*'s attempts to capture the audience's attention through a "Romeo and Juliet 'star cross'd lovers' conceit" has its values, orately speaking, given that such folkloric motifs require little in the way of discrete or autonomous interpretation.[16]

To be sure, multiple reasons might account for *Titanic*'s global reach, including the "verisimilitude of its special effects," its "liberatory impulses," even its sex scenes.[17] But these alone do not sufficiently explain its having been a "national entertainment sensation"—and in multiple nations and regions, including Egypt, the United Kingdom, the Middle East, and Indonesia.[18] In India, *Titanic* was jocularly described as a Hindi film in Western wear—a comparison that conceivably underscores its mutual grounding in orate attributes.[19] *Titanic* was also a major, if bootlegged, hit in Afghanistan, a country with one of the lowest literacy levels worldwide.[20] So, while some spectators might impugn that Hollywood blockbuster for its affective and, even, bathetic overreach, for viewers ensconced in an oral or orality-privileging environment, characters who are *not* schematically heightened, who do *not*, as the saying goes, wear their hearts on their sleeves, may appear *less* accessibly human rather than more.

Consider likewise the way that these global blockbusters lean away from moral complexity. Much as with orature, their worlds are best—or, at least, ultimately—grounded in straightforwardly readable oppositions, such as black and white, good versus evil, virtuous versus vicious, Jack's righteous bravery versus Cal's sneering villainy. Or, consider the original *Star Wars,* with its black-cloaked Darth Vader yearning, with the aid of Nazi-like stormtroopers, to undo blond, white-wearing Luke Skywalker—who, with the aid of the mystical Force, will ultimately destroy that nemesis's Death Star. While today the racialized connotations of such encounters can prove ideologically unsettling, some psychologists argue that humans have a natural-born propensity for dualistic thinking.[21] It is *alphabetic literacy* that has facilitated our retreat from polarity as a cognitively organizing device and our entry into moral terrains (and even psyches) that are evermore subtle and abstruse—cast in those hazy, nebulous grays endemic to modernist literature and film.

Memory retention might explain, too, the material excesses in which these global blockbusters affectively indulge, whether through setting, visual style, or props and costumes. Yes, these films may be berated for offering "spectacle in the place of substance,"[22] but as Eric Havelock reminds us apropos Homeric epic, what better than striking imagery to reinforce a spell over a storyteller's listeners?[23] In fact, the more conspicuous that imagery—whether as sumptuous homes, intergalactic battles, or magically iridescent jungles; whether in the form of gargantuan dinosaurs or, by turn, a gargantuan ship on which we can lose ourselves in the lavish wealth of its stiff, upper-deck patrons (but no less in the rousing affability of the poor communally dancing beneath)—the better the spell's chance of future recollection.

Similar motivations apply to these films' emphasis on action rather than on the promotion of audience reflection, on a kinetic engagement that does *not* mandate an abstracted, contemplative plumbing on our part. Nowhere is that more evident than in these blockbusters' frequent climactic capitulations: the Avengers' epic face-off with the alien warlord Thanos; the military's rapacious attempts in *Avatar* to bulldoze The Hometree on Pandora. Such edge-of-your-seat showdowns viscerally arrest us—seize every fiber of our being—rather than demand that, by virtue of a visual-acoustical *in*action onscreen, we *think* in anti-operational terms about what we are supposed to be seeing or responding to. True, the Freudian film critic may read audience attraction to such fetishized display as reflecting sublimated atavistic impulses or a desired gratification of the "pleasure principle." But recall the gruesome clashes that pervade *Beowulf* or the *Mahabharata*. Indeed, the much-cited concept of a "cinema of attractions," with its emphasis on spectacle that is visually arousing, exhibitionistic, and "indifferent to realism," is, I would argue, an extension—or, at least, an importation—of storytelling aligned with orature.[24] Such traits, after all, reinforce the narrative spell in a manner that is emotive, intelligible, and not dependent on some private hermeneutical unpacking.

So, while *Star Wars* may traffic in a set-apartness that is futuristically outer-spatial, its narrative orientation is cognitively styled in a fashion that is as old as the hills. By the way, hardy, time-tested platitudes and clichés—like "as old as the hills" precisely—are an additional form of mnemonic packaging that best safeguards information's transmission through time. Indeed, savvy readers may by now be gleaning the extent to which the content of myth, both ancient and otherwise, is highly entangled with the mnemonic devices that serve to ensure that myth's survival.[25] Or, to put it more accurately, contemporary analysts have never quite managed to disentangle the two—a disentanglement no doubt hampered by our increasingly literate retreat from myth's original housing in the acoustical.

ACOUSTICAL COMMUNION

In cultures or communities not predicated on the written word, the utterance is the locus of truth. The sensory organs of privilege are the ear and the voice, not the eye, as in the literate—and even literately cinematic—context. Because speech is the central method of communication, with all exchanges therefore necessitating a party of at least two, the self is naturally *outwardly* directed—oriented toward *others*. Thus can we find Luke Skywalker, even when in isolated peril, conveniently and unabashedly asking himself out loud, "Will this never end?," much as, elsewhere, he will let us know, unreservedly on point, "I'm never going to get out of here."

Moreover, because characters' utterances, let alone a bard's, must be powerful enough to induce memory, speech is often relayed in amplified manner, via sententious exchanges; emphatically delivered oaths; or ripe displays of love, piety, distress, or even vengeance. Indeed, if melodrama has served as the "characteristic form of narrative and dramaturgy in societies undergoing the transition to modernity," as Wimal Dissanayake posits, its connection to the orally acoustical realm crucially elucidates why.²⁶ Such extrinsic—and, so, too, exoteric—display is the most practical means of ensuring knowledge's safe passage through time. But sensationalized delivery is hardly exclusive to developing societies. The purportedly "over-the-top melodrama" of *Titanic*, coterminous with (or arguably induced by) its "ludicrous dialogue," makes sense if one considers that the film might be operating in—and as—language primarily governed by oral principles.²⁷

The same might be said of the morality play–like pleas that are rife in many of these global blockbusters. In *Avatar*, for instance, when earthling Jake counsels Pandora's Na'vi tribe about the rapaciousness of his own people, "[They] have sent us a message," he declares, "that they can take whatever they want—that no one can stop them. Well, we will send them a message that they cannot take whatever they want! And that this . . . this is our land!" Especially when involving a group's most cherished principles or values, such climactic petitions are pretty much always delivered in a manner that is, as the bromide goes, "clear as crystal." In fact, formulary kernels of knowledge in the form of commonplaces—proverbs especially—are frequently the stuff *of* such moralizing, as they not only prudently safeguard the wisdom of the community but also tie the expressed ethical appeals directly to tradition.

Meaning, as we can glean from the above, is best when it arrives "already interpreted"—a prevalence witnessed not only in many of the aforementioned blockbusters but virtually all children's films, too. While film scholars may forgive a youth-oriented film like *The Lion King* (1994, dir. Roger Allers and Rob Minkoff) for the transparency of its narrative palette, they can sometimes prove less sympathetic when it comes to a film like *Titanic*, which similarly nests in "emotional clarity . . . undampened by the murky ambivalence of contemporary irony."²⁸ But murky ambivalence and, even more, irony demand a semantic engagement that is inefficacious for individuals whose thinking is based in "practical utility," in situations *not* divorced from everyday reality, as A. R. Luria discovered in his 1930s fieldwork with nonliterate Uzbek and Kirghiz peasants.²⁹ In fact, based on Luria's findings, we might safely infer that the very textual elements that critics like Roland Barthes and Umberto Eco venerate—erotic gapes, openness—would prove baffling, if not existentially impenetrable, to oral percipients.³⁰

A provision of already interpreted meaning extends no less to the visual and acoustical dynamics of these globally top-grossing movies. Camera movements, editing, music, and sound effects can all be conveniently deployed to cue viewers that "this means danger"; or "feel the pain"—or "the love"; or "laugh"—or "relax and enjoy the whimsy." A rapid zoom in on a face can articulate shock, much as the emphatic musical leitmotifs in *Star Wars* instantaneously impart, "Here comes Luke, who is good," "There goes Darth Vader, who is bad." While ostensibly more "sophisticated" viewers might deem these emotionally manipulative, they operate, from the orate standpoint, as technical extensions of verbomotor speech, as formulary devices that, not unlike clichés, economically conserve and articulate meaning rather than conceal or suppress it.[31]

In the orate context, meaning survives—can only survive—if passed down through direct encounters between the generations. Might that help to explain the frequent and even reflexive incorporation of intergenerational relationships in these global blockbusters? *Titanic*'s sinking, for example, is recounted by an elderly survivor in the presence of her grandniece, with the flashbacks to her story operating analogically as visual representations of memory. And in the original *Star Wars*, knowledge of the Force passes from the wise and wizened Jedi Master, Obi-Wan Kenobi, to the youthful novice, Luke, with subsequent episodes of the franchise continuing that theme. In this way, *who-we-are-now* functions integrally as an extension of, and, in fact, must be compressed with, *who-we-were-before*—at least if the past is to remain alive.

In other words, this is not some historically verifiably "real" or data-driven past. As Walter J. Ong reminds us, that sort of past owes its existence to alphabetic literacy.[32] Instead, this past—or Past, rather—is the sacred domain of one's ancestors. Accordingly, orate narratives, not to mention the above-mentioned blockbusters, temporally slide into the realm of the "anti-historical" (to borrow Ashis Nandy's descriptor for late twentieth-century Bollywood films).[33] Why? Because, in the orate context, the "now" is an *ontological* locale binding past and present. Thus do their endings fold that "now" into exemplary ethical patterns of human relations: the annihilation of an aggressor (think the disintegration of Thanos in *Avengers: Endgame,* with Iron Man sacrificing himself in the process); or the valiant martyrdom of the hero in the face of tragedy (think Jack Dawson willing himself to the icy waters of the North Atlantic after the *Titanic*'s sinking, so that his love interest, Rose, can survive).

For similar reasons, any dissension or threat impeding a social suturing (to appropriate that Lacanian term for a very different purpose) is put to rest *before* these films' resolutions. In advance of the credits rolling, the immediate danger is vanquished, with the bad expunged (even if only temporarily), the good reunited, and the ideal social-cum-moral order restored. The eventual reconstitution of individuals "into a communal subjectivity" is vital in the oral milieu, as Keyan G. Tomaselli, Arnold Shepperson, and Maureen Eke argue, because, otherwise, the community would be endangering itself: its survival into the future, its continuity as a collective.[34] In much the same way, spectators of these global blockbusters leave the theater in a spirit that is ultimately "life-affirming,"[35] surefire in the knowledge that they—we—have not only survived, but have safeguarded our identity and, so, will carry on.

Yes, this may demand some major papering over of tensions pertaining to ethnicity, gender, class, nation, and so forth, but that is the cost of returning to an "orbit of the normative and morally acceptable," as Ravi Vasudevan describes with respect to Hindi popular film—a description perfectly transferrable to global blockbuster cinema, which equally capitulates to "something like a joint family."[36]

THE ETHICS OF FILM ETHICS, IN LIGHT OF ORATE FILM

Can moral philosophy find comfort in a historical formula whose language of ethics is almost exclusively based on a *literate* sensibility, on a *literate* way of knowing and engaging with the world?[37] Pair this with Robert Solomon's query regarding why the "sentimentality of kitsch" is not only condemned as art but *as ethics,* and the *ethics of* film ethics is brought painfully to the fore.[38] Thus might some spectators, as if from a "natural" standpoint, decry a film like *Titanic* for casting a cheap spell over its audience, not realizing that they, too, are under a spell—only one kindled by literacy, which has trained them in how privately to negotiate calculated ambiguity, inner amplitude, Deleuzian "thinking images," and the like.[39] If anything, it is this latter form of engagement that is unnatural—and also not cheap, requiring, as it does, decades of instruction in reading and writing. So, we should probably remain provisional when making judgments about *art cinema,* since we may be responding in the image of those afforded a rigorous training in the higher-order goals seminal to educational literacy.

This is especially the case if we are prone to maintaining, as the film ethicist Robert Sinnerbrink does, that "aesthetic and ethical dimensions of film are increasingly understood as complementary, even coincident, features of our experience of movies."[40] Alas, orate films, operating as they do from a different epistemic center of gravity, cannot always share the same aesthetic dimensions apparent in the films that Sinnerbrink privileges.[41] Films that operate on the basis of a more oral way of knowing, expressing, and engaging with the world cannot mnemonically afford to reside in the subtlety, ambiguity, and "deeper intersubjective understanding of the characters' situations" that presumably provoke philosophical thinking.[42] (To be fair, Sinnerbrink himself acknowledges that students need to be *educated* into reading films this way.)

Consequently, we should attend more sensitively to how *all* sorts of audiences engage with and value films—global blockbuster films, perhaps especially. To rely exclusively on theorizations by schooled intellectuals can only ever lead to partial knowledge. The unspoken *sine qua non* of becoming a film scholar is literacy, after all, and this can lead to dangerous blind spots, especially given the extent to which orature is *not* a familiar concept in film studies. Could this be why limited phenomenological attention has been granted to how lay audiences, both lettered and not, respond to mainstream cinema? For instance, how might exclusively oral individuals differently assess the films that they not only enjoy watching but deem meaningful, purposeful, powerful, even *beautiful*? I stress that word because two of Kant's conditions for the aesthetic judgment of beauty hinge on an artwork's nonpurposiveness and disinterestedness—which, as we have seen, are basically *contra* orature. Given that any critical assessment depends in part on one's epistemic location vis-à-vis film narrative, how might exclusively oral individuals distinguish "good" orate films from "bad" ones? More empirical audience research would not only remind us but *require* us "to avoid overly generalizable statements" that do not "recognize the fundamental diversity of audience responses," as Matthew Reason worthily exhorts.[43] Such research would also productively force a more holistic consideration of *whom* specifically we are talking about when we talk about film's value or "good." In fact, in light of the pressures that orality can place on spectators and so, too, on their film preferences, research along these lines might just prove the *ethical* thing to do.

NOTES

1. Satyajit Ray, *Our Films, Their Films* (New York: Hyperion, 1994), 84.
2. For global literacy rates, see Réka Vágvölgyi, Andra Coldea, Thomas Dresler, Josef Schrader, and Hans-Christoph Nuerk, "A Review about Functional Illiteracy: Definition, Cognitive, Linguistic, and Numerical Aspects," *Frontiers in Psychology* 7 (2016): 1–13.

3. Christopher Collins, *Paleopoetics: The Evolution of the Preliterate Imagination* (New York: Columbia University Press, 2013), 214.
4. Ngũgĩ wa Thiong'o, *Globalectics: Theory and the Politics of Knowing* (New York: Columbia University Press, 2012), 72.
5. Thiong'o, *Globalectics*, 73.
6. These are adjusted for inflation. While the top-grossing film in this category is *Gone with the Wind* (1939, dir. Victor Fleming), that film, along with several others, falls outside the last fifty years, which is when the category of the "blockbuster" conceptually began.
7. Pyramidal plots do not appear to subvert orally inflected noetic accessibility. According to one theorist cited by David Bordwell, "comprehension and memory are best when the story conform[s] to the drive-to-a-goal pattern." David Bordwell, *Narration in the Fiction Film* (Madison: University of Wisconsin Press, 1985), 35.
8. Vivian Sobchack, "'Surge and Splendor': A Phenomenology of the Hollywood Historical Epic," *Representations* 29 (1990): 24–49, at 24. While there may be some intersection here with Miriam Hansen's theory of "vernacular modernism," Hansen does not etiologically or paradigmatically account for the "everyday" discourse undergirding Hollywood cinema's engagement with modernism. See Miriam Bratu Hansen, "The Mass Production of the Senses: Classical Cinema as Vernacular Modernism," *Modernism/modernity* 6, no. 2 (1999): 59–77, at 60.
9. Sobchack, "'Surge and Splendor,'" 24–35.
10. See, e.g., Archita Kashyap, "Why the Indian Moviegoers Prefer Hollywood Over Bollywood?," *Tehelka*, April 3, 2021, http://tehelka.com/why-the-indian-%E2%80%8B%E2%80%8Bmoviegoers-prefer-hollywood-over-bollywood/. Accessed July 9, 2021.
11. Robert Sinnerbrink, *Cinematic Ethics: Exploring Ethical Experience through Film* (New York: Routledge, 2016), 136. This is not to suggest that there are *not* also film ethicists who look to Hollywood and mainstream cinema for ethical lessons.
12. Wheeler Winston Dixon, *Disaster and Memory: Celebrity Culture and the Crisis of Hollywood Cinema* (New York: Columbia University Press, 1999), 3–4.
13. Geeta Kapur, "Mythic Material in Indian Cinema," *Journal of Arts and Ideas* 14–15 (1987): 79–108, at 70. Here, Kapur is describing characters typical of twentieth-century Hindi cinema.
14. Sobchack, "'Surge and Splendor,'" 36.
15. Eric Havelock, *Preface to Plato* (Cambridge, MA: Harvard University Press, 1963), 119.
16. Dixon, *Disaster and Memory*, 3–4.
17. Barbara Klinger, "Contraband Cinema: Piracy, *Titanic*, and Central Asia," *Cinema Journal* 49, no. 2 (2010): 106–124, at 118.
18. Klinger, "Contraband Cinema," 113 and 110.
19. Sheila J. Nayar, *Cinematically Speaking: The Orality-Literacy Paradigm for Visual Narrative* (New Delhi: Sage, 2014), 213.
20. Stephen Farrell, "Movies Return to Kabul," *The Montreal Gazette*, November 2, 2001, B1.

21. Paul Bloom quoted in Blakey Vermeule, *Why Do We Care about Literary Characters?* (Baltimore, MD: Johns Hopkins University Press, 2010), 90.
22. Dixon, *Disaster and Memory*, 3.
23. Eric Havelock, "Some Elements of the Homeric Fantasy," in *Homer's The Iliad*, ed. Harold Bloom (New York: Chelsea House Publishers, 1987), 93–109, at 98.
24. Nayar, *Cinematically Speaking*, 26. For more on the cinema of attractions, see Tom Gunning, "The Cinema of Attractions: Early Film, Its Spectator and the Avant-Garde," *Wide Angle* 8, nos. 3–4 (1986): 63–70, at 63.
25. Collins, *Paleopoetics*, 195.
26. Wimal Dissanayake quoted in Ravi Vasudevan, "Addressing the Spectator of a 'Third World' National Cinema: The Bombay 'Social' Film of the 1940s and 1950s," *Screen* 36, no. 4 (1995): 305–324, at 308.
27. Nayar, *Cinematically Speaking*, 47. The ascriptions "over-the-top melodrama" and "ludicrous dialogue" come from Vivian Sobchack, "Bathos and Bathysphere: On Submersion, Longing, and History in *Titanic*," in *Titanic: Anatomy of a Blockbuster*, ed. Kevin S. Sandler and Gaylyn Studlar (New Brunswick, NJ: Rutgers University Press, 1999), 189–204, at 191. Sobchack is here describing on what bases the film was critically attacked upon its release.
28. Sobchack, "Bathos and Bathysphere," 191.
29. A.R. Luria, *Cognitive Development and Its Social Foundations*, ed. Michael Cole, trans. Martin Lopez-Morillas and Lynn Solotaroff (Cambridge, MA: Harvard University Press, 1976), 59.
30. Nayar, *Cinematically Speaking*, 105.
31. Nayar, *Cinematically Speaking*, 45.
32. Walter J. Ong, *Orality and Literacy: The Technologizing of the Word* (London: Routledge, 1982), 96.
33. Ashis Nandy, "The Popular Hindi Film: Ideology and First Principles," *India International Centre Quarterly* 8, no. 1 (1981): 89–96, at 91.
34. Keyan G. Tomaselli, Arnold Shepperson, and Maureen Eke, "Towards a Theory of Orality in African Cinema," *Research in African Literature* 26, no. 3 (1995): 18–35, at 26.
35. Klinger, "Contraband Cinema," 113.
36. Ravi Vasudevan, "The Cultural Space of a Film Narrative," *Indian Economic and Social History Review* 28, no. 2 (1991): 305–324, at 183.
37. I have here tweaked the intentions and words of Havelock, *Preface to Plato*, 121.
38. Robert C. Solomon, *In Defense of Sentimentality* (Oxford: Oxford University Press, 2004), 239–241.
39. Gilles Deleuze, *Cinema 2: The Time-Image* (Minneapolis: University of Minnesota Press, 1986).
40. Sinnerbrink, *Cinematic Ethics*, 81.
41. See J. Edward Chamberlin, "Boasting, Toasting, and Truthtelling," in *Orality and Literacy: Reflections Across Disciplines*, ed. Keith Thor Carlson, Kristina Fagan, and Natalia Khanenko-Friesen (Toronto: University of Toronto Press, 2011), 21–41, at 34.

42. Sinnerbrink, *Cinematic Ethics*, 101.
43. Quoted in Judith Thissen, "Beyond the Nickelodeon: Cinemagoing, Everyday Life and Identity Politics," in *Audiences: Defining and Researching Screen Entertainment Reception,* ed. Ian Christie (Amsterdam: Amsterdam University Press, 2012), 45–65, at 70.

23

... Love of Community and Reality

On André Bazin and the Good of Cinema

DUDLEY ANDREW

THE WORLD VIEWED AND THE CINEMA REVIEWED: A CAVELLIAN PRELUDE

"What is cinema good for?" This question was implicit in the years just after 1968, when I found myself among those wresting a place within the university for cinema, an artform desperate to look respectable. A budding scholar, I looked first to Rudolf Arnheim and Siegfried Kracauer, whose theories, though smart and logical, felt distant and rather bloodless. Erwin Panofsky would have been a better source. Also a Jewish German intellectual, he clearly cared about the overall good "the moving pictures" brought to art and to culture. Stanley Cavell relied on him in 1971, when he declared his reasons for an allegiance to film. On the second page of *The World Viewed,* he states, "The answer to the question 'What is the importance of art?' is grammatically related to, or is a way of answering, the question 'What is art?'" And then he asks outright, "Why are the movies important?"[1]

I listened to Cavell because he dared to take cinema as seriously as he did arts that clearly count, like Shakespearean theater in the Renaissance and grand opera in the nineteenth century. Like them, cinema today is at once the most personal and social of the arts; like them it is tied to one's memory of specific experiences and to the conversations one has about films right after seeing them; and like them the movies (this term says a great deal, and it is the one Panofsky used) are designed

FIGURE 24. Catherine (Jeanne Moreau) in *Jules and Jim* (1962, François Truffaut).

to be shared, yet are privately meaningful.[2] At least this was the case in the classical period that formed Cavell's views. Modernist films choose a more select audience and are candidates for essentially private screenings. As he points out in his preface, this fact seems to have occasioned Cavell's reflections, for the very category of art films broke the natural relation the movies had earlier maintained with its audience. Cavell needed to consider first what had been lost and then how the modern works he admired somehow allowed him to regain his footing.

This natural relation, which can still take hold of us, though no longer routinely, enlivens life by giving it to us a second time, projecting it on a screen so that we can see, relish, and evaluate experiences and feelings that we misapprehend in a first go-round. Cavell found *Jules et Jim* (1962, dir. François Truffaut) to be a modernist emblem of this classical flirtation with loss and recovery. Catherine (Jeanne Moreau), an incarnation of an Attic statue, lives blithely with Jules and Jim, but then is successively lost, only to be repeatedly restored. Often stilled by photography, she breaks out in exuberant bursts of song, sexuality, and dramatic leaps. Her final suicidal leap is held in Jules's memory, from which comes the film's wistful, world-wise narrative tone. Cavell would formalize this power of cinema to hold and release, then hold again, in *Pursuits of Happiness: Comedies of Remarriage*.[3] Cinema is a remarriage machine, restoring our disenchanted world so we can enter into a more mature marriage with it. *The World Viewed* aims to recover, through memory and analysis, a natural relation to the movies, now distanced as philosophical "reflections on the ontology of film," his volume's subtitle.

"The Ontology of Film" is a phrase that brings André Bazin instantly to mind. Indeed, Cavell's preface divulges that encountering *What Is*

Cinema? in 1968 was crucial to motivating his book. My own encounter with Bazin that year was, I venture, equally decisive, launching my dissertation prospectus. For a long while Cavell's ideas struck me as pale in comparison to those of Bazin. Cavell was an ivory-tower speculator wrapped up in his own (self)reflections, whereas Bazin had made sense of cinema every single day as he came to terms with what was on the Paris screens. He watched films constantly, whereas Cavell confessed that the more he wrote about movies, the less he attended the cinema. Still, at base, they both held to the belief that any notion of the cinema had to include a huge range of titles, not just masterpieces, and these had to be taken as addressing everyone, not just the refined sensibility of the critic. Cinema is good for the individual to the extent that films in general are good for people in general.

ANDRÉ BAZIN, MYTHOGRAPHER OF POPULAR CINEMA

"People in general" is more a philosopher's locution than a critic's. Writing for several journals with different readerships required Bazin to reckon with various values the cinema holds out. Why would this or that group bother to read him unless he addressed what they cared about in going to the cinema? Why would they pay attention to his urgings or reservations about what to see, or check their views against his? What was cinema good for in the case of each public? By considering the type of audience targeted by each of the journals that paid for his criticism, one can survey distinct ways cinema was valued in his day. And in previous eras, too, since Bazin was by instinct and training a historian, and he knew that cinema's appeal—its social and psychological worth—was not the same in 1905 as in 1955 or as it would be in 1975, for audiences are specific and subject to history and class.

Most of Bazin's readers were paid subscribers of *Le Parisien libéré*, the most popular of the capital's dailies; others were cinephiles who waited each week for *L'Écran français* to come out (Bazin wrote more than 100 articles for it), or each month for *Cahiers du Cinéma* (120 articles). After 1950, in addition to *Cahiers*, he wrote regularly with the readers of two highly successful cultural weeklies in mind, *L'Observateur* (300 articles) and *Radio-Cinéma-Télévision* (now *Télérama*, more than 400 articles), both still appealing to a rather educated base. And then there was *Esprit*, his intellectual home base, where, among his fifty or so pieces, one finds those that are most far-reaching, most influential. Shortly before the war, when at the École Normale Supérieure, he had joined an *Esprit* study group, subscribing to its leftist Catholic politics and to the place it accorded literature and the arts in an overall social program. He had particularly liked Roger Leenhardt's film criticism, epitomized in a series of short articles, "La Petite École du Cinéma." Leenhardt had known exactly who his pupils were, the 5,000 *Esprit* subscribers, and perhaps 15,000 dedicated readers who shared a parti pris he generally agreed with.

After the war, Bazin stole Leenhardt's rubric, "Petite École du Cinéma," for a syllabus all his own, a dozen brief articles. These, however, were not destined for *Esprit*'s intellectual readership, although Leenhardt had ceded him the role as its film critic and its print run had reached 12,000, outstripping that of its rival *Les Temps Modernes*.[4] Bazin's little school was meant instead to educate the popular classes who picked up *Le Parisien libéré* every day, glancing through it, usually before tossing it away. Launched just after Charles de Gaulle entered Paris in the summer of 1944, and known as the paper of the concierges because of its catchy headlines, quick summaries of the news, its *faits divers* and gossip, its crude cartoons, and its practical information about city life, *Le Parisien libéré* paid Bazin to keep its thousands and thousands of readers in touch with Paris's unparalleled film offerings, something he did for more than fourteen years, almost fourteen hundred times altogether.[5]

Becoming a critic during the Occupation meant that Bazin began reviewing films in crowded theaters, where most spectators were happily taken away for a couple of hours to an imaginary or distant time and place, where they could watch familiar stars navigate intricate intrigues or pursue high-minded aspirations. Even films that were poorly put together fed a need that the historical moment made quite apparent: a need for tacit social cohesion. No matter how anonymous, each spectator imbibed with all the others some myth that the cinema purveyed like no other medium. You can call it ideology if you like; Bazin preferred the prevalent term "myth." And while he recognized that, like ideology, myths feel so satisfying that they may discourage critical thought, fostering passivity if not wild illusions, he counted them as extraordinarily valuable. For myths, thanks to their mystifying and displaced logic, speak to everyone in a society, eliciting a cohesiveness even among those likely to be at odds over their interpretations. Films, like myths—indeed, *as* myths—don't demand explanation, just the assent of those digesting them. But they do consist of elements that make up a vocabulary through which a kind of critical self-reflection is possible. Bazin knew how to deploy this vocabulary.

Rather than reflect on his personal reactions, he adopted a transpersonal view by recognizing where his readers were coming from when they entered the movie theater for a two-hour interruption of their day, as they paid to be astonished, or at least entertained. His mission: to extend and complicate the experience so they would, upon emerging, be able to recognize anew, or recognize something new, about their world and perhaps be able to articulate it to themselves and to those around them. Bazin became an extraordinary "ordinary man of cinema."[6] Whatever cinema was good for, it needed to be good for everyone, not just the connoisseur.

In a dissertation aimed at the politics implicit in Bazin's writings, Syed Feroz Hassan focuses on Bazin's treatment of cinema as instrumental to the common good of "aesthetic politics."[7] In quite a similar way to Hannah Arendt's simultaneous reflections on totalitarianism, Bazin insisted on the importance of the "love" and "imagination" requisite to bringing about a community of hope. Love names the acceptance, even among disputants, of the situation all are in, while imagination provides the space needed to consider reordering that situation. Love of cinema (cinephilia) must lead to love of the community of viewers who are lifted briefly out of the necessities of existence into a realm of pleasurable speculation.

This realm Bazin thought of as Myth, and he entered it again and again (The Myth of Total Cinema, The Myth of Jean Gabin, The Bardot Myth, The Myth of Chaplin, etc.). The term was rife in France in the 1940s and 1950s when Claude Lévi-Strauss, Roger Caillois, Roland Barthes, and Edgar Morin wrote about it. Later it would be identified as ideology, or as the political unconscious, terms that emphasize its blindness to the conditions on which it feeds.[8] Bazin understood the blindness of myth (see his devastating attack on "The Stalin Myth in Soviet Cinema"), but he marveled at the way it distills the complexities of social life for an entire society.[9] Myths organize confusion into categories and units, complete with names and valences. Myths may exist full blown, as in the Western or the gangster film, or crop up piecemeal in references to literary types and figures, in the names of stars, and so on. Myths thrive in a space where the community (the masses, if you will) might begin to identify the contradictions under which they live. Hassan reminds us that myth is a concrete instance of what Arendt claimed was essential for politics, "a small non time-space in the heart of time," enabling people living under certain conditions to imagine how those conditions operate and might be transcended or altered.[10]

Bazin was not alone in believing that even the most inane genre film could open up such a space, and project a utopia beyond the present. While his more cynical contemporary, Barthes, demonstrated that myths cement existing social structures by naturalizing history, Bazin felt that their broad, sometimes universal, appeal projected a community, one that could be reshaped through the effort of (critical) reflection within that tiny space of imaginative freedom represented by the movie theater. In that space, Gabin was indeed Everyman, as was Charlie Chaplin and as was Jacques Tati. Their aspirations, and especially their defeats, in film after film, should be treasured as a genuine good. Bazin displaced his love of genre films, a cinephilia that utterly absorbed his less political friends at *Cahiers*, into a love for the indefinitely large and variegated audience that breathes such films as second nature, that lives with them unconsciously. Especially in France after four years under totalitarian Occupation, myths were needed, the cinema was needed, as a vast carpet on which people of various classes and political tendencies could walk together into the future. The figures in that carpet certainly look different from different angles, causing rifts in interpretation, but the carpet's existence makes individuals recognize each other's presence. Cinema exists as a site for a people to gather, for a politics from the ground up.

In his role as citizen-critic, Bazin reined in his refined taste. He titled one article "No Gulf between 'Elite Cinema' and 'Popular Cinema,'" claiming that only cinema required critics to take all works seriously, without a hierarchy of genres.[11] Its social role is so prominent that if a hierarchy exists it puts subject matter before form. In "Un bon film sur de bons sentiments" ("A good film about good sentiments"), reviewing a film forgotten today, *Le Vrai Coupable* (1951, dir. Pierre Thévenard), he acceded to the de facto priority of ethics over aesthetics. *Le Vrai Coupable,* produced by a medical doctor, took up the subject of abortion, thus joining a large number of films where "if it's not only appropriate but in fact eminently desirable that cinema should put its extraordinary didactic capacities, its exceptional power of persuasion, at the service of fundamental problems of social morals or prevention, [then] inevitably in this kind of undertaking, 'form' comes second after 'content.'"[12]

And so Bazin willingly served on France's censorship committee from 1954 to 1958, when what was at stake had everything to do with what content was admissible on French screens. A study of his tenure there concluded that in the negotiations over what children (or the nation) should be allowed to watch, he seldom promoted one position over another; instead, he fostered debate by keeping open the complexities and multiple dimensions of every case the commission took up.[13] Ever consistent, as a public critic Bazin concerned himself less with whether a given film was good or bad; rather, it was cinema itself he cared about, and in his era cinema served as a place for imagination and politics, a place where, as he proclaimed in a brilliant essay, "every film is a social documentary."[14]

However, Bazin recognized that social history was accelerating and so cinema would pass into something else, as one era slipped into or beneath a new one rising up. He even predicted cinema's demise, as the myths of religion and literature that it has purveyed so powerfully would migrate to newer technologies.[15] We can congratulate him for his perspicacity, but he was only partly correct. Cinema remains alive, having proved mythical itself. Anyone living after *Star Wars* can attest to that. Technology, demography, competing cultural expressions, and world events like the recent pandemic may have altered the landscape to such a degree that the myth of cinema as bearer and maker of myths can no longer be what it was in 1950. But when scores of thousands of viewers pack theaters around the world to experience a *Star Wars* sequel almost simultaneously, one must recognize the extraordinary potential cinema retains to gather undifferentiated multitudes on its magic carpet. Whether for better or worse, this remains something cinema is good at, and good for.

CINEMA, AN ART AT THE EDGE OF CULTURE

Of course, the indiscriminate address of popular theatrical cinema, like that of mass-market newspapers such as *Le Parisien libéré,* no longer holds in the same manner in today's streaming environment, where innumerable channels distribute images to screens of all sizes. In truth, even in Bazin's day the dominance of the big studios and distributors had lots of competition. A network of film clubs catered to fans of political or religious or amateur films. And the Cinémathèque Française served those devoted to cinema itself. In the 1950s, a circuit of small theaters, grouped together as "Art et Essai," received special treatment from the government just to keep a discriminating audience alive. These curated sites, replicated in a modest number of art houses in major American cities, formed a particular niche, rather the way the Criterion Channel or MUBI does today.

Bazin wrote for this niche audience, too, doing so in *L'Écran français* during the late 1940s and in *Cahiers du Cinéma* from its birth in 1951 until his death in 1958. This is where he reported on and encouraged the emergence of a modern cinema capable of measuring and challenging both art and society. He referred to edgy films, including neorealism, as "La Nouvelle Avant-garde," situating it beyond the reach of genre cinema and the mass audience, but within reach of anyone devoted to the history of cinema and cheering its development.[16] When, early in the 1960s, Cavell found himself torn about his adhesion to cinema, this arrival of *la nouvelle avant-garde* was to blame; it intentionally made the viewer self-conscious. Yet Cavell recognized its value and responded deeply to many of its better examples. These films were good for something other than providing the kind of reassurance about the world that he (like everyone, he argued) found in classical Hollywood. But exactly what were difficult films good for?

Coming to cinema in the 1960s, I ought to know. Despite growing up in Pacific Palisades with film people, including stars, all around, and even working at Universal Studios for a summer job, I was relatively indifferent to movies until I found an art house (soon, five or six) to which I could drive. The auteurs they programmed were crucial to my maturation. In my final year of high school, I watched and discussed films with a couple of friends as if they were the great or cutting-edge novels we were simultaneously reading. In college, I quickly attached myself to the film society, collecting tickets at an Orson Welles series that permitted me to see six of his films three times each. During its single year of publication, I read each of the monthly issues of Andrew Sarris's *Cahiers du Cinéma in English* cover to cover. This wasn't my scenario alone. How could it be? Institutions like art theaters, college film societies, *Cahiers in English*, served and depended on a new generation of filmgoers, distinct from "the public."

Although I had yet to hear of him, Bazin had already identified what we found so valuable in European and Japanese auteurs, or in Satyajit Ray and John Cassavetes. This "avant-garde," unlike the main body of movies, actively discovered the pressure points of life—life in general, but also life in the Cold War era. These auteurs put their fingers on those points until you could feel them in the act of feeling these concerns. Cinema had indeed reached maturation, proving itself capable of exploring and expressing inchoate personal and social experience. Like the novel, with which it ran in a cultural relay race, cinema dared to push beyond politics, beyond society, into the magma of the Real.

And it did so better than the novel, or so we thought. Ingmar Bergman and Akira Kurosawa produced the look of anguish, François Truffaut the sensation of desperately pursuing a lost secret. Jean-Luc Godard was even more direct; he winked at us in our seats, then affronted us in a way no novel could. Modern cinema, *la nouvelle avant-garde,* spoke to a 1960s audience that felt itself to be avant-garde. That's why we went to specialized theaters. We were onto something, and the cinema was leading us on. When *What Is Cinema?* appeared in English, many of us, evidently Cavell included, could more clearly understand cinema's irreplaceable asset, that which made it incalculably valuable. Because it is technologically bound to the physicality of the Earth's time and space, cinema could ground its fictions in reality, no matter how far those fictions might drift with the imagination of their creators. Whatever one thinks of "the ontology of the photographic image," it identifies an attribute or effect of the medium—call it the documentary function—that ought to work against every myth, except the myth of total cinema.

For the next half-century I tried to articulate what Bazin had intuited when he experienced *The Rules of the Game/La Règle du jeu* (1939, dir. Jean Renoir), *Citizen Kane* (1941, dir. Orson Welles), and *Paisà* (1946, dir. Roberto Rossellini) just after the war: cinema may be an art, at least some of the time, but even its purest creators (Robert Bresson, Tati, Bergman) caught fire through the heat of friction when their pure creative intention rubbed up against the impurities of a recalcitrant reality. Essentially, in my view, that is *"what cinema is,"* what it is good for.[17]

Cinema needed its own half-century to recognize what was there at its origin, the marriage of Lumière and Méliès, as Godard put it. The freshness of its modernist moments, so evident in its various new waves, recovered this twin capacity for discovery and invention. Auteurs can be credited with this resurrection, and I remain on the lookout for them: Jia Zhangke, Apichatpong Weerasethakul, Claire Denis, Arnaud Desplechin, Pema Tseden. But perhaps the era of auteurs has passed; cinema may now be evolving not in response to the novel but to manga, video games, and social media that seem to arise not from a single artistic mind but from groups and networks of developers, and even from artificial intelligence.

This would not have troubled Bazin, for even if the "politique des auteurs" grew out of his orientation toward art (which he owed largely to André Malraux), cinema was to him a much larger phenomenon than its auteurs. He explicitly rebuked his disciples—the Hitchcocko-Hawksiens—for their narrowness. Films were valuable, he felt, because they concentrate, like nothing else, an array of forces that solicit all the disciplines and that therefore can educate any viewer about the interconnectedness of the universe. Angela Dalle Vacche has arranged these forces into Bazin's three lines of inquiry, "Art, Science, Religion."[18] A Renaissance man, Bazin followed these lines as they led him into the intricate bodies of films, where he exulted in finding out what goes into and what comes out of them. Cinema should make one hungry to understand life. For Bazin this amounted to an informal, yet comprehensive anthropology.

It makes sense that so many of his most fascinating essays show up in the two weeklies where he served as the mainstay critic, *L'Observateur* and *Radio-Cinéma-Télévision*. Their readers were likely to be educated and inquisitive. Yet, his deepest, most thoughtful essays were reserved for *Esprit,* with its readership of left-leaning intellectuals. This is where he made the case for Italian neorealism, focusing on *Paisà* and later on *Bicycle Thieves/Ladri di biciclette* (1948, dir. Vittorio De Sica), then on De Sica himself. Auteur studies you may call them, but these *Esprit* essays are much, much more. Bazin applauds a style-less style that abdicates authorial cunning and reduces bias without discarding perspective. The result is that famous "ambiguity" from which no clear moral can be drawn, other than the "love" that accepts and invests in the situation away from which the camera refuses to turn. Neorealism was initially a literary movement, but it found its power in cinema thanks to the impervious eye of the camera which takes in more than art can handle (a postwar landscape of broken buildings and broken lives), while presenting that "more" in the frame of art. It articulated raw situations without advocating what to do about them. Today we would say it "figured" what language had yet to name, doing so, Bazin dared to say, out of sheer love. This love, in which humans recognize each other as they come to recognize even impossible or tragic situations, is the basis for the politics Bazin believed in and that he sought in all kinds of films, well beyond the neorealist moment. But, as Hassan points out, this moment—1948—crystallized the politics not just of Bazin but of Arendt as well, and, I would add, was countersigned by the Universal Declaration of Human Rights.[19] In 1948, cinema was good for quite a lot. If we have outgrown it, it is to our shame.

NOTES

1. Stanley Cavell, *The World Viewed: Reflections on the Ontology of Film* (Cambridge, MA: Harvard University Press, 1979 [1971]), 4.

2. Erwin Panofsky, "Style and Medium in the Motion Pictures," published originally in 1936, its ultimate revision came out in *Critique: A Review of Contemporary Art* 3 (1947): 5–28.

3. Stanley Cavell, *Pursuits of Happiness: Comedies of Remarriage* (Cambridge, MA: Harvard University Press, 1981).

4. Michael Scott Christofferson, *French Intellectuals Against the Left* (New York: Berghahn, 2004), 77n40.

5. Hervé Joubert-Laurencin published a census of Bazin's complete works, "André Bazin et les revues," in *La Revue des revues* 33 (August 2003): 41–55. His figures would need to be updated as additional items have been discovered, a few even after he edited *André Bazin, Ecrits complets* (Paris: Macula, 2019).

6. I take this phrase from Jean-Louis Schefer, *L'homme ordinaire du cinéma* (Pairs: Gallimard, 1980), trans. Max Cavitch, Noura Wedell, and Paul Grant as *The Ordinary Man of Cinema* (Cambridge, MA: Semiotext[e], 2016). Schefer, as Nico Baumbach notes, believes cinema "acts on every social being as if on a solitary being," a cipher as in Kafka, where intimations of meaning well up begging to be articulated, but remaining just beyond clarity. In this, too, cinema behaves as do myths. Baumbach's review is in *Artforum* (May 2017), https://www.artforum.com/print/201705/jean-louis-schefer-s-ordinary-man-of-cinema-67915. Accessed August 24, 2021.

7. Syed Feroz Hassan, "Surviving Politics: André Bazin and Aesthetic Bad Faith," PhD diss. (University of Michigan, 2017).

8. Hassan, "Surviving Politics," 77.

9. André Bazin, "The Stalin Myth in Soviet Cinema," in *Movies and Methods: An Anthology,* vol. 2, ed. Bill Nichols (Berkeley: University of California Press, 1985), 29–40.

10. Hassan, "Surviving Politics," 175

11. Bazin, "Pas de fossé entre un 'cinéma de l'élite' et un 'cinéma populaire,'" *Radio-Cinéma-Télévision* 124 (June 1, 1952), reprinted in Joubert-Laurencin, *André Bazin, Ecrits complets,* 940–941.

12. Bazin, "Un bon film sur de bons sentiments," *Radio-Cinéma-Télévision* 79 (July 22, 1951), reprinted in Joubert-Laurencin, *André Bazin, Ecrits complets,* 751 (translation mine).

13. Marc Vernet, "Bazin the Censor?," in *Opening Bazin,* ed. Dudley Andrew (Oxford: Oxford University Press, 2011), 234–239.

14. André Bazin, "Tout film est un documentaire social," *Les Lettres françaises* 166 (July 1947). An English version translated by Sis Matthé is on the website *Sabzian* (October 10, 2019), https://www.sabzian.be/text/every-film-is-a-social-documentary. Accessed August 9, 2021. See also Marco Grosoli's fine discussion of this essay in *New Readings* 11 (2011): 1–16.

15. See André Bazin, "Is Cinema Mortal?" in *André Bazin's New Media,* ed. and trans. Dudley Andrew (Oakland: University of California Press, 2014), 313–318.

16. Bazin wrote four articles promoting formally audacious feature films. See, esp., "Découverte du cinéma: Defense de L'avant-garde," *L'Ecran français* 182 (December 21, 1948), reprinted in Joubert-Laurencin, *André Bazin, Ecrits complets,* 486–487.

17. Dudley Andrew, *What Cinema Is!* (Malden, MA: Wiley-Blackwell, 2010).

18. Angela Dalle Vacche, *André Bazin's Film Theory: Art, Science, Religion* (Oxford: Oxford University Press, 2020).

19. See Hassan, "Surviving Politics." Arendt's *The Origins of Totalitarianism* was published in 1951, the same year as Bazin's essay on Stalin. Arendt's ideas about politics in a blighted Europe gestated like his in the immediate postwar era. See Louis Menand, *The Free World* (New York: Farrar, Strauss, Giroux, 2021), 92–114, esp. 104.

PART SIX

Medial Goods

24

... Projection and Protection

On Cinemagoing as Playing Hide-and-Seek with Reality

FRANCESCO CASETTI

GERBI'S DELIGHTS (AND FEARS)

One of the most beautiful testimonies of the values attached to filmgoing is Antonello Gerbi's "Initiation to the Delights of Cinema."[1] Gerbi's essay, published in 1926 in the authoritative Italian journal *Il Convegno,* and only recently returned to the attention of film scholars, highlights the fascination exerted both by projected images and the setting in which they are projected—a dual focus that almost fifty years later Roland Barthes would reiterate in his famous contribution "Leaving the Movie Theater," with which Gerbi's essay can be rightly associated for its orientation and sensitivity.[2]

Gerbi starts by describing not the spectators' exit, as Barthes would do, but their entrance into the theater. There is an economic transaction: "The delights of the cinema begin immediately after buying your ticket" (p. 836). And there is a physical transition: "They begin as soon as the usher, seeing you arrive across the lobby, opens the velvet curtain so that you can enter [the theater] without having to slow down, without a moment of pause or the smallest obstacle" (p. 836). Those who go to the cinema must cross a threshold, both real and symbolic. The boundary is less pronounced when the spectator enters before the beginning of the film: in this case, the "tangible and three-dimensional reality" (p. 841) is left behind through successive steps, which begin with the waiting for the film and end with the gradual fading of the theater's

FIGURE 25. A cinema scene in *Sherlock Jr.* (1924, Buster Keaton).

architectural elements: "Absorbed by the darkness, first every shape, every outline, every structure disappears: farewell, plastic forms!" (p. 841). The boundary, on the other hand, appears much more marked when the spectator enters during the show. Here we have a "sudden leap" (p. 841) between two profoundly different universes, marked respectively by light and darkness, and in open struggle with each other. Not by chance, the usher who stands at the door of the theater

> opens the jaws of the shadows . . . just a little bit—I don't know if it's out of fear that the outside light would disturb or wound the sacred darkness, or that the darkness collected in the room, having found some small opening would spread out into the lobby, would hinder a careful checking of tickets, would pour out into the street and would shortly flood the entire city. (p. 837)

If the light of the world threatens the room, the darkness of the room threatens the world. This is why we need a closed space, separated from the world. We need an anti-world, capable of "swallowing up the real, mundane world" (p. 838).

Once in the theater, the spectator's gaze "springs to the security lights, grazes the luminous reflections that touch the rows of patrons' heads, and settles trustingly on the screen" (p. 838). The already settled spectators, "subdued by the darkness," seem to escape the new audience member's gaze. In return, the latter is especially attracted by the cone of light that comes out of the projection booth. It is "a very sharp electric ray, which with a shock awakens the little images in their squared cells of celluloid, and one after another, in rapid succession, throws them out of the little window only to flatten themselves out—enlarged by terror—against the canvas" (p. 841). This divine, essential light is "a sort of domestic Milky Way that contains in embryonic form billions of worlds" (p. 840). These worlds blossom when they are projected onto the screen—"a large cut of canvas" that is "ready to take in all of the impressions, and ready to forget them" (p. 839), and which in this game of conquest and abandonment reveals its masculine nature: "Impassable and untiring, the screen is the last incarnation of the spirit of Don Giovanni" (p. 839).[3]

Devoid of images, the screen "is so stupid and useless that it is irritating. It doesn't justify itself. It doesn't explain itself" (p. 839). But when the light from the projector hits it, the screen transforms: "What was a large bandage strewn with talcum powder is reborn as an altarpiece for the liturgies of the new times" (p. 840). And like an altarpiece, the screen returns in all its richness the reality that spectators have left behind them, or even a reality that they have never experienced. Indeed, the canvas, miraculously, "changes color, trembles, grows pale, flees into the background, approaches in close-ups right under the nose of the worshipper, passes through a number of hurried and temporary reincarnations, changes its face and soul a hundred times a minute" (p. 841). What takes shape on the screen is the flowering of life.

Such a transformation of the screen is fully apparent at the beginning of the screening. If the title of the film and the names of the actors could still evoke literature and theater, with the first images it starts a completely different experience. "Spectators make themselves comfortable in the deep of their chairs; their eye governs the focus of their gaze; their feet finally find the support they were looking for; their elbows marry the line of the armchairs" (p. 842). From their seats, without "the light murmur of a prayer," and in "perfect adoration," they now witness the appearance of a "new Epiphany" (pp. 840 and 842).

Despite the delights, however, there is no shortage of reasons for concern. Waiting for the film to start, for example, creates anxiety: it is then when we experience "the unexpected sensation of finding ourselves suspended between two worlds—the fantastic one of cinema and the real one" (p. 842). A similar anxiety emerges when the projection is not well centered on the screen: "Everyone yells 'Frame! Frame!' with the same anguish of a person who sees a crazed horse coming from the end of a deserted street and yells 'Stop! Stop!'" (p. 845). An even stronger anxiety takes shape when, for whatever reason, the pace of the projection slows down: "No patience could resist the slow, corroding, continuous dripping of images" (p. 843). The projection can even stop: "A yawn. Just one. But in that boundless yawn the entire Universe will be swallowed up. That is how I imagine the end of the world" (p. 843). This fear that the world on the screen may dissolve, giving way to nothing, has its perfect counterpart in the terror that the world on the screen may instead become real and merge with the everyday world. Here Gerbi's imagination becomes apocalyptic: "The night-time-reveling phantasms would come down from the screen and would attach themselves, deformed, contorted, grimacing, to the bodies of the spectators, to the bare walls, to the skin of the ladies, to the backs of the chairs, to people's heads, to their collars, to the newspapers" (p. 845). A direct projection toward open space instead of a screen would produce the same effects:

> If a projection took place without the screen—onto open space—where would it end up? Seemingly it would vanish into the air, it would dissolve into a vague, luminous nebulosity. But if it is true that nothing is lost in the Universe, how can characters who are so alive and so animated disappear like that? Their fate worries me. If you were to find them close to you, so thin and silent, one night when you're returning home, there would be quite a bit to be afraid of. (p. 846)

The materialization of images is frightening.

THE PROJECTION/PROTECTION COMPLEX

Gerbi's description, full of literary and religious echoes, hits the mark. Cinema is not just a movie: it is an optical-spatial *dispositif* that couples an enclosed space, separated from the everyday world, and a screen whose moving images reestablish contact with the reality from which spectators have been severed, or to which they never had access. Conveyed by a powerful beam of light, and in sharp contrast with the darkness of the theater, images acquire unusual intensity and strength. Hence the idea of a miraculous epiphany: the world on the screen ends up being more detailed and more encompassing than what a direct sight can capture.[4] The consequence is that what has been lost is given back with interest.

Spatial deprivations that encourage reconnection with actual or transcendental worlds are common to other situations, starting from religious rituals and theater. Yet cinema makes this arrangement special. Its

Projection and Protection | 293

enclosure is deeply artificial: it depends on architectural, economic, logistic, and organizational thresholds, as Gerbi recalls. And filmic images are produced and reproduced by a technical apparatus. Gerbi praises the electric light that holds together the screen, projector, and audience and makes them work in unison.[5] Cinema belongs to the age of machines. If we want to track cinema's affiliations, we can find them, on the one hand, in the phantasmagoria, which in the late eighteenth century first linked an intentionally closed space with a relatively sophisticated system of projection that materialized ghosts, and, on the other hand, in the personal "bubbles" in which we seek refuge when we isolate ourselves from our physical surroundings and concentrate on our laptop or smartphone.[6] Despite their apparent divergences, they, too, rely on the convergence of a forced enclosure and technical images, whose sensorial fervor compensates for spatial deprivation.

But why this optical-spatial arrangement? At stake are not only practical needs—to accommodate spectators or users and to increase attention toward images. As Gerbi's worries suggest, there is something more: the necessity to distance oneself from reality for fear of coming into direct contact with it. This contact triggers discomfort, as spectators reveal when at the beginning of the screening they still linger in their everyday world, or even worse, when they experience images that can be mistaken for actual people. Reality can be threatening, hence the need for some sort of distance and reconnection.

It is worth mentioning that the fear of a close contact with the world is not uncommon in the twentieth century. In addition to Gerbi, it emerges in several cinephobic texts of the time, which ask cinema to stay away from the crudest aspects of life.[7] Beyond the cinema, it is at the core of philosophical anthropology, which underscores the threats of the environment for that "underdeveloped animal" that is man.[8] Martin Heidegger connects this fear to our anxiety of being-in-the-world—exposed to a reality that, in turn, exposes itself to us.[9] Walter Benjamin associates it with an age marked by traumatic events that leave the individuals astounded and often speechless.[10] Paul Virilio attributes its resurgence to a technological progress that shrinks our space and accelerates our time to an unprecedented scale.[11] If we take into account this theoretical background, and especially its references to the modern experience, the reasons behind the convergence of artificial enclosures and technical images in cinema become even clearer: against the perceived risk of full exposure, the restricted place of the theater works like a shelter and the screened images work like a filter.[12] By doing this, they not only enhance the mediation with the world, allowing spectators to explore it in its detail and in its extension through images that look like "epiphanies," but also make this mediation harmless. Instead of an increasingly risky face-to-face confrontation with things and events, this optical-spatial arrangement offers an encounter with reality that preserves liveliness and adds layers of defense, thanks, respectively, to representations that can be taken for perceptions and delimited settings that introduce distances and deferrals.[13] The outcome is a "mediated immediacy" that combines connections and thresholds—and that ultimately discloses how, in the modern condition, immediacy is a by-product of mediation itself.[14] Such a state of security makes it possible to reintroduce the fears from which the optical-spatial arrangement attempted to protect its users. The images can be frightening, yet they are not threatening unless they change their status and become physical entities, as Gerbi ironically remarks.

This perspective allows us to rethink the *dispositifs* that connect an artificial enclosure with screened images, starting from those of cinema. These *dispositifs* ultimately embody what I want to call the *projection/ protection complex,* in which "projection" does not necessarily stand for the presence of a projector, easily replaceable by other screening devices, but rather for the presence of a surface that hosts impermanent images on behalf of viewers that turn their attention to them. The projection/protection complex is a mechanism that plays hide-and-seek with reality: while alluding, in a sealed space, to the fear of immediate contact with the world, it provides a safe reconnection with what it severed thanks to successful representations. Consequently, individuals regain an interaction with the reality that they were encouraged to relinquish; they can continue and even increase their engagement with the world, though by other means. Rooted in a recurring anthropological configuration that finds its archetype in Plato's cave, with modern media the projection/protection complex becomes a techno-environmental technique that helps mediate a reality that is increasingly perceived at once as more aggressive and more elusive.

BETWEEN DISCIPLINE AND IMMUNITY

Gerbi bears full witness to the mode in which the projection/protection complex works.[15] In his essay, the delights of cinema emerge when the viewer leaves the everyday world behind and reconnects to it thanks to images that represent a magnified reality. Anxieties, on the contrary, are linked to a sudden return to a direct interaction with the world, due to either a delay in the projection or a materialization of projected images. Yet, Gerbi astutely adds a further stroke to the picture. When filmic characters become real entities, either because they "come down from the screen" and invade the theater, or because they reappear in the night after the projection was lost in the sky, they not only elicit a distressing confrontation with spectators but also uncover how cinema, instead of reconnecting its audience to the world, can turn into a self-sufficient reality that entraps the audience in its own perimeter. In this case, cinema becomes an arrangement from which we are not able to escape—a machine that ultimately ensnares its spectators.[16]

Gerbi's further stroke raises a question. What kind of protection is one that not only reiterates frightening motifs through harmless images, but also elicits new fears—the fears of the protective machine itself? Moving away from Gerbi, the answer can be twofold. On the one hand, the protection elicited by cinema, as well as by the phantasmagoria and the electronic bubbles, appears to be a counterpart of *disciplinary strategies*. As Michel Foucault showed, discipline largely involves the partitioning of space, with the creation of borders, cells, positions, ranks, and so on.[17] The result is a physical and social environment that is at once efficient and safe from surprises. This perfectly applies to the settings that characterize our three media. Their enclosures subject spectators and users to a set of predefined actions and norms, and in exchange give them a sense of safety. Screened images complete this process, eliciting forms of focalization that delimit the elements at stake and ease the beholders' interaction with them.[18] The need for order can also elicit a sort of *state of exception*.[19] In this case, spectators and users experience their confinement as a suspension of their usual ways of coping with reality, a suspension imposed upon them under the pretext of combatting a potential danger.[20] Such a proximity with disciplinary strategies reveals how deeply entrenched the projection/protection complex is in a political dimension.

On the other hand, the apparently paradoxical protection promised by our media echoes an *immunization process*. While the enclosure offers a barrier against external dangers, the screened images, with their fearsome but not deadly content, provide a vaccine against them. Less than ten years after Gerbi wrote "Initiation to the Delights of Cinema," Benjamin developed this argument in a crucial passage of the second version of his "Work of Art" essay: the images of the most aggressive behaviors, once projected in a film theater, trigger antibodies that fight the tendencies that those behaviors seem to imply.[21] The paradigm of sovereignty gives way to biopolitics.

Hence, a dramatic choice that the projection/protection complex faces: is it a form of repression or a pharmacological answer to an endemic threat? Is it a turning point in the balance of powers or a mitigation of the risks involved in coping with the world? Such an alternative does not necessarily imply a binary situation. Both the disciplinary strategies and the immunization processes have a hidden face. Despite the creation of docile bodies, discipline brings to the fore the presence of potentially active political subjects, and an autoimmune disease can lead to the destruction of the organism that it is supposed to protect.[22] Outcomes depend on the ecology of elements in which each *dispositif* operates and on the kind of reply it offers. Born to avoid the uncertainties related to the direct exposure to the world, the projection/protection complex eventually discovers the need to deal with the world's density and convolution.

We find an even more radical indetermination at the very heart of the mechanism. While promising a safe interaction with the world, the projection/protection complex puts forward the idea of a detachment from reality and the idea of fears triggered by reality. What if the detachment is something intrinsic to all processes of mediation—something that modern technical media just amplify? To mediate does not only mean to hold together but also to split the terms of the mediation.[23] If splitting from reality is constitutive of our coping with it, the promise of a full reconnection is just a myth. And what if the fears triggered by the exposure to reality are the product of the mediation itself, which in this way finds its own rationale? Indeed, shelters and filters not only offer a shield, but also materialize the risks of being exposed to the exterior—they "create" the panic of the outside through their own presence. Consequently, protection becomes like the Platonic *pharmakon:* it cures and poisons at once. These dilemmas give the projection/protection complex a veneer of ambiguity: it no longer appears as a unilateral and deterministic mechanism. Once again, the circumstances that the single instantiations face offer them a solution.

While drastically reframing the idea that screened images, starting with those of film, provide an unproblematic experience of reality, the projection/protection complex fosters an approach that takes into consideration all aspects of the mediation process, including the fears that it raises, the settings where it takes place, the bifurcations that it creates, and the reversals that it encounters.[24] Yet, it is the conjunction of radical choices and sensitivity toward the whole ecology of elements that ultimately makes the complex the exemplary mechanism through which we can gain a better understanding of the moral and political accountability of modern media.

NOTES

1. Antonello Gerbi, "Iniziazione alle delizie del cinema," *Il Convegno* 7, nos. 11–12 (November 25, 1926): 836–848. Gerbi's essay is unpublished in English: I will quote here from a translation by Siobhan Quinlan, whom I thank. In the main text the page numbers of Gerbi's essay are subsequently indicated in brackets.

2. Roland Barthes, "Leaving the Movie Theater," in *The Rustle of Language*, trans. Richard Howard (Berkeley: University of California Press, 1986 [1975]), 345–349.

3. In a gendered prose, Gerbi describes the negative film stock as female: "The negative, which allows itself to leave its mark with the first ray of light that comes by, and then jealously always keeps the imprint of it, has something feminine about it." Gerbi, "Iniziazione," 839.

4. In a silent parallel with Jean Epstein and Béla Bálazs, Gerbi describes the slow movement as able to capture bodies, things, and events with unprecedented precision: "A microscope applied not to points in space but to moments in time, slow motion examines the phases of each act with an equal love for all of them, and with an equal, very attentive zeal." Gerbi, "Iniziazione," 844.

5. "The band of rays that keeps the images bridled on the screen gives unity to the three essential elements of the cinema: it holds the screen, the audience, and the projection booth together in a collected and peaceful order." Gerbi, "Iniziazione," 843.

6. On phantasmagoria's history, see Laurent Mannoni, *The Great Art of Light and Shadow: Archaeology of Cinema* (Exeter: University of Exeter Press, 2000), and Mervyn Heard, *Phantasmagoria: The Secret Life of the Magic Lantern* (Hastings: Projection Box, 2006). The bubble as a personal space in which an individual can take refuge is explored by Michael Bull, "'To Each Their Own Bubble.' Mobile Space of the Sound in the City," in *Mediaspace: Place, Scale, and Culture in a Media Age*, ed. Nick Couldry and Anna McCarthy (New York: Routledge, 2004), 275–293. For visual bubbles, see Francesco Casetti and Sara Sampietro, "With Eyes, with Hands: The Relocation of Cinema into iPhone," in *Moving Data: The iPhone and the Future of Media*, ed. Pelle Snikars and Patrick Vonderau (New York: Columbia University Press, 2012), 19–32. Peter Sloterdijk has expanded the concept of the bubble to include social, architectural, and psychological formations: see the trilogy *Spheres*, respectively *Bubbles*, *Globes*, and *Foam*, trans. Wieland Hoban (Los Angeles: Semiotext[e], 2011, 2014, 2014).

7. For the cinephobic trends in the early film theories, see Francesco Casetti, "Why Fears Matter: Cinephobia in Early Film Culture," *Screen* 59, no. 2 (Summer 2018): 145–157.

8. See Arnold Gehlen, *Man, His Nature and Place in the World,* trans. Clare McMillan and Karl Pillemer (New York: Columbia University Press, 1988).

9. Heidegger distinguishes between fear (oriented toward an object and raised by an impending threat) and anxiety (a fear without an object, tied to our general being-in-the-world). See Martin Heidegger, *Being and Time,* trans. John Macquarrie and Edward Robinson (Oxford: Blackwell, 1962), 179–182 and 228–235.

10. Walter Benjamin, "Experience and Poverty," *Selected Writings* 2.2 (Cambridge, MA: The Belknap Press of Harvard University Press 1999), 731–736. On modern shocks, see "On Some Motifs in Baudelaire," *Illuminations,* ed. Hanna Arendt (New York: Shacken Books, 1968), 155–200.

11. Paul Virilio, *The Administration of Fear* (Los Angeles: Semiotext[e], 2012).

12. Stanley Cavell captures this status of the screen when he writes: "The world of a moving picture is screened. The screen is not a support, not like a canvas. . . . A screen is a barrier. What does the silver screen screen? It screens me from the world it holds—that is, makes me invisible. And it screens that world from me—that is, screens its existence from me." Stanley Cavell, *The World Viewed* (Cambridge, MA: Harvard University Press, 1979), 24.

13. The idea of "representations taken for a perception" has been expansively explored by Jean-Louis Baudry, "The Apparatus: Metapsychological Approaches to the Impression of Reality in Cinema," in *Narrative, Apparatus, Ideology,* ed. Philip Rosen (New York: Columbia University Press, 1986), 299–318.

14. On immediacy and mediation, see David Jay Bolter and Richard Grusin, *Remediation* (Cambridge, MA: MIT Press, 1999).

15. Gerbi was not alone. In the same years, while condemning cinema for dissociating spectators from reality, the Italian playwright and novelist Luigi Pirandello also described the modern world as increasingly uncomfortable and challenging. The mechanical copies of reality provided by cinema, quite paradoxically, can make spectators aware of their lives as they have been shaped by modern progress. See Luigi Pirandello, *Shoot! The Notebooks of Serafino Gubbio, Cinematograph Operator,* trans. C. K. Scott Moncrief (New York: E. P. Dutton, 1926). Walter Benjamin in his "Work of Art" essay—which not by chance quoted Pirandello—noted that modern technology—the "second technology"—relies on an accentuated distance from nature; this is even more true for film, whose capacity to capture reality depends exclusively on a technical apparatus that deeply affects what is to be shot. This separation is redeemed by images that give the opportunity to rejoin reality, through new forms of apperception that echo the impact of technology on nature. See Walter Benjamin, "The Work of Art in the Age of Mechanical Reproduction, Second Version," in *The Work of Art in the Age of Its Technological Reproducibility, and Other Writings on Media,* ed. Richard Levin, Michael W. Jennings, and Brigid Doherty (Cambridge, MA: Harvard University Press, 2008).

16. "There is no further escape. It is impossible to detach from oneself the shadow which is as threatening and restless as remorse. . . . It is impossible to flee: the passages are like canals filled with corpses." Gerbi, "Iniziazione," 845.

17. Michel Foucault, *Discipline and Punish: The Birth of the Prison* (New York: Random House, 1975).

18. On the role of modern attention and its complicity with disciplinary strategies, see Jonathan Crary, *Suspension of Perception: Attention, Spectacle, and Modern Culture* (Cambridge, MA: MIT Press, 2001).

19. See Giorgio Agamben, *State of Exception,* trans. Kevin Attell (Chicago: University of Chicago Press, 2005).

20. For this interpretation, see Giorgio Agamben, "Lo stato d'eccezione provocato da un'emerganza immotivata," *Il Manifesto* (February 26, 2020), https://ilmanifesto.it/lo-stato-deccezione-provocato-da-unemergenza-immotivata/. Accessed February 27, 2020.

21. Benjamin, "The Work of Art, Second Version," 38.

22. See Jacques Derrida, "Autoimmunity: Real and Symbolic Suicides," trans. Pascale Anne Brault and Michael Naas, in *Philosophy in a Time of Terror,* ed. Giovanna Borradori (Chicago: University of Chicago Press, 2003), 123–124. On the complexity of the immune paradigm, see Roberto Esposito, *Immunitas: Protection and Negation of Life* (Cambridge: Polity, 2011); and Roberto Esposito, "The Immunization Paradigm," trans. Timothy Campbell, *Diacritics* 36, no. 2 (2006): 23–48. A recent discussion of the immune paradigm in cinema is Francesco Vitale, *La farmacia di Godard* (Naples: Orthotes Editrice, 2021).

23. On the process of mediation, see Richard Grusin, "Radical Mediation," *Critical Inquiry* 42 (Autumn 2015): 124–148.

24. For a critical revision of the trend to see screened images as providing an unproblematic experience of reality, see Malcolm Turvey, *Doubting Vision: Film and the Revelationist Tradition* (Oxford: Oxford University Press, 2008).

25

. . . An Animated and Animating Medium

On Hegel, Adorno, and the Good of Film

NICHOLAS BAER

The spirit is an animating law in union with the manifold which is then itself animated.
—G. W. F. Hegel

To make an anachronistic comparison, Hegel's publications are more like films of thought than texts.
—Theodor W. Adorno

The good of film experience is addressed nowhere more famously than in the epilogue to Siegfried Kracauer's magnum opus, *Theory of Film: The Redemption of Physical Reality* (1960). For a divergent perspective on the value of cinema, we can turn to a contemporaneous book by Kracauer's longtime friend and interlocutor, Theodor W. Adorno. In *Hegel: Three Studies* (*Drei Studien zu Hegel*, 1963)—a work that remains all but unknown among cinema and media scholars—Adorno makes repeated reference to moving images, characterizing G. W. F. Hegel's writings as "films of thought." Such cinematic language is not only anachronistic but also highly unexpected from the harsh and unsparing critic of the culture industry who once proclaimed, "Every visit to the cinema leaves me, against all my vigilance, stupider and worse."[1] As I will nonetheless suggest, Adorno's reflections on Hegelian phenomenology can offer important insights into the good of film

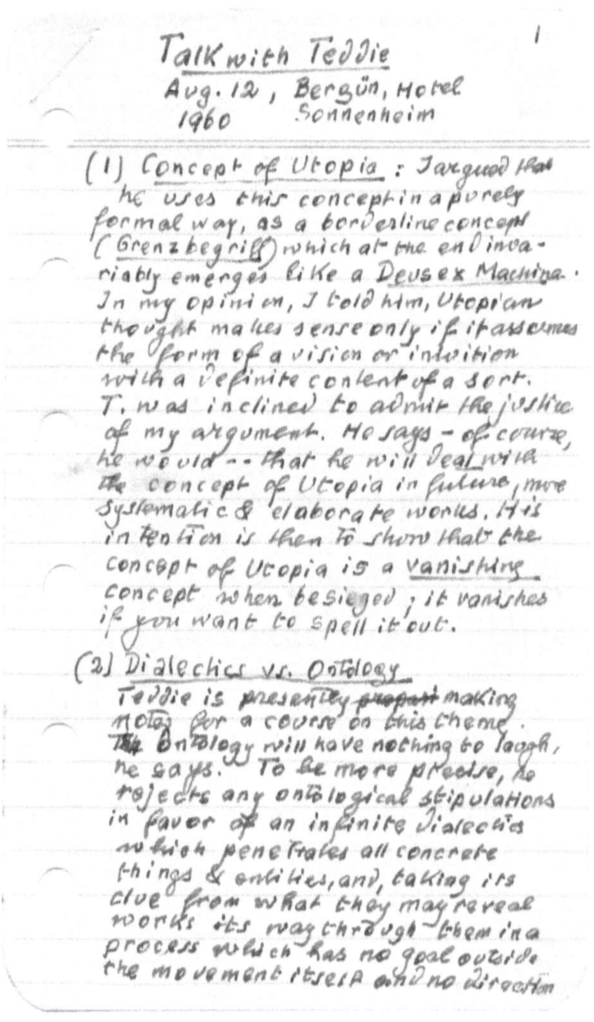
Talk with Teddie 1

Aug. 12, 1960 Bergün, Hotel Sonnenheim

(1) Concept of Utopia: I argued that he uses this concept in a purely formal way, as a borderline concept (Grenzbegriff) which at the end invariably emerges like a Deus ex Machina. In my opinion, I told him, Utopian thought makes sense only if it assumes the form of a vision or intuition with a definite content of a sort. T. was inclined to admit the justice of my argument. He says — of course, he would — that he will deal with the concept of Utopia in future, more systematic & elaborate works. His intention is then to show that the concept of Utopia is a vanishing concept when besieged; it vanishes if you want to spell it out.

(2) Dialectics vs. Ontology

Teddie is presently ~~prepar~~ making notes for a course on this theme. The ontology will have nothing to laugh, he says. To be more precise, he rejects any ontological stipulations in favor of an infinite dialectics which penetrates all concrete things & entities, and, taking its clue from what they may reveal works its way through them in a process which has no goal outside the movement itself and no direction

FIGURE 26. Siegfried Kracauer's handwritten notes from an August 12, 1960, meeting with Theodor W. Adorno. Deutsches Literaturarchiv Marbach.

experience, particularly as cinematic spectatorship assumes unfamiliar new guises in today's digital mediascape.

Kracauer and Adorno formulated their views on film and Hegelian philosophy in dynamic, often-contentious intellectual exchange. At a meeting in Bergün, Switzerland, on August 12, 1960, Kracauer articulated his objections to Adorno's dialectics in terms of shot scale:

> I compared Teddie's [Adorno's] dialectics with a film made up exclusively of close-ups. Such a film is of course imaginable, I said; but the close-ups of which it consists would be completely undefined and, hence, puzzling rather than revealing, were they not every now and then, interrupted by "establishing" shots relating them to the reality with which we are confronted after all and thus defining, however tentatively, their approximate position. Otherwise expressed, the radical immanence of dialectical process [sic] will not do; some ontological fixations are needed to imbue it with significance and direction. I spoke of "*ontologischen Würfen*" within this context and remarked that Hegel's dialectics moved toward, or implied, an ontological end. This was a bit careless of me, for Teddie knowing my lifelong aversion to Hegel, immediately exploited the situation by saying that Hegel never committed the sin of orienting the dialectical process toward anything allegedly "Objective" outside that process.[2]

For Kracauer, Adorno's dialectical procedure was dizzying in its lack of objective elements, remaining purely immanent throughout its infinite movement. More concerned with ontological stipulations, Kracauer's *Theory of Film* favored fixed, deductive postulates (e.g., the "basic aesthetic principle") over the vertiginous, "Bacchanalian revel" of Hegelian dialectics.[3] In subsequent years, Adorno would critically engage with Kracauer's ideas in private correspondence along with well-known publications such as "The Curious Realist" ("Der wunderliche Realist," 1964), "Art and the Arts" ("Die Kunst und die Künste," 1966), and "Transparencies on Film" ("Filmtransparente," 1966).[4] Yet, already in 1963, his *Hegel: Three Studies* marked an indirect response to his spirited conversation with Kracauer in Switzerland. In the third of his three studies, "Skoteinos, or How to Read Hegel" ("Skoteinos oder Wie zu lesen sei"), Adorno adopted Kracauer's filmic approach to philosophy, yet he signaled a differing understanding of moving-image media and the good of cinematic experience.

Where Kracauer was a critic and theorist of film over multiple decades, Adorno maintained an enduring suspicion of the technologically based mass medium on account of its profit dependency and its seemingly immediate relation to empirical reality, with insufficient potential for subjectivity, intentionality, and aesthetic autonomy. To the extent that Adorno modified his understanding of cinema in the 1960s, he revised his assumptions in productive tension with Kracauer's *Theory of Film*, which he faulted for its elision of sociological and economic considerations, invocation of a "decline of ideology," and reified conception of the "concrete."[5] In the epilogue to *Theory of Film* ("Film in Our Time"), Kracauer had cited a waning of common beliefs and a prevailing abstractness, locating the good of film in its capacity to record, reveal, and redeem the material world by enabling "the experience of things in their concreteness."⁶ While Adorno's "Skoteinos" likewise suggested an experiential aesthetics of film, it emphasized temporality and dynamism rather than photographically subtended realism. Adorno's essay thus poses a challenge to Kracauer's work and to later film-theoretical paradigms that rely on the indexical trace and an ethics of realism as their Archimedean point.

This essay will use Adorno's "Skoteinos" as a lens through which to analyze Hegel's *Phenomenology of Spirit* (*Phänomenologie des Geistes*, 1807), focusing on "Sense-Certainty: or the 'This' and 'Meaning'" ("Die sinnliche Gewißheit; oder das Diese und das Meinen"). Developing Adorno's reflections, I will demonstrate that the temporality of the *Phenomenology* becomes integral to Hegel's treatment of time, necessitating a cinematic mode of reading. I then turn to the issue of perspective, indicating that the dynamism of subject/object relations affords neither a stable vantage point nor a fixed, "photographable" object. The third section examines Hegel's ruminations on deictic words and problems of indexicality, especially with regard to the ever-shifting "Now." As I will argue, the good of film for Adorno arises from the medium's challenge to Cartesian standards of distinct, unambiguous clarity. With its temporal dynamism and perspectival mobility, cinema suggests a dialectical relation between the subject and object, which are both in motion. In this way, Adorno's study of Hegel can intervene in contemporary debates on filmic indexicality and the rapidly changing nature of cinematic experience, providing an apt model as scholars confront the dizzying landscape of twenty-first-century media and spectatorship.

TEMPORAL DYNAMISM

In "Skoteinos," Adorno writes that both the substance of Hegel's philosophy and its mode of expression are processual in character.⁷ Elaborating on this strongly mimetic approach, Adorno draws an analogy between Hegel's writings and the medium of film: "To make an anachronistic comparison, Hegel's publications are more like films of thought than texts. The untutored eye can never capture the details of a film the way it can those of a still image, and so it is with Hegel's writings. This is the locus of the forbidding quality in them, and it is precisely here that Hegel regresses behind his dialectical content."⁸

Reappropriating Kracauer's cinematic comparison from their 1960 meeting in Switzerland, Adorno likens Hegel's writings to fleeting and elusive moving images.[9] While Adorno characteristically identifies the filmic quality of Hegel's publications as their locus of regression behind "dialectical content," he later deploys cinematic diction once again to describe the twofold mode of reading demanded by Hegel—a mode of reading, Adorno adds, which is "not ill suited to the nature of the dialectic."[10] According to Adorno, the reader should not only "float along, to let himself be borne by the current and not to force the momentary to linger," but also attempt "to develop an intellectual slow-motion procedure, to slow down the tempo at the cloudy places in such a way that they do not evaporate and their motion can be seen."[11] Rather than seeking to fix or still Hegel's writing, then, the reader must both surrender him- or herself to it and place its opaque passages in a "slow-motion procedure" that maintains their dynamic quality. Adorno notes that these two procedures are seldom part of the same act of reading.

The first section of *Phenomenology of Spirit,* "Sense-Certainty: or the 'This' and 'Meaning,'" exemplifies how Hegel lends the reader a perpetual sense of dispossession in movement. At the outset of the section, Hegel contends that in a study primarily or immediately concerned with knowledge, the knowledge that is the object of study must itself be "immediate knowledge itself, a knowledge of the immediate or of what simply *is*."[12] By the same token, according to Hegel, one must adopt an immediate relation to the object: "Our approach to the object must also be *immediate* or *receptive;* we must alter nothing in the object as it presents itself. In *ap*prehending [*Auffassen*] it, we must refrain from trying to *com*prehend [*Begreifen*] it."[13] In the following paragraph, Hegel states that the "concrete content" of sense-certainty makes it appear as boundless and complete knowledge, or "the *richest* kind of knowledge" and "the *truest.*"[14] Switching his pair of superlative adjectives, however, Hegel proceeds to write, "This very *certainty* proves itself to be the *most abstract and poorest truth.*"[15] As Hegel asserts that sense-certainty only knows "the sheer *being* of the thing," and that neither subject (*Ich*) nor object (*die Sache*) has "the significance of a complex process of mediation," he destabilizes the reader's own sense of certainty of his previous claims.[16] Just as Hegel declares that one should refrain from grasping an object of study while apprehending it, he prevents the reader from fixing or isolating any thesis or statement in his own work, which—as Adorno notes—requires time for its development and for the demonstration of its truths.

PERSPECTIVAL MOBILITY

While, for Adorno, the temporality and dynamism of Hegel's writings warrant comparison with the aesthetic properties of film, calls for epistemological clarity assume a Cartesian model analogous to still photography. Adorno states:

> Clarity can be demanded of all knowledge only when it has been determined that the objects under investigation are free of all dynamic qualities that would cause them to elude the gaze that tries to capture and hold them unambiguously. The desideratum of clarity becomes doubly problematic when consistent thought discovers that the object of its philosophizing not only runs right over the knower as though on some vehicle but is inherently in motion, thereby divesting itself of its last similarity with the Cartesian *res extensa*, matter extended in space. The correlate of this insight is that the subject too is not static like a camera on a tripod; rather, the subject itself also moves, by virtue of its relationship to the object that is inherently in motion—one of the central tenets of Hegel's *Phenomenology*. Faced with this, the simple demand for clarity and distinctness becomes obsolete.[17]

The dictate of epistemological clarity thus presupposes that the object of knowledge lacks a dynamism that would elude the gaze's grasp. The inherent motion of the object challenges Descartes's model of substance dualism, and the subject itself moves on account of its relation to the moving object. Echoing a remark from "The Essay as Form" ("Der Essay als Form," 1958), Adorno expresses this central tenet of Hegelian phenomenology in negative relation to photography: the subject—"*not . . . like a camera on a tripod*"—is itself dynamic, and as soon as consciousness regards objects of knowledge "*not . . . as pinned down and identified like things—photographable, as it were,*" it defies Cartesian standards of clarity and distinctness.[18] For Adorno, then, the criterion of photographability is associated with the demand for congealed, graspable objects of knowledge, or products of reified consciousness.

In Hegel's discussion of "Sense-Certainty," the mobility and mediation of both subject and object resist a static, unidirectional photographic gaze. Refuting his earlier claim that neither subject nor object undergoes a process of manifold mediation, Hegel writes that "neither one nor the other is only *immediately* present in sense-certainty, but each is at the same time *mediated*."[19] Sense-certainty is thus mutually constituted through a process of intermediation between subject and object. Taking up the categories of time and space, which Kant had identified as fundamental coordinates of experience and conditions of intelligibility, Hegel tests basic indices of both—"the Now" and "the

Here"—and observes their mobility and promiscuity. Thus, an ostensible truth (e.g., "'Now is Night'") that a subject writes down is later negated, and another truth ("'Here' is, e.g. the tree") vanishes as the subject pivots.[20] Furthermore, when one shifts perspective from this subject to another, the truth claim of the former ("'Here' is a tree") disappears in that of the latter ("'Here' is not a tree but a house instead").[21] According to Hegel, each index or deictic word—"Now," "Here," and "I"—is thus a "universality" or "mediated simplicity," and Kantian attempts to "deduce, construct, find *a priori,* or however it is put, something called 'this thing' or 'this one man'" face the problem of specifying their very object of analysis.[22] In his philosophical prose, Hegel enacts the mobility and promiscuity of these indices, thereby shaking the reader's own epistemological confidence. Indeed, Hegel's written claims—like the ostensible truths he invokes—are soon negated, subjects and objects of knowledge are reversed, and seemingly fixed and stable perspectives are suddenly shifted.

PROBLEMS OF INDEXICALITY

Acknowledging that sense-certainty loses its immediacy at a temporal or spatial distance, Hegel states that one must enter into the same point in time or space as "the one who knows with certainty" to access this truth.[23] In so doing, however, one always confronts problems of indexicality:

> The Now [*Itzt*] is pointed to, *this* Now. "Now"; it has already ceased to be in the act of pointing to it. The Now that *is* [*ist*], is another Now than the one pointed to, and we see that the Now is just this: to be no more just when it is. The Now, as it is pointed out to us, is Now that *has been* [*ein gewesenes*]; and this is its truth; it has not the truth of *being*. Yet this much is true, that it has been. But what essentially *has been* [*was gewesen ist*] is, in fact, not an essence that *is* [*kein Wesen*]; *it is not,* and it was with *being* that we were concerned.[24]

In this paragraph, Hegel highlights the discrepancy between the time of indication and the time actually indicated. As the "Now" ceaselessly shifts, the act of pointing is always belated, losing the "Now" at the moment of pointing to it. Hegel stylistically emphasizes this temporal lag and the elusiveness of the "Now" by shifting between the present and perfect tense and between the active and passive voice ("is pointed to [*wird gezeigt*]" versus "has already ceased [*hat schon aufgehört*]") as well as by referring to the two "Nows" with different sets of grammatical constructions ("the Now," "another," and "*being*" versus "the one pointed to," "Now that *has been*," and "what essentially *has been*"). Furthermore, he enacts the futile, asymptotic quality of attempts to pinpoint or reach the immediate "Now" by reiterating the term with a definite article, demonstrative article, and finally on its own ("The Now . . . ; this Now. 'Now'") and also by repeatedly placing the near-homonymic words "Now [*Itzt*]" and "is [*ist*]" in close rhythmic succession. The very linearity of Hegel's text necessitates the perpetual rewriting of the word "Now" and calls the reader's attention to the gap between Hegel's initial and later identification of his own point of focus: "it was with *being* that we were concerned."

Like other deictic words (e.g., "Here," "This") that point to seemingly self-evident objects or properties, "Now" is a universal that reveals an undifferentiated plurality at the moment of specification. Hegel writes that each indexical speech act follows a similar trajectory: (a) one points to a true "Now" that has always already vanished; (b) one claims its pastness as its truth; (c) one recognizes that "what was" is not "what is" and returns to the initial claim: "that the 'Now' is [*daß Itzt ist*]."[25] According to Hegel, the time of indication and the time indicated are dialectically constituted such that neither is "something immediate and simple," but rather "a movement which contains various moments."[26] One is thus unable to assume an unmediated relation to the "Now," which—through this three-step process of movement and negation—becomes what Hegel calls "something that is reflected into itself [*ein in sich Reflektiertes*]" rather than "something immediate [*ein Unmittelbares*]."[27] In this way, the true "Now" always contains a plurality of "Nows," untethered to a particular moment and infinitely divisible: "a Now which is an absolute plurality of Nows. And this is the true, the genuine Now, the Now as a simple day which contains within it many Nows—hours. A Now of this sort, an hour, similarly is many minutes, and this Now is likewise many Nows, and so on."[28] Hegel suggests an infinity within the "Now" not only by dividing a day into ever-smaller temporal units, but also through the repetition of the words "many" and "Now," the accumulation of clauses, and the final conjunctive adverb and dash—a horizontal stroke in which "thought becomes aware of its fragmentary character," as Adorno claimed in his essay on "Punctuation Marks" ("Satzzeichen," 1956).[29] For Hegel, the act of pointing is itself the movement that expresses the true multiplicity and universality of the "Now." More broadly, simple empiricism always confronts problems of indexicality and of the nondescriptive, indifferent referentiality of its terms.

AN ANIMATED AND ANIMATING MEDIUM

Let me "now" shift my own mobile, intermediated gaze to scholarship on film and digital media, suggesting how Hegel's and Adorno's writings might contribute to recent debates on indexicality and the changing nature of cinematic experience. Charles Sanders Peirce's theory of signs entered cinema studies through semiotic film theory in the late 1960s, and his concept of the index—understood as a physical or existential connection between sign and object, a trace fixed in time since the moment of inscription or registration—became a primary marker of cinematic realism, medium specificity, and disciplinary boundaries.[30] The concept was invested with new significance at the turn of the twenty-first century in response to the perceived potentialities and threats of digital media. A reductive concept of indexicality, referring to film's analogical, photochemical base, was often posited against digitality as commentators apprehensively heralded the "end of cinema"— and with it, their object of disciplinary study. Numerous scholars challenged these alarmist accounts by calling attention to instances of media competition, transfer, and interchange throughout film history; highlighting genres or modes of filmmaking (e.g., animation) marginalized by ontological claims about indexicality; and emphasizing aesthetic continuities in illusionism, motion, and stylistic practice. Furthermore, returning to Peirce's writings, many noted the index's oft-overlooked deictic forms and functions, the diversity of Peirce's examples, and cinema's semiotic heterogeneity within his broader triadic system.[31]

Classical film theory gained renewed interest in this context, as scholars considered the ongoing relevance of early/mid-twentieth-century writings following the digital turn. Acknowledging the problems of Kracauer's essentializing, medium-specific claims about film's "photographic nature" in *Theory of Film,* Miriam Hansen shifted attention to his theorization of film experience: "What *Theory of Film* can offer us today is not a theory of film in general, but a theory of a particular type of film experience, and of cinema as the aesthetic matrix of a particular historical experience."[32] In this essay, I have instead focused on how Adorno formulated his own experiential aesthetics of film that placed emphasis on temporality and movement rather than "camera-realism."

As I have contended, not only did film experience serve as a point of comparison for Adorno's privileged approach to reading Hegel, but Hegelian phenomenology also assumed a key, overlooked role as Adorno developed his late film aesthetics, based on "a subjective mode of experience that film, irrespective of its technological origin, resembles and that constitutes its artistic character."[33] Where Hansen attributes Adorno's more capacious and differentiated sense of film aesthetics to the writer-filmmaker Alexander Kluge and New German Cinema, I have stressed the formative impact of his intellectual exchange with Kracauer, particularly on the nexus of cinema and Hegelian dialectics.[34]

Diverging from Kracauer's understanding of moving-image media, Adorno located the good of film in its break with Descartes's substance dualism. While Kracauer characterized still photography as the ontological basis of film, Adorno associated photography with a static model of knowledge formation, whereby objects are pinned down and unequivocally captured. And if film scholarship has often defined indexicality in terms of the enduring trace or imprint of an object that appeared before the lens at the past moment of recording, Adorno focused on the deictic function of cinema, which directs the spectator's gaze to a specific, unique object in the "here" and "now" that may shift or disappear in the moment of its identification. For Adorno, cinema's deictic function was crucial for its affinity with Hegelian phenomenology as well as its challenge to the long-standing Cartesian split between the thinking subject (*res cogitans*) and the extended substance (*res extensa*). Positing a more spatiotemporally dynamic, intermediated relationship between the cognizing subject and object of cognition, Adorno proposed a dialectical, post-Cartesian approach to film as an *animated* and *animating* medium. Much as the Hegelian spirit is "an animating law [*belebendes Gesetz*] in union with the manifold that is then itself animated [*alsdann ein belebtes*]," cinema places moving images and beings in a living, mutually implicated relation with one another that implies the transformation of each in time.[35]

In "Skoteinos," Adorno suggests that the dialectical movement of Hegel's philosophy resists Cartesian standards of distinct, unambiguous clarity. For Adorno, the "praxis of knowledge" clings to such standards "out of excessive zeal for the specialized activities of the individual disciplines, which establish their objects and object domains without reflection and set dogmatic norms for the relationship of knowledge to its objects."[36] Writing before cinema studies became an "individual discipline" and at a time when cinematic spectatorship demanded greater self-surrender, Adorno nonetheless evoked tendencies apparent more recently as film scholars have confronted the dizzying environment of new media. While some have claimed photographic, analog representation as an ontological or specific property of the medium—and, by extension, as a flag of disciplinary territory—others have looked to Henri Bergson and his commentators (most notably, Gilles Deleuze) to emphasize the irreducible movement of the cinematic image. Yet for Adorno, Hegel stands in "oblique relationship" to Bergson, who—for all his critical opposition to scientific positivism—eschewed contradiction in favor of *"unmediated* acceptance of the so-called given as a firm basis of knowledge."[37] In my reading, Adorno suggests an animated and animating understanding of cinema, whereby both film and spectator are in motion by virtue of a complex, dialectical process of mediation. Taking up Kracauer's question of the good of film experience, Adorno "points" toward a distinctive approach to the medium, one concerned less with ontological stipulations or fixed, deductive postulates than with phenomenological insight into an experience that, in Hegel's words, "has already ceased to be in the act of being pointed to."[38]

NOTES

Epigraphs: G.W.F. Hegel, "Fragment of a System," trans. Richard Kroner, in *Early Theological Writings* (Philadelphia: University of Pennsylvania Press, 1975), 309–319, at 311; Theodor W. Adorno, "Skoteinos, or How to Read Hegel," in *Hegel: Three Studies,* trans. Shierry Weber Nicholsen (Cambridge, MA: MIT Press, 1993), 89–148, at 121.

1. Theodor Adorno, *Minima Moralia: Reflections on a Damaged Life,* trans. E.F.N. Jephcott (London: Verso, 2005), 25.

2. Siegfried Kracauer, "Talk with Teddie," in Theodor W. Adorno and Siegfried Kracauer, *"Der Riß der Welt geht auch durch mich": Briefwechsel 1923–1966,* ed. Wolfgang Schopf (Frankfurt am Main: Suhrkamp, 2008), 514–517, at 515. On the friendship between Adorno and Kracauer, see Martin Jay, "Adorno and Kracauer: Notes on a Troubled Friendship," in *Permanent Exiles: Essays on the Intellectual Migration from Germany to America* (New York: Columbia University Press, 1985), 217–236; and Johannes von Moltke, "Teddie and Friedel: Theodor W. Adorno, Siegfried Kracauer, and the Erotics of Friendship," in *Criticism* 51, no. 4 (Fall 2009): 683–694.

3. G.W.F. Hegel, *Phenomenology of Spirit,* trans. A.V. Miller (Oxford: Oxford University Press, 1977), 27. On this point, see also Jay, "Adorno and Kracauer," 228, 312n48.

4. See Adorno and Kracauer, *Briefwechsel;* Theodor W. Adorno, "The Curious Realist: On Siegfried Kracauer," trans. Shierry Weber Nicholsen, *New German Critique* 54 (Autumn 1991): 159–177; Theodor W. Adorno, "Art and the Arts," trans. Rodney Livingstone, in *Can One Live after Auschwitz? A Philosophical*

Reader, ed. Rolf Tiedemann (Stanford, CA: Stanford University Press, 2003), 368–387; and Theodor W. Adorno, "Transparencies on Film," trans. Thomas Y. Levin, *New German Critique* 24–25 (Autumn 1981–Winter 1982): 199–205.

5. See Adorno and Kracauer, *Briefwechsel,* 628–629, 633, 636, 639, 642, 688. Adorno went so far as to advocate the exclusion of the epilogue to Kracauer's *Theory of Film* from its German-language edition.

6. Siegfried Kracauer, *Theory of Film: The Redemption of Physical Reality* (Princeton: Princeton University Press, 1997), 296.

7. On the "processual" and its relation to aesthetic experience, see Theodor W. Adorno, *Aesthetic Theory,* ed. Gretel Adorno and Rolf Tiedemann, trans. Robert Hullot-Kentor (London: Continuum, 2002), 175–178.

8. Adorno, "Skoteinos," 121.

9. For discussions of "Skoteinos" between Adorno and Kracauer, see Adorno and Kracauer, *Briefwechsel,* 583, 585, 586, 591–592, 633. Adorno explained to Kracauer that the Greek term "means the Obscure and is the old epithet of Heraclitus" (Adorno and Kracauer, *Briefwechsel,* 592). For a discussion of Adorno's engagement with the "language character" of film, see Miriam Bratu Hansen, *Cinema and Experience: Siegfried Kracauer, Walter Benjamin, and Theodor W. Adorno* (Berkeley: University of California Press, 2011), 229–236. Magisterial as it is, Hansen's book neglects Adorno's "Skoteinos" essay.

10. Adorno, "Skoteinos," 123.

11. Adorno, "Skoteinos," 123.

12. Hegel, *Phenomenology,* 58.

13. Hegel, *Phenomenology,* 58.

14. Hegel, *Phenomenology,* 58.

15. Hegel, *Phenomenology,* 58 (emphases added).

16. Hegel, *Phenomenology,* 58.

17. Adorno, "Skoteinos," 98–99. See related comments by Adorno in "Notes on Kafka," in *Prisms,* trans. Samuel and Shierry Weber (Cambridge, MA: MIT Press, 1983), 243–271, at 246: "[Kafka's] texts are designed not to sustain a constant distance between themselves and their victim but rather to agitate his feelings to a point where he fears that the narrative will shoot towards him like a locomotive in a three-dimensional film"; and "The Handle, the Pot, and Early Experience," *Notes to Literature,* ed. Rolf Tiedemann, trans. Shierry Weber Nicholsen (New York: Columbia University Press, 2019), 466–473, at 470: "Philosophically, [Ernst Bloch's *Spirit of Utopia*] indicates a change of attitude toward the object. The object can no longer be contemplated peacefully and with composure. As in emancipated film, thought uses a handheld camera."

18. Adorno, "Skoteinos," 99, 100 (emphases added). See also Theodor W. Adorno, "The Essay as Form," trans. Bob Hullot-Kentor and Frederic Will, *New German Critique* 32 (Spring–Summer 1984): 151–171, at 166. Obvious counterexamples to Adorno's claims about photography include Marey's chronophotography and Bragaglia's photodynamism. For more complex accounts of the relation between Cartesian perspectivalism and photographic technology, see, e.g., Jonathan Crary, *Techniques of the Observer: On Vision and Modernity in the Nineteenth Century* (Cambridge, MA: MIT Press, 1990);

and Martin Jay, *Downcast Eyes: The Denigration of Vision in Twentieth-Century French Thought* (Berkeley: University of California Press, 1993).

19. Hegel, *Phenomenology*, 59.
20. Hegel, *Phenomenology*, 60.
21. Hegel, *Phenomenology*, 61.
22. Hegel, *Phenomenology*, 61, 62.
23. Hegel, *Phenomenology*, 63.
24. Hegel, *Phenomenology*, 63.
25. Hegel, *Phenomenology*, 63.
26. Hegel, *Phenomenology*, 64.
27. Hegel, *Phenomenology*, 64.
28. Hegel, *Phenomenology*, 64 (translation modified).
29. Theodor W. Adorno, "Punctuation Marks," in *Notes to Literature*, 106–111, at 108.
30. Peter Wollen is commonly cited as the scholar who introduced Peirce's semiology to the study of film; see Wollen, "The Semiology of the Cinema," in *Signs and Meaning in the Cinema* (Bloomington: Indiana University Press, 1969), 116–154.
31. Key texts in the recent debates over cinematic indexicality and technological change include Mary Ann Doane, "The Indexical and the Concept of Medium Specificity," *differences: A Journal of Feminist Cultural Studies* 18, no. 1 (2007): 128–152; Tom Gunning, "Moving Away from the Index: Cinema and the Impression of Reality," *differences: A Journal of Feminist Cultural Studies* 18, no. 1 (2007): 29–52; Gertrud Koch, "Carnivore or Chameleon: The Fate of Cinema Studies," *Critical Inquiry* 35, no. 4 (Summer 2009): 918–928; Lev Manovich, *The Language of New Media* (Cambridge, MA: MIT Press, 2001); and Laura Mulvey, *Death 24x a Second: Stillness and the Moving Image* (London: Reaktion Books, 2006).
32. Hansen, *Cinema and Experience*, 255. On Kracauer's conception of film experience, see also Johannes von Moltke, *The Curious Humanist: Siegfried Kracauer in America* (Oakland: University of California Press, 2016).
33. Adorno, "Transparencies on Film," 201 (translation modified).
34. See Hansen, *Cinema and Experience*, 210, 249. See also Nicole Brenez, "T. W. Adorno: Cinema in Spite of Itself—But Cinema All the Same," trans. Olivier Delers and Ross Chambers, *Cultural Studies Review* 13, no. 1 (March 2007): 70–88, at 76: "In the sixties, Adorno's observations on cinema undergo a sea change as a consequence of his discovery of the work of Godard and the New German Cinema, but also of an experimental film by Mauricio Kagel."
35. Hegel, "Fragment of a System," 311. On this passage, see also Judith Butler, "To Sense What is Living in the Other: Hegel's Early Love," *dOCUMENTA* 13 (Ostfildern: Hatje Cantz, 2012), 16.
36. Adorno, "Skoteinos," 99. See also Charles Sanders Peirce, *Collected Papers*, vol. 5, ed. Charles Hartshorne and Paul Weiss (Cambridge, MA: Harvard University Press, 1934), 392: "It appears that there are certain mummified pedants who have never waked to the truth that the act of knowing a real object alters it."

37. Theodor W. Adorno, "The Experiential Content of Hegel's Philosophy," in *Hegel: Three Studies,* trans. Shierry Weber Nicholsen (Cambridge, MA: MIT Press, 1993), 53–88, at 55 (emphasis added); on the contrast between Hegel and Bergson, see 72–73.

38. I would like to thank Judith Butler, Matthew Noble-Olson, and the editors of this volume, Julian Hanich and Martin Rossouw, for their invaluable comments on versions of this essay.

26

... The Bigger Picture

On Watching Films on a Cinema Screen

MARTINE BEUGNET

Is the big screen finally losing the battle? Has watching films in a movie theater merely been, as one media historian provocatively put it, "a brief parenthesis ... a brief encounter that today we are all the more inclined to remember nostalgically for its transience?"[1] If television and the VHS player did not manage to kill the cinema (film watched collectively, on a large screen), DVDs and streaming, the computer, the tablet, and finally the mobile phone, may succeed in consigning it to the past. Media archaeologists have pointed out that there is nothing inherently new about this evolution.[2] After all, protocinematic technologies entailed a large variety of modes of reception, public and domestic, aimed at mass audiences or the individual viewer. From the flip-book to the mobile phone for instance, the connection is even more easily established that access to the content extends to the way the single viewer interfaces with the image—from thumbing to swiping.[3]

However, filmmakers and film scholars have rallied in defense of the specificity and value of the cinematic mode of reception. From the late 1990s onward, reception became both a popular field of study and a topic of debate between film theorists, historians of the arts, and media theorists.[4] If film theorists were intent on defending the experience of watching film in the cinema as irreplaceable, art historians were eager to downplay its uniqueness and incorporate film, now a fit object for the museum, in a broad field of art history, while media theorists similarly explored the various ways in which the experience of watching

FIGURE 27. Georges Méliès's early cinema in *Hugo* (2011, Martin Scorsese).

films might be successfully "relocated" elsewhere than in the cinema.⁵ For those who have come to equate going to the cinema with an exclusive cinephiliac practice, such "relocation" was the sign of a welcome democratization of content and access.⁶ Yet, the discourse that appears to prevail ultimately mirrors the dominant consumerist ethos: the demise of the cinema both participates in and results from the generalized ownership of individual screening devices (synonymous with planned obsolescence and endless replacement), and the attendant subscription to streaming platforms.

There is no denying factual reality: fixed and portable smaller screens are occupying an ever-increasing part of our watching time. For the "digital natives," the smaller screens are becoming the primary mode of reception of films (among other content): the habit and urge to see a given film on a large screen first has largely disappeared. The Covid-19 pandemic may well put the last nail in the coffin: with confinement and the temporary or final closing of cinemas everywhere in the world, the default size is, overwhelmingly, that of the domestic screens.

Does it matter? As I write this piece, in 2021, Parisian cinemas have been shut, on and off, for almost a year. I miss going to the cinema. Is it primarily a question of generation? A futile nostalgic indulgence and snobbish "hang-up" for an outmoded cultural practice? I am well aware of such views, yet I still cannot help but wonder about what might effectively be lost as we renounce watching films on a big screen. In particular, and though the debate on film reception has become a rather tired trope, I observe that questions of aesthetics never played as large a part as one would expect in the discussion. To put it simply: are some of the things film is good for not best experienced on the cinema screen? And if so, does this not, in turn, suggest that it is important that filmmakers continue shooting films for the big screen, films that are exhibited in cinemas? In what follows, I would like to briefly consider the relationship between the cinematic film (distinguished from moving-image productions originally shot for a different mode of exhibition) and the large screen, focusing on three, interconnected aspects of the experience of watching films on a big screen: film as a mirror for the collective, haptic immersion, and offscreen space.

THE MULTITUDE, OFF- AND ONSCREEN

From the beginnings of the cinema, filmmakers and film theorists alike agreed on one particular ability of film that no other spectacle or art form could rival: a spectacle for mass audiences, film was the first medium to offer its spectators a mirror image of themselves as a collective—as a group, a crowd, the masses.[7] In contrast to the theater, cinema did not even need to rely on extras: a director could simply set the camera alongside city streets, or at the entrance of a factory, to capture the reality of the individual as part of an anonymous throng or a community of people.[8] Film's power of evocation as a mass medium was diversely appraised as a tool of hateful propaganda or social liberation and advancement. Disparaged by the established powers who feared its revolutionary potential, embraced for the opposite reasons by some of the avant-gardes and by militant filmmaking ever since, it has also been an object of ambivalent consideration for progressive observers, in particular in the wake of the catastrophic spread of fascisms.[9] The point I would like to stress, however (a point that might help weigh out these contrasted arguments), is that this particular ability of film to portray human beings or animals as a collective or as a mass is only truly effective on a large screen.

Depending on the kind of scene depicted, the collective identification encouraged in the cinema might foster a feeling of empathy or rejection. However, whether people are portrayed as an anonymous group or crowd, as a collective protesting for their rights, as a deadly army or a destructive mob, not only the question of the size of the bodies on screen, but that of the occupation of a shared space, on screen and in the cinema, are key.

In her writing on the subject of public protest, Judith Butler insists on the performative role of demonstrations as the marching or sitting together of a multitude of bodies.[10] Demonstrations have a performative function insofar as the bodies assembled together result in an actual appropriation or reappropriation of public space, as well as the setting in motion of an efficient form of agency rendered possible by the incorporation of the individual in the crowd. The space that matters, Butler points out, is not only the space as place (that is, as historically situated and signifying) but also the space between the bodies that the sitting or marching together invests with meaning and purpose. She further observes that if this is true of any public protest, for the performative function of a particular event to become effective in the long term, in its specificity and historicity, it needs to be recorded and broadcast.[11]

It is a sign of the continuing importance of embodied practices such as depicted by Butler that even in the age of social media and the online "swarm," people still feel the need to gather (and are repressed by the powers that be for doing so).[12] It is on our television and computer screens that we are most likely to encounter accounts of ongoing protests. On such screens, however, crowds are never human size, and the resulting descaling, in which assembled bodies end up looking like insects, figurines, or dots, works to objectify the human figure, just as it objectifies the animal figure. The solitary spectator's domestic space also does not offer itself as a meaningful, performative counterpart to the representation of spaces that are wrongly seized and occupied, or, conversely, reclaimed or simply shared by a crowd or a community of people. This is not to deny the incomparable capacity for raising awareness of the instant, mass dissemination of video content on social networks (and, contrariwise, its incomparable capacity for disinformation). But whether documentary or fictional, film has a role to play both in the historicizing of events and in fostering collective identification.[13] The issue is not merely a discursive one—a question of retrospective narratives and their inscription in collective memory—but one of aesthetics. The alternation of shots of various scales that represents the individual, simultaneously or in succession, as a singular figure and as part of a crowd, arguably works whatever the size of the display. In the cinema, however, not only does the space extend toward the audience (3D cinema likes to occupy this connecting zone, with images that appear to reach out for us), but combined with the camera work, the scale of the image allows the spectator to project themselves into the diegetic space, in the midst of the depicted group of people (I am here talking about the standard size of cinema screen, rather than the outsized panoramic image of the IMAX).[14] As a result of, and contributing to, this fluid form of incorporation, the "pluralism" of "the cinematic subject," afforded by the multiplicity of potential points of view produced by the mobile camera and the editing, comes fully into play.[15] Furthermore, only in the presence of a cinema screen do the conditions of reception (a collective audience watching a collective character or characters as a collective) allow for a form of performative, collective identification—as, and with, a crowd or a group of people occupying space. It is not unreasonable, therefore, to think that the kind of co-present, embodied perception encouraged by film watched on a cinema screen contributes to a sense of shared awareness and agency and the elaboration of a social imaginary.

In a context where many film theaters struggle to survive, some might contend that the cinema experience should be maintained primarily for art films and their audiences. One might also argue, however, in defense of a popular form of cinemagoing that continues to provide, to as wide an audience as possible, a gateway to a culture of collective film spectatorship.[16] But such considerations are inseparable from a more general appreciation of the film image viewed in its large, cinematic format.

THE IMAGE ON THE BIG SCREEN

We do not need oculometric studies to realize that watching a film on a large and on a small screen not only changes the meaning of what we view but that it amounts to a different aesthetic experience.[17] If film derives some of its most powerful effects from its capacity to alter the scale of things, the mode of display can amplify or reverse such effects. To revisit Sergei Eisenstein's classic example of cinematic enlargement in the contemporary context of the multiplication of screening devices is to relativize his classic observation on the power of the film close-up. If the close-up projected on a large screen has the ability to transform mere cockroaches into elephant-sized monsters, when viewed on a mobile phone screen, the cockroaches revert to their insect-like size.[18]

But such rescaling also has an impact on our appreciation of film's material appearance. Smaller screens allow images to be "seized" instantly and consumed as a whole by our gaze. Because the more reduced screen space also artificially increases definition, we "read" the content more efficiently and immediately: the figurative and narrative dimensions of the image are foregrounded. In contrast, the expansive cinema image fills the periphery of our vision and invites the eye to wander and lose itself in the depth of the field, the shallow background, or in the uncertain zones that form its borders.

I am not interested in playing one mode of reception against the other (I have argued elsewhere that small screens produce their own spectatorial pleasures).[19] Rather, in stressing the differences between them, and the need to remain "dispositive conscious,"[20] I wish to advocate for the cohabitation rather than the replacement of one technology or mode of reception by another. In other words, I contend that to merely follow a strategy of planned obsolescence amounts to a significant impoverishment of our aesthetic experience.

The emergence, in the late 1990s, of a strand of film studies rooted in phenomenology has helped to reemphasize aesthetic dimensions of film and film spectatorship that had been explored by early theorists but downplayed by later, narrative, and semiology-driven approaches. In a visual culture that arguably privileges a distanced, optical form of visuality, certain images offer a reprieve to the eye, the possibility of reconnecting with a more synaesthetic perception supported by forms of haptic visuality.[21] From high definition to the "poor" image, the encounter with a variety of qualities of images, displayed in diverse sizes and levels of resolution, encourages us to exercise our haptic gaze.[22] In this regard, the cinematic image, displayed on a large screen, offers a distinctive spectatorial experience. Whether it relies on the crispness of lines and the depth of field, or, on the contrary, on the softening of contours and blurriness, or on a combination or succession of both, the film image, viewed on the big screen, invites a versatile synaesthetic gaze, associating vision with a form of tactility, and beyond, a multisensory perception. Even in the case of the most conventional of films, in which the filmmaking systematically works to guide the viewer's gaze spatially and narratively, the large image still allows for the gaze to "graze" its surface, to appreciate the changing textures, contrasts, and colors.[23]

On the one hand, because, and thanks to, the combination of a powerful projector and large size of display, cinema screenings produce a quality of image that cannot be emulated in the domestic space: they offer high resolution but without the harsh contrast, not to say garish sharpness, of some of the digital screens available for home display. As a result, the large-scale image is more suited for the inclusion of the onscreen figure into its environment and fosters an awareness of the material properties of film. This is facilitated by cinema's specific affinity with the sublime: its capacity to blow things out of the proportions normally afforded by human vision.[24] From the extreme close-up to the extreme long or wide-angle shot, the film image can transform a body, or even part of a body, into a landscape on which the eye wanders or, on the contrary, reduce it to a mere speck, part of a wider setting that offers itself to the mobile gaze like a panorama or tapestry.[25] Aided by the surrounding darkness of the film theater, the "absenting" of the body, whereby awareness of our sentient body recedes so that we concentrate on the perception of an external object, contributes to the immersive quality of our engagement with a film watched on a large screen.[26]

THE OUT-OF-FIELD

Furthermore, the combination of darkness and the large screen allows for the manifestation of a phenomenon that is essential to the experience of film: the presence of the out-of-field. The space demarcated by the borders of the image, and, in turn, the limits of the screen onto which it appears, has been an object of continuing fascination for film theorists. Defined by movement both in and of the frame, the film image appears inherently centripetal, hence its relation to what lies beyond (actual or virtual, diegetic or fantasized) is as constant as it is fluid. As such, the nature of its out-of-field is dual: on the one hand, it describes that part of the set that is not (not anymore, or not yet) included in the frame but forms an extension of the diegetic space beyond the edges of the frame. On the other hand, it stands for the existence of the "whole in which it is integrated."[27] In the first instance, the out-of-field thus designates "that which exists elsewhere, to one side or around" (the diegetic offscreen space, *hors-champ* in French). In the second instance it "testifies to a more disturbing presence, one which cannot even be said to exist, but rather to 'insist' or 'subsist,' a more radical Elsewhere."[28] The auditorium (and beyond it, the world at large), and the production space, once occupied by the filming crew and later translated into the spectatorial space, are both part of such an out-of-field (the *hors-cadre* in French). Yet the existence of a "radical Elsewhere" cannot be so precisely delimited, and its origins cannot be so strictly identified: a manifestation of the permeability between off- and onscreen worlds, it is jointly produced by the spectator's imagination and the vision that the film constructs.[29] The edges of the frame and, in turn, the cinema screen form an ill-defined, precarious liminal space, both physical and mental: a space of potentiality that may never be actualized.[30]

Such a versatile definition of the out-of-field is dependent on the big screen, the limits of whose expansive surfaces fade into darkened surroundings.[31] In many ways, smaller screens appear devoid of the power to conjure the "radical Elsewhere" that Gilles Deleuze assigns to the cinematic image. From television to computer to mobile phone, the domestic and portable screens rescale the profilmic as well as its image to fit within the narrower confines of their casements. The last-named, in particular, allows us to "grasp" the image both literally (in the way we handle such tactile devices) and figuratively (in the way we see and "consume" the small image instantaneously), and thus encourages a regime of the possessive gaze.[32] The always potentially intruding presence of the reality that surrounds the viewer—living room, street, or subway: spaces and environments that are neither designed for, nor dedicated to, the watching of film—further denies the existence of the image's invisible extensions, its out-of-field.

Hence, André Bazin's classic distinction between the regimes of vision established by painting and cinema appears to gain a renewed pertinence in the era of multiple screen sizes. In Bazin's oft-debated comparison, the cinematic image stands as the record of a portion of reality that continues beyond its edges while, in contrast, in traditional painting, the frame delimits the boundaries of a world in itself.[33] Small display devices appear to draw even the moving image toward our experience of conventional painting: the smaller the image, the greater the sense of a self-contained microcosm and the weaker the presence of an out-of-field (whether it be the diegetic offscreen/*hors-champ* or the fantasized space of the *hors-cadre*).[34] Hence, even as we become engrossed by the spectacle that unfolds on the computer, television, or mobile-phone screen, no matter how discreet, the casement or frame functions as more decisive boundary.

In the cinema, the size of the screen, the immobility of the spectator, and the surrounding darkness produce a greater affinity with the loosely defined frame of the natural, limited, human scope of vision. Such capacity of the big screen to uphold the film image's out-of-field appears valuable in many ways. An essential part of the pleasures of film spectatorship, the out-of-field is both a crucial dimension of the cinematic imaginary (part of our active engagement with the film) and more broadly of our relation to the world we perceive. Seen on a large screen, films encourage us to relate to the field of the visible not as fully and instantly legible and consumable, but—and this is part of the appeal of the cinematic experience—as elusive and forever incomplete.

Ultimately, to watch a film in a cinema is to envision oneself, as well as the image, as part of a larger, shared reality.

The movie theater brings out key dimensions of what film is good for. I highlighted three such dimensions, connected to watching film on a big cinema screen. It does not follow that one should return to, or insist on, a single, or a dominant, mode of reception. Rather, these characteristic features of film watched in a cinema point to the importance of maintaining a variety of screening scales and modes of reception. Indeed, there is one more feature, one more dimension of what film is good for, that comes to the fore on the big screen, in the context of the current multiplicity of display modes and devices. Thanks to its expansive, encompassing scale, film, when viewed on a large screen, has a unique ability to account for the complexification of the field of the visible: increasingly, the composition of its images incorporates, and plays on, the presence of the smaller screens.[35] Frames within frames, superimpositions, doubling . . . the possibilities are endless, as is the performance of new gestures, attitudes, and modes of communication that come to challenge and enrich the language of film, from acting to cinematography and montage. In absorbing the other screens within the larger, more inclusive space of its cinematic appearance, film is not merely documenting and reflecting on the changing reality around us, it is also experimenting with new forms, reinventing itself.

NOTES

1. Gabriele Pedulla, *In Broad Daylight* (London: Verso, 2012), 79.

2. Eric de Kuyper, however, warns us against such historical short cuts: "L'Autre Histoire du cinéma, ou la perte du spectacle: qui gagne, qui perd?," in *At the Very Beginning, at the Very End*, ed. Francesco Casetti and Jane Gaines (Udine: Forum, 2010), 143–151. See also Martine Beugnet, *Le Cinéma et ses doubles: L'image de film à l'ère du foundfootage numérique et des écrans de poche* (Bordeaux: Le Bord de l'Eau, 2021).

3. See part IV of Pepita Hesselberth and Maria Poulaki, eds., *Compact Cinematics: The Moving Image in the Age of Bit-Sized Media* (New York: Bloomsbury, 2017); and Martine Beugnet, "Touch and See? Regarding Images in the Era of the Interface," *InMedia* 8, no. 1 (2020), http://journals.openedition.org/inmedia/2102. Accessed November 2, 2021.

4. Julian Hanich, *The Audience Effect: On the Collective Cinema Experience* (Edinburgh: Edinburgh University Press, 2018). See also Daniel Biltereyst and Philippe Meers, "Film, Cinema, and Reception Studies: Revisiting Research on Audience's Filmic and Cinematic Experiences," in *Reception Studies and Audiovisual Translation*, ed. Elena Di Giovanni and Yves Gambier (Amsterdam: John Benjamins Publishing Company, 2018).

5. Raymond Bellour, *La querelle des dispositifs: Cinéma, installations, expositions* (Paris: POL, 2012). In contrast with Bellour, art historians are claiming film as part of an expanded concept of the history of the arts. Luc Vancheri, *Cinémas contemporains: Du film à l'installation* (Lyon: Alias, 2009), as well as the polemical manifesto by Philippe Dubois, *Oui, c'est du cinéma: Formes et espaces de l'image en mouvement* (Pasian di Prato: Companatto Editore, 2009). On the erasure of the collective audience and recouping of popular culture by "high" art, see Beugnet, *Le Cinéma et ses doubles*. On "relocation," see Francesco Casetti, "The Relocation of Cinema," *NECSUS* (November 2012), https://necsus-ejms.org/the-relocation-of-cinema. Accessed November 2, 2021.

6. See for instance, Kata Szita, "New Perspectives on an Imperfect Cinema: Smartphones, Spectatorship, and Screen Culture 2.0," *NECSUS* (July 2020), https://necsus-ejms.org/new-perspectives-on-an-imperfect-cinema-smartphones-spectatorship-and-screen-culture-2-0/. Accessed November 2, 2021.

7. Walter Benjamin, "The Work of Art in the Age of Its Technological Reproducibility," *Grey Room* 39 (Spring 2010): 11–37, at 34.

8. Sergei Eisenstein emphasized films' unique ability to portray the masses: "Here is real unity: Of mass and individual, in which the mass is genuine, and not a handful of participants in a 'crowd scene,' hurrying around back-stage in order to reappear from the opposite wings to give a 'bigger' impression." Sergei Eisenstein, *Film Form: Essays in Film Theory*, trans. Jay Leda (New York: A Harvest Book, 1949), 182.

9. Benjamin, "Work of Art"; and Michael Tratner, *Crowd Scenes: Movies and Mass Politics* (New York: Fordham University Press, 2008).

10. Judith Butler, "Bodies in Alliance and the Politics of the Street," in *Notes toward a Performative Theory of Assembly* (Cambridge, MA: Harvard University Press, 2015), 66–98.

11. Butler, "Bodies in Alliance," 83, 87, 98.

12. Byung-Chul Han, *In the Swarm: Digital Prospects*, trans. Erik Butler (Cambridge, MA: MIT Press, 2015).

13. On the institutional monitoring of popular film audiences, see Jon Burrows, "Penny Pleasures: Film Exhibition in London during the Nickelodeon Era, 1906–1914," *Film History* 16, no. 1 (2004): 60–91, and "Penny Pleasures II: Indecency, Anarchy, and Junk Film in London's 'Nickelodeons,' 1906–1914," *Film History* 16, no. 2 (2004): 172–197.

14. Haidee Wasson, "The Networked Screen: Moving Images, Materiality, and the Aesthetics of Size," in *Fluid Screens, Expanded Cinema*, ed. Janine Marchessault and Susan Lord (Toronto: University of Toronto Press, 2008), 74–95.

15. John Jervis, "Cinematic Sensation: The Sublime and the Spectacle," in *Sensational Subjects: The Dramatization of Experience in the Modern World* (London: Bloomsbury Academic, 2015), 123–140, at 127.

16. Erika Balsom, for instance, welcomes the potential disappearance of mainstream productions from theaters: "The crowd hurries to the narcotizing spectacle as a distraction from its misery. This is certainly a major way cinema has functioned throughout its history, but it is one that might be on the wane today. . . . Entertaining films will continue to be made, of course, mostly as

'content' to be consumed in private on digital platforms. Where does this leave the crowd of the movie theatre? One possibility: still there, just a little smaller, concentrated in fewer places, and watching different films, better films." Erika Balsom, "The Crowd is Dead, Long Live the Crowd!," *Cinema Scope* 85 (2021), https://cinema-scope.com/features/the-crowd-is-dead-long-live-the-crowd/. Accessed June 29, 2022. Such a vision, however, consigns whole classes of spectators to streaming and smaller screen watching, and risks turning the cinema into yet another elitist practice. Taking into account the complex entanglement of high and low in economic, artistic, and sociocultural terms, we may recall that throughout its history cinema has offered itself as an accessible experience of the theater as collective spectacle, with velvet seats and red curtain, to those who are initially barred from high-art culture for sociocultural as well as economic reasons.

17. Wasson, "Networked Screen"; Pascal Bonitzer, *Le Champ aveugle* (Paris: Éditions du cinéma/Gallimard, 1982), 25; and Sergei Eisenstein, *Au-delà des étoiles,* trans. Jacques Aumont, Bernard Eisenschitz, and Sylviane Mossé (Paris: Union générale d'éditions, 1974), 112.

18. Eisenstein, *Au-delà des étoiles;* and Martine Beugnet, "The Gulliver Effect: Screen Size, Scale, and Frame, from Cinema to Mobile Phones," *New Review of Film and Television Studies* 20, no. 3 (2022): 303–328.

19. Martine Beugnet, "Miniature Pleasures: On Watching Films on an iPhone," in *Cinematicity,* ed. Jeffrey Geiger and Karin Littau (Edinburgh: Edinburgh University Press, 2014), 196–210.

20. "[M]ore than ever it's necessary to become dispositive conscious—even *dispositive conscientious.* . . . We have to investigate—and teach—what particular media and their dispositives make possible for us and what they prevent us from." Julian Hanich, "An Invention with a Future: Collective Viewing, Joint Deep Attention, and the Ongoing Value of the Cinema," in *The Oxford Handbook of Film Theory,* ed. Kyle Stevens (Oxford: Oxford University Press, 2022), original emphasis. Adrian Martin, *Mise en Scène and Film Style: From Classical Hollywood to New Media Art* (Houndsmills: Palgrave Macmillan, 2014), 189.

21. Laura U. Marks, *The Skin of the Film: Intercultural Cinema, Embodiment, and the Senses* (Durham, NC: Duke University Press, 2000), 169.

22. Hito Steyerl, "In Defense of the Poor Image," *e-flux journal* 10 (2009), http://www.e-flux.com/journal/10/61362/in-defense-of-the-poor-image/. Accessed November 2, 2021.

23. Martine Beugnet, *L'Attrait du flou* (Crisnée: Yellow Now, 2017).

24. Jervis, "Cinematic Sensation."

25. Martine Beugnet, *Cinema and Sensation: French Film and the Art of Transgression* (Edinburgh: Edinburgh University Press, 2012); and Beugnet, "Gulliver Effect."

26. Drew Leder, *The Absent Body* (Chicago: University of Chicago Press, 1990), 70–71.

27. Gilles Deleuze, *Cinema 1: The Movement-Image,* trans. Hugh Tomlinson and Barbara Habberjam (Minneapolis: University of Minnesota Press, 2013 [1983]), 15.

28. Deleuze, *Cinema 1,* 17.

29. As Vivian Sobchack puts it, "The frame . . . is a limit, but like that of our own vision it is inexhaustibly mobile and free to displace itself. Although the frame is visible to *us*, it functions as the 'secret' boundary of the film's act of vision." Vivian Sobchack, *The Address of the Eye: A Phenomenology of Film Experience* (Princeton: Princeton University Press, 1992), 131.

30. Pascal Bonitzer talks of the "ghosts of the gaze and the voice that haunt the hallucinatory confines of the image." Bonitzer, *Le champ aveugle*, 107. See also Louis Seguin, *L'espace du cinéma: Hors-champ, hors d'œuvre, hors-jeu* (Toulouse: Ombres, 1999); and Beugnet, "Gulliver Effect."

31. Christian Metz, "The Fiction Film and Its Spectator: A Metapsychological Study," trans. Alfred Guzzetti, *New Literary History* 8, no. 1 (Fall 1976): 75–105.

32. Possessiveness expands the concept as defined by Laura Mulvey in relation to the use of the remote control. Laura Mulvey, *Death 24x a Second: Stillness and the Moving Image* (London: Reaktion Books, 2006).

33. André Bazin, *What is Cinema?*, trans. Hugh Gray (Berkeley: University of California Press, 2004), 166. Bonitzer, *Le champ aveugle*, 115. The metaphor of the window inherited from Alberti has continued to flourish in our contemporary technological imaginary; see Anne Friedberg, *The Virtual Window: From Alberti to Microsoft* (Cambridge, MA: MIT Press, 2009).

34. Beugnet, "Gulliver Effect."

35. Beugnet, *Le cinéma et ses doubles*.

... Quality Time

On Resisting What's Next, or Staying with the Credits

TIAGO DE LUCA

You may have experienced this before: you are watching a film on a streaming platform, the credits start rolling and, before you realize it, or have had time to grab the remote control, the service has taken you to something else, most probably a trailer of a film or series the algorithms think you might like based on your recent viewing history. If you were watching a series, the same would happen, the difference being that it would take you to the next episode, interrupting the credits of the previous one. Unless, that is, you were fast enough to find your remote control and press the right button. And I mean *really* fast. Though the time given by streaming platforms for you to make up your mind as to whether you want to watch credits will vary, it is usually literally a matter of seconds, visualized as an ominous countdown icon at the bottom of the screen.

Although end credits might be deemed by many an expendable part of the film experience, there is something perturbing when the time you are given to decide if you want to leave the credits rolling is so little as to be almost nil. In other words, you are given a choice in theory, but the streaming platform forcefully reminds you that it really wants you to watch a new film, immediately after the one you have just watched, and so on ad infinitum. The equivalent of "recommended buying options" on Amazon, the assumption underpinning this phenomenon is that ideally you should continue *consuming* films until there is no tomorrow.

FIGURE 28. Screenshot from the Netflix credit sequence of *Children of Men* (2006, Alfonso Cuarón), announcing *Wild Things* (1998, John McNaughton).

It is this assumption that I would like to explore in this essay, with all the implications that it poses for an understanding of film as something that is only as good as the next film in line—a situation that in this particular scenario lasts only a few seconds. By treating this default mechanism of streaming platforms as the symptom of a larger phenomenon in which time and experience are antithetical to frenetic and insatiable consumption, my aim is to demonstrate that, in this context, to watch film credits constitutes an ethical decision that directly contravenes the temporal mandates of late capitalism. At the same time, I want to use this opportunity to reflect on closing film credits as something that is often sidelined as unworthy of attention—whether in film auditoriums, one's own living room, or film scholarship. By casting a long, hard glance at film credits, we may become equipped to uncover not only larger systemic structures that often dictate the way in which time is regulated in our day-to-day lives, but also some aspects of the film experience that often go unnoticed, or at least unremarked upon.

SIGNING CREDITS

On the most superficial level, we may champion the right of closing film credits to exist, and more specifically their right to exist for the time that it takes to unroll them, on the basis of the fact that they make visible the vast number of personnel needed to make a given film possible: from the artistic and creative side of the spectrum through to the logistical and practical one. Cast, production assistants, production managers, catering teams, recording mixers, colorists, gaffers, set dressers, art directors, and so on and so forth: every person who has contributed in some way to the making of a film is usually listed, or should be listed, in its closing. That it takes a while for credits to unfold is a testament to the fact that scores of people were involved in its making and that it was the result of their work. In some cases, this can become a political statement. Recent Brazilian films prove that. Since President Jair Bolsonaro took office in 2019, his government has systematically dismantled the cultural and art industries in Brazil. The intent was, of course, ideological, but the argument used is that such industries are not properly relevant from an economic perspective. In response, the closing credits of *Bacurau* (2019, dir. Kleber Mendonça Filho and Juliano Dornelles) state that "this film directly and indirectly generated 800 jobs," a move that has been followed by a number of other Brazilian films. The fundamentally collective character of film production as listed in the credits becomes in this context the evidence that cinema is also economically important, as it secures and sustains the livelihood of numerous people on a very practical level.

Closing credits, by dint of its enumerative features, act as a welcome counterpoint to the myth of the auteur, the idea that the director is the genius behind the film and that a film's success (or downfall) should be solely attributed to his mind (I use the male pronoun advisedly given the gendered connotations implicit in the concept as originally conceived by the *Cahiers du Cinéma* critics). No doubt, the fact that the director's name usually appears at the film's opening, sometimes in the guise of "a so-and-so film," is proof of the enduring allure of auteurism. Personal creativity and artistry are factors that must, of course, be considered in the evaluation of any given film. But, if anything, closing credits tell us that it takes more than personal genius to make a film. If the director writes with the camera in the same way that a novelist writes with a pen, to recall Alexandre Astruc's famous aphorism, closing credits ask us to see this process as a collective form of writing.[1] It is no coincidence, in this context, that one of the hyper-auteurs of our time, the Taiwan-based Tsai Ming-liang, has since his third feature-length film decided to end his films with his signature in handwritten form. Not content with his inimitable signature visual style, Tsai felt that such a signature must be itself literalized, "at once assuming responsibility and claiming ownership" of his films, as Song Hwee Lim puts it.[2] That this signature appears at the beginning of closing credits is therefore significant in its symptomatic acknowledgment that the credits about to unfold may contradict the claim of individual ownership that the signature is supposed to legitimize.

The scarce attention devoted to closing film credits may be justifiable or perhaps expected: they are often devoid of narrative content. In some measure, this sits in contrast with openings, which have received comparatively more attention. As a transitional and relatively autonomous form, with its own internal rules of coherence, the opening-title sequence would seem to favor experimentation and abstraction in a manner that is often unthinkable in the film proper. Openings are often malleable in terms of how they intersect the dull task of listing people with the more noble task of conveying information about the story world that is about to open up before our eyes. For Georg Stanitzek, the opening title sequence is "an eminent space of cinematic intertextuality" on which sounds, songs, live-action and animated elements, lettering, and design all playfully converge in order to "deal with the systematic hiatus between titling and diegesis in the form of a lead-in into the film."[3] Deborah Allison strikes a similar chord by noting that the opening prepares "the audience for the viewing experience" and that its analysis remains "a shamefully underused resource in film studies."[4] Closing credits would appear in this instance as an overlooked feature of films within the already overlooked field of title sequences.

SIGNIFYING CREDITS

But is it true that closing credits give us nothing new in terms of narrative information and aesthetic experience? A generalization: closing credits simply scroll up the names of all people involved in the production of a film; unlike openings, this is an exhaustive list that includes everyone who worked for that film. Most often, these credits roll against a black background, the size of the words is tiny, and a song can be heard on the audio track, not infrequently the film's musical theme. The simple act of replaying that song may have an impact upon how we will process the film. If a different song is heard, and perhaps one that has not been played previously and whose tonality contrasts with the overall mood of the film, this too may add to and perhaps even modify our judgment of that film. Conversely, where a director chooses not to play any song during the closing credits, this can likewise amplify the experience. Given that silence is often rare during closing credits, its presence becomes conspicuously, sometimes ominously, felt. It is no coincidence that most films directed by Michael Haneke conclude with silent credits. The silences closing his films enhance the harrowing experience that Haneke meticulously planned for us. Silence here is therefore not simply silence but a potent aesthetic decision that intensifies the film's sensory fruition, and one that needs the closing credits in order to assert its invisible presence.

Yet, not all closing credits end against a black background. In addition to various manners of diegetic elaboration, some films choose to introduce extradiegetic images that illuminate the film's world by providing a counterpoint against which that world is to be judged and understood. A case in point is Lars von Trier's *Dogville* (2003), which ends with a series of photographs, some of them iconic, of poverty-stricken US citizens by Dorothea Lange and others to the sound of David Bowie's "Young Americans." These documentary and historical pictures contrast with the film's stripped-bare theatrical setting, while the inclusion of Bowie's song infuses the end with more than a dose of irony. Other films may choose to replay or introduce new scenes during the closing sequence. As David Bordwell, Kristin Thompson, and Jeff Smith observe: "Sometimes key scenes will be replayed under the final credits, or new plot action will be shown," which reminds us that "an enterprising filmmaker may exploit every moment of the film's running time to engage our narrative expectations."[5] Comedy and action films, from the Jackie Chan movie franchise through to *10 Things I Hate About You* (1999, dir. Gil Junger), use end sequences as a way of playing "bloopers" or "outtakes" that reveal funny mistakes made in the shooting of selected scenes, thereby adding a humorous, self-referential layer to the viewing experience. The inclusion of scenes during or after the end credits is also a common and significant feature of Marvel films, in that such scenes often foreshadow future releases in the franchise and thus engage our narrative expectations *across* a vast body of films.[6]

Other films may confound the viewer as to whether the film has really ended. Haneke provides us with another good example. His *Caché* (2005) ends with a static frontal shot of a school where the protagonist's son studies, and its meaning is as ambiguous as it is in line with the film's questioning of the veracity and source of images. Is this image a reproduction, much like the film's opening image, whose sudden rewinding tells us that it is not the film's image but a film-within-the-film's image? This blurring of lines is never resolved, and that is the whole point. Yet as a film intent on interrogating the power of images, its closing credit sequence is part of the game, refusing to cut itself off from the film's world. Alfonso Cuarón's *Roma* (2018) similarly ends with a low-angle shot pointing toward the sky. In the film's last image, we see the main protagonist, the maid Cleo (Yalitza Aparicio), ascending the stairs with a bunch of clothes and, as she walks onto the terrace and leaves the frame, the credits begin. The image and sound never fade, meaning that while the film has technically ended, its diegetic world hasn't, with airplanes and the whistling sounds of camote street vendors—visual and aural tropes throughout the film—finding a new, lingering resonance before the film finally fades to black, which is not until the credits have completely ended.

Roma was distributed by Netflix. Incidentally, its credits are shown in their entirety on the streaming service without any interruption or suggestions regarding what to watch next. This confirms that, for Netflix, a film is still a film if there is an image onscreen: content. Was Cuarón's decision to style the credits this way perhaps a strategy to stop Netflix from tampering with his film, in the same way that its panoramic scale, meticulous mise-en-scène, and gliding tracking shots continually remind the viewer that this is a film best watched in the film theater? One will probably never know the answers to these questions, yet the relationship of Netflix with the idea and concept of "content," and how this dictates the mutilation of anything that is considered superfluous and extraneous to that content, is one worth examining.

SKIPPING CREDITS

At this point it might be helpful to bring in Netflix's favored content, that is to say, series rather than films. Here, we may note that the same principle not only applies, but it is in some ways doubled insofar as the trimming of credit sequences extends, as a possibility, to both openings and closings. Stanitzek muses: "It is interesting to imagine what it would be like if, as a matter of convention, movies always did without any kind of titles, either opening or closing. Or even if it were an option: that versions on digital media, like on DVD, had title sequences as a 'feature' to be turned on or off."[7] As far as series are concerned, this is already a reality on Netflix, and judging from the contempt with which closing film sequences are treated, it is not far-fetched to imagine that film openings could soon be in jeopardy, too. Whereas end credits in series are, like their filmic counterparts, given only a few seconds to assert their will to live until the service abruptly interrupts them on our behalf, a similar function appears in the series' opening sequences through a "skip intro" button—although, it must be noted, without the imposition we encounter in the end sequences, where the option is not to *skip* the credits but, rather, to opt in to watch them. In turn, these opening and closing excisions subscribe to a larger phenomenon Netflix has greatly helped popularize over the last decade: the binge-watching experience. Rather than releasing episodes one by one, Netflix lands them all together in a bid to stimulate that such episodes be viewed continuously rather than episodically. In this sense, the elision of credits, be it at the opening or closing of an individual episode, makes sense: the series is to be experienced as one continuous watch, in a single sitting.

Could it be the case, then, that Netflix and other streaming services want us to experience series as (long) films? Discussions on the "cinematic quality" of current "prestige" TV series might lead us to believe so, as might one of the creators of *Game of Thrones* (2011–2019, HBO), who put forward the controversial claim that the series is, in fact, "a 73-hour movie."[8] Whatever the case, the fact is that even if you binge-watch a ten-episode season in one go, the algorithms regulating streaming services take no rest and they want you to take no rest either: at the end of the season, you can be sure that something else will be suggested for you to watch. Which leads us to conclude that it is not so much the case that the skipability of openings and closings is meant to ensure the experience is one of continuity. Rather, the purpose here is to ensure that one never turns off their viewing device: the ideal viewer anticipated by the algorithms is one who never stops watching content; one who presumably never sleeps or does anything other than be the recipient of moving images.

Why do streaming platforms want to cultivate such a spectator? Isn't it the case that, unlike broadcasting, these services—and Netflix, in particular—are not dependent upon the revenues generated by advertisement or public funds? As Amanda Lotz tells us: Netflix is strictly a "subscriber-funded video service" and its "primary goal is to expand the number of people who subscribe to its service and maintain those that already do so."[9] This means that the service "does not aim to make series that are likely to attract all, or even a significant portion of its subscribers"; rather, "Netflix makes a variety of series distinctly targeting specific taste cultures," and the same applies to the films it produces and acquires.[10] In this sense, it is imperative for the service to make sure that subscribers do not stop subscribing; hence, the need to entice them with new things to watch *all the time.*

This is different from traditional broadcasting in the sense that Netflix is unencumbered by the demand to attract the largest possible audience to watch a specific program at a particular time, but it is not that different when we consider the distinct attention economy with which television has been historically associated. As Zoë Shacklock argues, as much as Netflix tries to distance itself from broadcasting in its self-mythologizing promotional tactics, it is still highly embedded in "foundational features of television," including a reliance upon "continuous viewing," which "has been part of the television landscape for decades."[11] One needs only remember (as does Shacklock) Raymond Williams's influential concept of "televisual flow," according to which the television experience must be understood in terms of a concatenation of programs, trailers, and advertisements rather than discrete units with a clear start and end time. For Williams, this mode of organization was dictated both by "the financing of television by commercial advertising" and the concomitant necessity to include trailers of programs so as to capture and retain the viewer's attention for an indefinite amount of time.[12] One of the consequences of this process, as far as the broadcasting of films is concerned, is the mutilation of films into several sections, which "were not made to be 'interrupted' in this way."[13]

As Williams's remarks demonstrate, however, the capturing of attention instigated by traditional television and streaming services differs significantly when it comes to experiencing films on the TV screen. For, unlike the interruption of films that has been part of the television experience due to commercial imperatives, the "flow" of streaming services is instead predicated upon the absence of any interruption between shows, to the point that even credit sequences are considered a hindrance to the continuity of the viewing experience. The flow envisioned here is therefore one in which different audiovisual content is stitched together in succession but without the "bizarre disparities" Williams locates in a normal broadcasting evening as a result of the confluence of radically disparate materials.[14] Yet, even when considering the traditional television experience, closing credits have not been absorbed as part of the televisual flow either, with many networks opting to simply cut or speed up end sequences so as to quickly make room for something more appealing.[15] Whether in its broadcast or streaming variations, then, credits are time wasted.

SAVORING CREDITS

To be clear: I am not opposed to films being watched on television. I am also not suggesting that cinema, the most industrial of all art forms, has no commercial or financial imperatives of its own. One may even argue that the fact that the lights come on as soon as credits start rolling in a film theater, as an invitation for people to start leaving, is in itself proof that credits are not valorized in that setting either—even if here the credits will roll until their very end regardless of how many people stay in the auditorium. But since we do watch more and more films at home, on streaming platforms, we would do well to interrogate the wider premises informing algorithmic strategies to capture and maintain our attention nonstop, and what this might mean to the experience of cinema and the good of film viewing. This seems especially paramount because these strategies are often cloaked in a hyperbolic promotional rhetoric of increased autonomy and interactivity, which on closer inspection proves fallacious.

In his riveting *24/7: Late Capitalism and the Ends of Sleep* (2013), Jonathan Crary notes: "Billions of dollars are spent every year researching how to reduce decision-making time, how to eliminate the useless time of reflection and contemplation. This is the form of contemporary progress—the relentless capture and control of time and experience."[16] For Crary, capitalism is defined by "the continual simulation of the new," and television, as "only the first of a category of apparatuses with which we are currently surrounded that are most often used out of powerful habitual patterning involving a diffuse attentiveness and a semi-automatism," is the symptom of "larger strategies of power in which the aim is not mass-deception, but rather states of neutralization and inactivation, in which one is dispossessed of time."[17] He concludes: "One of the forms of disempowerment within 24/7 environments is the incapacitation of daydream or of any mode of absent-minded introspection that would otherwise occur in intervals of slow or vacant time."[18] As we now find ourselves being able to watch anything anywhere—on the train, in the park, at a bus stop—capitalism infiltrates every aspect of our lives: no matter where we are, at what time of the day or night, we will always be able to consume.

Crary does not speak of closing credits. Yet, his reflections on a world that relentlessly provides viewers—consumers—with choices, to the point that for him sleep becomes the last refuge where capitalism is unable to interfere in our capacity to simply experience time as it unfolds unfettered, finds, I believe, a useful correlation with how films are valued and valorized in current streaming services.[19] As he notes: "Visual and auditory 'content' is most often ephemeral, interchangeable material that, in addition to its commodity status, circulates to habituate and validate one's immersion in the exigencies of twenty-first-century capitalism."[20] The aim of streaming services is to make sure the spectator's attention is continually sustained via the accumulation of content, ideally 24/7; hence, the expurgation of unproductive time, the time of credits. For the time of credits is, precisely, a time when we find ourselves in daydream mode, a transitional time of Crary's "absent-minded introspection" where we are given the opportunity to assimilate what we have just seen and adjust ourselves to the physical reality that awaits us either in the heightened materiality of our living room or the outside world beyond the film theater (all the more so if we emerge into daylight). It can be a time of unproductive—yet valuable—reverie, drifting, repose.[21]

In this context, the forceful, indeed violent, curtailing of the possibility of watching film credits in streaming platforms is yet one more instance of "the relentless capture and control of time and experience" to which we are subjected today. Or, to put it differently, such curtailing is proof that cinema is, according to the logic underpinning such platforms, no longer an "experience." Experience takes time; experience, as a qualitative and transformative state, is inseparable from an awareness of time passing; experience needs time to be processed, remembered, rationalized. And cinema, as a medium of time, doubles down on the stakes of temporal experience. Content, on the other hand, is fleeting, additive, quantitative: it can be replaced, accrued, rejigged, potentially indefinitely. In their formulation of credits as a temporal residue that must be eliminated, streaming services are telling us that they don't care about the qualitative and experiential dimension of film viewing. They care about quantity. Letting the credits roll thus constitutes an ethical act of resistance, even defiance: cinema, after all, deserves more of our time.

NOTES

1. Alexandre Astruc, "The Birth of a New Avant-Garde: La Caméra-Stylo," originally printed in *L'Écran Française,* March 30, 1948, http://www.newwavefilm.com/about/camera-stylo-astruc.shtml. Accessed July 22, 2021.

2. Song Hwee Lim, *Tsai Ming-liang and a Cinema of Slowness* (Honolulu: University of Hawaii Press, 2014), 46.

3. Georg Stanitzek, "Reading the Title Sequence (Vorspann, Générique)," *Cinema Journal* 48, no. 4 (2009): 44–58, at 45, 57. It must be noted Stanitzek deploys the expression "title sequence" to refer both to opening and closing film credits; however, his article focuses almost entirely on the former.

4. Deborah Allison, "Title Sequences in the Western Genre: The Iconography of Action," *Quarterly Review of Film and Video* 25, no. 2 (2008): 107–115, at 107.

5. David Bordwell, Kristin Thompson, and Jeff Smith, *Film Art: An Introduction,* 12th ed. (New York: McGraw-Hill Education, 2020), 96.

6. My thanks to my colleague James Taylor for alerting me to this.

7. Stanitzek, "Reading the Title Sequence," 48.

8. Mareike Jenner, "Binge-Watching: Video-On-Demand, Quality TV, and Mainstreaming Fandom," *International Journal of Cultural Studies* 20, no. 3 (2017): 304–320; and Julia Alexander, "*Game of Thrones* Showrunners Ignite Debate Over Whether It's a TV Show or a Movie," *Polygon* (2007), https://www.polygon.com/tv/2017/3/13/14911318/gameof-thrones-tv-movie. Accessed June 1, 2021.

9. Amanda Lotz, "What's Going On? Netflix and the Commissioning of *Sense8*," in *Sense8: Transcending Television*, ed. Deborah Shaw and Rob Stone (New York: Bloomsbury Academic, 2021), 31–40, at 32.

10. Lotz, "What's Going On?," 36.

11. Zoë Shacklock, "You Are No Longer Just You: Netflix, *Sense8*, and the Evolution of Television," in *Sense8: Transcending Television*, ed. Deborah Shaw and Rob Stone (New York: Bloomsbury Academic, 2021), 41–56, here at 42, 45.

12. Raymond Williams, *Television: Technology and Cultural Form*, ed. Ederyn Williams (London: Routledge, 2005 [1974]), 86.

13. Williams, *Television*, 84.

14. Williams, *Television*, 84.

15. Stanitzek, "Reading the Title Sequence," 48–49.

16. Jonathan Crary, *24/7: Late Capitalism and the Ends of Sleep* (London: Verso, 2013), 40.

17. Crary, 24/7, 40, 88.

18. Crary, 24/7, 88.

19. Disturbingly, the recent news story that the beer company Coors was testing "target dream incubation" to advertise its products confirms that not even our dreams might be safe from capitalism's insatiable drive. "Corporations Want to Put Advertisements in Your Dreams," *The Byte*, https://futurism.com/the-byte/corporations-advertisements-in-dreams. Accessed October 25, 2021. My thanks to Martin Rossouw for pointing this out to me.

20. Crary, 24/7, 52.

21. On "cinematic daydreaming," see Julian Hanich, "When Viewers Drift Off: A Brief Phenomenology of Cinematic Daydreaming," in *The Structures of the Film Experience by Jean-Pierre Meunier: Historical Assessments and Phenomenological Expansions*, ed. Hanich and Daniel Fairfax (Amsterdam: Amsterdam University Press, 2019), 336–352.

PART SEVEN

Unsettled Goods

28

. . . Wanton Destruction

On Cinema's Antisocial Thrills

ADRIAN MARTIN

What are the most memorable elements in any youth or JD [juvenile delinquent] film? Their capacity for outlining the social dilemma of youth? No! It's all the sex, swearing, violence, and action—those bits where youth is at its most reckless and disconnected from social and family ties.
—Philip Brophy

Art, like sarcasm, is one of the forms of recognition of the meaninglessness of reality, because what we usually call "art" is anything which is not assigned with a certain meaning. It remains a free sphere. . . . Art corresponds to the human tendency to self-destruction. . . . Art denotes chaos, and opposes itself to established meanings and orders. And our desire for death, or self-destruction, is associated with our fondness for chaos and the transgression of established meanings and orders.
—Julie Reshe

In 2004, I happened to watch (as part of my professional job, at the time, as weekly film reviewer for a newspaper) the strange American black comedy, *Duplex* (2003). It is directed by Danny DeVito and features Ben Stiller and Drew Barrymore, but all that star power hardly amounts to much in this modern variation on a very old formula: the anxieties, for a young married couple, of getting and holding onto a

FIGURE 29. A scene of wanton destruction in *The Patsy* (1964, Jerry Lewis).

prime piece of real estate. House moving: a common, everyday catastrophe. DeVito plays it for all the predictable laughs. It's the type of dark comedy in which nobody wins and everyone is foiled in the end; the lesson would appear to be, as Nick Cave once sang, "People just ain't no good."

Nonetheless, I felt an odd, escalating elation as I took in *Duplex*. The film—with its veritable catalog of venal, cruel, and exploitative actions that the couple inflicts on the elderly tenant of the cheap duplex they crave, most of which painfully backfire on them—builds to its only possible, logical conclusion: the complete, physical destruction of the home. When that shell ultimately falls to pieces, I was ecstatic. The thought, the incipient theory, crystallized in my mind in that instant: *movies are made for this.*

Let it burn, let it crash. Down with it all! An outlet, an unleashing of all the so-called bad vibes of daily life, all the pent-up resentments and frustrations, all the petty hatreds and disdains. I include in this spectacle not only every kind of destruction, but also the many forms of "bad behavior" (such as that of juvenile delinquents) associated with this sort of anarchy. Cinema has given us many genres and subgenres that revel in the orgy of such a demise: from burlesque comedies (Jerry Lewis's *The Patsy* [1964], Steven Spielberg's atypical *1941* [1979]) to smash-'em-up car or truck movies (*The Gauntlet* [1977, dir. Clint Eastwood]), from entropic, satiric visions of hellish office life (*Waydowntown* [2000, dir. Gary Burns]) to icy art films (by Marguerite Duras or Béla Tarr) that slowly drain all signs of vitality away. And, above all, in grand cartoons of the Roadrunner versus Wile E. Coyote variety, so beloved of my childhood parked in front of a TV set.

This feeling is more than an abstract, universal, existentialist nihilism; it is a cry of rage aimed at the constriction in which you find yourself trapped, in any place or time. Faith in the world, belief in the system (whichever social system it may be), trust in a deity (of whatever religion) = zero. No more ethics or morality. Just wanton destruction and devastation, as gratuitous and excessive in its spectacle as it can possibly be: that is the antisocial thrill of cinema.

IMAGINING DISASTER

In her celebrated 1965 essay "The Imagination of Disaster," Susan Sontag trawls through several different ways of explaining the popularity of disaster movies—which, at that time, essentially meant science fiction tales of either alien invasion and/or planetary annihilation, with the occasional option of gigantic creatures like Godzilla and Mothra duking it out in the midst of a consequently ruined major metropolitan city like Tokyo or New York.[1]

Sontag's essay is admirable for the breadth of viewing it demonstrates, at least two decades before a pedagogy of cultural studies was institutionalized in universities: everything from high-art cinema to the lowliest B or Z movie is regarded on a more-or-less equal footing of value. The piece is equally prescient in relation to the types of intellectual methodologies it deftly juggles within the context of highbrow magazine journalism: sociology, myth criticism, film aesthetics.

Sontag's interpretive line on the entire phenomenon of disaster cinema tends, however, to waver as she unfolds it. As might be expected in the wake of her even more celebrated "Notes on Camp" essay in *Partisan Review* the previous year, Sontag finds plenty to be amused at in these movies—especially the cheapest-made ones. What she dubs the "charm" of the films sometimes shrinks to the "monumental but often touching banality" of dialogue that is "wonderfully, unintentionally funny." But, for the most part, Sontag sticks doggedly to ferreting out what she perceives as "painful and in deadly earnest" in disaster movies.

What I wish to refocus from "The Imagination of Disaster" is an attitude that Sontag only glancingly acknowledges and also seems to briefly share: that it is not only superior camp fun but intensely *pleasurable* to watch what she describes as "great acts of destruction" on screen. (Incidentally, she detected the exact same kind of joy in the avant-garde performance art of 1960s Happenings.) It is precisely in this pleasure, I believe, that we can begin to understand what film is good for: paradoxically, its antisocial drive to negate and tear everything down. All the arts can partake in this drive, but cinema is especially well-suited for the task, exactly for the reason that Sontag gave to explain the superiority of science fiction in filmic form over its literary equivalent: the medium's capacity for surface "sensual elaboration" of cataclysmic events (especially in comparison to the more detached rationality of science fiction in literary form) in both image and sound, given to every artificial exaggeration for the sake of eliciting an emotion.

Sontag takes this line of thought further still. In her view, cinema allows us to "participate in the fantasy of living through one's own death and more, the death of cities, the destruction of humanity itself." An intriguing fantasy, indeed! Linking the 1960s' cycle of science fiction movies back to the original *King Kong* (1933, dir. Merian C. Cooper and Ernest B. Schoedsack) and the "big sword, sandal, and orgy color spectaculars set in Biblical and Roman times," she exclaims, "There is nothing like the thrill of watching all those expensive sets come tumbling down"—as if she were describing my experience of watching *Duplex* almost four decades later. Along this line, she evokes "the aesthetics of destruction, with the peculiar beauties to be found in wreaking havoc, making a mess." She even evokes "primitive gratifications"! As her language implies, there is a sovereign, childlike, timeless, and universal glee that we can all visit (or revisit) in witnessing—and enjoying—such destruction.

As we would say today, Sontag's take on screen disaster ultimately proves to be *symptomatic,* the sign of a larger issue—for a critic who hoped to get "beyond interpretation," she eventually plumbs for an interpretative reading, after all. There is a grave social problem with science fiction, in Sontag's view. Disaster cinema signals a sociocultural safety valve: it both excites and neutralizes our collective anxieties over the (then) imminent possibility of global nuclear devastation. Fantasy turns out to be an ambivalent term in Sontag's critical lexicon. Screen fantasy is good—it's fun, it's aesthetic, it gives gratification, it "releases one from normal obligations"—and it's also bad—an ideological lure, an evasion, or mystification. She draws a line in film and cultural history. Where pre-1950s films "still have an essentially innocent relation to disaster," the 1960s crop exhibits "a decided grimness." How many cultural commentators, down the years, no matter their nominal topic, have diagnosed a similar end to collective innocence at some chosen point in history? Dipping into Heideggerian philosophy, Sontag further asserts that, ultimately, "Science fiction films invite a dispassionate, aesthetic view of destruction and violence—a *technological view.*" Note how the word "aesthetic" has already changed its connotative stripe here, from pleasure to pain.

HOW I HATED THEM

Let's stay with science fiction for a moment longer. One of the most striking passages of popular cinema from the past three decades arrives at the very end of Abel Ferrara's gruesome *Body Snatchers* (1993), the second of three remakes (so far) of the classic Cold War–era, science fiction movie *Invasion of the Body Snatchers* (1956, dir. Don Siegel), a film to which Sontag referred as offering a dark vision of "the wave of the future, man in his next stage of development." All versions (as well as the original 1954 source novel, *The Body Snatchers,* by Jack Finney) tell roughly the same story: members of a mysterious, alien species replace humans one at a time by inhabiting their bodies, after first incubating their simulacra in a pod—and there is no way to reverse the process. As Ferrara rightly stated in interviews publicizing his film, you can take that basic story template as the metaphor or allegory of whatever you choose: capitalism, communism, religious mania, consumerist fads . . .

In the closing scene of the 1993 version, teenage Marti (Gabrielle Anwar) rides high in a helicopter; she has just thrown, in the nick of time, her "snatched" little brother (Reilly Murphy) from the chopper into oblivion. Below Marti, on the ground, is an extraordinary, almighty conflagration: hundreds of body snatchers are burning and dying under the impact of military carpet-bombing. And what is our teen heroine's response to this disquieting apparition? We learn it from her intimate thought-track delivered in memorable voice-over narration: "They had destroyed everyone I loved. Our reaction was only human. Revenge, hate, remorse, despair, pity and, most of all, fear. I remember feeling all those things as I watched the bombs explode. *How I hated them.*" What a way to conclude a film!

This screen spectacle, so lovingly conjured by Ferrara, surely raises a question about the moral-ethical framework in which we might find ourselves enjoying it (as I, for one, most certainly do), as well as about the particular regime of aesthetic value and taste that could manage to embrace, rather than dismiss, it. After all, this is more than just a matter of Sontag's "expensive sets come tumbling down"; it involves depictions of (fictional) life and death, of (alien) oppression and (human) comeuppance.

Let's first canvas what I consider to be the opposition to my positively antisocial theory of film. I once heard the respected Australian screenwriter Ian David (the fact-based TV miniseries *Blue Murder* [1995] is among his prime achievements) outline a model for what he considered to be the most *satisfying* type of narrative.[2] Satisfying as aesthetic and emotional experience, and also as moral lesson. *Body Snatchers,* assuredly, would not pass his test. According to David (and many other authorities he cites from narratology, psychology, neuroscience, philosophy, and religion), a story needs to gradually progress from the base but "high-arousal" emotions (such as resentment, envy, agitation, lust, fear, and hatred)—those that Sontag calls the "cruel and amoral feelings"—to the morally higher feelings and states (forgiveness, pity, wisdom, love, redemption) that bring calmness and self-knowledge. Rather predictably, Shakespeare's plays provide persuasive examples of this model. Art (according to this view) should actively tutor our higher sensibilities, not simply (or nihilistically) rub our noses in the horribleness of all things.

Tales of revenge, for instance, should not simply end with the planned, bloody retribution carried out—although try telling that one to Quentin Tarantino. We need to reach a more *elevated* plane, according to David, otherwise narrative art (in whatever medium it arises) is stunted, adolescent, flattering only our lowest and least civilized senses of self. Art, ultimately, must transcend such pettiness if it wishes to reach a properly cathartic sense of wholeness and resolution. What David calls the optimum "emotional rhythm" must be correctly plotted and achieved. That classical ideal of audience *catharsis* operates on a higher plane than a merely mechanical *cathexis,* which, in the annals of psychoanalysis, signifies a release or discharge of energetic emotion.

As a film lover—and as someone rather fond of a bit of cheap emotional cathexis—I must confess that I am more than a little uneasy with this noble-sounding model. Sure, I appreciate profound tales of redemption, insight, peace, and utopia—the cinema boasts many classics of this kind, as do all the arts. My personal favorites in this class would include *Sansho the Bailiff/Sanshō Dayū* (1954, dir. Kenji Mizoguchi), *Gertrud* (1964, dir. Carl Dreyer), and *Fanny and Alexander/Fanny och Alexander* (1982, dir. Ingmar Bergman). But there is more to be said about—and valued in—the base emotions of art, whether that art be conventionally designated as high or low in the spheres of culture.

FINICKY, BITTER, AND HARD

For a very different account, I turn now to a special American film critic, Manny Farber—but not to one of his film reviews. Farber, who was also a renowned painter, wrote a review of the publication *The Complete Etchings of Goya* (which comes with a foreword by Aldous Huxley) in 1944.[3] What Farber found most praiseworthy in this art can strike the casual reader as unusual: "The consistent purity of Goya's hatred through his later works is an amazing fact in itself."[4]

Farber repeats this keynote of his review many times over. By the end of the *Caprichos* series, for instance, the artist's "loathing becomes more acutely directed."[5] Or his description of *Los Disparates,* also known as *Proverbios:* "Goya epitomizes all the pain, fear, and degeneracy of human beings in his greatest and last work."[6] For Farber, the "judgements" brought to bear by Goya upon "human badness" and social arrangements alike are "terrifying and magnificent." Not much higher-level transcendence here! The furthest Farber will allow himself to go is to credit Goya, at the end of his life, with a "passionate sorrow." But, even there, it is the turbulent passions that insist, not their pacific resolution. Extrapolating from this reading, we could say that Farber and Goya would happily sit alongside Marti for the final helicopter ride of *Body Snatchers*, helping her hurl that pesky pod-kid into free fall before his total immolation.

It was not only the clear allegorical content or philosophical worldview in Goya's drawings that Farber admired in 1944. The "emotional experience for the spectator" is also a matter of material technique. As if comparing the artist's work to the tough, American B-movies of the 1940s and 1950s (by Samuel Fuller, Nicholas Ray, Phil Karlson, and many others) that he loved, Farber exclaims: "These designs are like tightly clenched fists." Goya's evident "intensity," his "dogged insistence," his "impatient and abrupt" attack led him to create a new style, one that is "finicky and bitter and hard." We are close, here, to the beating heart of a certain cinephilia that has always willingly lost its rational head in the face of a stylized spectacle of *paroxysmic* violence.

MOVIES JUST AIN'T NO GOOD

My line of argument in this essay genuflects to a particular tradition in art, life, and thought: let's call it the *punk* tradition. I can recall many formative moments when the proud, publicly transgressive expression of punk sentiments—usually taking the form of a *détournement* of some venerable, sickly platitude—moved me to the core of my being. The aforementioned pop/rock star Nick Cave, for example, declaring that the role of an artist is not to grow old gracefully but disgracefully. Or a distinguished scholar of media studies, Stuart Cunningham, stating during a 1987 Australian seminar on documentary filmmaking that cinema should not be for our own good but for our own evil. Or, along that same line, Bill Routt's feverish championing of the significance of the most degraded and despised B movies, and of our lustful gaze upon them as spectators: "The tiny commitment of my look, shift of eyes from there to here, is enough to evoke the freedom by which, within which, Sin is done. It engages me in rehearsal of what once was possible, reminds me that even today some things begin despite the common pretense that they do not. And, gazing upon what has been outcast, what is not sound—unsweet, unstrong—I Sin with it."[7]

Cinema: good for nothing, for nothing other than nothing, good only for negation. Do I trade in outrageous exaggeration here? In arguments that are willfully exclusive, terroristic, myopic, contrarian? Of course, as I have no less than the philosopher Norman O. Brown to back me up on this, judging from his 1990 retrospective consideration of his own past extreme arguments and wild language: "'Nothing other than': it is the exaggeration which grabbed me. Years later I discovered the epigram of Theodor Adorno, 'In psychoanalysis the only true thing is the exaggerations.' That I now recognize as the cornerstone of a Dionysian epistemology."[8]

A Dionysian epistemology involves—among the many things it contains—an element of joyful destruction. And an aspect of this drama, in the specificity of historical time and place, is the ongoing contestation and reversal of established aesthetic values. In the context of cinema and cinephilia—the cultivated love of cinema, which includes turning it into a cultural battering ram or war machine—this contestatory maneuver regularly necessitates outsize, polemical gestures[9] Recall François Truffaut—a connoisseur of lyrical and violent paroxysm in film—who, as a young man back in 1955, flung at his readers the gauntlet that, if they cannot detect the art in either of two Westerns, *The Big Sky* (1952, dir. Howard Hawks) or *Johnny Guitar* (1954, dir. Nicholas Ray), then they should just "never go to the movies again, never see any more films"—an attitude he self-praised as "wonderful certainty."[10]

Another regularly contrarian film scholar, Paul Willemen, once struck an equally fine pose by announcing that "frenzy, madness, neurosis, extravaganza, monstrosity, etc." should be valued as "positive values" in works of art.[11] Willemen was opposing himself, in that passing provocation, to an entire tradition of predominantly humanist commentary in arts criticism. That tradition is back with us today, in the 2020s, under a new guise: the broad area of identity politics, which often results in the denunciation of mere, plastic, two-dimensional stereotypes (of gender, race, age, sexual orientation, and so on) and the concomitant demand for authentic, well-rounded, relatable human subjects on screen. People with whom we can identify! Emilio Estevez may have been a decade or so ahead of this curve when he proclaimed that his film *The Way* (2010)—a fictional account of the traditional pilgrimage of a group of folk along the Camino de Santiago in Spain—is "pro-people, pro-life, not anti-anything."[12]

But cinema was meant for the anti-everything, for disconnection from social agendas and obligations, for merry sin and evil. Sontag, in 1965, admitted as much: "There is a sense in which all these movies are in complicity with the abhorrent. . . . It is no more, perhaps, than the way all art draws its audience into a circle of complicity with the thing represented."[13] That is what we identify with in cinema, this circle of complicity with the abhorrent and the antisocial—not with characters, or moral lessons, or noble sequences of low-to-high emotion leading to chaste enlightenment. Let it all fall down, like that house in *Duplex;* from there, we can rebuild for the next apocalypse.

NOTES

Epigraphs: Philip Brophy, "Juvenile Delinquents," *The Video Age* (October 1985): 10–11, reprinted in Brophy, *ReStuff: Horror—Gore—Exploitation* (Melbourne: Stuff Publications, 1988), 40–41; and Svetlana Gusarova, "Depressive Realism: An Interview with Julie Reshe," trans. Duane Rousselle, *3:AM Magazine,* May 2, 2021, https://www.3ammagazine.com/3am/depressive-realism-an-interview-with-julie-reshe/. Accessed August 31, 2021.

 1. Susan Sontag, "The Imagination of Disaster," in *Against Interpretation and Other Essays* (New York: Picador), unpaginated and undated e-book edition.

 2. Ian David's keynote lecture was delivered in September 2012 at the Screenwriting Research Network conference in Sydney, Australia. My remarks are based both on notes taken during the talk, and David's subsequent published version, "Screenwriting and Emotional Rhythm," *Journal of Screenwriting* 5, no. 1 (2014): 47–57.

 3. *The Complete Etchings of Goya* (New York: Crown Publishers, 1943).

 4. Manny Farber, "83-Year Tantrum," reprinted in *Manny Farber: Paintings and Writings,* ed. Michael Almereyda, Jonathan Lethem, and Robert Polito

(Los Angeles: Hat & Beard Press, 2019), 74–76. Farber's review originally appeared in *The New Republic,* January 31, 1944.

5. Farber, "83-Year Tantrum."

6. Farber, "83-Year Tantrum," 76. All subsequent citations also come from this page of the essay.

7. Bill Routt, "Creature," *Stuffing* 1 (June 1987): 85.

8. Norman O. Brown, *Apocalypse and/or Metamorphosis* (Berkeley: University of California Press, 1991), 179.

9. See Adrian Martin, "Cinephilia as War Machine," *Framework* 50 (2009): 221–225; republished online in *Sabzian* November 29, 2013, https://www.sabzian.be/article/cinephilia-as-war-machine. Accessed August 31, 2021.

10. François Truffaut, *The Films in My Life* (New York: Simon & Schuster, 1978), 143. The author omitted from that version the "wonderful certainty" line that concluded (and provided the title for) his original review (published under the pseudonym of Robert Lachenay) in *Cahiers du Cinéma* 46 (April 1955): 38–40.

11. Paul Willemen quoted in *Frank Tashlin,* ed. Claire Johnston and Paul Willemen (Edinburgh: Edinburgh Film Festival, 1973), 17.

12. Marilyn Beck and Stacy Jenel Smith, "Charlie Has Goddesses, but Emilio and Martin Have Angels," *Dallas–Fort Worth Tribune,* March 7, 2011, https://web.archive.org/web/20120313024104/http://www.gouverneurtimes.com/dfw-section-f-artsentertainment/29594-charlie-has-goddesses-but-emilio-and-martin-have-angels.html. Accessed August 31, 2021.

13. Sontag, "Imagination of Disaster."

29

... Alienating Interventions

On What the "Bad" in David Lynch's Films Is "Good" For

ANNIE VAN DEN OEVER AND DOMINIQUE CHATEAU

IN THE LUMBER ROOM OF OUR EXISTENCE

At the very end of *Theory of Film: The Redemption of Physical Reality* (1960), in a series of concluding remarks on "the good" of film, Siegfried Kracauer reminds his readers that "Buñuel's involvement in the cruelties and lusts which fill the *lumber room* of our existence" is yet one of many "legitimate propositions" in the field of film.[1] There are pressing reasons to halt for a moment and examine this remark more closely. For one, Kracauer is well aware that viewers respond differently—perhaps stronger—to the "cruelties and lusts" evoked in a film by Buñuel than, say, to a thief's "everyday life" as pictured in a typically neorealist film such as *The Bicycle Thieves/Ladri di biciclette* (1948, dir. Vittorio De Sica). Of course, Kracauer, too, assumed that film viewers might wonder what "good" the cruelties are in *Un Chien Andalou* (1929). And what about Federico Fellini's "preoccupation" with the "shelterless" individual, or Georges Franju's "dread of the abyss that is everyday life"?[2] Kracauer's argument goes as follows: regardless of whether a film director is evoking the good or the bad (cruel, perverse, abysmal), *in film* all these options are equally valid; they are *legitimate propositions*.[3]

Being in the *lumber room* of our existence is a metaphor worth unpacking in this realm, not only because *lumber* and the semantic fields it activates play a central role in Kracauer's argument, but also

FIGURE 30. The Log Lady (Catherine E. Coulson) in David Lynch's television series *Twin Peaks* (1990–1991 and 2017).

because *lumber* plays a substantial role in films by David Lynch and most clearly in *Twin Peaks* (which we treat as film, as he does himself).⁴ Kracauer speaks about *lumber* as a substantive referring to big bulky pieces of wood used for heating or construction, but also to miscellaneous stored (bulky) articles. *Lumber rooms* are rooms where such bulky things are kept. The verb *to lumber* means to move in a slow, heavy, awkward way. The adjective *lumbersome* means bulky and awkward to handle or use. Metaphorically, *lumber* is associated with awkwardness and what is hard to handle. The *lumber room* of our existence, then, is the place where we keep things which are awkward and not easy to handle. David Lynch set some of his stories in a North American lumber town, among them *Blue Velvet* (1986). *Twin Peaks* (1990–1991, ABC; 2017, Showtime), too, is set in a lumber town, and there is lumber all over the place: a lumber mill, lumberyards, lumberjacks or woodmen; even a Log Lady (Catherine E. Coulson), Madonna-like, holding a piece of lumber as if it were her baby.

Kracauer's *Theory of Film* is so interesting to the field today because he did not develop a "theory of realism" or representation, as Miriam Hansen so aptly argued, but a phenomenological theory of the film experience and an anti-hermeneutic approach to film, one in which the study of the sensory-perceptual qualities of the film experience take center stage.⁵ This includes the study of the technology-induced effects that can be strong enough to subvert biological and ontological categories, which may force us to rethink "our relationship to the world." Paul Valéry, Walter Benjamin, Edmond Couchot, Hansen, and others helped to put on the research agenda what Kracauer called the "alienating intervention of technology."[6] In line with it, we pay attention to Lynch's phantasmagorical use of (extreme) close-ups and his mutual contamination of dream and story levels—not only to help understand how the film experience—any film experience—can be dreamlike and *on the verge of consciousness,* as Kracauer argued, but, more specifically, to pay attention to the uniquely "Lynchian" method to achieve this.

LYNCHIAN

Lynchian is a term coined in 1996 by the then-young American writer David Foster Wallace, in "David Lynch Keeps His Head," written while he was on the set of *Lost Highway* (1997).[7] Key in his testimony is that Lynch's *Blue Velvet* changed the idea of film for him and his generation, if only because Lynch demanded his viewers take on new roles as spectators and value films filled with weird and grotesque characters, objects, and behaviors as *equally legitimate,* to use Kracauer's words. *Lynchian,* then, is defined by Wallace as a combination of "the very macabre and the very mundane," yet what seems particularly apt is that he qualifies the combination as revealing "the former's perpetual containment within the latter."[8] In other words, the macabre is suppressed by the everyday. Today, *Lynchian* is in the Oxford English Dictionary. In this foundational piece, Wallace uses the term *Lynchian* twenty-three times. In combination with *Lynchian,* he uses words like *weird, creepy, creepy-comic, surreal-banal*—and *grotesque,* a term he uses seven times. For instance, he speaks of "Lynchian figures—grotesque, enfeebled, flamboyantly unappealing, freighted with a woe out of all proportion to evident circumstances," and he argues,

> that a sudden grotesque facial expression won't qualify as a really Lynchian facial expression unless the expression is held for several moments longer than the circumstances could even possibly warrant, until it starts to signify about seventeen different things at once.[9]

Among the many connotations that come with the predicate *Lynchian* are notions of this weird, upside-down world, in which all things "good" and "bad" take on different meanings.

RADICAL LITERALIZATION AS AN ALIENATING TECHNIQUE

There isn't a storyworld in Lynch's films that isn't multilayered. There are parallel universes, some of which coexist in separate dimensions without communicating with each other, and others interfere with one another in different and often complex ways. In *Twin Peaks,* the relationship between the first level of reality—the primary storyworld in which agent Cooper (Kyle MacLachlan) investigates a murder—and the second level of reality—the Black Lodge—constantly oscillates between the separation of the worlds and their mutual interference. The moment Cooper leaves the Black Lodge, his character undergoes a doubling, even a tripling which adds to his first personality of FBI agent an antinomic couple of bad guy/good guy: an agent of the evil, physically dark and psychologically cruel; and a guardian angel, awkward and dumb, yet surprisingly charismatic.

The parallel universe of the Black Lodge is a lumber room, of the kind where one collects "fantasies" that, reading Freud or some of his followers, we can define as images that we both love and hate, that we want to forget but cannot—"imagined fulfilments of frustrated wishes," as Elizabeth Spillius writes.[10] *Lumber room* is aptly translated into French by the term *débarras,* a deverbal noun derived from *débarrasser,* which means "to rid" or "to free" oneself, for example, of an unwanted person or thing. Extensively, *débarrasser* also refers to the fact or the action of being freed from a certain discomfort or constraint caused by something or someone, and the physical or moral relief it brings. This sense of "getting rid" of something is also found in *débarras,* then, a room in which old or temporarily unused objects are stored. The French *cabinet de débarras* describes a special room, generally a bit removed from the rest of the house. It recalls in some ways the *cabinet of curiosities,* or the *Wunderkammer* in German (literally, chamber of wonder), in which one would store a wide range of objects, artifacts, dead animals, and other curiosities—especially during the Renaissance—with a particular tinge of the rare, the exotic, and the esoteric.[11]

The lumber room is both a place of ridding and of keeping, of personal things hidden and held on to. Keeping such things "in the lumber room of our private life" means they can suddenly show up to peep into our everyday existence.[12] Going into the lumber room of Lynch's films means stepping into the place where the fetishes and fantasies are kept "in waiting" for agent Cooper to investigate. This is the lumber room

Cooper's and Lynch's viewers share. To further complicate this argument, we must acknowledge that maybe Cooper is dreaming, maybe the film itself is dreaming.[13] Probing the trope of the film experience as a dream, Kracauer argued that "memories of the senses" return to the viewer, an "absentee dreamer," brought back to forgotten layers of the self by a film.[14] Key is his Freudian understanding of the viewers in their dreamlike state, which provides film easy access to the unconscious. Another key is his "material aesthetics" of film, and his understanding of the film technologies as alienating the viewers from the world as they know it.[15] Film can make them experience the "material phenomena in their otherness, their opaque singularity," as Hansen writes in *Cinema and Experience* about the special form of "redemption" film has to offer according to Kracauer.[16] This is not to say that all films have a redemptive power, only that film is particularly well-positioned to show the *material phenomena in their otherness,* moreover, to catch viewers off balance, in a dreamlike state, vulnerable to experiences of the uncanny while confronting them with an alienated world.

As to Lynch's method: *radical literalization* is the alienating technique par excellence used by Lynch in his films. Wallace happens to have explained the technique for literature on another occasion, not incidentally, with reference to Kafka.[17] He argues that some of Kafka's stories depend on the "radical literalization of truths we tend to treat as metaphorical," and that "some of our most profound collective intuitions seem to be expressible as expressions only, as figures of speech," which is "why we call these figures of speech *expressions.*"[18] If we want to understand "what is really being expressed when we refer to someone as *creepy* or *gross* or say that he is forced to *take shit* as part of his job," Wallace recommends to just take a look at *Die Verwandlung/The Metamorphosis*.[19] Unsurprisingly then, *radical visualization* proves a potentially even greater technique to lay bare the deeper truth of expressions. For example, think of Kafka imagining himself being "cut to pieces," as the expression has it, and then take a look at the drawing made by the underground cartoonist Robert Crumb for *Introducing Kafka:* a hatchet as used by a lumberjack or a butcher cuts slices from Kafka's head.[20]

What can we learn from this? Perhaps that literalization and visualization can make us experience the deeper value of "collective intuitions" as found in some utterances.[21] Perhaps also that visualizations may create strong viewing experiences because the film camera is able to convey "category-crossing" experiences (of the psychomaterial dimensions of an object) better than any other medium.[22] This strikes us as significant, also with reference to the grotesque. The film camera can reverse (put upside down) the literal/figural relation simply by *showing* the thing, for instance, *lumber* from the otherwise figural "lumber room of our existence." *Seeing the thing,* over and over again, as in a film by Lynch, may easily bring back to viewers an experience of the *interpenetration* of the figural and the literal (material). For instance, what to think of the Log Lady? What is she holding or holding onto? Is it a log? Or a baby? Literalization, then, proves to be an ideal technique to confront viewers with subversions of the biological and ontological categories, the very technique on which the aesthetics of the grotesque, and the Lynchian no less, thrives.[23]

Pivotal to Kracauer's "material aesthetics," it seems to us, is that though he does not cover the grotesque, he acknowledges "the alienating intervention of technology" (e.g., light, framing), through which all material objects can be made to return their "gaze."[24] It is evident that Benjamin's notion of the *optical unconscious* penetrates Kracauer's thinking. He is keenly aware of the experiential effects of visualization, in general, and the *alienating* powers of the (extreme) close-up, in particular. These enlargement effects are used differently from the closeness effects and *erotic* powers of the close-up as known from Hollywood's "male gaze" system of looks.[25] Kracauer's focus is on the "alienating" powers of, for instance, a woman's hands as framed by Griffith. Being enlarged to a gigantic (screen) size, being zoomed in on, they "metamorphosize" into a landscape with a skin texture, thus typically creating a *human/nonhuman* category problem and a leap into the grotesque. In Kracauer's argument, it is a leap into the unconscious triggered by the extra-imaginative appeal these hands gained in close-up; as a result, the "viewer's imagination becomes an important part of the projection."[26]

Lynch's phantasmagorical close-ups are emblematic for such category problems and alienation effects, and for an understanding of the Lynchian grotesque. See, for instance, the famous ear in *Blue Velvet*. Similar to the extreme close-up of the ear in Sergei Eisenstein's *Strike* (1925), it demonstrates how an otherwise normal ear (though decaying, in *Blue Velvet*) can be made *monstrous,* dreamlike, fantastical, unreal, deformed, deceptively unhuman, and full of optical illusion. At heart, it poses a category problem. Is it an ear, literally, materially, or is it a crater or an abyss? Such a fusion of the biological and ontological categories is typical of the grotesque.[27] Claiming that Lynch is *grotesque* is just another way to say that his films present a confusing and alienating experience of an otherwise normal world being turned into something dreamlike and monstrous.

THE PHANTASMAGORICAL FUSION OF STORY LEVELS AND DREAM LEVELS

Lynch is also typically interested in a phantasmagorical fusion of story levels and dream levels, and the interpenetration of the parallel and extradimensional worlds into which he plunges his characters. For example, agent Cooper sees the Red Room in a dream even *before* the Black Lodge appears in the primary storyworld. In other words, this parallel world, emerging from a dream, underlines the incessant balancing between oneirism and realism in *Twin Peaks*. The layered storyworld moves within the realm of the mise en abyme. The Red Room is embedded in the Black Lodge, which finds its counterpart in the White Lodge. Red, Black, and White are overdetermined colors in Lynch's world. In *Twin Peaks*, Season 3, Episode 4, FBI agent Windom Earle (Kenneth Welsh), acting as Cooper's maleficent double, describes the White Lodge as "a place of great goodness," where "gentle fawns gamboled amidst happy, laughing spirits," and where "the sounds of innocence and joy filled the air." His true fascination though is with the *Black* Lodge. The White Lodge is much too sweet to his taste, a "wretched place of saccharine excess," in his words. He prefers the opposite:

> a place of almost unimaginable power, chock full of dark forces and vicious secrets. No prayers dare enter this frightful maw. The spirits there care not for good deeds or priestly invocations, they're as likely to rip the flesh from your bone as greet you with a happy "good day." And if harnessed, these spirits in this hidden land of unmuffled screams and broken hearts would offer up a power so vast that its bearer might reorder the Earth itself to his liking.

The world of the "good" is white, or pink, and soothing, and as sweet as candy. Like the good witch in *Wild at Heart* (1990, dir. David Lynch) and in its main intertextual point of reference, the *Wizard of Oz* (1939, dir. Victor Fleming), they are fairy-tale material. One wonders, therefore, whether Earle isn't right about the *saccharine excess:* is the "good" also the best, or is it just kitsch? The world of the "bad," on the other hand, proves to be highly attractive too, because its "dark forces and vicious secrets" lend boundless power to the imagination.

Back to the Black Lodge then and, more precisely, the Red Room, because this is the place pivotal to the understanding of the kind of lumber room—and fiction film—with which we are dealing. The Red Room, also called "the waiting room," is an *ante chamber* meant to provide access to a larger room, yet it is somehow difficult to leave it. Kept in limbo in this "waiting room" are weird individuals and "objects," among them The Arm, an abnormal tree, and two typically North American *lumberjacks*. The Red Room is also the place where the doppelgangers of the characters are born. It is the very heart of this great cabinet of fiction, a kind of diegetic dictionary where the basic so-called real world is reformulated in a phantasmagorical way, one which penetrates, disturbs, and deranges our real-world perceptions. It is as weird and dark as it is enchanting. It is the fiction film's *Wunderkammer* loaded with the motives found in his films.

The doubling of characters, personalities, and situations is part of an endless, diegetic dynamic in Lynch's work. In the spectator's mind, opposites that would otherwise be mutually exclusive, or simply successive, come to be superimposed—particularly the dualism of good and evil, thus inviting the viewers to an experience of distancing that either satisfies their taste for playful exploration or disorients those spectators who are clinging to their ordinary sense of logic. However, the problem is not only the mental state of the viewers. It is also and more deeply a problem of representation in the sense of a "technesthetic" operation (according to the concept of Couchot inspired by Valéry and Benjamin).[28] It artificially generates the realistic impression (*effet de réel*), while prolonging a sense of being not only "here," but also "there," in more esoteric or poetic spheres, at the same time. A particularly striking example of this may be found in *Lost Highway*: one cannot tell whether the character named "The Mystery Man" (Robert Blake) really exists in an (already dislocated) diegesis upon encountering him, or whether he is merely the product of the imagination of the—apparently schizophrenic—main character Fred Madison (Bill Pullman).

Are we in an embedded dream? Or at the primary level of the diegesis that continues to unravel? Regardless, the various scenes of the film demonstrate a fundamental property of cinema in general: that what is shown, even narrated as if in the past, is offered to the audience in the present at the moment of projection. This is the cinema's unique, *technesthetic* quality. It is a property that has set the medium of cinema apart from that of photography.

At a reception, having a drink near the bar, Fred is accosted by a man with a shallow face, slick hair, grinning enigmatically, Nosferatu-like. It is the Mystery Man who claims to have met him before. Fred denies it, but the Mystery Man insists that they met in his house, adding: "As a matter of fact, I'm there right now!" Fred does not understand what he means by "there," and the Mystery Man replies: "At your house!" Fred: "That's fucking crazy, man." The Mystery Man then takes a phone out of his pocket (a kind of "antique" cell phone) and says: "Call me. Dial your number. Go ahead." The phone rings, someone on the other end picks up and says: "I told you I was here." This is the Mystery Man's voice. Fred: "How'd you do that?" The Mystery Man in front of him: "Ask me!" Fred does, and the Mystery Man's voice answers by phone: "You invited me. It is not my custom to go where I'm not wanted." Then Fred asks him, by phone: "Who are you?" The Mystery Man in front of him tells Fred with a throaty laugh similar to his phone voice: "Give me back my phone!" The Mystery Man then ends the scene with the standard phrase: "It's been a pleasure talking to you!"

This *Lost Highway* scene is driven by the Mystery Man's freak character, an expression of Fred Madison's Mephistophelian mental state, and the disturbing contamination of human ubiquity (as evoked in literature) and technological ubiquity, a mode of "being present in the world" that is facilitated by technological teletransmission. It recalls the famous Valéry prophesy of a new medium allowing the ubiquity of all things (often cited in the early days of television): "It will be possible to send anywhere or to re-create anywhere a system of sensations, or more precisely a system of stimuli, provoked by some object or event in any given place. Works of art will acquire a kind of ubiquity.... I do not know whether a philosopher has ever dreamed of a company engaged in the home delivery of Sensory Reality."[29]

The technesthetic implications of the hypothesis struck Benjamin, in particular how the ubiquitous "tele presence" of the cinematic image, thanks to the passage through the audiovisual channel, would evoke the sensations from which sprang these very images.[30] In Lynch's work, the duality between conscience and unconscious plays out in this process. More often than not, it is a dream or a fantasy that invites the viewers in. As in the declaration of the assassin of Laura Palmer in *Twin Peaks*: "I saw him in my dreams. He asked me if I wanted to play. He opened me and I invited him and he came inside me."[31]

WHAT THE "BAD" IN DAVID LYNCH'S FILMS IS "GOOD" FOR

It seems to us that Lynch, as the Surrealists, situates himself beyond good and evil while playing with them. "Some ideas arrive in the form of a dream," as the Log Lady states.[32] Lynch situates his playing in his dream worlds, as the Surrealists do. Most of Lynch's dreams are alienating, hallucinatory, uncanny, as Buñuel's and Salvador Dalí's dreams. All are drawing from the sixteenth-century grotesque image tradition, a relation that was first made explicit by Wolfgang Kayser, who argued that the Surrealists were *the true twentieth-century heirs of the grotesque* and their evocations of an "estranged world" an attempt to "subdue the demonic aspects of the world."[33] All of them are "[f]ascinated with the dark side lurking in and amongst the everyday."[34] Crucially, though, the "sixteenth-century artists [e.g., Hieronymus Bosch, Lucas Cranach] ultimately put their monsters within a moral framework; the surrealists did not."[35]

If there is a value in playing with good and evil outside of a moral framework, it is the ethical value of discussing what is good. However, more important is perhaps that Lynch's work, being the epitome of lumber-room "fantasies," can offer the viewer a cathartic experience of sorts, in the sense of Freud, releasing strong or repressed emotions, ultimately leading to sublimation. By constantly opening up new pathways without ever closing them, making viewers linger in what Kracauer called *the lumber room of our existence,* Lynch's films can offer a "working through" of the "fantasies" we stick to and want to get rid of, want to forget but cannot.

NOTES

1. Siegfried Kracauer, *Theory of Film: The Redemption of Physical Reality* (New York: Oxford University Press, 1960), 310. Kracauer alternatively speaks of "the lumber room of our private life," 56.
2. Kracauer, *Theory of Film,* 310.
3. Kracauer, *Theory of Film,* 310.
4. *Twin Peaks,* created by David Lynch and Mark Frost, ran for two seasons on HBO in 1990–1991 and had a third season in 2017. Lynch regards *Twin Peaks* as a *film,* not a series; we, too, do not distinguish between his films and work for television. See also Dominique Chateau, "The Film that Dreams: About David Lynch's *Twin Peaks* Season 3," in *Stories,* ed. Ian Christie and Annie van den Oever (Amsterdam: Amsterdam University Press, 2018), 119–142, at 138.

5. Miriam Hansen, *Cinema and Experience: Siegfried Kracauer, Walter Benjamin, and Theodor W. Adorno* (Berkeley: University of California Press, 2012), 271.

6. Hansen unpacks some of Proust's images that inspired Kracauer, and she claims, "[f]or Kracauer and Benjamin, the only viable method of adapting the magic of Proust's madeleine is through the 'alienating intervention of technology.'" Hansen, *Cinema and Experience*, 270. Marcel Proust—his magic lantern images, his madeleine—was also the source of inspiration to Paul Valéry, Henri Bergson, and Edmund Couchot for their reflections on the impact of technologies on experience.

7. David Foster Wallace, "David Lynch Keeps His Head," *Premiere Magazine* (September 1996), http://www.lynchnet.com/lh/lhpremiere.html. Accessed March 1, 2021.

8. Wallace, "David Lynch Keeps His Head."

9. Wallace, "David Lynch Keeps His Head."

10. Elizabeth Spillius, *Journeys in Psychoanalysis: The Selected Works of Elizabeth Spillius* (London: Routledge, 2015), 124.

11. Gaston Bachelard, *Poetics of Space* (Boston: Beacon Press, 1994), 74–89.

12. Kracauer, *Theory of Film*, 56.

13. See Dominique Chateau, "Film that Dreams," 139–142.

14. Kracauer, *Theory of Film*, 165–166.

15. Hansen, *Cinema and Experience*, 253.

16. Hansen, *Cinema and Experience*, 271.

17. Wallace, "Funniness," originally a 1999 speech for PEN, which was published after his death in 2008 as a short text in *The David Foster Wallace Reader* (London: Hamish Hamilton, 2014), 849–853.

18. Wallace, "Funniness," 851 (original emphasis).

19. Wallace, "Funniness," 851 (original emphasis).

20. David Zane Mairowitz and Robert Crumb, *Introducing Kafka* (Cambridge: Icon Books, 2006 [1993]), 3.

21. Wallace, "Funniness," 851.

22. Hansen on Kracauer in *Cinema and Experience*, 253.

23. On the topic of technology-induced effects leaping into the grotesque and monstrous, see Annie van den Oever, "The Medium-Sensitive Experience and the Paradigmatic Experience of the Grotesque, 'Unnatural' or 'Monstrous,'" *Leonardo* 46, no. 1 (2013): 88–89. *Monstrous* is the term most often used as a synonym for grotesque.

24. Hansen, *Cinema and Experience*, 270–275.

25. Laura Mulvey, "Visual Pleasure and Narrative Cinema," *Screen* 16, no. 3 (1975): 6–18.

26. See Hansen on the close-up in *Cinema and Experience*, 270–273.

27. Wolfgang Kayser, *The Grotesque in Art and Literature* (Bloomington: Indiana University Press, 1963 [1957]).

28. On *technesthetic*, a concept developed by Couchot, following Valéry and Benjamin, see Dominique Chateau, "The Philosophy of Technology in the Frame of Film Theory: Walter Benjamin's Contribution," in *Technē*

/Technology, ed. Annie van den Oever (Amsterdam: Amsterdam University Press, 2014), 29–49, at 36, 40, 45.

29. Paul Valéry, "The Conquest of Ubiquity," in *Aesthetics*, trans. Ralph Manheim (New York: Pantheon Books, 1964 [1928]), 225–228, at 225.

30. Chateau, "Philosophy of Technology," 29–49.

31. *Twin Peaks*, Season 2, Episode 16.

32. *Twin Peaks*, Season 1, Episode 2.

33. The phrasing is taken from the art historian Frances Connelly's recent expert comments on Kayser's chapter on Surrealism. See her *The Grotesque in Western Art and Culture: The Image at Play* (New York: Cambridge University Press, 2014). See also Kayser, *Grotesque in Art and Literature*, 170–172, 184, 188.

34. Connelly, *Grotesque in Western Art and Culture*, 142, 144

35. Connelly, *Grotesque in Western Art and Culture*, 144.

30

... Dangerous Situations

On Whether Cinema Is Poisonous

MICHEL CHION

"Free the vipers," exclaims the strange J. Hovah (*sic*), played by the no less strange Severn Teakle Darden Jr. in *Vanishing Point* (1971, dir. Richard C. Sarafian), when he opens and empties the small wicker trunk full of rattlesnakes caught for him in the Nevada desert by an old prospector (Dean Jagger). The latter catches them with a snare at the end of a stick, exchanging them with the priest for coffee and sugar, and, along with the hero Kowalski (Barry Newman), whose car has run out of gas, we witness the impressive and dangerous operation. Why did this priest, with his little band of musicians singing a hymn in the desert, surrounded by a handful of worshipers who had come by car, want snakes, I asked myself (answer a few lines further down)? And why does he no longer want them now?

It was only recently that I watched *Vanishing Point,* that cult film in which the protagonist, an ex-policeman, tears along in his tricked-out car to make the trip from Denver to San Francisco, a distance of nearly two thousand kilometers, in fifteen hours. He is pursued by the police; meets colorful characters and poetic, benevolent bikers riding the same motorized mounts as the heroes of *Easy Rider* (1969, dir. Dennis Hopper); and, above all, is supported on his journey by the voice of a blind radio host, Super Soul (Cleavon Little), who programs songs, advice, and messages for him. The film is brilliant, poetic, dynamic, sometimes touching, and, in my opinion, worthy of its reputation. But does that mean this film is *without danger?*

FIGURE 31. Venomous vipers in *Vanishing Point* (1971, Richard C. Sarafian).

When I watched it for the first time and got to the precise moment matching the image above, one of the film's delayed surprises, I startled a bit—as if the snakes were going to land, not offscreen, outside the frame, which they do, but in my home, in my workroom. A sort of miniature echo of the panic that is said (it's probably just a legend) to have overtaken the first viewers of the cinematograph, as the Lumière brothers' train hurtled toward them.[1] Then I wondered what, in the world of the film, would become of the reptiles, which we then see slithering away again, and if they would kill people? So I thought about what I call *profilmic reality*. And, of course, as the film is about speeding, albeit on mostly deserted roads, I reflected on the problem of *risk:* the risk run by the character, the risk he makes others run, and the problem his example poses for those viewers with a driving license who, at the end—spoiler alert!—see the hero perish, through no fault of his own, but that of the police. As if one could do all these stunts and all this speeding without putting oneself in danger or risking running someone over.

CINEMA, A KINETIC ART!

This question of the danger of reproducing in reality particular behavior that we witness in films, where it is devoid of serious consequences, was born with the cinema and its car chases, which were often the highlight of the Keystone films produced by Mack Sennett. Cinema is so expressive on a kinetic and gestural level, as its very name indicates. In these chases, filmed with stuntmen who were often the actors themselves, and where the film was shot in slow motion so that afterward, at 16–18 frames per second, the vehicles appear to be whizzing past like racing cars, nothing serious ever happened, no one died or became paraplegic. Road accidents on screen are not that common, and if James Dean, Jayne Mansfield, Françoise Dorléac, and Grace Kelly died at the wheel or in the passenger seat, it was not in their films but in reality: the characters they played on the screen often escaped far more dangerous situations.

From this point of view, some of my favorite films, like *The Blues Brothers* (1980, dir. John Landis), set the worst example, with their road-speeding excesses that were treated as mere stock-car gags. These films could be accompanied by a warning speech: don't copy these people! We need to make a distinction that I have found in the experience and discourse of psychoanalysts: that between dangerousness and badness. Films that show people driving very fast or taking hard drugs without any fatal consequences are not bad, but they may be "dangerous."

What am I getting at with this theme of dangerous films that would no longer be dangerous if they were shown or analyzed properly? Oh yes, I wanted to answer an odd question that I was asked by Julian Hanich and Martin Rossouw for this collection: "what is film good for?" By turning the question around, *what would film not be good for?*, I see the "good" in cinema everywhere: in pleasure, beauty, landscapes, faces, storytelling, childhood, sex, emotion, travel, joy, the meeting of human beings from all countries and all eras, and also, beyond the actual films, the exchanges they may trigger and that allow us to rediscover ourselves. Plus, the small pleasures of erudition and commentary. These are also good, provided, of course, that we don't resort to hasty generalizations and moral stereotypes in our efforts to understand ourselves. The pleasure of seeing a film you like in a movie theater is great, but so is the pleasure of seeing it as a couple at home, or with family members. And in some cases, I can watch alone those films that are not my wife's cup of tea, for example, dinosaur films, and that gives me another type of pleasure. And for me personally, films were good because they gave me various jobs (journalism, writing, teaching, seeking grants) that allowed me to earn a living without having to do it by composing concrete music, which would have been much more difficult. What are films not good for?

Films are, however, haunted by the question of evil, by the discourse about them, and by the reactions they provoke: for example, the killing of an animal for the sake of an image. On several occasions I have witnessed scenes of goldfish lifted out of their aquarium on a screen, while the camera focuses on them dying on the ground, zooming in on their convulsive movements, as their mouths open in vain, and horses shot down by arrows and bullets in a Western or a war film.[2] These things are less acceptable today, hence the disclaimer at the end of the film: no animal was harmed in the making of this film. In the end, André Bazin was right: the question of reality, and the confusion between true/not true, is at the heart of the ontology of cinema. Not only from a moral point of view, of course.

That said, depending on the era, on personal inclinations and responsibilities, everyone sees evil and danger where someone else would see nothing wrong.

CINEMA, AN EVIL ART?

A close and very open-minded friend of mine, but who had daughters who were still very young, was concerned about some of the films they might see, not because they were violent or sexually disturbing (this she could easily discuss with them and help them figure out the cause of the turmoil provoked by the films), but because a character was made to seem attractive while, without being evil or malicious, spreading death and destruction around him. She did not condemn these films morally, but thought it useful to warn her children, especially when the actor was popular. For example, she warned them about the character played by John Travolta in Brian de Palma's *Blow Out* (1981). At the time, after the worldwide success of the high school musical *Grease* (1978, dir. Randal Kleiser), Travolta was the idol of little girls and not-so-little girls alike. His character may have been a nice guy, but he was nonetheless deadly because, by repeating a technical mistake he had already made once before and which had been fatal for someone else, he led his friend Sally (Nancy Allen) into a very dangerous game in which she loses her life. True, it is not Travolta, but his sound engineer character, whose name everyone, even me, who wrote about this film several times, soon forgot—Jack Terry, says Wikipedia, which I have just consulted—but on the screen, it is Travolta who brings about the death of the woman who loves him and whom he loves. And since one can be attracted to someone who brings death and perdition, even in his kindness, it is better to warn one's children that this can happen and to be wary of this attraction. Moreover, this friend had complimented me for having spotted that this tragic ending was inscribed in Jack's subconscious, in my review in *Cahiers du Cinéma* 333 (which she found too indulgent all the same).

I remember my own hostile reaction when I saw Clint Eastwood's Western *High Plains Drifter* (1973) in 1976. The story was classic enough: a mysterious, unnamed stranger (played by Eastwood) encourages villagers, who are being terrorized by bandits, to defend themselves. But it doesn't turn out the way it did in Akira Kurosawa's *The Seven Samurai* (1954), or its American remake, *The Magnificent Seven* (1960), directed by John Sturges, both of which have villagers trained to fight by those they hire, and both of which end well. At the end of Eastwood's film, there has been even more death and destruction than at the beginning, and the stranger rides off quietly on his horse. It's a bit as if Lucky Luke, at the end of the comic book, mounting Jolly Jumper and whistling as he rides off into the desert, leaves behind a town in the hands of the Dalton brothers, and in a worse state than he found it. I remember saying to myself in 1976: really, this film—written by Ernest Tidyman, the author of the script for *French Connection* (1971), which William Friedkin directed—is stupid! And that I thought it was morally stupid, and therefore bad (I haven't seen it again since). These are criteria that are debatable but that come to mind sometimes.

At the same time, I am aware that films that fascinate me and seem grandiose can be just as morally confused as the one I have just mentioned and sometimes create disturbing imitations: this is the well-known case, or one that deserves to be, of Martin Scorsese's *Taxi Driver* (1976), scripted by Paul Schrader. I met Schrader in Basel, Switzerland, at a screenwriting conference where he was the guest of honor. Very neat, well-dressed, and rigid, he made me feel almost as uneasy as the Travis Bickle character played by Robert de Niro on screen, in his Marine jacket and with his unshaven loser look. We know that a madman named John Hinckley Jr., after seeing the film about fifteen times in theaters, shot President Ronald Reagan in 1981, without killing him. Hinckley said he did it to attract the interest of Jodie Foster, who plays the young prostitute Iris in the film. But why had the Schrader/Scorsese film, and not another, impacted on this lonely, troubled character? In his book *American Cinema/American Culture*, John Belton offers a convincing hypothesis: it is through its very (apparent) incoherence that the film was able to "impact" somehow. Indeed, the character commits an unbelievably revealing blunder when, for their first date, he takes the blonde and respectable Betsy, played by Cybill Shepherd, to see a porn film, a gaffe on which he curiously does not reflect—even though he keeps a diary—and it is not clear why he sets out to assassinate the politician Palantine, which he gives up before killing Iris's "pimp." To quote Belton: "The film struck a nerve in middle America. One of its repeat viewers was John Hinckley, the ultimate incoherent spectator, who fell in love with Jodie Foster and shot the politician, President Ronald Reagan, rather than the pimp, in an attempt to rewrite the film and give it a better (that is, more coherent) ending."[3] I really like this idea of a viewer trying to rewrite a film through reality because its possible incoherence is unacceptable. The danger, the great danger, as can be seen in the history of peoples and utopias that went wrong, often comes from those who try to make reality totally coherent and consistent.

I also notice that Belton, in the hundreds of films he quotes in his book, starts every time by doing what I always do myself, something that critics and cinema enthusiasts in France tend to scorn: it consists of first following the letter of the story told. This then makes it possible to analyze how the effect produced by a given scene is specifically cinematographic, and irrational, often distinct from the effect foreseen in the screenplay. The editing, the size of the shot can give events a scale of importance and gravity that upsets the balance initially calculated. But first, the letter—what I call the *literal script*. For example, those serpents whistling round our heads as viewers in Sarafian's film were not initially a metaphor. As Wikipedia tells me:

> the use of snakes in Christian religious worship emerged in the late nineteenth and early twentieth centuries, at the height of the Pentecostal movement in the United States. It is part of a literal reading of the Bible, including the Gospel according to Mark: And these signs shall follow them that believe; In my name shall they cast out devils; they shall speak with new tongues; They shall take up serpents; and if they drink any deadly thing, it shall not hurt them; they shall lay hands on the sick, and they shall recover. (Mark 16:17–18) It was the American Pentecostal George Went Hensley (1880–1955), a minister in the Cleveland Church of God from 1915 to 1922, who introduced the practice of handling poisonous snakes during services.[4]

In this sense, just before its conclusion, the Gospel according to Mark gives a piece of advice, spoken by the resurrected Jesus, that we may not consider malicious but certainly dangerous. Moreover, I read in another Wikipedia article—yes, it exists!—entitled "Snake handling in religion," that there were several cases of fatal accidents during Pentecostal services.[5]

I was very interested to learn this, but that's because it's 2021, and there's Wikipedia to give me all sorts of information from which to draw, which is obviously not always infallible but can be verified by reasoning and cross-checking. So the effect of a film is a function of the context in which it is seen and the exchanges during which it is discussed. In this sense, there would be no or no more dangerous films, if they were well contextualized and well discussed. The vipers that the film unleashes on us do not carry any harmful venom if we take this film and its context at face value, with care to learn before judging. Which has never been so easy, and sometimes seems to me to be less and less practiced.

Obviously, Sarafian's idea of filming his snake release from this angle, with the small trunk open toward the viewer, is not a coincidence. I think it is a reminder that there is always something dubious, unpredictable, and potentially contagious in a film. We know the impact of certain film effects, which imprint themselves on us, become embedded, beyond their place in the story that is being told. Nevertheless, we cannot pretend to escape the story and the path it marks out.

How to conclude? I would say that the "good" that comes from films often also comes from the questions we ask ourselves about them, the worlds they open up to us. But it is up to us to complete the films, to make them more alive, by what we write and say, and by the discussions they inspire.

Translation: Naomi Morgan, University of the Free State

NOTES

1. The Lumière train legend is discussed in Martin Loiperdinger, "Lumiere's Arrival of the Train: Cinema's Founding Myth," *The Moving Image* 4, no. 1 (2004): 89–118; and Stephen Bottomore, "The Panicking Audience? Early Cinema and the 'Train Effect,'" in *Historical Journal of Film, Radio, and Television* 19, no. 2 (1999): 177–216.

2. Vivian Sobchack deals with the implications of the death of a rabbit in Jean Renoir's *Rules of the Game/La Règle du jeu* (1939) in her book *Carnal Thoughts: Embodiment and Moving Image Culture* (Berkeley: University of California Press, 2004), see, e.g., 245–247 and 268–272.

3. John Belton, *American Cinema/American Culture,* 4th ed. (New York: McGraw-Hill, 2013), 377.

4. https://fr.wikipedia.org/wiki/Manipulation_de_serpents_dans_la_religion_chr%C3%A9tienne. Accessed July 8, 2021.

5. https://en.wikipedia.org/wiki/Snake_handling_in_religion. Accessed July 8, 2021.

31

... Good for Nothing?

On How Films Help Us through the Night

TOM GUNNING

When first faced with this topic—"what film is good for"—I bristled. In the current atmosphere, a desire to do good, after a long period dominated by the threat of disease and death, and suffused by a constant discourse of division, disdain, and discord from the former president of my country, a ritual purification seems imperative. Shouldn't everything, especially the arts, be marshaled in an attempt to make things better—including film? I recalled a rhetorical question a friend had posted on Facebook: "If art doesn't make people better, what's it for?" I had replied, "Something else." Is being "good for" the same thing as "being Good," or, to use a phrase from the British humorist Saki (H. H. Monroe) in his fable on the nature of storytelling, "*Horribly* Good."[1] Before I retired from teaching at the University of Chicago, I served on a committee that awarded grants to projects in which the arts and scholarship interacted. One called "Poetry for Mental Health" wanted to explore the way writing poetry could be used therapeutically. I groped for a way to indicate my discomfort with such an obviously good-intentioned project. Luckily, a poet on the committee put it better than I could. Echoing Socrates in the *Phaedrus,* he said, "Well, poetry, done well, drives you crazy." But doesn't this run against recent claims that poetry can help us heal?

So I initially refused to contribute to this collection of essays, feeling I was being asked an aesthetic and political form of the old saw, "Have

Good for Nothing? | 369

FIGURE 32. Sullivan (Joel McCrea) and a trustee from the chain gang (Jimmy Conlin) in *Sullivan's Travels* (1941, Preston Sturges).

you stopped beating your wife yet?" Like Saki, I inherently distrust the "horribly good." What I consider evil (and I do believe such a thing exists) most often proclaims itself to be good. While I imagine an ethical discourse exists (and I have a philosopher friend who is expert in it), my own discourse as a critic tends to be ironic, aware of the distance between what we can say and what it means. Speaking broadly, I believe that irony is the mode of art, if we understand by that term a constant awareness of the devious paths of poetic language and a suspicion of direct discourse. I distrust art in the service of an end, what we might call "useful art." The complexity of this issue can be explored through the ambivalence that lies at the root of the rhetorical term *allegory*, which, through its Greek roots—*allos, agora*—literally means "speaking otherwise." But allegory has come to mean almost the opposite of this: allegories, such as the *locus classicus* of Bunyan's *Pilgrim's Progress*, refer usually to artworks that point to a lesson, convey a doctrine through figures whose meaning can be clearly interpreted. This slippage in meaning shows how tricky the terrain of artistic language I am trying to survey can be. The tradition I embrace stresses the *allos* of allegory rather than the shared *agora* of public discourse. This tradition stretches from Socratic irony, through the German Romantics to the Russian Formalists. It claims art speaks and acts contrary to common language, takes forking paths, and wanders through forests of adventure and, frankly, danger.

INTRANSITIVE ART: WHAT YOU SEE IS WHAT YOU GET

Tzvetan Todorov stresses the Romantic's differentiation between allegory as an extended metaphor devised to deliver a moral or religious meaning, and the Romantic symbol, whose meaning was obscure, possibly even ineffable, open to multiple interpretations. An art founded on this understanding of the symbol resists translation and complicates the communication of meaning.[2] It is, in Todorov's term, "intransitive"; it cannot serve simply as a means to an end. As the German theorist of *Sturm und Drang* Karl Philipp Moritz stated in 1785, "true beauty consists in the fact that a thing signifies nothing but itself, designates only itself, that it is a whole realized in itself."[3] Here we see the roots of a modern understanding of art as self-contained, and beauty, as Kant declared in the *Third Critique,* as fundamentally impassive beyond serving a simple practical purpose. I find the most powerful modern articulation of this tradition in the Russian Formalist Viktor Shklovsky's concept of *ostrannenie,* "making it strange" or "defamiliarization."[4] According to Shklovsky, while the language of direct communication tries to achieve a rapid and unambiguous conveying of information, artistic language, in contrast, involves "speaking otherwise": "The language of poetry is, then, a difficult, roughened, impeded language."[5] Instead of serving as the express train of meaning, art makes the observer slow down, consider ambiguities, and remain open to receiving mixed messages.

So does this mean art—and therefore, film—is good for nothing?

I agreed ultimately to write this essay because, as committed as I am to the uniqueness of artistic discourse, I felt that there might be a difference between asking what art is *good for* and asking how art can *do good.* The difference between these two phrases embodies the fork in the path that defines art, its wandering away from the purpose of communication, education, or indoctrination. Further, I was being asked "what *film* was good for," not "art" in its most general forms. I don't see this focus on film as calling for an inventory of all the ways film could be a means of education, information, or persuasion, although I think probing this might lead to some surprising discoveries, as an initial investigation of so-called educational film (instructional films, travelogues, procedural films, or the still ambiguous realm of "documentaries") has shown me. "Good for" may imply the instrumental, but perhaps I could bend its meaning to a sense of an "affordance": what does film allow or enable, in a unique manner? A version, therefore, of our eternal question: "What is Cinema?"

ONE GOOD: CINEMA COMPANIONS

If I can detour around the utilitarian assumption of an ethical purpose for film, I might phrase this question as: What do we use film for, how does it enrich our lives? Although the video revolution (from television, through DVDs, to screening on demand) has seemingly privatized the experience of film viewing (especially during the Covid era), the public nature of film exhibition—from the theatrical premieres of Cinématographe and the Vitascope at the end of the nineteenth century, to the anticipated post-Covid survival/revival of the movie theater—constitutes an essential aspect of film spectatorship. Cinema does not take place exclusively on screen but in a shared social space. Asking what film is good for, rather than directing our attention to how film can serve an agenda, should consider the transaction between films and viewers. I want to stress the plural nature of that transaction, not just the film "spectator" in abstract individuality but an "us," the audience.

Jack Kerouac once described his writing as "a tale told for companionship." I believe films are good for fostering companionship. Traditionally we go to the movies in groups or couples. Novels and movies have chronicled communal film watching, from Bigger Thomas and his pals watching *Trader Horn* (1931, dir. W.S. Van Dyke) in Richard Wright's *Native Son* to Anna Magnani's lyrical discussion with her husband in Luchino Visconti's *Bellissima* (1951) of the images they watch on the screen from *Red River* (1948, dir. Howard Hawks). The great innovation of the projection of film images in 1895 and 1896 throughout the world moved cinema from Thomas Edison's peep-show Kinetoscope with its single viewer to images shown in an auditorium on a large screen to an audience sharing moving images *en masse*. But it isn't just crowding folks into a theater during the film's projection that I want to emphasize but the culture of film*going*. Following a theoretical distinction introduced in the 1970s, I am not just talking about film—what appears on the screen—but *cinema,* the whole social institution that surrounds film viewing. We go to the movies often in a group, and we certainly leave in a crowd, even if we came alone. The communal space of cinema includes not only the auditorium but also the lobby, the stairways and corridors, the concession stand, even, as Tsai Ming-liang's *Goodbye, Dragon Inn* (2003) shows us, the restrooms. Michel Foucault described the movie theater as one of society's heterotopias, a world within a world, a demarcated space that asserts its otherness from ordinary space. The movie theater is a space where other spaces are juxtaposed on the screen and which has its own temporality, the screening schedule, the cinema program. Foucault indicates, "Heterotopias always presuppose a system of opening and closing that both isolates them and makes them penetrable."[6] The protocols of filmgoing shape our communal film experience, especially, as Roland Barthes teaches us, around the act of going to and leaving the movie theater. Settling into our seat, we inhabit an atmosphere, as Barthes details, with many dimensions, both erotic and intellectual.[7] Yuri Tsivian's brilliant discussion of the role of the movie-theater lobby, in which personas are assumed and enacted, contacts made or refused, reveals the many things we draw from the movies.[8]

I bring up this issue of communal filmgoing partly because it has a unique modern aspect. In contrast to the communal role of live theater from the Greeks on, perceptive theorists have claimed that cinema dwells within a culture of anonymity and alienation, offering a lack of companionship more than its celebration. Christian Metz phrased it, "Cinema was born much later than the theater, in a period when social life was deeply marked by the notion of the *individual*."[9] In contrast to the traditional theater experience, cinema viewing according to Metz became private: "The feast, once again, is not shared—it is a furtive feast not a festive feast."[10] Metz and André Bazin both claimed, in contrast to the highly social theatergoer, that the cinema spectator seems to be a voyeur viewing the world through a keyhole.[11] Bazin anticipated Metz's analysis of the contrast between theatergoing and film watching, saying, "Crowd and solitude are not antinomies: the audience in a movie house is made up of solitary individuals. Crowd should be taken here to mean the opposite of an organic community freely assembled."[12] Certainly any moviegoer knows both the alienation and the pleasure of going to a movie alone, of sinking into the anonymity of the auditorium, communing with the film images as the rest of the crowd fades into darkness, intoning William Carlos Williams's narcissistic dirge: "I am lonely, lonely. I was born to be lonely, I am best so!"

True, and yet . . . this delicious isolation is not always dominant; the conversations based around a shared film may be delayed; they may not take place in the theater or lobby or even a walk home, but can sprout up later as we recall or retell film (think of Manuel Puig's 1976 novel *The Kiss of the Spider Woman/El beso de la mujer araña*). We *have* shared something, and even the privacy as we take in the images does not necessarily stick to us. As we ease into the comforting, isolating darkness, as Barthes describes it, something other than simple privacy comes over us. "In this darkness of the cinema (anonymous, numerous, populated—oh the boredom, the frustration of so-called private showings!) lies the very fascination of the film (any film)."[13] We sense the many-headed yet faceless beast surrounding us that we are both part of and cut off from. The movie theater represents a modern sort of crowd, like the one that Siegfried Kracauer found in the hotel lobby (that of the era of Grand Hotels, now viewable primarily in old movies like *The Maltese Falcon* [1941, dir. John Huston]). Kracauer contrasts the hotel lobby not with the traditional theater but to the House of God, where worshipers gather. Kracauer claims, "In the hotel lobby, equality is based not on a relation to God but on a relation to the nothing. Here, in the space of unrelatedness, the change of environments does not leave purposive activity behind, but brackets it for the sake of a freedom that can refer only to itself and therefore sinks into relaxation and indifference."[14] But if the lobby represents the ultimate waiting room where strangers gather awaiting something else, the movie theater clearly appears as an escape attempt, where it is hoped that the keyhole may open onto some other type of chance encounter. It is lodged between the limbo of the lobby and the promise of the House of God.

MAKING TIME FLY

If the movie theater bears the promise of, or at least the impulse toward, a type of companionship, it also offers the deliverance from the waiting rooms of eternity with the possibility of passing of time. Besides companionship, movies are good for passing time. The motto of the Mutual Film Corporation, the early film company which at one point employed D. W. Griffith and Charles Chaplin, proclaimed, "Mutual Movies Make Time Fly." If the modern promise of companionship offered by the movies reveals a general sense of alienation, the ability of movies to make time fly reflects film's relation to modern boredom. As Theodor Adorno and Bernard Stiegler have tried to demonstrate, the movies as a pastime don't so much overcome boredom as imitate it.[15] However, I distrust the disdain these theorists express for these modern forms of entertainment as much as I abhor a "Hooray for Hollywood" celebration. The alienation of the movie crowd and the boredom that drives us into the theater exemplify a revolt against our modern situation as much as they mirror it. Films, I would say, are good for displaying the modern condition, even as they offer palliatives and perhaps alternatives to it.

GOOD TO THINK WITH

In trying to turn the question "what are films good for" away from exploring film's possibilities as a moral agent, I was inspired by Claude Lévi-Strauss's famous phrase, "animals were good to think with."[16] If the phrase has become a cliché and even been attacked by animal-rights activists, I still find it—well—good to think about. And this might be my strongest claim for the good of film: that they are good to think with. To think about, for sure, but also to think *with*. It would be hubristic to try to define the way films foster thought. Certainly, on the one hand, the stories and incidents in films give us plenty to think about. But beyond that unbounded topic, I am claiming there are affinities between the way films unwind and the way we think. As soon as film appeared, it offered a new model for the process of thinking, or at least a new metaphor. Consider the passage from Frank Norris's novel *The Octopus,* written in 1900 soon after films appeared, that describes a character's thoughts in these terms: "a series of the day's doings passed before his imagination like the roll of a Kinetoscope [Edison's first cinematic apparatus]." I do not have space in this brief essay to explore the ways this comparison has developed, but combining images with movement, giving them a temporal dimension through transformation, made cinema appropriate as an image of thought, imagination, or memory. I need not move through the more narrativized devices for portraying memory such as visual or aural flashbacks.[17] But my point is not that films can portray thought, rather it is that the nature of film images provides a way to think about thinking.

It must be evident that in thinking about what film is good for I am focusing on the nature of the cinematic moving images and sound in their most basic aspects, rather than specific movies, stories, characters, themes, or genres. But I do not intend to approach films simply as abstractions. Indeed, to get at what films are best for, I would return to Shklovsky's concept of "making it strange." For Shklovsky, defamiliarization was not simply an avant-garde device for making things appear weird. Art as a device eschewed the pragmatic purposes of communication or persuasion, but it did have a task, one that made it artful rather than practical. Art intends a renewal of perception; it defamiliarizes in order to strip off our habits of thought and perception, and open us to new experiences. "The purpose of art is to impart the sensation of things as they are and not as they are known." The technique of art is to make objects "unfamiliar, to make forms difficult, to increase the difficulty and length of perception because the process of perception is an aesthetic end in itself and must be prolonged."[18]

Film has often been described as the acme of realist representation. Not only does film capture images with the accuracy of photographic reproduction, it also records their movements and their temporality, and, combined with sound, it has been claimed to provide a complete illusion. My intention in citing Shklovsky is not to deny this realist impulse but to complicate it. Certainly film is good for capturing the world as we know it. But precisely because of its mastery of resemblance I would also claim films differ from our ordinary perception. The things we see on film look like our world, the one we know, and yet . . . This margin of the unfamiliar makes film's realism uncanny, unsettling, and that is something film is good for.

Films give us something we can share, but what that shared aspect is cannot be taken for granted. Its discussion forms the basis for the companionship I mentioned. I could write pages here about scenes in the films I love that have made me think about moral values or the significance of things as it seems only film can reveal them. But everyone owns a few of these, and I don't for the moment want to offer mine up for amused perusal. Film does allow us to think about our alienation and our boredom and perhaps confront it. It provides an image of the world familiar enough for recognition, but strange enough for speculation. I have avoided here stating what would seem obvious: that films are good for telling stories. I avoid it because too often it segues from a discussion of film into an analysis of characters and their actions that drive stories and a consideration of whether they are good or bad. I don't deny the value of this, but especially in the current climate, where films are being subjected to ideological tests, I find it too tempting, too easy, and too often an act of bad faith.

But speaking of bad faith, I must confess I do believe that films can reflect profoundly on values—on what makes life worth living. But I can't paraphrase their insights without considering how the film-viewing experience makes a line of dialogue, a gesture, a plot, or a scene meaningful. There is a scene from a film that eloquently displays the things I think films are good for, while maintaining a delicious sense of irony about what films are good for. It forms the climax of a film that more or less explicitly poses this question: Preston Sturges's *Sullivan's Travels* (1941).

You know the plot, I hope. Sullivan, a successful director of film comedies such as *Hey Hey in the Hayloft* and *Ants in Your Pants of*

1939, wants to make a film of social significance, revealing the harsh realities of life, but his studio bosses, fearing a commercial flop, convince him he knows nothing about harsh reality. He sets out, therefore, on the road as a hobo, to experience, as Thoreau put it, "the whole and genuine meanness of life."[19] He ends up in a prison camp after a struggle with a brutal railway dick. He encounters sadistic guards and cruel treatment. Toward the end of the film, his chain gang is invited to an African American church.

The entrance of prisoners shuffling into the Black church, chains and leg-irons clanking as the choir sings "Let My People Go," poses a sort of allegory. But it comes with an ironic reversal, the former slaves hosting current prisoners of state. Another reversal follows: after the hymn, instead of a sermon, a cartoon is projected, the image of Mickey Mouse appearing in aureole like a holy image. The sacrament of universal laughter follows, shared by prisoners and parishioners alike, even the sadistic guard. Sullivan initially reacts to this hilarity with confusion and perhaps incredulity. But then he begins laughing, and asks his fellow prisoner to confirm it, "Am I laughing?" This scene of merriment is followed by an explicitly ironic plot twist of a burlesque resurrection as Sullivan, believed by his studio to be dead, is discovered alive and liberated from the camp. He returns to Hollywood where the executives announce that with all the publicity of his case, they are now delighted to produce his socially significant film, "Oh Brother Where Art Thou." But Sullivan astounds them by declaring "with some embarrassment" he wants to make a comedy, adding, "There's a lot to be said for making people laugh. It's all some people have. It isn't much, but it's better than nothing in this cock-eyed caravan."

One could, of course, see this resolution as a self-serving justification of Hollywood's refusal to use films to accomplish good. But if we read this ending fully, its ironic reversals forbid any simple message, and the concluding montage of faces laughing hysterically (including sick children in hospitals) is hard to take simply as cheerful. We could hardly conceive of a more alienated film audience than shackled convicts and impoverished Black people; or a more compromised image of communal viewing than the entrance of prisoners into a fog-enshrouded version of Plato's cave, captivated by the projected shadows on its wall showing the antics of Pluto the pup. We might ask, what good is this? As Sullivan himself admits, "it isn't much." And yet some transformation does happen here, and I find it impossible to not be moved by it, even if I can't define it. But it *is* better than nothing.

NOTES

1. Saki [H.H. Munro], "The Storyteller," in *Selected Stories*, ed. Diana Secker Tesdell (New York: Everyman's Library, 2017), 229–235, at 230.
2. Tzvetan Todorov, *Theories of the Symbol*, trans. Catherine Porter (Ithaca: Cornell University Press, 1982), 198–221.
3. Quoted in Todorov, *Theories of the Symbol*, 161.
4. Viktor Shklovsky, "Art as Technique," in *Russian Formalist Criticism: Four Essays*, trans. and ed. Lee T. Lemon and Marion J. Reis (Lincoln: University of Nebraska Press, 1965), 3–24.
5. Shklovsky, "Art as Technique," 22.
6. Michel Foucault, "Of Other Spaces," *Diacritic* 16, no. 1 (1986): 22–27.
7. Roland Barthes, "Leaving the Movie Theater," in *The Rustle of Language* (Berkeley: University of California Press, 1989), 345–349.
8. Yuri Tsivian, *Early Cinema in Russia and Its Cultural Reception* (Chicago: University of Chicago Press, 1998), 32–46.
9. Christian Metz, *The Imaginary Signifier: Psychoanalysis and the Cinema*, trans. Celia Britton, Annwyl Williams, Ben Brewster, and Alfred Guzzetti (Bloomington: Indiana University Press, 1982). 95.
10. Metz, *Imaginary Signifier*, 96.
11. Metz, *Imaginary Signifier*, 95; and André Bazin, "Theater and Cinema," in *What Is Cinema?*, trans. Hugh Gray (Berkeley: University of California Press, 1967), 76–124, at 95.
12. Bazin, "Theater and Cinema," 99.
13. Barthes, "Leaving the Movie Theater," 346.
14. Siegfried Kracauer, "The Hotel Lobby," in *The Mass Ornament: Weimar Essays*, trans. and ed. Thomas Y. Levin (Cambridge, MA: Harvard University Press, 1995), 173–185, at 179.
15. Theodor W. Adorno, "Free Time," in *The Culture Industry: Selected Essays on Mass Culture*, ed. J.M. Bernstein (London: Routledge, 1991), 187–197, at 168; and Bernard Stiegler, *Technics and Time*, vol. 3, *Cinematic Time and the Question of Malaise* (Stanford, CA: Stanford University Press, 2011). For an extended treatment of film as passing time, see my essay "A Machine for Killing Time," in *The Oxford Handbook of Film Theory*, ed. Kyle Stevens (Oxford: Oxford University Press, 2022).
16. Claude Lévi-Strauss, *Totemism*, trans. Rodney Needham (London: Merlin Press, 1964), 89.
17. See Berthold Hoeckner's Film, Music, Memory (Chicago: University of Chicago Press, 2019) for a subtle discussion of the way film sound, and especially music, can evoke memory.
18. Shklovsky, "Art as Technique," 12.
19. Henry David Thoreau, *Walden*, ed. Jeffrey S. Cramer (New Haven: Yale University Press, 2004), 88.

32

. . . Medium-Sized Matters

On Whether Cinema Has Made
Any Difference

MARK COUSINS

I wrote a lot of the following when I was 42. I'm now 56. More than a decade of living, losing, changing. I've a beer belly now and I didn't have one then. But I've worked with Jane Fonda in those last twelve years, and worked in countries I'd never expected to—Albania and Belarus. I've directed fifteen films since then, and cast my net wide. The question that I asked back then—has cinema made a difference?—still matters to me. I'm not sure that, a dozen years later, my answers will be better, or my writing will be better. But I'm going to give it another go.

I'm taking a print-out of the original article on a walk, from my flat in Edinburgh, through a park, past an extinct volcano—Arthur's Seat. After that, I'll walk to, and end up at . . . I was going to say where, but maybe I'll not do so, here, at the start.

For the sake of honesty, and to play a little, everything that I write today will be in italic.

My partner works for the National Health Service. She's a psychotherapist who treats people who have suffered assault, torture, and other major traumatic experiences. I'm a movie guy, a filmmaker. When we go somewhere I am, therefore, the light relief. She gives me gravitas, I give her a hint of showbiz, a bit of bling.

I'm used to being the bauble. *When the Covid-19 pandemic hit, jobs were reordered according to social use. My partner was a frontline worker. People watched more films under lockdown, and I was asked to*

FIGURE 33. A mobile-phone photo of Jamie from the third part of the Bill Douglas Trilogy (1972–1978), taken by Mark Cousins.

do lots of talks on Zoom. I did what I could, but as I spoke to filmmakers or students in different countries, I always wondered how useful it was. I compared my work to health workers. I might not be here if doctors had not treated the jaundice I caught as a child. Politics builds the tracks on which we run. Science, economics, education, religion, transport, agriculture, and philosophy shape how we live and think. In comparison, is cinema not a smaller thing? It's just 125 years old. And it's entertainment, too. It is young and disposable. It can't extend lives or treat pain or build bridges or grow cabbages.

But cinema, at its best, is an art—an arriviste art—and a multibillion-dollar business. Movies seem to shape aspiration. They were one of twentieth-century America's and India's most striking exports, an exertion of their soft power. Certainly they seem responsive to national psychology. If you want to know what we are scared of, look at our movies. They are like Freudian parapraxes.

This all makes me feel more plugged into life. I'm on the longest walk I've done in ages. I like thinking about movies as I walk. I'm leaving the built-up part of Edinburgh and have just crossed into the wilder bit. I look into the faces of the dog walkers and joggers. I smile at them and they seem to smile back, more than they did before the storm came.

As I walk and look and smile and enjoy being out and about, as I look at the hawthorn and the bramble flowers that will become blackberries, I think about the role cinema has played in one individual life, my own.

I was a nervy little boy. Being brought up in Belfast in the 1970s, during the war, made me somewhat more so. The world felt both generally and, because of the Troubles, specifically, a bit scary. Then I went to the movies. Sitting in the auditorium, before the lights went down, before the film started, I could feel my nervous system ease. Those almost empty, dark movie houses, which would soon light up with projected vistas and faces, made my voltage drop.

But cinema as a relaxant does not take us very far. The human nervous system has always, surely, enjoyed a vicarious thrill and the melting away of fear. Cinema hasn't created radically new psychological experiences. It has just been extremely good at upgrading old ones. It's claimed sometimes that we live in an escapist age and, if cinema is very good at escapism, and very popular, then Hollywood and so-called Bollywood are partly to blame, but this is to forget that Christianity, Hinduism, and Islam, for example, are star systems and story factories too, as were Egyptian cosmology and the Greek deities.

If, therefore, the physical experience of watching the screen hasn't changed human experience at all, what about what appears on the screen? The ubiquity of cinema makes the issue of how it represents real life a matter of concern. A torrent of books, articles, and film studies courses worry over the ethics and politics of such representation. Many of them start with things like fashion. In the Jazz Age in particular, when cinema was highly designed and massively attended, the cupid's bow lips of Clara Bow, pillbox hats, pencil skirts, and box jackets leaped straight from the screen to the girls on Broadway and Mayfair. Bauhaus-influenced black-and-white sets and polished floors told millions what utopian living might look like. In my own case, after seeing Dennis Hopper's film *Colors* (1988), I immediately bought a pair of mirror shades like those sported by Sean Penn in the film and wore them for weeks. Why? To try to look as good as Penn, I suppose. Because I misrecognized myself in him. In order to nick some of his attitude and pass it off as my own. Such borrowings happen all the time and tell us something about human narcissism or the instability or acquisitiveness of identity.

A small, striking example of such elision of, or collision between, movies and life is that several generations of men in India, when they dance at weddings, do so in the manner of the Indian megastar actor and producer Amitabh Bachchan. Another example from my own life is more embarrassing. I can't remember at what age I first saw Martin Scorsese's film *Taxi Driver* (1976), but I do recall that when Robert De Niro took off his shirt I immediately decided that his chest hair was *exactly* how chest hair should be. And so I started shaving mine to look more like Travis's. If circumstances had been different I might well have seen a shirtless man in real life and made the same aesthetic judgment, but I doubt if it would have pricked me so much. The power of cinema made the moment stick. It dodged my defensive bullets. The film took advantage of the fact that I had submitted myself to it and, without intending to, led to a change in my body hair.

As I walk, my limbs begin to tire. I can feel my body working, pushing forward, and I recall an argument I had with an American film critic. I have said that, for me, reading a book is perhaps a more acute intellectual pleasure than watching a film, but it's far less physical. My senses are so alert when I go into a cinema. I feel like I'm entering a cave or a church. I move into a space, from one realm to another, just like this walk is taking me from Georgian Edinburgh to the suburbs, to the housing schemes. The critic argued the opposite, that he turns his body off when he's at the movies, that it's more inward than reading. But, surely, cinema is more like walking than reading?

Sex is but a block away from such things. I'm sure the fact that I was watching Kim Novak in *Vertigo* (1958, dir. Alfred Hitchcock) and Tippi Hedren in *The Birds* (1963, dir. Alfred Hitchcock) as I was going through puberty fixed some elements of my erotic imagination. At such formative times, of course, many things are grist to the erotic mill, but, again, it was surely the power of film and its seemingly direct dial to my brain stem that locked in the sexual buzz of a well-tailored suit and heels. The fact that I was an equal-opportunities luster—I wanted to be with Novak or De Niro—triangulated things in heady ways. From talking to friends I could see that they weren't bisexual (I rued their disadvantage) and, it began to dawn on me, neither was the world in general. Yet cinema, it seemed to me, most definitely was. When Hitchcock photographs Novak in a state of undress, her hair hanging down, in *Vertigo*, he doesn't invite just the men in the cinema to imagine the moment we have not seen—James Stewart taking her clothes off—but the women, too. When De Niro takes his shirt off in *Taxi Driver*, women and men see his body from the same distance and with equally privileged access. It is quite possible to imagine a film in which the screen splits at such moments of erotic appeal, the left half being for people who fancy women, the right for those who fancy men, but I have not seen this done, and it would be needlessly divisive. For years film theory talked about how movies coerced viewers into gendered responses to sexual display—Cameron Diaz's slow-motion appearance in *The Mask* (1994, dir. Charles Russell) makes us all lusty guys—but for me, in my early teens, I was both a boy and a girl in the cinema, and that was great.

Looking back, this was part of why cinema mattered to me. It made the world legible. The Northern Ireland in which I was growing up was wrong about sex, and cinema was right. If I had had to learn about the vectors and valencies of sexuality from the Ballymena of Ian Paisley and the St. Louis nuns who ran the school I attended, I would have been seriously screwed up. Theirs was an impenetrable medieval lexicon of sex, whereas cinema spoke plain erotic English.

This was exciting. Cinema was like Google Translate. You type in a paragraph in a foreign language and it translates it into your own. In her memoir, Temple Grandin—the autistic, activist, American, cattle-handling machine designer and lecturer—says that as a girl, when she heard the word "underneath" she had to translate this into a little video in her head of her getting underneath a table. Cinema did something like that translation for me. And judging by my conversations with cinephile directors like Martin Scorsese and Tsai Ming-liang, and with Tilda Swinton, it did so for them, too. Novels could never have unscrambled life for me in the same way. Scorsese would never have been a novelist. Cinema matters because it unlocked life for people like him and Swinton and me. Which is only to say that it matters to those for whom it matters. And even then only in a vague, Chomskyan, "my brain is structured like cinema" kind of way.

To get back to something more concrete, how about this for a claim? If I am not racist, it is substantially because of cinema. Where I grew up was almost exclusively white. The popular TV programs we watched as kids were full of racial stereotypes and sometimes overtly racist, and I had no opportunity to observe the agency, subjectivity, or volition of real nonwhite people. I've read novels by Naguib Mahfouz, Toni Morrison and J. M. Coetzee, and most of James Baldwin's writing. The work of Frantz Fanon and Edward Said gave me some perspective on my own whiteness and Western-ness. And yet none of this particularized nonwhite people for me like the movies of Djibril Diop Membéty, Ousmane Sembène, Youssef Chahine, Souleymane Cissé, Moufida Tlatli, Haile Gerima, Idrissa Ouédraogo, Safi Faye, and Med Hondo in Africa; Fei

Mu, Yuan Muzhi, Xie Fei, Chen Kaige, Zhang Yimou, Tian Zhuangzhuang, Zhang Nuanxin, Wong Kar-wai, Lou Ye, King Hu, Hou Hsiao-hsien, Tsai Ming-liang, Edward Yang, Cecile Tang, and Anne Hui in the Chinese-speaking world; or Yasujirō Ozu, Kenji Mizoguchi, Mikio Naruse, Kinuyo Tanaka, Akira Kurosawa, Nagisa Ōshima, Ogawa Shinsuke, Shōhei Imamura, Kazuo Hara, or Hirokazu Kore-eda in Japan. It's not just that I've gotten to know the world through these directors. When I first started meeting people from Ethiopia, for example, I knew something of their country's landscapes and politics from Gerima's movies.

But to say that sounds naive. Yes, those filmmakers helped me understand societies beyond the one in which I was born, but of course the films didn't change much. They didn't end institutional racism. They didn't lead to reparations for colonial plunder. I'm a few miles East of Edinburgh now, in Craigmillar, a series of working-class housing schemes like the places in which I grew up. Not the sort of place that tourists see. Not the place that visiting filmmakers film. There are far more BAME people here, and more on disability scooters, than in the city center. And, near here, one of Scotland's greatest filmmakers was born. The real purpose of my walk is to see if a plaque on the wall of a miner's cottage in Newcraighall, two miles further on, is still there. The plaque says that Bill Douglas was born there. I drove past it recently and couldn't see it. Has it been taken down? Bill Douglas's Trilogy is why cinema matters to me. It's so much about class and sex and creativity. It's . . . but no, wait. I'll say something more about it when I get to the plaque. If it's there.

Craigmillar has made me start to think about things beyond my own life. How has cinema effected not individuals, but groups or nations?

I think of *Gregory's Girl* (1981, dir. Bill Forsyth). When I saw it for the first time, I felt that it was about me, but when I talked to Scots, it was clear that Gregory (John Gordon Sinclair) was theirs, his humor and hairstyle and manner of speaking was theirs. The film's success boosted the confidence of the Scottish cottage film industry. But, more than that, the fact that a lad from Cumbernauld was up there, on the silver screen, where Carrie Fisher and De Niro lived, legitimized Scottishness. It made it something you boasted about rather than hid.

Success in football and pop music can reinforce group identities in similar ways but not to the same degree. David Beckham was inspiring but nonnarrative. The confidence of young English lads—and lads around the world—is boosted by his meritocratic example. But Beckham soared up and away from his background like a rocket. Gregory, being fictional and cinematic, took his 1980s Scottish world with him when he burst into life on the big screen. Or perhaps that's back to front: When *Gregory's Girl* is screened, it's a time and place that we see and then, only then, one of its most likable citizens, Gregory.

The film *Walkabout* (1971, dir. Nicolas Roeg) reinforced a strain of Australian identity just as *Gregory's Girl* did in Scotland. There had been Aboriginal characters onscreen before it, but the wise, beautiful, taciturn youth who the two white children meet in the outback not only launched the acting career of the extraordinary David Gulpilil, but took Aboriginalism from a current affairs issue into the realms of recognition and fulfillment. Likewise, *Gadjo Dilo* (1997), made by Tony Gatlif, an Algerian director of Romany descent, made Romany people proud and others interested. Gregory, Gulpilil, and Gatlif created performed selves in the symbolic, charmed, exciting realm of cinema for three marginalized identities. These and countless other examples show what a great witness-bearer cinema can be, and that matters.

Zoom out further, from groups to whole nations, and it's immediately clear that cinema's record as witness-bearer is mixed. Let's look at the plus side first. In *Cinema of Unease* (1995, dir. Sam Neill and Judy Rymer), a documentary he made about New Zealand's film history, actor Sam Neill argued convincingly that success in cinema was central to the country's growing confidence as a nation. To see the first good Indigenous New Zealand movies on the big screen was to think, *my god, at last*. In Britain, films like *In Which We Serve* (1942, dir. Noël Coward and David Lean) and Humphrey Jennings's documentaries depicted the wartime common cause across class divides—the British spirit—which, though idealistic and somewhat contentious, played a part in the slow erosion of class barriers that was one of the stories of Britain's twentieth century. The critic Jean-Michel Frodon argued that for André Malraux, France's culture minister from 1959 to 1969, cinema was a "diplomatic tool" that enhanced the shining of France in the world. The poetic humanism of Iranian cinema since the mid-1980s stood in winning counterpoint to the audiovisual clichés about the country on Western television.

These are "good" examples of film helping a nation to find a place in the world, but cinema has, of course, reinforced beliefs in far less edifying ways. The list is depressingly long: Africans in Tarzan movies, Jewish people in Nazi cinema, African Americans in Hollywood cinema until the 1960s, Chinese people in Japanese film and vice versa, middle-class people and intellectuals in Maoist and Soviet movies, Mexicans in American cinema until the 1970s, et cetera. These slurs were not invented by cinema, but it took to them with alacrity.

Nearly everything I've said so far has been about cinema as an identity machine. What has become clear is that cinema matters because it is great at first person, it fuels it, it is an antidepressant of first person, it is an identity steroid—whether that identity is the individual self, the ethnic or social group, or the nation. But what about when it isn't boosting types of selfhood? Does it have an impact on other aspects of social or political life?

Yes, but usually in alliance with its sometime sparring partner, TV. In the United Kingdom, Ken Loach's *Cathy Come Home* (1966) is regularly cited for the outrage it generated about homelessness, and the fact that it helped create the charity Shelter. *Heshang*, the "River Elegy," a series of Chinese documentaries, not only benefited from the relative freedom of thought in China in the 1980s, but helped broaden that freedom until the Tiananmen clampdown. In these and many other cases, the language of film told disruptive stories, but it was TV's ability to deliver these stories to mass audiences that created the impact. Other films changed the world without having to rely entirely on TV broadcasts: Michael Moore's *Bowling for Columbine* (2002) convinced Walmart to stop selling certain types of bullets, and Marcel Ophuls's *The Sorrow and the Pity/Le Chagrin et la pitié* (1969) helped convince France to face up to its wartime collaborationism. Japanese activist film in the 1970s was particularly effective in setting up alternative exhibition circuits, in community halls, village venues, schools, and so on, to challenge the government on issues such as environmental damage and transport.

As I rethink these thoughts, I see, on the ground, a cigarette packet. On it is a photograph of an eye with what looks like a cataract. A warning of blindness. I take a photograph of the photograph . . . I had a cataract removed at the end of last year, and now I can see far better. It strikes me that cinema is a warning against blindness.

There's a final lens, beyond questions of individuals, groups, nations, or specific social change, in which cinema's impact can be looked at: its imaginative fidelity. The degree to which it has told the truth, or effectively conjured the themes of our lives.

Take war, for example. I believe that because cinema looks like real life, and watching a movie feels like watching a parallel universe very like our own, but a bit more glamorous and structured more like a story, movies almost inevitably fail to capture the immersive agony of war at its worst. As well as being brought up in Belfast, I was in Sarajevo during its siege and Iraq during its war and, in each case, the feeling was of drowning in war, being in the conflict like a fish is in water. Cinema certainly hasn't shied away from trying to depict war—as either a heroic stage or an ignoble mess. And yet I can think of only two sequences in the whole of movie history that have given me that fish-in-water feeling: a celebrated scene in Elem Klimov's Soviet film *Come and See/Idi i smotri* (1985), when a boy and girl escaping the Nazis in Belorussia wade through and almost drown in a black bog that sucks at their bodies; and the first flashback sequence of Omaha Beach in *Saving Private Ryan* (1998, dir. Steven Spielberg). And in each case, I'd argue, it's the physicality rather than the "war-ness" of the scene that creates its impact.

Cinema inevitably understates the most intense real experiences. Yes, documentaries about Vietnam introduced a dose of reality into America's national perception of its misadventure there, but they could only do so because Washington and TV had painted such a fake picture of the fighting in the first place. The Vietnam documentaries marched America halfway back from its self-deluding untruth, but *only* halfway. Years ago, when I had photographs I'd taken in India developed, I realized a blindingly obvious fact. Photography doesn't capture smell. My pictures of the slums of Mumbai, the biggest in Asia, did not convey how terrible they are, partially because of my limited skills as a photographer, and partly because the medium itself is "optimistic" in the sense that it can't convey just how bad troubling things really are. A still or moving image of Mumbai's worst living conditions, even with sound, will always fail to capture their cacophony, their sensory overload, their enduring effect. Apply this thought to the question of war in cinema and words like "glamorize" and "sanitize" seem to be appropriate.

Which is, of course, to indict the medium I love. And no art form is really up to war—not *Guernica,* not *War and Peace,* not Benjamin Britten's *War Requiem,* not Käthe Kollwitz's sculptures. Take other themes, however, and cinema scores more highly. It is very good at travel and wanderlust—think road movies and Westerns. It is excellent at psychological flashback, trauma, and fear—in movies as diverse as Mai Zetterling's *Loving Couples/Älskande par* (1964), Krzysztof

Kieślowski's *Three Colors: Blue/Trois couleurs: Bleu* (1993), and Eduardo Sánchez and Daniel Myrick's *The Blair Witch Project* (1999).

I've been walking for some time now, and my mind turns to loneliness. Cinema is very good at loneliness. Movies, the kingdom of shadows, are its Mecca. I think of the Bill Douglas Trilogy (1972–1978), Billy Wilder's *The Apartment* (1960), most of the films of Chantal Akerman, Cissé's *Brightness/Yeelen* (1987), Kira Muratova's *Asthenic Syndrome/ Astenicheskiy sindrom* (1989), Agnès Varda's *Vagabond/Sans toit ni loi* (1985) or *Cléo from 5 to 7/Cléo de 5 à 7* (1961), Ingmar Bergman's *Winter Light/Nattvardsgästerna* (1963), or Mikio Naruse's *Flowing/ Nagareru* (1956). All about loneliness. Stick an individual up on the big screen, put a frame around them, watch them in the dark, and the experience is often about being alone. While it is defeated by war, the art of film is well placed to capture, to depict, and to celebrate things like human fear and loneliness. And, therefore, it matters.

And talking of which, I'm arriving at the cottage of one of the greatest filmmakers of loneliness, Bill Douglas. And . . . the plaque is still there right there on the wall! I must have missed it as I whizzed by. Relief. Markers matter.

As I look at his house, I scroll back on my phone at photos I took some years ago. The third part of his trilogy. Jamie, the wee boy whose life we've followed, who grew up where I'm standing, a fictional version of Bill, has grown up a bit. His painful shyness, his introversion, his carapace has softened a bit. It has softened enough for him to put his head on the shoulder of a posh, literate English man he's met . . . It's just a moment in the film, but it's revelatory. A rare tenderness in a film about harshness and coldness.

I thought about harshness and coldness as I did this walk. I think cinema is harsh and cold at the big things, but, when it sticks close to questions of self, confidence, and eros, of who rather than how; when it's about medium-sized things like aloneness and fear; when it doesn't bite off more than it can chew; when it does these things, film matters.

Today, as I walk in the sunlight, I can be seen from afar. But, in a cinema, I am unseen, unaware of myself, what Emerson called the transparent eyeball, what Virginia Woolf meant when she said, in her essay "Street Haunting," that "the eye is not a miner, not a diver, not a seeker after buried treasure. It floats."

Is that true of cinema, too?

Afterword

RADU JUDE

I am not a philosopher. So I don't see it as my place to offer any ideas or concepts to the question "what film is good for," or to state philosophically whether going to the cinema or, more broadly, film viewing, has any value. What I'd like to offer instead is a brief and modest recollection of how it all began for me and where I stand now—as a viewer.

We all know that the filmmakers and critics associated with the Nouvelle Vague started by watching films in ciné-clubs and in the Cinémathèque Française of Henri Langlois. Like painters who would go to museums to study the Old Masters, like young writers reading the classics, these people were going to the new museum of cinema and, as Jean-Luc Godard put it, they knew "that Griffith comes before Rossellini, that Renoir comes before Visconti and the exact moment of your appearance in a history that could already be recounted."[1]

I now realize that, because of the accidents of history, my film education had more or less the same shape as the one above: in my case, it was the Cinemateca Română in Bucharest, mostly. I come from a place and I belong to a generation that found itself at the beginning of their teenage years in the middle of a big change brought by the 1989 revolution: from a communist dictatorship to a more open society—call it democracy, capitalism, whatever. It was a time of big changes, anyway, and one of the institutions that changed was the Cinemateca Română. While before 1989, as I heard, it was a place very hard to get into, reserved for the elite of the regime, it reopened in 1993 and everybody

FIGURE 34. Vittoria (Monica Vitti) in *L'Eclisse* (1962, Michelangelo Antonioni).

could get access—yet almost nobody was interested in it anymore. A high school colleague who came from an intellectual family took me with him, and that was the beginning of a long-lasting passion. I started to go there as often as possible, avoiding, because of my shyness, the evening screenings, where I would have to encounter students, preferring, instead, the morning and daytime screenings, often skipping classes. Many times I was alone or only with two or three other people. Who were they? Cinephiles, of course, but also madmen, homeless people looking for shelter, retired people who didn't know what to do with their spare time, many lonely people. And, of course, there was no Mr. Langlois to present the films. The copies were sometimes okay, but most of the time they were black-and-white versions (I am speaking about films that were originally in color) or bad VHS tapes screened with a video projector. It was a special experience, because in those years—1993 to 1995, and less and less thereafter—there was still no real commercial television in Romania, and it was hard, if not impossible, to see those films in another medium (like VHS, which was mostly reserved for commercial films).

What has all this offered? In retrospect, I would say that the poor cinema screen wasn't the Athena's shield Siegfried Kracauer mentions—not at all. You might recall that at the end of his *Theory of Film*, Kracauer recounts the myth of the Gorgon Medusa, whose horrible face turned everyone who saw it into stone. When the goddess Athena asks Perseus to kill Medusa, she warns him not to look at the monster directly but rather at the mirror reflection in the shield she gave him. For Kracauer, the moral of the myth is that we can't face actual horrors directly because they would petrify us with fear. To know them, we need images that reproduce them accurately. Like Perseus, we need, so to speak, mirror reflections: "Now of all the existing media the cinema alone holds up a mirror to nature. Hence our dependence on it for the reflection of happenings which would petrify us were we to encounter them in real life. The film screen is Athena's polished shield."[2] In my film *Bad Luck Banging or Loony Porn* (2021), I raise this idea, quoting Kracauer.

But as far as my personal history with the cinema goes, at least, that perhaps sounds too important, too serious. My experience was mostly a joyful one. I would say it offered me something other than a shield. First, the cinema gave me eyes to see reality differently. After I watched Michelangelo Antonioni's *The Eclipse/L'Eclisse* (1962) and went out into the summer sun, the empty streets all of a sudden started to mean something else, and this feeling is still with me. It offered a certain kind of knowledge as well, even basic knowledge. If I know something about how an igloo is built, it is because of *Nanook of the North* (1922, dir. Robert J. Flaherty); all I know about African art has its origin in Alain Resnais, Chris Marker, and Ghislain Cloquet's film *Statues also Die/Les Statues meurent aussi* (1953); and tuna fishing exists for me only because of *Stromboli* (1950, dir. Roberto Rossellini). Of course, this kind of knowledge is not without its dangers. What can one learn about Native Americans if he or she watches only the classic Westerns? But, most important, and I know it might seem too much of a cliché—sorry for that, I cannot avoid it—cinema showed me that other people really exist. With their problems, with their bodies, with their language, with their faces, with their lives. Of course, one can get that knowledge from real life or maybe from television and Facebook nowadays, but there something is lacking: the solitude of *this* encounter and especially the intensity of *this* perception. And, I might add, that this intensity is often related to scarcity, which links it to my experience of Langlois's Cinémathèque. Many films were rarely screened and, when all of a sudden, after waiting for months, if not years, one could see a Murnau film, our attention was at its maximum. This doesn't happen to me as of late, when my hard disks are full with thousands of films I would never watch. Could this be also because of aging?

And now? What does cinema offer us today? As someone who makes films in a world so different from the one mentioned above, I can now understand Abbas Kiarostami, who said he never watches a film from the beginning to the end, only fragments. I read this many years ago, and I was puzzled by it. But now I do the same; it is enough to watch three minutes from a film of any kind. Even more, not only films, but all kinds of images do the job—an ad, a surveillance-camera monitor, a YouTube or a TikTok clip. Could this mean that cinema offers a specific thinking, no matter its so-called artistic quality? When I am optimistic, I believe so. Naum Kleiman mentions that Sergei Eisenstein's bookshelves were organized not alphabetically, thematically, or chronologically, but on montage principles.[3] *Ulysses* was put next to *Alice in Wonderland,* and a biography of Napoleon next to a book about biological anomalies. This is cinema, too, and I guess my montage-like mixing of all kinds of moving images—regardless of artistic quality—is a continuation of the same impulse. So perhaps cinema practiced in this fragmented contemporary form is like a shield of Athena after all. It might not mirror nature. But it certainly reflects a lot about ourselves in this present age.

NOTES

1. Jean-Luc Godard, Transcript accompanying *Histoire(s) du cinéma,* trans. John Howe, ECM Records 1706-10, 4 vols. (1999): 65.
2. Siegfried Kracauer, *Theory of Film: The Redemption of Physical Reality* (Princeton: Princeton University Press, 1960), 305.
3. See Ada Ackerman, *Eisenstein et Daumier: Des affinités électives* (Paris: Armand Colin, 2014), 38.

Contributors

MICHELE AARON is Professor of Film and Television at University of Warwick in Coventry, United Kingdom, and director of *Screening Rights Film Festival*. Author and editor of several books, she collaborates frequently with colleagues, community groups, and artists to explore further the potential for film to affect personal, social, and political change. Her first monograph was *Spectatorship: The Power of Looking On* (2007), and her most recent is the award-winning *Death and the Moving Image: Ideology, Iconography, and I* (2014). Her latest article, "Love's Revival: Film Practice and the Art of Dying," won *Film-Philosophy*'s annual article award for 2021.

DUDLEY ANDREW is R. Selden Rose Professor Emeritus of Comparative Literature and Professor Emeritus of Film Studies at Yale University in New Haven, Connecticut. His books include the biography of *André Bazin* (enlarged edition: 2013, first published: 1978), whose ideas he extends in *What Cinema Is!* (2010), *Opening Bazin* (2011), and in his editing and translating of themed collections of Bazin. With two books on 1930s French Cinema, Andrew was named Commandeur de l'Ordre des Arts et des Lettres. He is a member of the American Academy of Arts and Sciences and gained the Lifetime Achievement Award from the Society for Cinema and Media Studies. His current projects include issues in world cinema and comparative arts.

NICHOLAS BAER is Assistant Professor of Media, Arts & Society in the Department of Media and Culture Studies at Utrecht University, the Netherlands. He is author of the forthcoming monograph *Historical Turns: Weimar Cinema and the Crisis of Historicism*, and co-editor of two volumes of film and media theory: the award-winning *The Promise of Cinema: German Film Theory, 1907–1933* (2016) and *Unwatchable* (2019). Baer has published on film and media, critical theory, and intellectual history in journals such as *Film Quarterly*,

Krisis: Journal for Contemporary Philosophy, Los Angeles Review of Books, NECSUS: European Journal of Media Studies, Public Seminar, and *October,* and his writings have been translated into six languages.

JAIMIE BARON is Professor of Film Studies at the University of Alberta in Edmonton, Canada. She is the author of *The Archive Effect: Found Footage and the Audiovisual Experience of History* (2014) and *Reuse, Misuse, Abuse: The Ethics of Audiovisual Appropriation in the Digital Era* (2020), as well as many journal articles and book chapters. She is the founder, director, and co-curator of the *Festival of (In)appropriation,* a yearly international festival of short experimental found-footage films and videos. She is also a co-founder and co-editor of *Docalogue,* an online space for scholars and filmmakers to engage in conversations about contemporary documentary, as well as the *Docalogue* book series published by Routledge.

MARTINE BEUGNET is Professor in Visual Studies at Université Paris Cité and a member of the Laboratoire de Recherche sur les Cultures Anglophones (LARCA). She has written articles on a wide range of film and media topics, as well as several books on cinema. The most recent include *L'Attrait du flou* (2017), the edited volume *Indefinite Visions: Cinema and the Attractions of Uncertainty* (2017, with Allan Cameron and Arild Fetveit), and *Le cinéma et ses doubles: L'image de film à l'ère du foundfootage numérisé et des écrans de poche* (2021). She co-directs, with Kriss Ravetto, the Edinburgh University Press series *Studies in Film and Intermediality.*

FRANCESCO CASETTI is Sterling Professor of Humanities and Film and Media Studies at Yale University in New Haven, Connecticut. He is the author of *Inside the Gaze: The Fiction Film and Its Spectator* (1999), *Theories of Cinema, 1945–1995* (1999), *Eye of the Century: Film, Experience, Modernity* (2005), and *The Lumière Galaxy: Seven Key Words for the Cinema to Come* (2015). His current research focuses on film theories, especially the cinephobic stances in the first half of the twentieth century, and on a multimedia reconsideration of the screen in its spatial connotations and as a component of our current "mediascape."

DOMINIQUE CHATEAU is Professor Emeritus of Aesthetics and Cinema at the Sorbonne School of the Arts at Panthéon-Sorbonne University, Paris I. His books include *Cinéma et philosophie* (2003), *Philosophies du cinéma* (2010), *Subjectivity* (ed. 2011), *L'invention du concept de montage: Lev Kouléchov, théoricien du cinéma* (2013), *La direction de spectateur* (ed. 2015), *Après Charlie: Le déni de la représentation* (2016), *Screens* (ed. 2016), *Contribution à l'histoire du concept de montage* (2019), *Esthétique de la recréation* (ed. 2019), *Une esthétique japonaise* (2019), and *Post-Cinema in the Post-Art Era* (ed. 2020).

MICHEL CHION is a composer of musique concrète, filmmaker, critic, and the author of numerous articles and books on film sound and perception, most notably *Audio-Vision: Sound on Screen* (1994), *Film, a Sound Art* (2009), and *Music in Cinema* (2021), all translated by Claudia Gorbman. He is Honorary Professor at the University of Buenos Aires. From 1994 to 2012 he lectured at

Paris III-Sorbonne Nouvelle and, since 1990, at the École supérieure d'études cinématographiques (ESEC). He was member of the Groupe de Recherches Musicales from 1971 to 1976 and a member of the *Cahiers du Cinéma*'s editorial team from 1982 to 1987. His blog can be found at http://michelchion.com/blog.

SARAH COOPER is Professor of Film Studies at King's College London. Her books include *Film and the Imagined Image* (2019), *The Soul of Film Theory* (2013), *Chris Marker* (2008), and *Selfless Cinema? Ethics and French Documentary* (2006). She has also edited special issues of the journals *Film-Philosophy*, "The Occluded Relation: Levinas and Cinema" (2007), *Paragraph*, "New Takes on Film and Imagination" (2020), and *Philosophies*, "Thinking Cinema—With Plants" (2023).

TIMOTHY CORRIGAN is a Professor Emeritus of Cinema and Media Studies at the University of Pennsylvania in Philadelphia. His books include *New German Film: The Displaced Image* (1983); *The Films of Werner Herzog: Between Mirage and History* (1986); *A Cinema Without Walls* (1991); *Film and Literature: An Introduction and Reader* (1999); *The Film Experience* (2004, co-authored with Patricia White); *American Cinema of the 2000s* (2012); and *The Essay Film: From Montaigne, After Marker* (2011), winner of the 2012 Katherine Singer Kovács Award for an outstanding book in film and media studies. In 2014 he was awarded the Society for Cinema and Media Studies Award for Outstanding Pedagogical Achievement and the Ira H. Abrams Memorial Award for Distinguished Teaching at the University of Pennsylvania.

MARK COUSINS is an Irish Scottish filmmaker and writer. His films—including *The First Movie* (2009), *The Story of Film: An Odyssey* (2011), *Atomic* (2015), *The Eyes of Orson Welles* (2018), and *Women Make Film* (2018)—have won the Prix Italia, a Peabody Award, the Stanley Kubrick Award, and the European Film Academy Award for Innovative Storytelling. They have premiered at the world's major film festivals. Their themes are looking, cities, cinema, childhood, and recovery. His books include *Imagining Reality: The Faber Book of Documentary* (1998, with Kevin Macdonald), *The Story of Film* (2004), and *The Story of Looking* (2017). He has walked across Los Angeles, Moscow, Beijing, and Mexico City.

TIAGO DE LUCA is Associate Professor (Reader) in Film Studies at the University of Warwick in Coventry, United Kingdom. He is the author of *Realism of the Senses in World Cinema: The Experience of Physical Reality* (2014) and *Planetary Cinema: Film, Media and the Earth* (2022). He is the editor (with Nuno Barradas Jorge) of *Slow Cinema* (2016) and (with Lúcia Nagib and Luciana Corrêa de Araújo) *Towards an Intermedial History of Brazilian Cinema* (2022).

JENS EDER is Professor of Dramaturgy and Aesthetics of Audiovisual Media at Film University Babelsberg KONRAD WOLF in Potsdam, Germany. His research focuses on narration, reception, societal relations, and current developments of audiovisual media. Some of his publications are available also in English, such as *Image Operations: Visual Media and Political Conflict* (co-edited with Charlotte Klonk, 2017) and the issue "#Emotions" of the journal NECSUS (co-edited with Julian Hanich and Jane Stadler, 2019). Two books are forthcoming: *Film Character: Theory, Analysis, Interpretation* and *Video-Activism in Social Media* (with Britta Hartmann and Chris Tedjasukmana).

MARYANN ERIGHA LAWER is Associate Professor of Sociology and African American Studies at the University of Georgia in Athens, Georgia. Her research examines the production and circulation of popular media messages about race. Her scholarship is situated at the intersections of race and racism, media and popular culture, and technology and society. She is particularly interested in African American cinema and Black digital studies. She is the author of *The Hollywood Jim Crow: The Racial Politics of the Movie Industry* (2018), which examines practices of racial inequality in Hollywood through the lens of film directing.

JENNIFER FAY is the Gertrude Conaway Vanderbilt Professor of Cinema & Media Arts and Chair of the Department of English at Vanderbilt University in Nashville, Tennessee. She is the author of *Theaters of Occupation: Hollywood and the Reeducation of Postwar Germany* (2008) and *Inhospitable World: Cinema in the Time of the Anthropocene* (2018), and co-author of *Film Noir: Hard Boiled Modernity and the Cultures of Globalization* (2010).

CHRISTIAN FERENCZ-FLATZ is a researcher at the Alexandru Dragomir Institute for Philosophy and teaches at the National University of Theater and Film. His research interests comprise classical German phenomenology, critical theory, as well as film and image theories. His most recent publications include the monographs *Phenomenology and Critical Theory: Polemics, Appropriations, Perspectives* (2023), *Sehen Als-ob. Ästhetik und Pragmatik in Husserls Bildlehre* (2016), and *Filmul ca situație socială* (2018), as well as three issues of *Studia Phaenomenologica*, "Film and Phenomenology" (2016, with Julian Hanich), "The Promise of Genetic Phenomenology" (2018, with Andrea Staiti), and "Gestures" (2022, with Delia Popa).

MIKE FIGGIS is an award-winning British film director, writer, composer, musician, and stage performer. His films include *Cold Creek Manor* (2003), *The Loss of Sexual Innocence* (1999), *One Night Stand* (1997), and *Internal Affairs* (1990). For *Leaving Las Vegas* (1995) he received Academy Award nominations for Best Director and Best Screenplay. His most experimental film is *Timecode* (2000). The film pioneered digital filmmaking and consists of four continuous 93-minute takes that were shot simultaneously by four cameras for the purpose of simultaneous projection on a screen divided into four quarters. Figgis has been Professor of Film at the European Graduate School in Saas-Fee, Switzerland, since 2008.

TOM GUNNING is Professor Emeritus in the Department of Cinema and Media at the University of Chicago. He is the author of *D. W. Griffith and the Origins of American Narrative Film* (1986) and *The Films of Fritz Lang: Allegories of Vision and Modernity* (2000), as well as more than 150 articles on early cinema, film history and theory, avant-garde film, film genre, and cinema and modernism. With André Gaudreault he originated the influential theory of the "Cinema of

Attractions." In 2009 he was awarded an Andrew A. Mellon Distinguished Achievement Award and in 2010 was elected to the American Academy of Arts and Sciences. He is currently working on a book on the invention of the moving image. His theater piece *Fantomas: The Revenge of the Image*, created in collaboration with director Travis Preston, premiered in 2017 at the Wuzhen International Theater Festival in Wuzhen, China.

JULIAN HANICH is Associate Professor of Film Studies at the University of Groningen, The Netherlands. He is the author of three monographs: *Friedrich Wilhelm Murnau: City Girl* (2022), *The Audience Effect: On the Collective Cinema Experience* (2018), and *Cinematic Emotion in Horror Films and Thrillers: The Aesthetic Paradox of Pleasurable Fear* (2010). With Daniel Fairfax, he co-edited *The Structures of the Film Experience by Jean-Pierre Munier: Historical Assessments and Phenomenological Expansions* (2019); and with Christian Ferencz-Flatz he was responsible for an issue of *Studia Phaenomenologica* on "Film and Phenomenology" (2016). His research focuses on cinematic emotions, film and imagination, film phenomenology, the collective cinema experience, and film aesthetics.

SEUNG-HOON JEONG is Assistant Professor of Film and Electronic Arts at California State University Long Beach. He wrote *Cinematic Interfaces: Film Theory after New Media* (2013), co-translated Jacques Derrida's *Acts of Literature* into Korean (2013), co-edited *The Global Auteur: The Politics of Authorship in 21st Century Cinema* (2016), guest-edited an issue of *Studies in the Humanities* on "Global East Asian Cinema: Abjection and Agency" (2019), co-edited Thomas Elsaesser's *The Mind-Game Film: Distributed Agency, Time Travel, and Productive Pathology* (2021), and wrote *Biopolitical Ethics in Global Cinema* (New York: Oxford University Press, 2023).

RADU JUDE is one of the leading Eastern European writer-directors. He studied filmmaking in Bucharest. In 2006, his short film debut, *The Tube with a Hat/Lampa cu căciulă*, won the main award at Sundance. His feature debut, *The Happiest Girl in the World/Cea mai fericită fată din lume* (2009), was selected by more than fifty international film festivals. At the Berlin Film Festival, he was awarded both the Silver Bear for *Aferim!* in 2015 and the Golden Bear for *Bad Luck Banging or Loony Porn/Babardeală cu bucluc sau porno balamuc* in 2021. He has also won major awards at the festivals in Locarno and Karlovy Vary. His latest feature film is entitled *Do Not Expect Too Much from the End of the World* (2023).

GEOFF KING is Professor of Film Studies at Brunel University London and author of books including *The Cinema of Discomfort: Disquieting, Awkward, and Uncomfortable Experiences in Contemporary Art and Indie Film* (2021), *Positioning Art Cinema: Film and Cultural Value* (2019), *Quality Hollywood: Markers of Distinction in Contemporary Studio Film* (2016), *Indie 2.0: Change and Continuity in Contemporary American Indie Film* (2014), *Indiewood, USA: Where Hollywood Meets Independent Cinema* (2009), and *American Independent Cinema* (2005).

KATHLEEN LOOCK is Professor of American Studies and Media Studies at Leibniz University in Hannover, Germany, and director of the research group

"Hollywood Memories: Cinematic Remaking and the Construction of Global Movie Generations," funded by the German Research Foundation (DFG). Her research focuses on film remakes, sequels and reboots, seriality, and the role memory and cultural repetition perform on the level of identity formation and for the construction and maintenance of imagined communities. She is author of *Kolumbus in den USA* (2014) and her forthcoming second book, *Hollywood Remaking* (2024).

LAURA U. MARKS, FRSC, is Grant Strate Professor in the School for the Contemporary Arts at Simon Fraser University in Vancouver, Canada. She works on media art and philosophy with an intercultural focus and an emphasis on appropriate technologies. Her fifth book, *The Fold: From Your Body to the Cosmos,* is forthcoming from Duke University Press. With Azadeh Emadi, she is a founding member of the Substantial Motion Research Network (htttps://substantialmotion.org). She programs experimental media art for venues around the world and founded the *Small File Media Festival* (https://smallfile.ca).

ADRIAN MARTIN is an arts critic and audiovisual essayist based in Spain, and Adjunct Professor of Film and Screen Studies at Monash University in Melbourne, Australia. He is the author of nine books, including *Filmmakers Thinking* (2021), *Mysteries of Cinema* (2018), *Mise en Scène and Film Style* (2014), *Last Day Every Day* (2012), *The Mad Max Movies* (2003), and *Once Upon a Time in America* (1998). He frequently provides audio commentaries for DVD/Blu-ray releases. His online archive covering more than forty years of work is at www.filmcritic.com.au.

LITHEKO MODISANE is Senior Lecturer in the Center for Film and Media Studies at the University of Cape Town. He is also a film review editor for *African Studies Review.* Modisane earned his Ph.D. at the University of the Witwatersrand in Johannesburg. Author of the award-winning *South Africa's Renegade Reels: The Making and Public Lives of Black Centered Films* (2013), Modisane has also written several book chapters and articles on South African film and media. His major research area is the intersection of film and public-sphere theory.

SHEILA J. NAYAR teaches in the Department of Film & Media Arts at the University of Utah in Salt Lake City. Her research interests include the interplay of narrative and phenomenology, especially in the context of orality and alphabetic literacy. Her publications in that regard include *Cinematically Speaking: The Orality-Literacy Paradigm for Visual Narrative* (2010), *The Sacred and the Cinema* (2012), and *Before Literature: The Nature of Narrative Without the Written Word* (2019), as well as articles in *Film Quarterly, PMLA,* and *JAAR* among others. Currently, she is working on a monograph on secularism and Hindi popular cinema.

CARL PLANTINGA is Arthur H. DeKruyter Chair of Communication and Professor of Film and Media at Calvin University in Grand Rapids, Michigan. His latest books are *Alternative Realities* (2020), a study of the porous distinction between realism and fantasy, and *Screen Stories: Emotion and the Ethics of Engagement* (2018), on the ethics of storytelling on screens. He is also co-editor of *The Routledge Companion to Philosophy and Film* (2009) and *Passionate Views: Film, Cognition, and Emotion* (1999). Plantinga is former president of the Society for Cognitive Studies of the Moving Image.

MARTIN P. ROSSOUW is head of the Department of Art History and Image Studies, University of the Free State, South Africa, where he teaches as Senior Lecturer in Film and Visual Media. He is the author of *Transformational Ethics of Film: Thinking the Cinemakeover in the Film-Philosophy Debate* (2021), as well as the editor of Brill's *Contemporary Cinema* book series. His most recent work appears in the publications *Literature/Film Quarterly*, *Short Film Studies*, *Akademisk Kvarter*, *Image & Text*, and *New Review of Film and Television Studies*.

ROBERT SINNERBRINK is Associate Professor of Philosophy and former Australian Research Council Future Fellow at Macquarie University, Sydney. He is the author of *New Philosophies of Film (Second Edition): An Introduction to Cinema as a Way of Thinking* (2022), *Terrence Malick: Filmmaker and Philosopher* (2019), *Cinematic Ethics: Exploring Ethical Experience through Film* (2016), *New Philosophies of Film: Thinking Images* (2011), and *Understanding Hegelianism* (2007). He is also a member of the editorial boards of the journals *Film-Philosophy*, *Film and Philosophy*, and *Projections: The Journal of Movies and Mind*.

GARRETT STRPKO is an award-winning filmmaker and graduate student in Communication Arts at the University of Wisconsin–Madison. His primary areas of interest range from film phenomenology to postwar American cinema and video game studies. His research currently focuses on how representations of history in different media situate the spectator's relationship with the past. His article "Most Decorated Soldier: Negotiating Combat Trauma in the Stardom of Audie Murphy" was recently published in the *Quarterly Review of Film and Video*.

MALCOLM TURVEY is Sol Gittleman Professor in the Department of History of Art and Architecture and Director of the Film and Media Studies Program at Tufts University in Medford, Massachusetts. He is also an editor of the journal *October*. He is the author of *Doubting Vision: Film and the Revelationist Tradition* (2008) and *The Filming of Modern Life: European Avant-Garde Film of the 1920s* (2011), and the co-editor of *Wittgenstein, Theory, and the Arts* (2001). His *Play Time: Jacques Tati and Comedic Modernism* was published in 2019.

ANNIE VAN DEN OEVER is Associate Professor of Film at the University of Groningen, The Netherlands, and Professor by special appointment to the chair in Film and Visual Media at the University of the Free State in Bloemfontein, South Africa. Her books include *Life Itself* (2008), *Ostrannenie* (ed. 2010), *Sensitizing the Viewer* (2011), *Foundational Questions for a Film and Visual Media Programme* (inaugural lecture, 2014), *Technē/Technology* (ed. 2014), *Exposing the Film Apparatus* (ed. 2016, with Giovanna Fossati), *Stories* (ed. 2018, with Ian Christie), and *Doing Experimental Media Archaeology: Theory* (2022, with Andreas Fickers).

THOMAS E. WARTENBERG is Professor of Philosophy Emeritus at Mount Holyoke College in South Hadley, Massachusetts. His main areas of focus are aesthetics, the philosophy of film, and philosophy for children. Among his publications are *Unlikely Couples: Movie Romance as Social Criticism* (1999), *Thinking on Screen: Film as Philosophy* (2007), *Big Ideas for Little Kids: Teaching Philosophy through Children's Literature* (2014), and *Thoughtful Images: Illustrating Philosophy through Art* (2023). His philosophy for children website, teachingchildrenphilosophy.org, was awarded the 2011 APA/PDC Prize for Excellence and Innovations in Philosophy Programs. He received the 2013 Merritt Prize for his contributions to the philosophy of education. He is the editor of film topics for the magazine *Philosophy Now*.

CATHERINE WHEATLEY is Reader in Film and Visual Culture at King's College London. She has published widely on questions pertaining to film, ethics, and aesthetics, and is the author of four monographs, the most recent of which is *Stanley Cavell and Film: Scepticism and Self-Reliance at the Cinema* (2019). She also writes regularly for *Sight & Sound* magazine and is a convenor of the BFI's *Philosophical Screens* series.

DANIEL YACAVONE has been Senior Lecturer (Associate Professor) and Director of the Film Studies Program at the University of Edinburgh; Senior Research Fellow at the Cinepoetics Center for Advanced Film Studies, Freie Universität Berlin; and currently holds a fellowship in residence at the Netherlands Institute for Advanced Study in the Humanities and Social Sciences (NIAS), Amsterdam, where he was also a fellow in 2020–2021. The author of *Film Worlds: A Philosophical Aesthetics of Cinema* (2015), he is currently writing a book on reflexivity, affect, and intermediality in cinema, and co-editing (with Steffen Hven) *The Oxford Handbook of Moving Image Atmospheres and Felt Environments*.

Index

10 Things I Hate About You (film), 330
12 Years a Slave (film), 94, 120, 184–85
24/7: Late Capitalism and the Ends of Sleep, 334–35
2012 (film), 19

abjection, 84–89
abject lives, 80–89
Aboriginal characters, 384
academia, 40–41, 121–22
access to film, 44
access to internet, 24, 30–31
action, emphasis on, 265–66
Act of Killing, The (film), 104
Adorno, Theodor W., 70, 300–310, 301*fig.*, 346, 373
aesthetic dimension of cinema, 60–61, 138–43, 159–60, 211, 216. *See also* attractiveness; beauty
"Aesthetic of Astonishment, An" (essay), 164
aesthetic worlds, 138, 140–42
affect, 31–32, 57–65, 105–9, 121, 141–44, 146–47, 201, 210–11, 218
affective empathy, 93–94. *See also* empathy
Afghanistan, 264
African American cinema, 239–40
African National Congress (ANC), 75–76
aggression. *See* violence
Ahmed, Sara, 189–91, 193–94
Akaret, Julie, 122

alienation, 49–50, 64, 193, 352–55, 372–73, 375
allegory, 108, 343, 369–70, 376
Allison, Deborah, 329
altruism, 96
ambiguity, 20, 75–76, 123, 181, 261–62, 269–70, 283, 296
American Cinema/American Culture, 365–66
American Son (film), 241–46
ANC. *See* African National Congress
Andrew, Geoff, 165–66
"anew, as if," 190–93, 195–96, 390
animals, killing of, 363–64
animated and animating medium, film as, 309–10
Annihilation (film), 178*fig.*, 180–81
Another Gaze, 44
"Another Screen" (streaming platform), 44
Anthropocene, 13, 18–20, 146. *See also* climate change
antisocial thrill of cinema, 339–47
Antonioni, Michelangelo, 389*fig.*, 390
anxiety, 17–19, 291–92, 294–95
apartheid, 71, 73–76
apocalyptic scenarios, 15–19. *See also* catastrophes
Aravamudan, Srinivas, 18–19
Arendt, Hannah, 184, 217, 278, 283, 285n19
Aristotle, 6–7, 10n16
Armstrong, John, 166, 170

Index

Arnheim, Rudolf, 141, 150, 274
art and indie films, 128–36, 275
"Art et Essai" (circuit of theaters), 280
art, film as, 70, 150–53, 191, 379
art historians, 314
art history, 165, 314
artistic beauty, 162, 170
Assassin, The/Cikè Nie Yinniáng (film), 163*fig.*, 171
Astruc, Alexandre, 328
atopia, 86–88. *See also* utopia
Attenborough, Sir Richard, 69, 74, 75
attention of viewers, 70, 109, 156, 158–59, 182–83, 333–35
attractiveness, 98–99, 364–65. *See also* aesthetic dimension of cinema; beauty
audiences, 70–71, 119, 276, 371–73. *See also* spectatorship
Australia, 384
auteurism, 281–83, 328
autism, 64–65
avant-garde, 141, 164, 281–82, 316, 341–42, 374
Avatar (film), 103, 262–63, 267
Avengers: Endgame (film), 262–63, 262*fig.*, 268
Avengers film series, 264
Awful Truth, The (film), 195

Baahuabli 2: The Conclusion (film), 262–63
Bachchan, Amitabh, 380
Bacurau (film), 328
Badiou, Alain, 82
Bad Luck Banging or Loony Porn (film), 390
badness, 340–41, 363–67
Balsom, Erika, 323n16
banning and censorship, 73–77, 279–80
Barthes, Roland, 169, 267, 278, 279, 289, 372–73
Batson, C. Daniel, 96
Baumberger, Christoph, 118
Baumgarten, Alexander, 141–42
Bazin, André, 54n4, 164, 218, 275–83, 321, 364, 372
"Beautiful Relaxing Music for Stress Relief" (YouTube video), 29
beauty, 7, 120, 162–71, 370. *See also* aesthetic dimension of cinema; attractiveness
"Beauty Is a Method" (essay), 170–71
Becker, Oskar, 150, 152, 159–60
Beckham, David, 383–84

"Beiträge zu einer Phänomenologie des ästhetischen Genusses" (essay), 152
Bellissima (film), 371
Belton, John, 365–66
Benjamin, Walter, 16, 154, 293, 295–96, 351, 354, 356, 357
Beowulf, 266
Berger, John, xii
Bergman, Ingmar, xiii, 281, 282, 344, 387
Bergson, Henri, 140, 310
Berliner, Todd, 131–33
Berlin Wall, fall of, 83
Biko, Steven Bantu, 74–75
Bill Douglas Trilogy (films), 379*fig.*
binge-watching, 221, 332
Birds, The (film), 381
Birth of a Nation, The (film), 92*fig.*, 96–97, 119
#BlackLivesMatter films, 237–41, 244–47
Black Panther (film), 104, 110
Blade Runner (film), 140
Blade Runner 2049 (film), 87
"blank" style, 130–31
Blaxploitation films, 239
Blissfully Yours (film), 151*fig.*
Bloom, Paul, 93–94, 97–99
Blow Out (film), 364–65
Blue Planet, The (film), 105
Blues Brothers, The (film), 363
Blue Velvet (film), 123, 350–51, 354
Blu-rays, 26
Body Snatchers (1993) (film), 343–45
Body Snatchers, The (novel), 343
"bold" film-philosophy, 209, 212
Bolsonaro, Jair, 328
Booth, Wayne, 121
Bordwell, David, 166, 330
boredom, 154–60, 373, 375
Borgen (television show), 119
Bourdieu, Pierre, 130, 133, 134
Bowie, David, 330
Bowling for Columbine (film), 385
Brazilian films, 328
Breaking Bad (television show), 123
Brecht, Bertolt, 89, 139, 193, 194
Bringing Up Baby (film), 195
Britain. *See* United Kingdom
Brophy, Philip, 339
Brown, Norman O., 346
Bryant, Ma'Khia, 241
"bubbles," 293, 295
Buñuel, Luis, 54n6, 199–200, 349, 358
Burgin, Victor, 186
Butler, Judith, 317

Caché (film), 330–31
Cage, John, xi
Cahiers du Cinéma, 276, 280–81, 365
capitalism, 13, 83, 85–86, 327, 334
Capitalism: A Love Story (film), 104
car chases, 362–63. *See also* driving
Carroll, Noël, 4, 5, 120, 201, 204, 206, 226
Casey, Edward, 178–79
catachronism, 19
catastrophes, 84, 85. *See also* apocalyptic scenarios
catharsis, 139–40, 344, 358
Cathy Come Home (film), 385
Cavell, Stanley, 3–4, 188–89, 193–96, 199–201, 207, 209, 220n32, 223, 226–28, 274–76, 281–82, 298n12
Cave, Nick, 340, 346
cell phones. *See* mobile phones
censorship and banning, 73–77, 279–80
Chan, Jackie, 330
Chang, Justin, 20–21
change, 253–54
Chaplin, Charlie, 22, 279, 373
characterizations in oral milieu, 264–68
Charlie Hebdo attacks, 82
Chaudhuri, Una, 54n3
Chauvin, Derek, 240–41
Chesterton, G. K., 188
chest hair, 381
childhood, 193–95
Children of Men (film), 86–87, 327fig.
Chinatown (film), 144
Cho, Francisca, 223
Cinema and Experience, 353
cinema of discomfort, 130–34
Cinema of Unease (film), 384
cinemas. *See* movie theaters, watching films in
Cinemateca Română, 388–89
Cinémathèque Française, 280, 388, 390
"cinematic ethics," 201–3, 210–11
Cinematic Ethics, 201–3
cinempathy, 201. *See also* empathy
cinephilia, 31–32, 218, 278, 315, 345–46
cinephobia, 293
Cineworld advertisement, 57–58, 65
Clarks marketing campaign, 193
climate change, 13, 15–22, 30. *See also* Anthropocene
climate fiction films, 17–18
close-ups, 302, 318–19, 354
closing credits. *See* end credits
closure, 181

CMOS scaling, 27
coduction, 121–22, 125
Coetzee, Carli, 73, 76
Cold War, 18, 82–83
collective viewing, 26, 140, 229, 316–18, 376
colonialism, 58–64, 71–74, 82
Colors (film), 380
Come and See/Idi i smotri (film), 386
comedy of remarriage, 194–95, 199–200, 227–28, 275
Comic-Con, 123–24
"coming to wonder," 188–89. *See also* wonder
communal viewing, 26, 140, 229, 316–18, 371–73, 376. *See also* spectatorship
communities, standpoint of, 245–46
companionship, 371–73, 375
compassion, 51, 84, 91, 93, 95, 106. *See also* empathy
Complete Etchings of Goya, The, 345
Congress of Traditional Leaders in South Africa, 76–77
connectedness, 43, 145–47
considered empathy, 99. *See also* empathy
consumerism, 326–27, 332, 334–35
contemplation, 145, 167–69, 226, 228, 334–35. *See also* moral reflection; reflection
"content," concept of, xii, 331, 335
contextualization, 178–79, 183, 367
continuity, 250–54, 258
"cool" media, 33
cosmopolitanism, 87–88
Couchot, Edmund, 351, 356
Covid-19 pandemic, 13–14, 36–38, 40–44, 185–86, 249, 315, 378–79
Crary, Jonathan, 334–35
credits. *See* end credits
Critchley, Simon, 38
critics, 122–23, 166, 277–79
Critique of Judgment, The, 370
Critique of Pure Reason, The, 201
Crumb, Robert, 353
Cry Freedom (film), 74–75
Cuarón, Alfonso, 86, 327fig., 331
Cube (art house cinema), 44
"Cult of Distraction" (essay), 153
cultural memory, 254–55. *See also* memory
Cunningham, Stuart, 346
Currie, Gregory, 91–92, 95, 99
Curzon cinemas, 37, 37fig.
cuteness, 98–99

404 | Index

Dalle Vacche, Angela, 283
Daney, Serge, 89
danger, 258, 268–69, 361–67
Danto, Arthur C., 162, 215
Dardenne, Jean-Pierre and Luc, 39–40, 80, 81fig.
David, Ian, 344
"David Lynch Keeps His Head" (essay), 351
Davis, Colin, 220n32
Day After Tomorrow, The (film), 104
death, 61–62, 85, 89, 184, 226, 240–41, 342, 364–65
deception of viewers, 205–6
"decolonial aesthesis," 60
decontextualization, 178–79, 183, 367
"deep" vs "superficial," 154–56. See also depth of experience
defamiliarization, 193, 370. See also "making strange"; ostran(n)enie
Deleuze, Gilles, 28, 62, 135, 140–41, 209, 220n32, 223, 310, 321
delinking, 60–61
Democratic Republic of the Congo, 28
demonstrations (protests), 317
De Niro, Robert, 365, 381, 383
depth of experience, 150–60
Derrida, Jacques, 86
Descartes, René, 189, 190, 193–94, 225, 305, 309
destruction, 339–47, 364–66
devices, individual screening, 30–31, 315, 318–19, 321–22
DeVito, Danny, 339–40
dialogue-free films, 20–21
diegesis, 182, 185–86
diegetic worlds, 139, 331
differently, seeing, 190–93, 195–96, 390
Dilemma (film), 74
Dill-Shackelford, Karen E., 123
Dionysian epistemology, 346
disaster films, 17–18, 341–43
discipline, 294–97
discomfort, 130–34
discriminating empathy, 99. See also empathy
disgust, 71, 84, 132
disinterestedness, 168, 270
displacements, 48–50
Dissanayake, Wimal, 267
Doc Society, 105
documentaries, 31–32, 39, 88, 104–5, 238–39, 386
Dogtooth/Kynodontas (film), 129fig., 133

Dogville (film), 139, 139fig., 330
Dome (film), 110
domination, 64–65
"double death," 85
Douglas, Bill, 379fig., 383, 387
dreams, 353, 355–58
driving, 242–43. See also car chases
dualistic thinking, 265
Duplex (film), 339–40, 347
Dussel, Enrique, 59–62
DVDs, 26–27, 40, 314, 331, 371
Dyer, Richard, 131, 133

Eastwood, Clint, 340, 365
Eastwood, Steven, 64–65
Ebert, Roger, 123
Eclipse, The/L'Eclisse (film), 389fig., 390
eco-disaster films, 17–19
ecological thought, 43
ecology of spectatorship, 42–44
economic issues, xii, 41–44, 50–52, 57, 328
Écran français, 276, 280
edgy films, 281
education, 40–41, 122
Eisenstein, Sergei, 88, 142, 318, 323n8, 354, 391
electricity, 26–30
electrons, 26–28
Elf (film), 193
elitism, 128–29, 212–13, 323n16
Elsaesser, Thomas, 2–4, 87
Elvira Madigan (film), 170
Emadi, Azadeh, 33
Emerson, Ralph Waldo, 3, 188, 194, 200, 227–28, 387
Emmerich, Roland, 17, 19, 104
emotions, 57–65, 106–7
empathy, 7, 8, 91–99, 109, 186, 238, 244–47, 316; affective empathy, 93–94; cinempathy, 201; considered empathy, 99; discriminating empathy, 99; empathy-avoidance behavior, 94; intelligent empathy, 99
emplacements, 47–48
end credits, 326–35, 327fig.
endings of films, 181
end of history, 81–82
engagement. See public engagement
Enrico, Robert, xiifig., xiii
"entertainment education," 104–5, 110
Entertainment Weekly, 123, 251
enthymemes, 120–21, 123
environmental problems, 43. See also climate change

epistemological clarity, 305–6
Erll, Astrid, 256
erotetic theory of film narration, 201, 204, 206
escapism, 41, 128, 380
Eskilsson, Tomas, 37, 38, 42
Esprit, 276–77, 283
Estevez, Emilio, 347
ethics of film, concept of, 1–10
Eurocentrism, 59–62, 109–10, 135
evil, 369
exaggeration, 342, 346
exhilaration, 132–34
"expansions of the self," 228
experience, 143–45, 150–60, 335
experimental films, 104, 191
extratextual memory, 255. *See also* memory

Facebook, 125
"face of the other," 86
families, 245–46
fan culture, 123–25, 258
fan fiction, 124–25
Fanny and Alexander/Fanny och Alexander (film), 344
Farber, Manny, 345
fashion, 380–81
feelings, 57–65, 106–7
feminism, 62, 194
Ferrara, Abel, 343
fictional worlds of films, 140–43
film, use of term, 8
film as philosophy debate, 223–24, 230
"Film as the Discoverer of the Marvels of Everyday Life" (essay), 178
Film History as Media Archaeology, 2–3
film noir, 49, 205–6, 226
film-philosophy, 39, 209, 211–16. *See also* philosophy
financial value of film, xii, 41–44, 57, 328
Finding Truth in Fiction, 123
Finney, Jack, 343
First Kiss (film), 189fig.
Fisher, Philip, 190–92, 197n20
Five Dedicated to Ozu (film), 163–66, 168
"flight from beauty," 164–67
Floyd, George, 240–41
Folding Ideas (YouTube channel), 125
Ford, John, 48–50
Formalism in Ethics, 152–53
form of films, 106–9
Foster, Jodie, 117, 118fig., 365–66
Foucault, Michel, 221, 229, 295, 371–72

fragmentation, 258, 391
frames, 320–22, 325n29
France, 384–85
Frankfurt School philosophers, 70
"fresh contact," 257
Freud, Sigmund, 154, 266, 352, 353, 358, 379
Fridays for Future movement, 110
friendship, 51, 64, 227
Frodon, Jean-Michel, 384
frontline workers, 378–79
Fruitvale Station (film), 238fig., 241–43, 245–46
Frye, Northrop, 195
Fundamental Concepts of Metaphysics, The (lecture course), 154–55
fundraising videos, 110

Gabriel, Teshome, 62
Gadjo Dilo (film), 384
Gaï, Djeïnaba Diop, 76
Game of Thrones (television show), 332
games, online, 32
Gans, Herbert, 134
Gatlif, Tony, 384
Geiger, Moritz, 150–54, 158, 159
gender, 76–77, 382
generations. *See* intergenerational relationships
genres, 46–53, 199–200, 238, 240, 279–80, 340–41
Geostorm (film), 19
Gerbi, Antonello, 289–95
Gertrud (film), 344
Get Out (film), 46–47, 52–53
Ghostbusters (film), 249–50
Ghostbusters II (film), 249
Ghostbusters: Afterlife (film), 249–52, 250fig.
Ghostbusters: Answer the Call (film), 249–50, 254
Gift, The, 191–92
Glawogger, Michael, 170
globalization, 81 87
global warming. *See* Anthropocene; climate change
Glory Road (film), 239–40
Godard, Jean-Luc, 146, 165, 282, 388
Godwin, Peter, 74–75
Goodbye, Dragon Inn (film), 17, 371
Goodman, Nelson, 213
good of film, concept of, 1–10
"Good of Film, The" (lecture), 3, 188–89, 194, 199, 232n17

Goya, Francisco de, 345
Graduate, The (film), 182
Grande Bellezza, La (film), 170
Grandin, Temple, 382
Grease (film), 364
Greco-Roman philosophers, 228
greenhouse-gas emissions, 18, 24, 30–31
Greenpeace, 29
"green world," 195–96
Gregory's Girl (film), 383–84
grotesqueness, 354–55, 358
group identities, 383–85
Guattari, Félix, 28
Gulpilil, David, 384
Gunning, Tom, 164, 197n20

Habel, Yiva, 71–72
Hadot, Pierre, 221, 228
Hall, Stuart, 238–39
Haneke, Michael, 330–31
Hanich, Julian, 26, 132, 158, 179, 229
Hansen, Miriam, 271n8, 308–9, 350–51, 353, 359n6
happiness, 169–70
hapticality, 61
haptic immersion, 316, 318–20
Harbord, Janet, 64–65
Harney, Stefano, 61, 62
Hartman, Saidiya, 61, 62, 165, 171
Hassan, Syed Feroz, 278, 283
Hate U Give, The (film), 241–43, 245–46
hatred, 343–45
Havarie (film), 104, 110
Havelock, Eric, 265
health workers, 378–79
Hegel, G. W. F., 144, 213, 300–310
Hegel: Three Studies, 300–310
Heidegger, Martin, 154–57, 159, 200, 293, 298n9, 343
Help, The (film), 239
Heshang (series of documentaries), 385
Hidden Figures (film), 239
High Plains Drifter (film), 365
high resolution, 31–32, 319
Himizu (film), 80–81, 85–87
Hinckley, John, Jr., 365–66
Hindi popular films, 269
His Girl Friday (film), 195, 227
Hole, The (film), 14fig., 17
Hollywood comedy of remarriage. *See* comedy of remarriage
Hollywood remaking, 249–58
homelessness, 51–52
homes, 48–52, 339–40

hooks, bell, 61
Hoolboom, Mike, 58fig., 63–65
Hopper, Dennis, 123, 163, 361, 380
Horkheimer, Max, 70
hotel lobbies, 373
"hot" media, 31–32
How to Do Nothing, 182–83
Huffington Post, 123
Hugo (film), 315fig.
human rights, 82–83
humility, 64, 183
Hunger Games, The (film), 104
Husserl, Edmund, 189

ICT. *See* information and communication technologies
I, Daniel Blake (film), 103
idealism objection to film-philosophy, 212–13
identifiable victim effect, 98–99
identity, 254–58, 383–85
identity politics, 347
I Don't Want to Sleep Alone (film), 14–15, 20–22
Il Convegno, 289
imagination: close-ups, 354–56; communal viewing, 277–80; disaster movies, 341–43; empathy and, 91–94; offscreen space, 181, 183, 320–21; political impact and, 106; reality and, 292; resolution and, 31; small-file movies, 33; thought-provoking films, 374; worlds of films, 139–41
"Imagination of Disaster, The" (essay), 341–43
"immunization," 294–97
implicating space, 186
imposition objection to film-philosophy, 212, 215–16
Inception (film), 104, 110, 146, 181
independent films. *See* art and indie films
indexicality, 306–8
India, 264, 380
indie films. *See* art and indie films
inequality, 41, 73, 77
information and communication technologies (ICT), 24
infrastructure, 25, 28–31, 33
in-group biases, 98–99
initiation ceremony (*ulwaluko*), 76
"Initiation to the Delights of Cinema" (essay), 289–95
innocence, 342–43

intelligent empathy, 99. *See also* empathy
"interestingness," 131–32
intergenerational relationships, 252–58, 268–69
internet access, 24, 30–31
Interpreting Films, 119
intertextual memory, 255
In the Heat of the Night (film), 239
"intransitive," 370
Introducing Kafka, 353
Invasion of the Body Snatchers (film), 343
In Which We Serve (film), 384
Inxeba (film), 76–77
Iranian cinema, 384
Irigaray, Luce, 189–90
irony, 369, 376
It Happened One Night (film), 200–201, 208n6, 226–27

Jameson, Fredric, 83
Japanese activist films, 385
Jazz Age, 380
Jennings, Humphrey, 384
Jensen, Jeff, 123
Jules and Jim/Jules et Jim (film), 275, 275fig.

Kaeslin, Hubert, 27
Kafka, Franz, 284n6, 353
Kant, Immanuel, 87–88, 131, 140, 159, 167–68, 200–201, 270, 305–6, 370
Kaplan, E. Ann, 17–18
Kapo (film), 88
Karmen Geï (film), 76
Kayser, Wolfgang, 358
Kelleter, Frank, 252–53
Kerouac, Jack, 371
Keystone films, 362
Kiarostami, Abbas, 163, 166, 391
King Kong (1933) (film), 342
Kivy, Peter, 119
Kleiman, Naum, 391
Klimov, Elem, 386
knowledge: Adorno on, 305–6, 309–10; of the arts, 133, elitism and, 212–15; of experiences, 216–17; from films, 390; geopolitics of, 60–62; Hegel on, 304; oral milieu, 264, 267–68; political, 102, 108
Koepnick, Lutz, 182, 190
Kracauer, Siegfried: alienation, 349–51, 353–54; depth of experience, 153; handwritten notes from meeting with Adorno, 301fig.; hotel lobbies, 373;

lumber rooms, 358; mirror reflections, 186, 389–90; offscreen space, 58, 178–79, 183, 186; *Theory of Film*, 3–4, 300–304, 308–10; on value of film, 135–36, 274
Kristeva, Julia, 84, 89
Ku Klux Klan, 96

Landless (film), 103fig., 106, 110
Langlois, Henri, 388, 389, 390
laws, 84
"Leaving the Movie Theater" (essay), 289
Leenhardt, Roger, 277
legacy, 249, 251, 257–58
Leibniz, Gottfried Wilhelm, 28
Lettres Persanes, 193
Levinas, Emmanuel, 38–42, 59–60, 82, 86–87
Lévi-Strauss, Claude, 278, 374
Lévy, Pierre, 140
LGBTQI+ sexualities, 76–77
liberal democracy, 82
Life of Pi (film), 86–87
Lilya 4-Ever (film), 170
Lim, Song Hwee, 328
Limelight (film), 22
Lion King, The (film), 267
literacy, 261, 269–70
literal scripts, 366
Livingston, Paisley, 209
Lloyd, Genevieve, 181, 183–84
Loach, Ken, 103, 385
Lobato, Ramón, 30
LoBue, Vanessa, 198
"local genres," 48
loneliness, 64, 170, 372, 387
long takes, 20–21, 182–85, 190
Los Olvidados (film), 199–200
loss, 102
Lost Highway (film), 356–57
Lotz, Amanda, 332
love, 278
lumber, 350, 354
lumber rooms, 349–50, 352, 356, 358
Luria, A. R., 267
Lynch, David, 3, 123, 146, 350–58, 350fig.
"Lynchian," 351, 354

M (film), 99
Ma, Jean, 17
Mad Men (television show), 123
Magnificent Seven, The (film), 365
Mahabharata, 266
"making strange," 374–75. *See also* defamiliarization; *ostran(n)enie*

Malick, Terrence, 120, 162, 165, 167, 171n1, 210*fig.*, 228–29
Malraux, André, 282, 384
Man and Boy Foundation, 76–77
Mann, Bonnie, 189, 194–95
Mannheim, Karl, 255–57
Man Who Shot Liberty Valance, The (film), 49
Mapantsula (film), 74–76
Marcus Aurelius, 226
marginalization, 81
Marsden, Eric, 74–75
Martin, Trayvon, 237, 242, 245
Martin-Jones, David, 62
Marvel films, 330
Masanet, Eric, 26–27
Mask, The (film), 382
material excesses in films, 265
Mathieu, Stephan, 63, 85
Matrix, The (film), 225
May, Todd, 38
Mbembe, Achille, 61, 165
McLuhan, Marshall, 31, 33
McQueen, Steve, 94, 120, 184
media archaeologists, 314
media psychologists, 104
media theorists, 314–15
mediation, 25, 294, 296, 305
Meditations, 225
Medusa, myth of, 389–90
Meena (television show), 104–5, 110
Méliès, Georges, 282, 314*fig.*
melodrama, 266–67
"Melodrama of the Unknown Woman" genre, 199–200
memory, 177–78, 186, 254–55, 258, 263–66, 270
mental depth, 105
Merleau-Ponty, Maurice, 189
metals, 28, 29
Metz, Christian, 182, 372
Micheaux, Oscar, 239
Mignolo, Walter, 60, 62, 135
mind-game films, 3, 225
"Mind-Game Film, The" (essay), 3
mirror reflections, 191–92, 390–91
Misek, Richard, 156–59
Mitry, Jean, 141
mnemonic communities, 252
mobile homes, 50–52
mobile phones, 157
modernity, 2–4, 60–65, 88–89, 135, 164, 223, 267, 275, 281–82
Monroe, H. H. *See* Saki

montage, 391
Montesquieu, 193
Moodysson, Lukas, 170
Moore, Michael, 104, 385
Moore's law, 27, 33
moral improvement, 198–207
morality, 10n17, 93–94, 96–99, 267
moral perfectionism, 199–201, 227
moral reflection, 91–93, 117–26, 265. *See also* contemplation; reflection
Moritz, Karl Philipp, 370
Morrison, Toni, 165, 382
Morton, Timothy, 43
Most Shocking Second a Day Video (fundraising video), 110
Moten, Fred, 61–62
Mouers, 76
Movement for Black Lives. *See* #BlackLivesMatter films
movie generations, 252–58
movie theaters, watching films in, 25–26, 36–37, 44, 314–22, 371–73
Mulhall, Stephen, 209, 223
multiculturalism, 82–83, 85
Mulvey, Laura, 24, 89, 164
Münsterberg, Hugo, 140–41, 144–45, 164
Mutual Film Corporation, 373
myths, 277–80
Mzamo, Ralph, 75–76

Nabokov, Vladimir, 191–92
Nandy, Ashis, 268
Nanook of the North (film), 390
"narrative paradigm scenarios," 120
"natality," 217
Native Son, 371
necropolitical, 61
Neer, Richard, 166
Negro Motorist Green Book, The, 242–43
Neill, Sam, 384
Nelson, Steven, 76
neorealism, 135, 281, 283, 349
Netflix, 32, 331–33
net neutrality. *See* internet access
New Argentine Cinema, 136
New World, The (film), 228–29
New York Times, 37–38
New Zealand films, 384
Ngũgĩ wa Thiong'o, 262
niche audiences, 280–81
Nicomachean Ethics, 6–7
Nixon, Rob, 19
Nomadland (film), 47*fig.*, 51–52

Norris, Frank, 374
nostalgia, 250–51, 254–55, 258
"Notes on Camp" (essay), 341
Nouvelle Vague, 388
"Now," 306–8
nuclear weapons, 18–19, 342
Nussbaum, Martha, 91

Obama, Barack, 245
"Oberflächen- und Tiefenwirkungen der Kunst" (essay), 151–52
objectification, 61, 317
Observateur, 276, 283
Occurrence at Owl Creek Bridge, An (film), xii*fig.*, xiii
Octopus, The, 374
O'Dell, Jenny, 182–83
OECD. *See* Organization for Economic Co-operation and Development
offscreen space, 177–86, 244, 316, 320–22, 362
Olson, Dan, 125
Ong, Walter J., 268
online games, 32
online teaching, 40–41
on-location filming, 16
ontology vs ethics, 39
opening-title sequence, 329, 331–32
Ophir, Adi, 102
Ophuls, Marcel, 385
"optical unconscious, the," 16, 354
oral milieu, 261–70
Organization for Economic Co-operation and Development (OECD), 30
ostran(n)enie, 193, 370. *See also* defamiliarization; "making strange"
othering, 61, 71, 82–87
Otherwise than Being or Beyond Essence, 38–39
outplacement, 50–52
overreading, 216, 220n32

Paik, Nam June, 222*fig.*, 222–25. *See also TV Buddha* (video installation)
pain and beauty, 169–70
pandemics, 13–16, 59, 84. *See also* Covid-19 pandemic
Panofsky, Erwin, 274
Paradise Now (film), 181
Parasite (film), 82
Parisien libéré, Le, 276–77
participatory films, 110
Partisan Review, 341
Patsy, The (film), 340*fig.*

Paul, Leslie A., 216–17
Paull, Jeffrey, 63–65
Peele, Jordan, 46–47, 53n1
Peirce, Charles Sanders, 308
Peretz, Eyal, 186
perfectionism, 3, 188, 199–201
performative contradiction objection to film-philosophy, 212, 214–15
personal transformation, 129, 209–18, 221–22, 224, 229
perspectival mobility, 305–6
phantasmagoria, 293, 295, 355–57
pharmakon, 296
Phenomenology of Spirit, 303–10
Philadelphia Story, The (film), 195, 227
philosophy, 39, 88, 200–201, 209–16, 218, 223–30
Philosophy of Liberation, 60
photography, 305, 309–10
physical attractiveness. *See* attractiveness
physical experience of films, 381
Pippin, Robert, 143–44, 146
pixels, 32, 33
Plantinga, Carl, 4, 5, 97
Plate, S. Brent, 223
Plato, 189, 192, 225, 294, 296, 376
playback mediums, 25–27
"pleasingness," 131–32
plot vs story, 185
poetry of the ordinary, 193–94
Point Zero (film), 25*fig.*
Poitier, Sidney, 239
polarity, 265
police brutality, 242–45
political art films, 110
political impact of film, 82–83, 87–89, 102–12, 183–85, 258, 283
"popular activist" documentaries, 110
portals, 14–15, 14*fig.*, 22
Porter, Edwin S., 193
Positioning Art Cinema: Film and Cultural Value, 129
postcolonial films, 73–76
post-traumatic stress disorder (PTSD), 18. *See also* anxiety
power imbalance, 64–65
premeditatio malorum, 226
"preparatory ethics," 200, 202, 212, 214–16
pretraumatic stress syndrome, 17–19. *See also* anxiety
Prettejohn, Elizabeth, 168
Pride (film), 239
Prinz, Jesse, 97–99

"Problem of Generations, The" (essay), 255–56
production companies, 105
"profilmic reality," 362
profound boredom, 155–60
projection/protection complex, 292–97
Promesse, La (film), 80–81, 81*fig*., 85–87
propaganda, 109
protests, 110, 317
proximity effects, 98–99
Psychology Today, 198
PTSD. *See* post-traumatic stress disorder
public engagement, 69–77
publicness of films, 69–71
"Punctuation Marks" (essay), 307
punk tradition, 345–47
"pure gift," 86–87
Pursuits of Happiness: Comedies of Remarriage, 275

Quaranta, Chiara, 156, 157–59
Quijano, Aníbal, 60

racial difference, 72–73
racism, 82, 239, 242–44, 382–83
"radical" films, 109–12
radical literalization, 352–55
Radio-Cinéma-Télévision (now *Télérama*), 276, 283
rainbows, 192
Ramaka, Joseph Gaï, 76
Rancière, Jacques, 83
rare metals, 28, 29
Ray, Nicholas, 345, 346
Ray, Satyajit, 261–62, 281
Reagan, Ronald, 365–66
reality, 4, 293–94, 386
Reardon, Nicholas, 241
Reason, Matthew, 270
reboots. *See* Hollywood remaking
Reclaiming Wonder, 181
Reddit, 125
Red River (film), 371
re-existence, 60–61
reflection, 143–47, 157–58, 334–35. *See also* contemplation; moral reflection
"reformist" films, 109–12
reframing exercises, 228
Reinhardt, Ad, xi
Reitman, Ivan, 249, 251
Reitman, Jason, 249, 250*fig*., 251
relaxant, cinema as, 380
religion, 76–77, 223
remakes. *See* Hollywood remaking

remembrance, 244–45, 247
renewable energy, 30
Renoir, Jean, 140, 261–63, 282
repetition of viewings, 230
Reshe, Julie, 339
resolution, high, 31–32, 319
revenge, 97
Rider, The (film), 51
risk, 362–63. *See also* danger
Rivette, Jacques, 89
road accidents, 363
road movies, 50–53
Road, The (film), 17
Rohmer, Eric, 164, 165
Roma (2018) (film), 331
Romania, 384, 389
Rose of Rhodesia (film), 71–72
Rossouw, Martin, 200, 211–16
Routt, Bill, 346
Roy, Arundhati, 13–16, 22
Rules of the Game, The/La Règle du jeu (film), 261–62
Ryan, Marie-Laure, 140–41, 148n7

Saint-Amour, Paul K., 18
Saki (H. H. Monroe), 368–69
salience effects, 98–99
Sansho the Bailiff/Sanshō Dayū (film), 344
Sarris, Andrew, 281
Saving Private Ryan (film), 120–21, 386
Scheler, Max, 152–53, 159
Schopenhauer, Arthur, 167–69
Schrader, Paul, 365
science fiction genre, 190, 341–44
Sconce, Jeffrey, 130
Scorsese, Martin, 315*fig*., 365, 381–82
Scotland, 383
Scrapbook (short film), 58*fig*., 63–65
screens, 178–79, 222–23, 291–95, 298n12, 389–90. *See also* movie theaters, watching films in; offscreen space
screen stories, 117–21, 123
Searchers, The (film), 49–50
"second-order seriality," 252–53
second-screen interactivity, 156, 157
Second World War, 49–50
Seeing Like the Buddha, 223
Seel, Martin, 218
self-destruction, 339. *See also* destruction
self-examination, 225
Selfless Cinema? Ethics and French Documentary, 39
"self-licensing," 95

self-transformation. *See* transformative experience, film as
Sembène, Ousmane, 69, 70*fig.*, 74, 382
Seneca, 226
Sennett, Mack, 362
sentimentality, 152, 251, 258
Separation, A/*Jodāi-e Nāder az Simin* (film), 202–3
September 11 attacks, 83–84
sequels. *See* Hollywood remaking
Sesame Street (television show), 103–4
Seven Samurai, The (film), 365
sexuality, 20–21, 76–77, 381–82
Shacklock, Zoë, 333
Shakespeare, William, 274, 344
Shams, Nadia, 25*fig.*
Sharpe, Christina, 165, 170–71
Shehabi, Arman, 26–27
Sherlock Jr. (film), 146, 290*fig.*
Shift Project, The, 30
"shipping," 124
Shklovsky, Viktor, 193–94, 370, 374–75
shock, 154, 268
Shohat, Ella, 61
Shoplifters/*Manbiki Kazoku* (film), 86–87
silence, 329–30
Silence of the Lambs, The (film), 117–18, 118*fig.*, 120
Singer, Tania, 94–95
Sinnerbrink, Robert, 4, 5, 91–92, 201–4, 207, 223, 228, 269–70
"Skoteinos, or How to Read Hegel," 302–10
slow cinema, 156–60, 167, 190
slowness, 145
Small File Media Festival, 25, 32–33
small-file movies, 32–33
smell, 386
Smith, Jeff, 330
Smith, Murray, 5, 92
Smith, Zadie, 165
snakes, 366–67
Sobchack, Vivian, 41–42, 134, 263–64, 325n29, 367n2
social impact entertainment, 105, 110
social justice films, 237–47
"socially conscious" films, 110
social media, 29, 32, 104, 125–26, 183
social organization, 105
social problem films, 238–40
social science researchers, 104–5
Socrates, 368–69
Soderbergh, Steven, xi–xii
Solomon, Robert, 269

songs, 329–30
Sontag, Susan, 166, 341–44, 347
Sorrentino, Paolo, 170
Sorrow and the Pity, The/*Le Chagrin et la pitie* (film), 385
soul-assemblages, 28–31, 33
South African Film and Publication Board, 77
"sovereign" violence, 84–85
spectatorship, 24, 36–44, 59, 65, 221, 224, 319, 371. *See also* audiences; communal viewing
Spence, Louise, 61
Spillius, Elizabeth, 352
Spinoza, Baruch, 28
spiritual exercises, 221–31
Stagecoach (film), 48
Staiger, Janet, 119
Stam, Robert, 61
Stanitzek, Georg, 329, 331, 335n3
Star Wars films, 262–63, 265–66, 268, 280
Statues also Die/*Les Statues meurent aussi* (film), 390
Stiegler, Bernard, 373
Stoicism, 228
storage mediums, 25–27
story levels vs dream levels, 355–57
storytelling, 108, 110–11, 344
story vs plot, 185
story worlds, 139
"strategic impact documentaries," 104
streaming media, 24–33, 36–37, 41, 44, 280, 315, 326–27, 331–35
Strike (film), 88, 354
Stromboli (film), 390
Sturges, John, 365
Sturges, Preston, 369*fig.*, 375–76
Sturken, Marita, 254
subscriber-funded video services, 332–33
suffering, 102–4
Sullivan's Travels (film), 369*fig.*, 375–76
Sunday Times (London), 74–75
Sunset Boulevard (film), 226
superficial boredom, 155–58
superficiality, 154–56
"superfluous evils," 102, 104
superiority, 130
supranational agencies, 110
surprise, 179
Surrealism, 358
Swinton, Tilda, 382

Tallis, Raymond, 145
tantalum, 28

Tarantino, Quentin, 97, 344
Taxi Driver (film), 365–66, 381
teachwithmovies.org (website), 122
"technesthetic" operation, 356–57
technology, xi–xiii, 25–27, 351, 371
Télérama. See *Radio-Cinéma-Télévision*
television, 26, 123, 230, 333–34, 385
televisual flow, 333
temporality, 105, 229–30, 303–5, 308–9
10 Things I Hate About You (film), 330
terrorism, 83–84
Thank You for the Rain (film), 106
theater, 372
Theory of Film, 3–4, 178, 300, 302–3, 308, 349–50, 389–90
Thin Red Line, The (film), 120, 171n1
"Third," 86–87
Third Man, The (film), 199*fig.*, 203–6
Thompson, Kristin, 330
thought experiments, 210, 216, 224–25
"Thought of Movies, The" (essay), 193
thought-provoking, 130–31, 133–35, 374–75
threats. *See* danger
Tidyman, Ernest, 365
Titanic (film), 262–65, 267–69
Todorov, Tzvetan, 370
tolerance, 82–83
Totality and Infinity, 38–39
To the Wonder (film), 210*fig.*
Touch of Evil (film), 183
Trader Horn (film), 371
traditional values, 48–50, 202
transformational ethics, 211–12, 221, 224, 230
transformative experience, film as, 129, 209–18, 221–22, 224, 229
transience of beauty, 169
Travolta, John, 364–65
tricking of viewers, 205–6
Trier, Lars von, 85, 130, 139, 139*fig.*, 330
Truffaut, François, 275, 275*fig.*, 281–82, 346
Tsai Ming-liang, 14–17, 14*fig.*, 19–22, 23n16, 151, 328–29, 371, 382, 383
Tsivian, Yuri, 372
TV. *See* television
TV Buddha (video installation), 221–23, 222*fig.*, 225–30
12 Years a Slave (film), 94, 120, 184–85
24/7: Late Capitalism and the Ends of Sleep, 334–35
2012 (film), 19
Twin Peaks (television show), 350, 350*fig.*, 352, 355–57

twist films, 225
Twitter, 125

ugliness, 98, 159, 170
UK. *See* United Kingdom
ulwaluko (initiation ceremony), 76
Uncle Josh at the Moving Picture Show (film), 193
uncomfortable experiences, 130–32
United Kingdom (UK), 384–85
United States (US), 122
unseen, 177–85, 195–96
Unthinking Eurocentrism, 61
US. *See* United States
utopia, 85–88, 169, 171, 279, 380. *See also* atopia

Valéry, Paul, 351, 356, 357, 359n6
value of film, concept of, 2, 4–9
values, traditional, 48–50, 202
Vanishing Point (film), 361–62, 362*fig.*, 366–67
Vasudevan, Ravi, 269
Vertigo (film), 381
Vertov, Dziga, 88
Vietnam, documentaries about, 386
viewers, 70–71, 119, 276, 371–73
Vinney, Cynthia, 123
violence, 84–85, 198, 207, 239–45
Virilio, Paul, 293
virtual worlds, 138, 140–43
"Visual Pleasure and Narrative Cinema" (essay), 164
"vital," 152–53, 159
Voortrekkers, De (film), 72–73, 77
Vrai Coupable, Le (film), 279

Walkabout (film), 384
Walker, Ben, 26–27
Wallace, David Foster, 351, 353
Walmart, 385
Walton, Kendall, 139–40
war in films, 386. *See also* Cold War; World War II
Wartenberg, Thomas, 4, 122, 209, 223, 225
Washington, Donna, 63–65
Way, The (film), 347
Wayward Cloud (film), 17
Webb, Amy, 124
Weber, Samuel, 16
Weerasethakul, Apichatpong, 151*fig.*, 156, 158, 282
Weigel, Sigrid, 256
"Western" context, 59–62, 109–10, 135

Westerns, 48–50, 53
Westworld (television show), 124
What Is Cinema?, 276, 282
"what's in it for me?," 38–39
"What's the Big Idea?" (website), 122
Whitehead, Alfred North, 28
Widerberg, Bo, 170
Wikipedia, 366–67
Wild at Heart (film), 355
Wilder, Billy, 226, 387
Wild Things (film), 327*fig.*
Willemen, Paul, 191, 346–47
Williams, James S., 165
Williams, Raymond, 333
Williams, William Carlos, 372
witness-bearer, cinema as, 384
Wittgenstein, Ludwig, 166, 189, 190, 217
Wizard of Oz (film), 355
Wolf Warrior 2/Zhàn Láng 2 (film), 262–63
wonder, 181, 183–86, 188–96
Woods, Donald, 75

Woolf, Virginia, 387
Workingman's Death (film), 170
"Work of Art in the Age of Mechanical Reproduction, Second Version, The" (essay), 295–96
"world-in" and "world-of" framework, 142–46
worlds of films, 138–47, 139*fig.*
World Viewed, The, 195–96, 274–75
World War II, 49–50

Xala (film), 70*fig.*, 74–75

"Young Americans" (song), 330
YouTube, 29, 32, 125

Zhao, Chloé, 8, 47*fig.*, 51
Zimmerman, George, 237
Zirimu, Pio, 262
Žižek, Slavoj, 82–83, 86
Zuma, Thando, 75–76

Founded in 1893,
UNIVERSITY OF CALIFORNIA PRESS
publishes bold, progressive books and journals
on topics in the arts, humanities, social sciences,
and natural sciences—with a focus on social
justice issues—that inspire thought and action
among readers worldwide.

The UC PRESS FOUNDATION
raises funds to uphold the press's vital role
as an independent, nonprofit publisher, and
receives philanthropic support from a wide
range of individuals and institutions—and from
committed readers like you. To learn more, visit
ucpress.edu/supportus.

www.ingramcontent.com/pod-product-compliance
Lightning Source LLC
Chambersburg PA
CBHW021333230426
43666CB00006B/279